The Force of Labour

The Force of Labour

The Western European Labour Movement and the Working Class in the Twentieth Century

Edited by
Stefan Berger
and
David Broughton

BERG
Oxford • Washington D.C.

First published in 1995 by
Berg Publishers Limited
Editorial offices:
150 Cowley Road, Oxford, OX4 1JJ, UK
13950 Park Center Road, Herndon, VA 22071, USA

Library of Congress Cataloging-in-Publication Data

A catalogue record for this book is available from the Library of Congress.

British Library Cataloguing-in-Publication Data

A catalogue record for this book is available from the British Library.

ISBN 0 85496 381 2 (Cloth)
1 85973 023 X (Paper)

Printed in the United Kingdom by WBC Book Manufacturers,
Mid-Glamorgan.

For Dick Geary

Contents

Preface

All the chapters contained in this book were first given as papers to a seminar series held at the School of European Studies, University of Cardiff (UWCC) between February and June 1992. They were subsequently revised in the light of comments received and discussed once more at a two-day conference in May 1993, again organised under the auspices of the School of European Studies, UWCC. Only after extensive revision did they reach the form in which they are presented here. We felt strongly that such a close degree of cooperation between all the contributors was essential if our aim of coherence and comparability was to be achieved.

On that basis, we must express our thanks to all our contributors for their patience and willingness to cooperate in our requests for yet further revisions and extra information, particularly for the appendix of this book. The whole project was encouraged and supported from the very start by Professor David Hanley as Head of the School of European Studies, and our gratitude to him must be fully acknowledged here. In the course of planning, developing, writing, re-writing and editing this book, a number of other individuals played vital roles. Above all, we would like to thank David Jackson for his unfailing belief in our work. The sterling efforts of Anett Pförtner in re-typing many of the chapters and helping us with the collating of the appendix were greatly appreciated. We must also thank the anonymous reader for his/her constructive comments. We believe they further improved the book. Any remaining errors are entirely our own responsibility.

We should also mention the particular help we received from Professor Dick Geary of the University of Nottingham. Dick attended the two-day workshop in May 1993 and his comments on the various draft chapters were both perceptive and constructive. The original plan was for Dick to contribute the comparative chapter for this book, but his recent illness prevented this. We are nevertheless grateful for his support at a crucial stage in the project's development. His comparative work on European labour movements has been an important inspiration to the editors and contributors of this volume. We therefore feel that it is appropriate to dedicate the book to him.

Stefan Berger
David Broughton

List of Abbreviations

ADGB	German General Trade Union Federation
AEU	British Amalgamated Engineering Union
AfA	Association for Questions Concerning Employees (intra-party pressure group within the German Social Democrats)
AJC	Dutch Social Democratic Youth Organisation
ANDB	General Union of Dutch Diamond Workers
ANV	Dutch White Collar and Civil Servants Union
ASF	German Association of Social Democratic Women
BdM	National Socialist Association of German Girls
CC.OO	Spanish Workers Commissions
CDA	Dutch Christian Democratic Party
CDU\CSU	German Christian Democratic Union\Christian Social Union
CFTC/CFDT	French Catholic Trade Union Federations
CGIL	Italian Communist Trade Union Federation
CGL	Italian National Trade Union Federation
CGT	Main French Trade Union Movement
CGTU	French Communist Trade Union Federation
CIL	Italian Catholic Trade Union Federation (pre-Fascism)
CISL	Italian Catholic Trade Union Federation (post-Fascism)
CNPF	French Employers' Federation
CNT	Spanish Anarchist National Labour Confederation
CNV	Dutch Christian National Trade Union Federation
Cobas	Italian rank and file trade union committees
DAF	German Labour Front
DFD	Democratic Women's Association (GDR)
DGB	German Trade Union Federation (post-1945 FRG)
EVC	Dutch Unity Trade Federation
FDG	Free German Youth (GDR)
FDGB	Free German Trade Union Federation (GDR)
FDP	German Free Democratic Party (Liberals)
FET de las JONS	Spanish fascist party under Franco (the only party allowed in Spain under the dictatorship)

FNV	Federation of the Dutch Trade Union Movement
FO	Force Ouvrière
GDR	German Democratic Republic
GPS	Italian Socialist Parliamentary Group
ILP	British Independent Labour Party
KAB	Dutch Catholic Workers' Movement
KAB	German Catholic Workers' Movement
KPD	German Communist Party
KVP	Dutch Catholic People's Party
LO	Swedish National Union Organisation
MSPD	German Majority Social Democratic Party
NAF	Dutch Labour Front
NAS	Dutch National Labour Secretariat
NKV	Dutch Catholic Trade Federation
NUM	British National Union of Mineworkers
NVV	Dutch Federation of Trade Unions
OS	French 'specialised workers' (census category)
OSE	Spanish Syndical Organisation
PCE	Spanish Communist Party
PCF	French Communist Party
PCI	Italian Communist Party
PDS	German Party for Democratic Socialism
PDS	Italian Party of the Left (former Communist Party)
PP	Spanish Popular Party
PPR	Dutch Radical Party
PSI	Italian Socialist Party
PSIUP	Italian Socialist Party Splinter Group
PSOE	Spanish Socialist Workers' Party
PSUG	Catalan Communist Party
PvdA	Dutch Social Democratic Party
RK Vakbureau	Dutch Roman Catholic Trade Union Bureau
RKWV	Dutch Roman Catholic Working Men's Federation
RMI	French Safety Net Minimum Income
SAC	Swedish Workers' Central Organisation
SAF	Swedish Employers' Federation
SDAP	Swedish Social Democratic Workers' Party
SDAP	Dutch Social Democratic Labour Party
SDB	Dutch Social Democratic League
SDP	British Social Democratic Party
SED	German Socialist Unity Party (East German Communist Party)
SER	Dutch Social and Economic Council
SFIO	French Socialist Party

SMA	Spanish Socialist Miners' Union
SPD	German Social Democratic Party
STO	French Forced Labour for Young Workers (Vichy regime)
TCV	Catalan Textile Federation
TGWU	British Transport and General Workers' Union
TUC	British Trades Union Congress
UGT	Spanish Socialist General Workers' Trade Union Movement
UIL	Italian Social Democratic Union Federation
USI	Italian Syndicalist Trade Union Federation
USPD	German Independent Social Democratic Party
VDB	Dutch Liberal Democratic League
ZAG	German Central Working Community Between Employers' Federation and Unions after 1918

Notes on Contributors

Tobias Abse Lecturer in Modern European History at Goldsmiths College, University of London. He is the author of *Sovversivi e fascisti a Livorno: Lotta politica e sociale (1918–1922)* (Milan, 1991), and has contributed several articles on twentieth century Italian history and politics to *New Left Review* and other journals.

Stefan Berger Lecturer in the School of European Studies at the University of Wales, Cardiff. His research interest concentrate upon the comparative history of labour movements and municipal socialism as well as historiography. He has published several articles on these topics and he is the author of *The British Labour Party and the German Social Democrats, 1900–1931* (Oxford, 1994).

David Broughton Lecturer in Politics in the School of European Studies at the University of Wales, Cardiff. He was Research Associate on the ESRC-funded project *A Study of the Labour Party Membership* at the University of Sheffield in 1989–1990. His research interests include Social Democracy, Christian Democracy and the internal organisation of political parties.

James Fulcher Senior Lecturer and Head of the Department of Sociology at the University of Leicester. He has had a long-standing interest in the history of the Swedish labour movement and the comparative study of British and Swedish industrial relations. He is the author of *Labour Movements, Employers and the State: Conflict and Cooperation in Britain and Sweden* (Oxford, 1991).

Susan Milner Senior Lecturer in European Studies at the University of Bath. She has written several articles on the French labour movement, and in *The Dilemma of Internationalism: French Syndicalism and the International Labour Movement, 1900–1914* (Oxford, 1990), she examined the relationship between French syndicalism and the international movement before 1914. Her research interests centre on comparative labour relations within Europe.

Angel Smith Lecturer in Modern Spanish History at the University of Southampton. In 1990 he completed his PhD thesis entitled 'Industry, Labour and Politics in Catalonia, 1897–1914'. He has since written several articles on Catalan labour history, and is at present working on a historical dictionary of modern Spain and a history of the Barcelona labour movement between 1897 and 1923.

Lex Heerma van Voss Lecturer in Social and Economic History at Utrecht University. He studied history at Utrecht and Paris and has written a dissertation on the economic and social consequences of the adoption of the eight-hour working day in the Netherlands. His current research topics include the social history of the Netherlands in the twentieth century.

Chris Williams Lecturer in Modern British and Modern Welsh History in the School of History and Archaeology at the University of Wales, Cardiff. His research interests concentrate on the history of the Labour movement in Britain, particularly in the South Wales coalfield, during the nineteenth and twentieth centuries. He has published articles in the Welsh Labour history journal *Llafur*, and his monograph on Labour politics in the Rhondda Valley is to appear shortly.

–1–

Introduction

Stefan Berger and David Broughton

Before his untimely death in 1989, Martin Broszat called on his fellow historians to develop analyses of the whole period of modern German history which would cut across the almost stereotypical chronological start and end points in twentieth-century historiography, namely, before the First World War, in the inter-war years and after the second World War.[1] Some time before Broszat's challenge, in 1978, Geoff Eley and Keith Nield had pleaded in a now famous article for the coming together of political and social history.[2]

This book accepts the advice of Broszat and the perspective of Eley and Nield in the area of European labour movements and working-class history. In the past, institutional and organisational accounts of the trade unions, political parties, cooperatives and other associations which formed the core of the labour movement in different countries have all too often ignored the experience of ordinary workers, those people who form the natural backbone of such organisations. Historians, at least up until the 1970s, tended to concentrate on the leaders of the labour movements rather than the rank-and-file members of these movements. On the other hand, one reaction to this kind of 'head office' approach to labour movement history has tended to throw the baby out with the bath water, in that suddenly in the historiography on working-class experience and working-class culture, there were no references whatever to the organised labour movement. It is therefore high time to bring working-class history and labour movement history together, and to begin to ask questions which concern themselves specifically with the link between the labour movement and the working class in Western Europe.

Furthermore, the neat periodisation of historical studies has so far prevented a *longue durée* consideration of the development of organised labour and the working-class experience. We do have valuable studies on European labour movements before 1914,[3] and on the working class experience in the inter-war years[4] as well as in the post-war years,[5] but there is nothing to date which takes the whole of the twentieth century into account in the same work. We hope that by focusing on the whole of the twentieth century, fresh perspectives can be provided as the old self-imposed chronological boundaries are questioned. Through this approach, long-term continuities can be seen as well as genuine discontinuities.

A major objective of this book is to permit and indeed foster comparisons in labour movement and working-class history. Richard Price has recently drawn attention to the insular outlook of much British labour history.[6] The same could be said for almost any other country in Europe. Despite frequent calls for the development of comparative labour history, it remains a field in which the implementation of such an approach is still relatively scarce. It is a positive sign that the 1980s have seen an increase in the number of genuinely comparative studies,[7] but on the whole comparison has remained rare because it is difficult. The way in which the historiographical profession is institutionalised in a European context and elsewhere means that history to a very large extent remains national history. Therefore, especially if more than two or three countries are to be analysed, the best way of proceeding is arguably to assemble material on different nation-states from specialists on the labour history of specific countries.

The immediate problems facing any editor with this aim in mind centre upon which countries to choose, and on how best to achieve a high degree of coherence and compatibility between the different national chapters and the particular questions addressed by each chapter in turn. In this book, we have concentrated on Western Europe. The book includes studies of all core Western European countries, namely Britain, France, Spain, Italy and Germany, as well as studies of two smaller nations, Sweden and the Netherlands. Sweden was chosen because of its record of having developed the most successful European labour movement in the twentieth century, whilst the Netherlands serves as an example of a strong labour movement in a small country riven for many years by religious division. The decision to concentrate on the countries of Western Europe is not an attempt to prolong the former Cold War division of the continent artificially; it is more a recognition of the fact that after 1945, under the conditions of the Cold War, the continent of Europe grew increasingly apart. As the work of Hartmut Kaelble has shown, the history of Western Europe in the twentieth century is characterised by long-term trends which have brought Western European societies closer to each other.[8] This process of convergence makes comparisons much easier, not only for the number of similarities which emerge, but also for the remaining differences which reveal important individual facets of Western European nation-states.

As editors, we developed and refined the analytical framework which each of the contributors of the country chapters was asked to follow. This framework was designed to produce a coherent feel to the book as a whole.

Consequently, all contributors followed clear guidelines as to the structure of their chapters. In particular, all the contributors were expected to address six major questions.

First, the development of labour markets in Western European countries had to be discussed. Each author was asked to trace the development of wage structures, processes of urbanisation, and industrialisation and its effects on the structure and outlook of the working class. Second, questions of occupation and class had to be investigated. Here the relationship between occupational classifications and class position had to be confronted, as well as the importance of differences between skilled and unskilled workers. Additionally, contributors were asked to critically examine the validity of labour aristocracy concepts as explanations for the development of labour movements. Third, the economic and political identity of workers had to be taken into account. The significance of employers' actions, attitudes, and ideologies for the development of the organised working class had to be considered, as well as the impact of strikes. Fourth, the relationship between the labour movement and other social classes, groups and institutions had to come under scrutiny; authors were asked to examine specifically any attitudes of 'them' versus 'us', the degree of inter-class cooperation and the extent of class barriers in any given society. Additionally, the role of the church, the army and the school system should be discussed.

Fifth, contributors were asked to consider the role of the state in the making of the Western European labour movement. The impact of legal and constitutional frameworks, and of the electoral system, were potentially important points in this section. Finally, authors were asked to discuss generational, geographical and cultural problems affecting the working class, and the labour movement in their countries. The importance of regions and localities for the identity of the working class and the degree of community feeling amongst the working class in different regions added a significant dimension to this last point.

This may look like an overly rigid and prescriptive approach to the study of European labour movements. We felt, however, that such an approach was necessary if a coherent and complementary volume would result from the project. Nevertheless, we did allow our contributors a degree of latitude concerning whether they adopted a chronological or topical approach to their respective chapters. This became a matter of some debate between the editors and the contributors, and in the end it was left to individual contributors to decide whether a chronological or a topical approach to their respective country would best enable them to employ the overall framework. In the event, the Swedish, British, Dutch, German and Spanish chapters follow a largely chronological approach, whilst the French and Italian chapters are structured by different topics with little regard for chronology.

We have compiled basic statistical data for all the countries discussed in this book and these are presented in comparative tables in an appendix. These tables provide information on the size of the working class and membership in trade unions and working-class parties as well as trade union density.

We now move on to the first substantive chapter of the book, a consideration of the development of the labour movement and the working class in Sweden in the twentieth century.

Notes

1. Broszat (1987), p. 172.
2. Eley and Nield (1980).
3. Katznelson and Zolberg (1986); Geary (1989); van der Linden and Rojahn (1990); Breuilly (1992).
4. Salter and Stevenson (1990); Wrigley (1993). Geary (1981) and Geary (1991) are exceptional in bridging at least the First World War divide. Compare also the remarkably broad Lipset (1983).
5. Fox Piven (1991); Paterson and Thomas (1977, 1986); Kendall (1975); Padgett and Paterson (1991).
6. Price (1991), p. 259.
7. For discussions of the pitfalls of comparative Labour history see Berger (1994), chapter one.
8. Kaelble (1993), pp. 173–200.
9. Kaelble (1990); for France and Germany see also idem (1991).

Bibliography

Berger, Stefan, *The British Labour Party and the German Social Democrats, 1900–1931*, Oxford, 1994

Breuilly, John, *Labour and Liberalism in Nineteenth-Century Europe: Essays in Comparative History*, Manchester, 1992

Broszat, Martin, *Nach Hitler. Der schwierige Umgang mit unserer*

Geschichte, Munich, 1987
Eley, Geoff and Keith Nield, 'Why does Social History Ignore Politics?', *Social History*, vol. 5, 1980, pp. 249–71
—— (ed.), *Labour and Socialist Movements in Europe Before 1914*, Oxford, 1989
Geary, Dick, *European Labour Protest 1848–1939*, London, 1981
——, *European Labour Politics from 1900 to the Depression*, London, 1991
Kaelble, Hartmut, *A Social History of Western Europe, 1880–1980*, London, 1990
——, *Nachbarn am Rhein. Entfremdung und Annäherung der französischen und deutschen Gesellschaft seit 1880*, Munich, 1991
——, 'Vergleichende Sozialgeschichte des 19. und 20. Jahrhunderts: Forschungen europäischer Historiker' *Jahrbuch für Wirtschaftsgeschichte*, 1993, pp. 173–200
Katznelson, I. and A. R. Zolberg (eds), *Working-class Formation: Nineteenth-Century Patterns in Western Europe and the United States*, Princeton N.J., 1986
Kendall, Walter, *The Labour Movement in Europe*, London, 1975
van der Linden, Marcel and Jürgen Rojahn (eds), *The Formation of Labour Movements 1870–1914: An International Perspective*, 2 vols., Leiden, 1990
Lipset, Seymour M., 'Radicalism or Reformism: The Sources of Working-Class Politics', *American Political Science Review*, vol. 77, 1983, pp. 1–18
Padgett, Stephen and William E. Paterson (eds), *A History of Social Democracy in Postwar Europe*, London, 1991
Paterson, William E. and Alistair H. Thomas (eds), *Social Democratic Parties in Western Europe*, London, 1977
——, (eds), *The Future of Social Democracy: Problems and Prospects of Social Democratic Parties in Western Europe*, Oxford, 1986
Piven, Frances Fox (ed.), *Labor Parties in Postindustrial Societies*, Cambridge, 1991
Price, Richard, 'The Future of British Labour History', *International Review of Social History*, vol. 36, 1991
Salter, Stephen and John Stevenson (eds), *The Working Class and Politics in Europe and America 1929–1945*, London, 1990
Wrigley, Chris (ed.), *Challenges of Labour: Central and Western Europe 1917–1920*, London, 1993

–2–

Sweden

James Fulcher

The Swedish labour movement has probably been the strongest and most unified socialist movement in the world. Its political wing, the Social Democratic Workers Party (SDAP), dominated Swedish politics from 1932 to 1991. The party has been closely linked to the national union organisation (LO), which may reasonably be described as the world's most powerful union federation. Union density has reached exceptional heights, and in 1992 actually rose to a new peak of 86 per cent.

The strength and unity of the Swedish labour movement have usually been explained quite simply in terms of the religious, ethnic and cultural homogeneity of Swedish society or Sweden's late industrialisation. The Protestant character of Swedish religion is also considered important, because the opposition of Catholic churches to socialist movements has been a divisive factor elsewhere.[1] There is undeniably much truth in these explanations, but they can all too easily lead to a deterministic, unproblematic, and over-simple account of the movement's emergence. The occupational sectionalism, ideological divisions, and conflicts of strategy typical of labour movements elsewhere were present in Sweden too, and an explanation of the strength and unity of the Swedish movement must show how and why these problems were overcome. The first part of this chapter is concerned with these issues.

The emergence of a powerful and unified socialist movement is one thing but the maintenance of its strength and unity are something else. These issues are examined in the second part of the chapter. The very success of a movement in developing a centralised organisation and securing prolonged political power may generate tensions between leaders and led, while 'labour' governments have generally found it difficult to reconcile their economic dependence on capital with their political dependence on labour and their socialist goals.

The rising costs of the welfare state and public sector expansion have gradually created an intractable fiscal crisis which can only be solved by tax increases or expenditure cuts, either of which is liable to erode a 'labour' government's traditional political base. This has in any case been shrinking as the decline of occupations involving manual work has reduced the size of the working class, as traditionally conceived. These accumulating problems have coincided with an intensification of international competition and global economic integration that have shifted power from labour to capital and made it ever harder to sustain the strength of a labour movement.

The Formation of the Swedish Labour Movement

Swedish industrialisation began in the early 1870s, but it was not until the 1880s that the first viable trade unions emerged amongst urban craft workers and it was the 1890s before labourers and factory workers became substantially organised. Socialism arrived in the 1880s from Germany via Denmark and the SDAP was constituted in 1889, before the LO, which was founded in 1898.

Late Industrialisation, Socialism and Union Structure

Proponents of the late industrialisation thesis argue that the Swedish movement escaped the conflict between craftworker and labourer that dogged the labour movements of nations which had become industrialised earlier, such as Britain or Denmark.[2] Instead of being divided between exclusive craft unions and general unions of the unskilled, Swedish workers were organised along industrial lines compatible with a unified and centralised federation. Similarly, late industrialisation facilitated a class solidarity conducive to socialism.

The problem with this approach is its neglect of the early stage of Swedish union organisation, when there was indeed a division between craft workers and general workers. According to Lindbom's standard account of the 105 unions that existed in 1885, 73 were in traditional crafts and another 12 in skilled-worker occupations.[3] Labour organisation did indeed result from the capitalist transformation of craft work rather than industrialisation; it was the concentration of craftsmen in large urban workshops, the abolition of craft restrictions, the introduction of 'free labour' agreements, and the development of individual employment relationships that stimulated workers to organise themselves.[4] In Stockholm, craftworkers continued to dominate the labour movement until the First World War.[5] Factory workers certainly became organised as Sweden industrialised, but rather more slowly. Their main union was the general Labourers' and Factoryworkers' Union of 1891, which briefly became Sweden's largest union in 1906.

Given the existence of a potentially divisive distinction between craft and general workers in the union movement, there are two main puzzles.

First, how can one explain the growth of industrial unionism and, second, how can one explain the early founding of a federation that rapidly assumed leadership of the movement?

The solution to the first puzzle lies largely in the emergence of a distinctive 'work-material' unionism that bridged the gap between skilled and unskilled workers. Two unions took this form, the Woodworkers' and, above all, the Metalworkers' unions. A work-material union was not a craft union, for although it had a core membership of craftsmen, unskilled workers could be members as well, but it was not an industrial union either, for its membership ranged across different industries. The work-material character of the Metalworkers Union was crucial in preventing the hardening of skill divisions in the engineering industry and the craft fragmentation that was certainly a danger at this time.[6]

How did such a union come into existence? The socialists played a key role, both in the founding of local ironworkers' unions that included unskilled workers and in the creation of a national organisation in 1888, the Swedish Iron and Metalworkers' Union as it was then called, which initially consisted of three ironworker and three craft unions.[7] This was but one instance of the important part played by socialists in building a unified labour movement which spanned the whole working class. The socialists encouraged 'open' organisations, set up local organising and coordinating committees, and put special effort into organising the unskilled workers who found it hardest to establish unions. At a time when craft unionism was strong and the opposed principles of craft and class were competing for worker loyalty, socialist influence may be said to have tipped the balance towards class.

This leads us to the answer to the second puzzle, for the SDAP continued and developed the socialists' organising role by providing a national organisation which extended and coordinated trade unionism. It was the party that established a class-wide organisation and demonstrated the need for such an organisation to the unions, which later created the LO to carry out this function more effectively. It is fundamental to the understanding of the Swedish labour movement that national political organisation preceded and generated national union organisation.

Party leadership of the labour movement caused problems, however, for party and union priorities could clash, while, additionally, many unionists were not socialists. Lindbom estimates that at the beginning of the 1890s only one-fifth of the unions had socialist majorities.[8] As the national unions built up their strength in the 1890s they became increasingly restless with the party's leadership of the movement.[9] Tensions were eased by the establishment of the LO, which grew out of union (and party) dissatisfaction with this situation, but the tensions were not entirely removed. The party insisted initially on the compulsory collective affiliation of LO union members, and this question threatened to split the federation until compulsory affiliation was abolished in 1900. Collective affiliation itself then became the issue until an individual right to disaffiliate was introduced in 1908 and the LO's constitutional obligation to work for collective affiliation was removed in 1909. Thus, the movement's unity depended on the functional separation of the unions from the party through a gradual process of organisational differentiation.

Given the resolution of these problems, socialist influence was fundamental to the emergence of a class-wide and organisationally-unified movement. Why were the socialists so influential? The paradox is that it was the relative backwardness of Swedish society at the time when the early socialists arrived that enabled them to be so influential. The significance of late industrialisation was not that it produced factories full of semi-skilled workers who naturally organised along industrial lines. It was rather that socialists originating from other countries where industry was more advanced could agitate and organise while Swedish workers were building their first unions.

It was not just the timing of industrialisation that mattered, however, but also the timing of democratisation. The democratisation of Sweden was exceptionally late and made little progress during the nineteenth century.[10] The constitutional reform of 1866 had created a two-chamber parliament but, as Rustow has put it, this merely 'brought oligarchy up to date by substituting property for status'.[11] Property and income qualifications for the vote meant that the franchise for the lower house extended to only one-fifth of adult males, whilst the composition of the indirectly-elected upper house was controlled by two per cent of the adult male population. This situation did not change until the constitutional reform of 1907–1909 removed income qualifications from lower house voters and extended the franchise to all males over the age of twenty-four.

Late democratisation meant that the socialists had to seek an industrial rather than a political base. They could only establish themselves by building unions and using them to create and support a party which could then press for electoral reform and seek representation in parliament. The political general strike became the labour movement's main weapon in its campaign for suffrage reform. Late democratisation forced socialists to immerse themselves in the formation of unions and the coordination of union activity, thereby leading them to play a much more prominent role in the shaping of union organisation than would otherwise have been the case.

Employer Organisation and the Labour Movement

The character of Swedish industrialisation was in many ways inimical to labour organisation because so much of it took place in isolated rural locations, as in the mining, lumber and paper industries, the ironworks and also to some extent in manufacturing and engineering. Single-plant communities, company control of housing, employer paternalism, and the ready availability of labour from surrounding areas were hardly conducive to worker organisation. Employers in the saw-works and the related pulp and paper industry fought hardest against union recognition, though there was also strong resistance in textiles, glass manufacture and mining. There were fewer battles in the paternalist ironworker communities (*järnbruk*), which were unionised after the struggle for union recognition had been won nationally.[12] Interestingly, paternalism could also be found in some cities, notably in Göteborg where, at the shipyards on the island of Hisingen, worker organisation was long delayed by the employer's patriarchal control of housing and welfare.[13]

One might expect that an employer paternalism of this sort would lead to the local inhibition of union organisation, but the employers did eventually play, through their organisations, a prominent role in the growth of a unified and centralised labour movement. Employer organisation was stimulated by the highly organised character of the labour movement, which by 1902 had only recruited a small part of the labour force[14] but was coordinated by a federation with a central strike fund (albeit for defensive use only) and able to mount a political general strike, as the 1902 strike for suffrage reform demonstrated. In response, in the same year the engineering employers' association was reorganised into a much more effective body and three general employers' associations including the Swedish Employers Association, the SAF, were founded. After the engineering employers were defeated by the unions in the 1905 lockout, a sustained trial of strength that lasted some five months and demonstrated that the unions could, with LO assistance, out-gun employer associations at industry level, the SAF took over the leadership of the employers and began to absorb the other associations. The employers now had a highly-centralised national association which could bring to bear the mighty weapon of a general lockout against the LO.[15]

The employers' new organisational superiority and an economic recession starting in 1906 shifted power from labour to capital, but the employers' strategy was now to use the unions rather than crush them. While many employers were ambivalent about collective bargaining, it had become a fact of life with the 1905 engineering industry agreement. It could also be turned to the advantage of the employers, if their prerogatives were written into collective agreements. In 1906, the SAF forced on the LO the so-called December Compromise, which recognised unions but required them to write into their agreements the employer's right to hire and fire and direct work, thereby giving union backing to an almost absolute employer authority at plant level and making it difficult for the unions to prevent the hiring of non-union labour and strike-breakers.[16]

It was the employer counter-attack that forced centralisation on the LO. The LO had been created by powerful national unions jealous of their independence and, until the events of 1906, it exercised little real authority over its members. In negotiating the December Compromise and then intervening in industrial disputes to enforce it, the LO exceeded its brief, albeit justifiably since economic conditions had changed and the unions were in no position to withstand an employer offensive. This pattern was repeated during the following three years, as the SAF-led employers' associations presented the LO with demands backed by the threat of general lockouts, and the LO found itself obliged to persuade its members to accept. Eventually the LO reacted by declaring a general strike in 1909, although it had no authority to do so. Proposals to formally centralise the LO followed, but the strike's disastrous failure led instead to a temporary de-centralisation. Nonetheless, one of the basic features of modern Swedish industrial relations, the centralisation of union authority under employer pressure had been established.[17]

The 1905 agreement in the engineering industry established collective bargaining as the norm, and employers holding out against the unions then faced joint pressure from the LO and the SAF to come into line. In 1906 the SAF refused to approve or support the six-month lockout at Mackmyra Sulfit AB, a last-ditch attempt to keep unions out of the paper industry, and worked with the LO to end it.[18] The 1905 agreement also meant that the *järnbruk*, with their close links to engineering, could no longer resist collective bargaining, although an agreement was concluded only after intervention by the LO and SAF to prevent open conflict between the Metalworkers Union and the iron industry employers.[19]

Employer organisation influenced union organisation in yet another way. Pressure from the industrially-organised employers' associations helped to push the Metalworkers Union from its intermediate 'work-material' status towards industrial unionism. Thus in 1908 the Engineering Employers Association's refusal to negotiate a new agreement unless all eight unions in the industry signed was followed by the Metalworkers' adoption of the principle of industrial unionism in 1909.[20]

The emergence of strong national unions and the building of a national federation had produced a labour movement able to put heavy pressure on the employers to accept collective bargaining. The employers responded by creating their own organisations, developing the lockout as a weapon and using collective agreements to strengthen their authority. The LO found itself turned into an agent of employer power, as the SAF used the threat of lockout to pressure it into bringing individual unions into line. This employer strategy entailed not the suppression of unions but rather the organisation of the whole labour market, the extension of collective agreements and the reorganising of the unions into industrial units matching the employers' associations. In spite of circumstances apparently facilitating employer resistance to worker organisation, the escalatory dynamics of class conflict meant that the employers themselves contributed to the formation of a centralised, national, industrially organised labour movement.

The State, the Employers and the Labour Movement

While there were clear instances of state repression, the labour movement was allowed to develop in a relatively unfettered way. The best known example of repression was the use of the military against striking saw-workers at Sundsvall in 1879, but Westerståhl's standard work on the Swedish labour movement concludes that such interventions were exceptional and only on rare occasions decisive.[21] In the 1880s and 1890s the *Riksdag* responded to the growth of the labour movement by passing punitive legislation that could be used against socialist agitation and the 'coercion' of other workers by strikers. Socialists and strikers were imprisoned but intermittently rather than systematically and, crucially, there was no legislation against unions as such, for the right to free association had been established by the constitutional changes of 1864.[22]

After the turn of the century, as conflicts became larger, attention switched to the regulation of conflict and a law was passed in 1906 to enable state mediation. The protracted general strike of 1909 was followed by an attempt to pass legislation that would make collective agreements legally binding, prohibit conflict during their period of validity, establish a Labour Court to administer the law, require notice of conflict and extend the existing punishment and mediation laws. After much debate and revision these proposals were rejected[23] by the *Riksdag*.[24] The employers were in any case ambivalent about them, for while they favoured punitive anti-strike laws, a general state regulation of industrial relations would inhibit lockouts as well as strikes.[25]

Why did the state, which was democratised so late, not do more to stop the growth of a socialist labour movement? One must first consider the character of the pre-industrial regime, which was a centralised and undemocratic monarchy but, on the whole, non-repressive. This was mainly, it seems, because of the dominance of a 'free' and largely self-governing peasantry in a homogeneous society where the aristocracy and the urban bourgeoisie were relatively weak, and internal conflicts that might involve the state were therefore minimal. Indeed, Swedish monarchs at times allied themselves with the peasantry in order to restrict the power of the aristocracy.[26] A further factor was the marginality of the Scandinavian societies, for their non-involvement in European warfare meant that the state was not under pressure to mobilise and control the population.

Secondly, however, why did Swedish capitalists not make greater use of the power of the state against the nascent labour movement? If class conflict had been muted in the past, it was becoming highly visible in the 1880s and after. The enactment of punitive legislation against strikers in the 1890s showed that the state apparatus could be used against the unions, and there were further attempts to legislate. Indeed, the 1905 proposals to introduce fines or imprisonment for strikers in private or public utilities, where strikes would have a serious knock-on impact on industrial production, and for strikers who threatened life or property, only narrowly failed to secure a majority.[27]

That they did so was due to the growing strength of the combined Liberal and Social Democratic parties, which were in a majority in the *Riksdag*'s lower chamber by this time. Critical here and in future parliamentary battles on such questions was the Liberals' belief that anti-worker legislation should not be passed while a restricted suffrage prevented the proper representation of workers in parliament. The Liberals were also allied with the SDAP in pursuit of constitutional reform. Paradoxically, Sweden's late democratisation actually prevented anti-labour legislation and it was only in 1928, after the completion of democratisation, that further such legislation was eventually passed.

Socialism and Liberalism

Late democratisation was also linked to the comparative weakness of Swedish liberalism, for this weakness eased the socialists' assumption of the leadership of the labour movement. Although the Liberal alliance became important to the Social Democrats once they had established themselves and had begun to build up their strength in an unreformed parliament, where they needed all the friends they could get, a strong Liberal Party with support in the working class could have been a serious obstacle to the establishment of the SDAP as the political party of labour. Liberals and socialists were enemies before they became allies.

A Liberal workers' movement did emerge in the 1860s and showed signs of national organisation with the 'First Swedish Workers' Meeting' in Stockholm in 1879. Multi-class in character, it involved intellectuals, employers and professionals, and only about half those at the 1879 meeting were workers. Much emphasis was placed on class cooperation but the problem of industrial conflict had to be faced, particularly at the 1879 meeting which occurred shortly after the dramatic events at Sundsvall, and there was a reluctant acceptance that strikes could be justified in some circumstances. The early 1880s programme of the Stockholm Central Union Committee was much influenced by Liberal ideas, although it was also influenced by the Lassallean producer cooperative notions of the socialist August Palm, who first visited Stockholm in 1881.[28]

During the 1880s, socialists took over the leadership of the labour movement. In 1885 an open competition began between Liberals and socialists for control of the Stockholm union committee. The socialists won and the committee adopted a more radical, more political programme in 1886, and elected a socialist as its chairman.[29] The Liberals planned to launch a Liberal workers' party in 1890 but in 1889 the socialists beat them to it by founding the SDAP at a meeting in Stockholm.

The socialist takeover was accomplished rapidly, particularly in comparison with Britain, for example, where the socialists faced a much harder fight to establish themselves.[30] There was undoubtedly much support for Liberal ideas in the craft unions, but the Liberals' ambivalent attitudes towards industrial conflict at a time when these unions were making frequent use of the strike weapon provided an opening for the socialists. The socialists also clearly outmanoeuvred the Liberals in the contest for the leadership of the labour movement in the later 1880s. It was, however, the general weakness of liberalism in Sweden that lay behind the Liberals' failure. The overwhelmingly agrarian character of Swedish society, the slowness of urbanisation[31] and a relatively monolithic elite did not provide good conditions for the emergence of a strong Liberal party.

This was hardly a hospitable environment for socialism either, apart from the fact that strikes were becoming much more common in the 1880s. But once the socialists had gained a foothold they were, as Stephens has argued,[32] in an excellent position to organise the working class as it emerged and lead the fight for parliamentary reform.[33] The SDAP was the first modern political party in Sweden. As a consequence, the Swedish Social Democrats faced less competition for worker votes from established bourgeois parties than labour parties elsewhere did. So far as the socialists were concerned, the late democratisation of Sweden was an obstacle that became an advantage.

Socialists, Anarchists and Communists

The SDAP was careful to pursue a moderate line in order to avoid upsetting non-socialist trade unionists and maintain the Liberal alliance, but there was then the opposite problem of preventing the secession of revolutionaries. The complete range of ideological positions could be found within the infant Swedish socialist movement.[34] Sweden's late democratisation meant, however, that all could agree that the movement's immediate goal was to achieve universal suffrage, even if they disagreed about the strategy that should be followed thereafter.[35] Furthermore, reformers such as Branting, who quickly came to dominate the party, accepted that it might be necessary to use revolutionary means to achieve suffrage reform.[36] Indeed, in 1894 the party was united behind the idea that the general strike should be used as a weapon to force through reform.[37]

The emergence of a new generation of radicals made it less easy to maintain the ideological and organisational unity of the labour movement. The SDAP leadership's actions alienated the radicals, notably through its decision to abandon the use of the strike as a political weapon and its reformist cooperation with the 1905 Liberal government which, in connection with the 'union crisis' over Norwegian secession, passed laws against pacifist propaganda. The SDAP leadership also suspended two anarchists from membership in 1906 and then expelled them in 1908.

The radicals gathered in the Young Socialist movement which was spreading at this time. The age composition of the industrial labour force, a quarter of which was under the age of twenty-five in 1900, and the high mobility of young workers had led to the rapid growth of a youth movement susceptible to radical ideas.[38] The Young Socialists had a particular impact on the industrial wing of the movement; their syndicalism led them to reject collective agreements, union centralisation and the LO's acceptance in 1906 of the 'employer's rights'. Discontent with the LO's leadership was growing during 1908 as this organisation, under heavy pressure from the SAF, sought to contain worker militancy and settle industrial conflicts. The Young Socialists exploited this and encouraged local union branches to disaffiliate from the SDAP. Eighty-six branches did so between July 1908 and August 1909, though these defections were as nothing compared with the halving of union and party membership after the unsuccessful general strike of 1909.[39] If this puts the Young Socialists' activities in perspective, they did nonetheless found in 1910 the syndicalist Swedish Workers' Central Organisation (SAC), which became a small but persistent rival to the LO.

By 1908 the Social Democratic Youth Association, formed by loyalist breakaways from the Young Socialists, had itself become an opposition organisation virtually independent of the party. A running battle developed with the party leadership, which criticised the Youth Association but did nonetheless strive to keep it within the fold. The party's electoral success in 1911, after the establishment of universal male suffrage in 1909, raised the possibility of SDAP participation in a Liberal government and led to renewed charges of opportunism from the left. This created a new organisational focus for its activities in the form of the Social Democratic Left Society, founded in 1912 just before the so-called 'Red Congress' of the Youth Association. Secession from the SDAP was in the air, but there was insufficient membership support for such a move and the congress eventually passed a 'unity resolution'.[40]

Towards the end of the First World War a more serious political and industrial opposition emerged that challenged the Social Democratic leadership of the labour movement until the mid-1930s. The leadership had declared a wartime truce with the 1914–1917 Conservative government, appointed after a royal intervention in defence policy that led to the resignation of the existing government and also 'implied rejection of a parliamentary cabinet system of government'.[41] This truce with an apparently retrograde government resulted in an intensified conflict with the left which was forced out of the party at the 1916 Congress and went on to found the Social Democratic Left Party in 1917. A series of communist-led organisations, starting with the Union Opposition of 1917, then appeared within the union movement. These exploited the growing worker discontent of the later war years when wages failed to keep pace with price increases, and the intensified industrial conflict generated by the employers' attempts to secure wage reductions during the years of depression and high unemployment in the 1920s and early 1930s.

The opposition certainly had some success. The SAC built up support initially in stone quarrying, which spread to construction, especially railway building, during the war period, and then to forestry. It attained its maximum membership, one-eighth that of the LO, in 1920. But during the 1920s and early 1930s it was the communists who were the more active opponents of the LO. Their Committee for Union Unity attracted numbers equivalent to one-tenth of the LO's membership at its conferences in 1926 and 1929, and in 1919 they gained brief control of two important unions, the Typographers and the Metalworkers. They also became influential in the unions in mining, the paper and wood industries, some branches of the building unions and amongst seamen.

These successes were short-lived and in the early 1930s major communist-led strikes were defeated, while the LO launched a counter-attack that resulted in the expulsion of communists from the unions. It was only in the particular 'isolated mass'[42] context of certain industries, such as forestry and mining, that the opposition was able to establish itself for any length of time, while its urban victories were always tied to specific circumstances that brought union leaders and members into conflict and gave the opposition a temporary boost.[43]

Why had the radicals failed to consolidate their gains and mount an effective challenge to the labour leadership? The centralisation of the LO, its cooperation with the SAF and the party's rightward drift towards participation in government might, after all, have been expected to create internal conflicts that would foster opposition movements. Opposition within the unions was, however, hard to sustain because of the employers' centralised organisation and their strategy of escalating conflict through widening lockouts, which made unions dependent on the LO.[44] On the other hand, the success of the party's reformist strategy, as it rapidly became the largest party in the lower house and as electoral and constitutional reforms were carried through, cut the ground from under the proponents of revolutionary change.

By the time that the internal opposition first became significant in 1908–1909, both the LO and the party were strong enough to ride out the challenge from the left, consolidate their authority and then counter-attack. It would have been a rather more serious matter if ideological divisions had crystallised earlier and weakened the labour movement before it had established itself and demonstrated its ability to both defend and advance the cause of labour. Hence the importance once again of Sweden's late democratisation, which blurred the boundaries between revolutionaries and reformers during the critical formative years of the movement.

Social Democratic Rule

Social Democratic Rule, Capitalism and Socialism

Although the Social Democrats formed short-lived minority governments in the 1920s, it was in 1932 that Social Democrat rule really began. In the 1930s the Social Democrats came to terms with capitalism but maintained, at least in the long term, their socialist goals. It has been argued that the party leadership abandoned its socialist beliefs in favour of a pragmatic welfare capitalism, but this was demonstrably not the case.[45] Indeed, the Swedish movement's capacity to reconcile its socialist goals with the successful management of a capitalist economy has been one of its striking features, as in the well-known Rehn-Meidner model of economic policy[46] and, less convincingly, the Employee Investment Funds of 1983.[47]

By the time of the 1932 election the idea that socialism involved the immediate taking of the means of production into public ownership had been dropped.[48] More positively, the Social Democrats came to recognise that the achievement of their goals depended on the profitability of industry and its international competitiveness. If it was to deliver employment, welfare and a high standard of living, the government needed to promote rationalisation and get Sweden's capitalist economy working more efficiently, even if this meant that labour would suffer in the short term. In the late 1930s a 'reform pause' was declared, taxes on profits were reduced and a series of joint state-industry committees to formalise cooperation was proposed. These proposals were overtaken by international events, though these led in any case to the emergence of an extensive wartime cooperation between employers and the state. Labour, on the other hand, required regulation, for strikes such as the troublesome strike in the building industry during 1933–1934 could impede government economic policies designed to promote full employment. Organised labour had to be made responsible and, after government attempts to extend state regulation had failed, the LO and the SAF signed the Basic Agreement of 1938 which provided the model for the post-war regulation of industrial relations.[49]

The shelving of socialisation, the pursuit of welfare and the encouragement of rationalisation did not, however, mean that the idea of a socialist transformation of society had been abandoned. Indeed, rationalisation could prepare the way for socialism since the concentration of ownership would make an eventual socialisation of ownership easier. Meanwhile, policies leading to the extension of state regulation and planning, the growth of collective saving and investment, and the involvement of labour in management would reduce the functions of capital until it was ripe for expropriation. The development of a welfare state was arguably not a way of integrating labour into a capitalist society but a means of promoting class solidarity by protecting labour from the divisive impact of market forces and enabling the labour movement to build up its power.[50]

A tension between socialism and capitalism remained and conflict flared up periodically. Although the Social Democrats had arrived at a *modus vivendi* with capital, the employers recoiled from the notions of industrial democracy, state-planning, wage equalisation and the collectivising of ownership which surfaced periodically in the party. If, on the other hand, the government cooperated too closely with capital, discontent built up within the labour movement, as the heyday of the 'Swedish model' in the 1960s showed.

Thus, cooperation during the 1950s and 1960s between the government, the employers and the labour leadership produced an economic growth providing full employment and high living standards for Swedish workers. However, the failure to achieve the labour movement's redistributive goals, the costs of an uninhibited pursuit of growth, the tensions created by the centralisation of authority in the unions and the powerlessness of workers to resist deteriorating conditions at plant level, all combined to generate a revolt with far-reaching consequences.

The long unofficial strike in the northern iron mines during the winter of 1969–1970 expressed this discontent, challenged the labour leadership and administered a considerable shock to the system. The strike rate rose sharply in these years and a shadowy opposition movement, based on mutually supportive strike committees, emerged. There were long battles in the docks and in 1972 the bulk of the dockers seceded from the Transport Workers Union to form their own. There was a general reaction against the pressures of increasingly widespread piecework methods of payment, and in 1975 a long unofficial strike occurred in the forestry industry over this issue. Swedish workers began to demand security of employment, lower levels of stress at work, more say in management and decision-making, a reform of labour law and a more responsive labour leadership.

This revolt showed some similarities with the inter-war opposition movements, since its more organised manifestations were rooted in the 'isolated mass' industries of mining, forestry and the docks, though it was less politicised and did not challenge the SDAP's leadership of the labour movement. On the other hand, discontent was more widespread; it could not therefore be dismissed as the product of communist agitation or crushed by expulsions, and consequently had a greater impact on the policy of both the LO and the SDAP.

The labour leadership was forced to radicalise its policies in ways that undermined what was generally known as the 'Swedish model'. The system of central bargaining, which had been established in the 1950s to contain wage demands, now became a means of equalising wages. The post-1938 settlement of issues through central agreements between the LO and the SAF gave way to legislative regulation as the government responded to labour demands by passing laws to provide security of employment, improved conditions of work and codetermination. The Co-determination Law of 1976 abolished the 'employer's rights' accepted by the LO in 1906; also in 1976, the LO adopted the Meidner Plan to transfer gradually but steadily the ownership of industry from capital to union-controlled funds.[51] Not only the institutions of the Swedish model but also the capitalist relations of production, indeed the capitalist ownership of the means of production, were now challenged and some thought that the Swedish labour movement was on the threshold of the peaceful transition to socialism that had eluded movements elsewhere.[52]

If this radicalisation of policy preserved the unity of the labour movement, for the LO's response to the rank-and-file and the SDAP's broad willingness to enact the LO's wishes maintained the movement's cohesion, it did so at considerable cost. The Social Democrats lost the 1976 election and found themselves out of office for six years, at least partly because of the unpopularity of the Meidner Plan. The use of central bargaining to equalise rather than restrain wages contributed to an employer disenchantment with this institution, which has led to a radical de-centralisation strategy ultimately undermining the LO's *raison d'être*. The assault on the 'employer's rights' and the Meidner Plan provoked a counter-attack from the SAF, aimed not only at circumventing the legislation of the 1970s but also at restoring employer power and carrying through a new 'bourgeois revolution' that would reverse the achievements of Social Democracy. The issue of the Meidner Plan was, indeed, the first since the 1930s that could not be resolved through compromise.

In the end the Social Democrats avoided legislation that might seriously interfere with the capitalist relations of production or damage the capitalist engine of economic growth. The 1976 Codetermination Act was formulated so as not to undermine employer authority or weaken management, while the version of the Meidner Plan legislated in 1983 posed no threat to the ownership of industry by private capital, even if the employers thought it did. The implementation of the wage solidarity policy, the 1970s legislation and the Meidner Plan had, however, wrecked both the machinery and the culture of the centralised corporatism that had made Social Democracy work.

The 1970s showed that there was a contradiction at the heart of the Social Democratic model. The Social Democrats had worked out a *modus vivendi* with capital that was mutually beneficial but ultimately unstable; the idea of a socialist transformation of society persisted, while cooperation with industry generated a labour revolt that forced the government to radicalise its policies in ways that destroyed the very *modus vivendi* which had been established.

From Peasant Alliance to Extended Working Class

As Przeworski has pointed out, the early socialist belief that workers would one day be in a majority was quite wrong. This presented Social Democratic parties with a dilemma, for a party seeking to govern must secure support from other social groups, but this would lead to the pursuit of welfare and the abandonment of socialism. Furthermore, 'when socialists seek the support of other people they erode the very sources of their strength amongst workers'.[53]

Others, such as Himmelstrand et al., Esping-Andersen and Tilton,[54] have argued that this problem can be solved. Classes should not be regarded as objective, economically-determined facts with fixed boundaries; on the contrary, they can be shaped by social policy. Thus welfare policies need not mean a retreat from socialism; if appropriately formulated on universalist lines, they could help to bring socialism about by protecting labour from market forces and establishing a common interest between workers and other exploited groups. It was possible for the Social Democrats to create an adequate political base without sacrificing their socialism or losing worker support.

The Social Democratic breakthrough into government was in fact based on a widening of the party's appeal through the concept of the *folkhem* or 'people's home', which is particularly associated with Per Albin Hansson, Prime Minister from 1932–1946. He believed that the SDAP could unite all the exploited classes – workers, peasants, elements of the middle class – against capitalism, without diluting socialist beliefs.

'For Per Albin, what made the labour movement socialist was not that it sought the welfare of the working class, still less that it tried to exalt worker interests over the general interest, but rather that it represented the general interests of society'.[55]

This notion fitted well with the Social Democrats' reliance on Agrarian Party support for a majority in parliament from the 1930s through to the 1950s. This party was detached from its bourgeois allies by the SDAP's willingness to protect agriculture and support food prices, though the Social Democrats had prepared for such an alliance as long ago as 1911 when the idea of socialising the ownership of land was dropped from the party programme.[56] The alliance with the SDAP was cemented by the involvement of the Agrarians in government.[57] The historic condition for a farmer-worker alliance was the predominantly small-holder character of agriculture and the ancient conflict between the peasantry and a bureaucratic urban elite, which prevented the emergence of a British-style Conservative Party with rural support.[58] The greater success of the Swedish 'labour party' has depended not only on the labour movement's strength but also on a divided right.

The governments of the 1930s were certainly not particularly radical through the deal with the Agrarians probably played only a minor part in this, for the emerging *modus vivendi* with capital and the threatening international situation also counselled moderation. The Agrarian Party did however exert a restraining influence, and it was only when the SDAP broke away from this alliance in the 1950s that the socialist potential of welfare policies was developed.

The crucial event was the SDAP's decision in the late 1950s to opt for a compulsory, state-funded and earnings-related supplementary pension scheme. The Agrarian Party opposed this scheme, but the SDAP designed it to attract the white-collar vote and made sufficient electoral gains to ensure its passage through Parliament and establish a clear parliamentary majority, after many years of gradually declining Social Democrat representation in Parliament. A universal welfare measure with income-related benefits, the pension scheme appealed to non-manual as well as manual labour and created a common interest in the development of the welfare state.

With pension reform, the Social Democrats moved in one bound from an alliance with the *petit bourgeoisie* to one with the new middle class, thereby both building on and creating an 'extended working class'. Furthermore, the new pension scheme provided the state with funds it could use to collectivise the ownership of industry. Far from sacrificing socialism to welfare, this reform opened up an opportunity for the Social Democrats to pursue socialist goals.[59]

Politically, this alliance was successful. Middle class support for the left rose during the elections of the 1950s and 1960s and, after stagnating during the 1970s, continued rising through the 1980s to 39 per cent in the election of 1988.[60] A community of interest between white-collar workers, largely employed in the public sector, and the SDAP, which continued to work to provide welfare and maintain full employment, underpinned the alliance. Industrially, the alliance was associated with a strong growth of white-collar unionism, which strengthened the labour movement as a whole in important ways. It provided the basis for an 'employee front' against capital, as in the 1970s campaign for industrial democracy; it also led to a very high overall union density, which insulated the labour movement against occupational changes that would otherwise have led to a declining union membership.

There was an important gender dimension to the alliance, for the growth of non-manual and service occupations which largely employed women meant that the overall strength of the labour movement depended on its success in recruiting them. The proportion of women in paid employment has reached an exceptional level in Sweden, with some 84 per cent of women aged between 16 and 64 years gainfully employed in 1991, as compared with 90 per cent of men.[61] Furthermore, although the expansion of women's employment in the 1970s was largely in part-time work, in the 1980s the balance shifted towards their employment in full-time work.[62] The labour movement has been remarkably successful in generating support amongst these women workers; their union density has been exceptionally high, and indeed now exceeds that of men, particularly in white-collar occupations.[63] Also, the loyalties of women voters have gradually shifted from the right to the left, and in the 1980s for the first time women voted preponderantly for the parties of the left. In the 1985 election, 46 per cent of women voters supported the Social Democrats, as compared with only 41 per cent of men.[64]

During the egalitarian 1970s, the political parties had competed to exploit the gender issue and generally advocated equality between the sexes at work, at home and also in politics, where women have achieved internationally high levels of representation. There was something of a consensus on the goal of gender equality but not on the means of achieving it,[65] and the Social Democrats acquired a certain advantage here by emphasising womens' participation and equality in the labour market and facilitating their employment by various means.

The separate taxation of women, legislated in 1971, greatly increased women's incentive to work while the provision of publicly funded daytime child-care and generous arrangements for leave of absence with parental benefit at childbirth and during the illness of children, legislated in the 1970s and extended in the 1980s, facilitated the employment of women. An important factor encouraging women's part-time employment was the long-standing entitlement of part-time workers to social benefits, from which they are frequently excluded in other countries; combined with other 1970s reforms, such as the partial pension of 1976, this entitlement made it financially easier to work part-time.[66] The labour movement's wage solidarity policy promoted the compression not only of occupational differentials but also those of gender, and this too encouraged women to enter employment. By 1985 women's wages had reached a level of 88 per cent of those of men, though the gap has since widened again.[67] On the demand side, the SDAP's commitment to public sector expansion has been crucial, for this is where women have largely been employed.

One should also note that Social Democrat egalitarianism has played an important part in integrating migrant labour into the working class. Immigration since the Second World War has certainly diminished the homogeneity of Swedish society. Migrants have accumulated through net immigration as follows: 134,000 in the 1940s, 106,000 in the 1950s, 235,000 in the 1960s, 155,000 in the 1970s and 178,000 in the 1980s. Migrants and their children now make up a significant proportion of the relatively small population of Sweden (currently some 8 million inhabitants). After a surge of migrants in the 1960s, many of them coming from Mediterranean countries, the entry of non-Nordic foreign workers was restricted in 1967 but they have continued to enter Sweden as refugees.[68]

The assimilation of migrants may have been eased by the large proportion coming from other Scandinavian countries with linguistic and cultural affinities,[69] but the Social Democrats also actively promoted equality for migrants and freedom of cultural choice. Legislation passed in 1975 gave all aliens, irrespective of citizenship, who are resident in Sweden for three years the right to vote and run for office in local and regional elections, while considerable effort has gone into special educational and cultural programmes aimed at both assimilating migrants *and* sustaining their native cultures. One should note, however, that a serious backlash against migrants has recently emerged and found political expression in the rise of the populist New Democracy Party and a more restrictive attitude, justified by reference to higher unemployment, in the Social Democratic Party itself towards the entry of refugees.[70]

In other ways, however, the labour movement's drive for greater equality has had more problematic consequences, for it collided with the growth of white-collar unions and opened up the whole question of wage relativities. The LO's attempts in the late 1960s to implement its wage solidarity policy put it on a collision course with the white-collar federations, and led to some spectacular industrial conflicts focused not on labour's relationship with capital but on wage differentials. The very centralisation of the Swedish labour market amplified these rivalries and by the 1970s they were completely dominating wage rounds, wrecking the wage restraint function of Sweden's famous institutions of central bargaining and alienating the employers who had largely created them. These rivalries were then increasingly complicated by a division between the private and public sectors; the result was four competing union power blocs which paralysed bargaining in the 1980s and helped to generate the upward spiral of wages that made Sweden increasingly uncompetitive.[71] The growing sectoral division also threatened the LO's cohesion, as the Local Authority Workers Union became numerically dominant and the Metalworkers Union joined with the engineering employers in breaking away from the central bargaining process which had become ever more crucial to the LO.[72]

The new strategy of the 1950s had apparently solved the problem of reconciling a working-class political base with the absence of a working-class majority. It provided the basis for constructing the world's most advanced welfare state, extended the labour movement into the ranks of white-collar labour, reinvigorated socialism and gave the SDAP a new lease of life. The egalitarian policies associated with this revival of radicalism benefited the lower-paid and integrated women workers and migrants. These policies also, however, interacted with the growth of white-collar unionism to stimulate an occupational sectionalism that wrecked the corporatist system of bargaining established in the 1950s. The sectional rivalries of an extended working class were amplified by centralisation and began to weaken the unity of the LO; this extended working class eventually became divided and unmanageable.

Social Democracy in One Country

While changes in occupational structure presented the Social Democrats with one set of problems, a bourgeois political revival during the 1970s challenged the whole Social Democratic project. The bourgeois parties won the election of 1976 and a bourgeois government was in power for the next six years. The Social Democrats weathered this political storm, however, returning to office in 1982 and remaining in government during the rest of the decade and, at least initially, continuing to implement socialist policies and develop the Swedish welfare state. Sweden apparently defied the international tendency of the 1980s for labour movements to decline and the New Right to dominate politics; indeed, Sweden seemed to show that there really was a viable Social Democratic alternative to Thatcherism and Reaganomics.

The explanation of Swedish exceptionalism lay partly in the political weakness of the right, for the bourgeois governments of 1976–1982 had been ineffective, divided and quite unable to make a break with the legacy of forty-four years of Social Democratic rule. Although popular support for the right had clearly increased, the 1976 bourgeois victory had resulted mainly from a reaction against the growing use of nuclear power, a reaction that was exploited very effectively by the Centre Party. There is little evidence in Sweden of an anti-tax, anti-welfare state backlash of the kind that had developed amongst British workers, before the end of the 1970s.[73]

This was not just a matter of the weakness of the right, however; there was also the organisational and ideological strength of the labour movement. Although issue voting was on the rise, as the importance of the nuclear energy and environment question in the 1976 election showed, the SDAP retained its hold on the working-class vote, continuing to attract around 70 per cent of the worker vote during the 1980s.[74] The Social Democratic Party maintained its remarkable capacity to mobilise and control working-class voters.

The historic strength of the SDAP in the working class, dating back, as argued earlier, to the circumstances of industrialisation and democratisation, laid the basis for this control but, crucially, the party's strength in the working class has been actively developed and renewed by organisational means. Party membership levels have long been very high in international terms[75] and in the 1980s a staggering one in six adult Swedes were members of the SDAP,[76] which, as Linton points out, is a rate of party membership some seven times greater than that of the British Labour Party.[77] The collective affiliation of union members accounted for roughly three-quarters of this membership, although this was only one element in a complex of reinforcing labour organisations.

Tensions between the youth movement and the labour leadership may have been a source of conflict during the labour movement's early years, as discussed above, but the party's youth section also became an important means of political socialisation that provided the party with cross-generational continuity. The SDAP's youth section had built up a membership of 64,000 by 1932, and this shot up to 104,000 in 1936 as the section organised protests against unemployment. This high level of membership was sustained for a time but declined after 1970, dropping to 45,000 by 1983, although this was nonetheless still an impressive figure when one recalls that the whole population of Sweden amounts to only about 8 million. Furthermore, political socialisation did not start with the youth movement; there was also the labour movement's Young Eagles organisation, founded in 1931, which by the mid-1980s had a membership of some 70,000 school children.

The women's section of the party expanded from 8,000 members in 1932 to 50,000 in 1948 and still had around this number in the mid-1980s. The cultural side of the worker's life has been catered for by People's Halls and People's Parks, originally founded in the 1890s and still flourishing in the 1980s. There are also extensive pensioners', tenants', consumer cooperative and housing cooperative movements, temperance and sports associations linked to the labour movement.[78] Other labour movements have of course developed a periphery of such organisations, but what is particularly striking about Sweden is their high membership levels and continued strength into the 1980s, in spite of well-known tendencies towards privatisation (in the 'private life' sense of this term) and individualism.

These organisational activities have been linked to a considerable informational and educational apparatus. The Social Democratic press included twenty-one locally-based daily newspapers in the 1980s and accounted for 20 per cent of the newspapers sold.[79] Adult education has long been a priority of the labour movement but this received a considerable boost in the 1970s. The proportion of the adult population taking part in 'study circles' organised by education associations increased from 19.5 per cent in 1968 to 32.2 per cent in 1981 and, although the bourgeois parties also run education associations, the largest of them, the Workers' Educational Association, is attached to the labour movement. It has been estimated that at the end of the 1970s roughly one and a half million workers were taking part in study circles organised by the unions.[80]

These study circles have been particularly important in cultivating and disseminating the labour movement's views on work environment and industrial democracy issues. Remarkably, when faced by the spectre of rising unemployment, the 1976 bourgeois government accepted the labour movement's proposal for state subsidies for workers involved in educational programmes at work. According to Heclo and Madsen, some 400,000 workers found themselves paid to study the application of the legislation recently introduced on these matters by the Social Democrats.[81] This was hardly the bourgeois counter-revolution the employers had been hoping for!

If all this testifies to the energy and activity of the labour movement, the movement was also dependent on an extensive system of state support built up by years of Social Democratic government. This applies to the Social Democratic Party itself, which like the other political parties has received considerable state funding since 1966, and the unions, whose members receive tax allowances to cover their subscriptions. The labour press was kept alive by state subsidies, notably by the law of 1971 that 'preserved choice' by giving financial support to the smaller newspaper in an area, which was often the labour paper.[82] Some 40 per cent of the costs of a study circle, so long as it meets certain basic requirements, are borne by the state and municipal grants cover part of the remainder.[83] The extensive labour legislation of the early 1970s created new flows of money to support the educational, health and environmental activities of the labour movement at plant level through a payroll tax on private and public companies. In 1977 a similarly funded Centre for the Study of Working Life was set up in Stockholm to monitor, research and develop industrial democracy and improvements in the work environment.[84]

The organisational vigour, capacity for mobilisation and state subsidisation of the labour movement were not seriously dented by the electoral setbacks of 1976 and 1979, or the six years of ineffectual bourgeois rule, and enabled the Social Democrats to return to power in 1982. The strength of the labour movement, the restoration of Social Democratic rule and the political weakness of the right concealed, however, the continued strength of employer organisation and a gathering SAF offensive. The labour movement's use of its political and industrial power to equalise wages and democratise industrial relations in the 1970s stimulated a broad employer counter-attack, aimed not only at curbing union power in the labour market and the workplace but also at reasserting employer ideological dominance by exerting greater influence on the media and education. The SAF underwent extensive reorganisation, sought to decentralise bargaining and became increasingly an opinion-forming and lobbying body. In the workplace some major companies adopted a strategy to integrate labour locally, thereby making the occupationally-demarcated and centralised union federations appear archaic. The bourgeois governments of 1976–1982 may have been a severe disappointment, but capital continued to support the Moderate Party, the most right-wing of the bourgeois parties as the political vehicle of a new bourgeois revolution.[85]

It was not just the employer offensive that threatened the labour movement but also the growing economic power of capital and Sweden's deteriorating economic situation, which combined to make it ever more difficult to maintain the Social Democratic model. While the labour movement may have regained political power, the trans-national organisation and ever greater mobility of capital meant that economic power was shifting from labour to capital.[86] Furthermore, although devaluation and favourable terms of trade shielded the economy for a time during the 1980s, it was clear that Swedish products were becoming uncompetitive. Swedish corporations increasingly moved capital abroad and set up mergers with foreign companies. At a time of growing international economic integration, the prospects were not good for a small, high-cost country with a more expensive welfare state, higher taxes and a better protected and more organised labour force than its competitors.

In the later 1980s the Social Democrats began to come to terms with economic realities and to abandon the Social Democratic model. Neo-liberal tendencies can be detected in the government's moves to make Sweden more competitive and more attractive to capital by abolishing foreign exchange and import controls, by introducing private capital to state-owned industries, by shifting from direct to indirect taxation and by reducing public expenditure. The SDAP, or its leadership at least, came to accept that Sweden should end its socialist isolation and enter the EU. So far as the welfare state was concerned, the government began to decentralise public services and introduce internal markets. It also met employer concerns over absenteeism by reducing sick-pay and agreeing to transfer responsibility for its payment during the first two weeks of absence to employers. As sectional rivalries drove up wages, the government became increasingly interventionist in wage bargaining, and during the political crisis of February 1990 it actually proposed a wage freeze, a two-year strike ban and massive increases in fines on strikers.[87]

All this placed a growing strain on the labour movement's cohesion, and internal tensions began to incapacitate the Social Democratic government. These tensions in fact go back to the LO's commitment to the Meidner Plan in 1976, which took the Social Democrats by surprise and proved a serious electoral liability which could not be easily jettisoned after its adoption by the LO's congress.[88] The LO did cooperate with government attempts to restrain wages after the 1982 devaluation, but later used its influence to block government attempts to deflate the economy after the incomes policy had failed. It was indeed the government's inability to deflate which precipitated the February 1990 crisis; initially the LO supported the crisis proposals but an outcry among the membership forced it to reverse its position, although the government could not in any case assemble a parliamentary majority for its proposals. Relations between the LO and the government deteriorated, and personal attacks on government members by the LO chairman did not help matters. What the media called a 'war of the roses' had developed between the political and industrial wings of the movement.

By the early 1990s the Social Democrats had little more to offer. They were abandoning socialist policies and their drift towards neo-liberal ones was alienating the labour movement. Their opinion-poll rating was tumbling, there was a widespread sense that it was time for a change and it was clear that the Social Democrats were heading for defeat at the 1991 election, which returned a radical and determined bourgeois government quite different in character to those of the later 1970s.

The new bourgeois government initially pursued its programme with some vigour and began to reverse the legacy of Social Democratic rule, not only through policy changes but also by ending the state subsidies for union activities at plant level and the tax allowances for union membership, at a time when economic crisis and a rapidly deepening recession severely strained the finances of the unions, the labour press and other organisations linked to the labour movement. The bourgeois government then ran into growing difficulties, in part because it was dependent for its majority on the unreliable populists of the newly born *Ny Demokrati* party, and in part because of its coalition character, but largely because of Sweden's worst economic crisis since the 1930s. In the autumn of 1992 the government turned to the Social Democrats to obtain their support for a crisis package.

The Social Democrats, who have remained much the largest party, were returned to government in autumn 1994 but this does not mean that the Social Democratic model can be restored, for the Social Democrats have themselves abandoned it. The great problem faced by the Social Democrats, and indeed by labour parties elsewhere, is to develop a viable post-socialist ideological alternative to neo-liberalism, an alternative that recognises the force of international economic realities but also generates a distinctive programme that can provide a still powerful movement with a new direction and motivation.

Conclusion

The world's strongest labour movement had emerged out of the circumstances of late industrialisation in a politically backward, if lightly governed, agrarian society that was relatively homogeneous and isolated from European conflicts. Furthermore, the industry that did exist was largely craft-dominated and much of it located in isolated rural communities. This was hardly a favourable environment for socialism, but once the early socialists had achieved a foothold they were able to exploit the advantages of being in at the start of industrialisation, democratisation and the growth of a labour movement. The weakness of Liberalism allowed the socialists to establish quickly their leadership of the labour movement, while late democratisation focused socialist energies on creating and shaping the industrial organisation of workers and minimised ideological fragmentation during the movement's formative years. The unified national organisation of labour then set off a pattern of escalating class warfare that stimulated, unified and centralised employer organisation; which in turn helped to extend, centralise and unify labour organisation.

Social Democratic rule began in the 1930s but it was the 1950s pensions reform that freed the SDAP from the constraints of its dependence on the Agrarian Party and created a new, potentially radical alliance with sections of non-manual labour. The labour movement now moved to more radical policies on wage equalisation and economic and industrial democracy, in part because of rank-and-file discontent, but the Social Democrats were too dependent on a capitalist economy to take the final steps to a socialist transformation. On the other hand, these policies, together with sectional rivalries, led to the collapse of the corporatist relationship with the employers and to an institutional breakdown which, combined with the inflationary consequences of full employment and the costs of public sector expansion, weakened Swedish competitiveness and sped up the flow of capital abroad. The government responded by becoming more interventionist, authoritarian and neo-liberal in its policies, but an increasingly strained relationship with the LO halted its drift to the right.

In the end the Social Democrats were immobilised by their abandonment of the socialist project and their inability to either tackle the problems generated by welfare capitalism or arrest the declining competitiveness of Swedish industry in an ever more economically-integrated world. In spite of the strength and unity of the Swedish labour movement, its ideological flexibility and its remarkable capacity to synthesise socialist policies with capitalist practices, Social Democracy in one country was not ultimately viable.

Notes

1. Korpi, for example, advances all these arguments to account for the distinctiveness of the Swedish labour movement. Korpi (1978), p. 74f.
2. Korpi (1978), p. 74; Stephens (1979), pp. 399, 406.
3. Lindbom (1938), pp. 62f., 127, 145.
4. Åmark (1986)), pp. 61–4; Berglund (1982), p. 298.
5. Cederqvist (1980), p. 123.
6. There was in fact some danger of this happening, for the union nearly broke up in the early 1890s. Disintegration was averted by an internal reorganisation into craft-based branches and a tightening of discipline, thereby accommodating craft interests and meeting craftworker complaints. Fulcher (1991), pp. 45–50.
7. Lindgren (1938), pp. 28–41, 48, 56, 162.
8. Lindbom (1938), p. 129.
9. Blake (1960), pp. 22, 29.
10. Elvander dates the breakthrough to parliamentary government at 1884 in Norway, 1901 in Denmark and 1917 in Sweden. In 1917, parliamentary opposition brought down the wartime Conservative government and finally established that government required parlimentary consent. Elvander (1980), pp. 29–33.
11. Rustow (1955), p. 25.
12. Lohse (1963), pp. 55–7.
13. This ironically meant that when the Metalworkers Union eventually organised the workers there 'from the outside', the kind of centralised, egalitarian, class-conscious unionism that resulted was, from an employer point of view, the worst kind. Strath (1982), pp. 100–112; Svensson (1983), pp. 106–14.
14. At the turn of the century between one-fifth and one-sixth of workers were organised. Lindbom (1938), p. 176.
15. Fulcher (1991), pp. 88–92.
16. Indeed, a little-known side of the industrial relations history of the time was the role of the SAF and the Engineering Employers Association in promoting 'non-socialist' unions and organising the recruitment of strike-breakers, in part supplied by these unions but also enlisted through employer-controlled labour exchanges. One prominent company, AB Separator, contributed the lion's share of the employers' financial support for 'non-socialist' activities. If the official policy of these employers' associations was to recognise the unions, they also pursued a covert policy that sought, unsuccessfully, to undermine them. Flink (1978), pp. 33, 98; Myrman (1975), pp. 95f., 109.

17. Fulcher (1991), pp. 76–9.
18. Lohse (1963), p. 55.
19. Lindgren, Tingsten and Westerståhl (1948), pp. 135f.
20. Ibid, pp. 198–208, 217, 221.
21. Lindgren, Tingsten and Westerståhl (1945), p. 13.
22. Rustow (1955), p. 15.
23. Most did later find their way into law, notably when laws were passed in 1928 to establish a Labour Court, prohibit conflict while a collective agreement was in operation and enforce collective agreements.
24. Westerståhl (1945), pp. 312–28.
25. Once the employers had become organised and had started to use the weapon of the general lockout, they were no longer so keen on the state regulation of industrial conflict. Thus, the larger employers in particular opposed the 1906 Mediation Law and were critical of state intervention in 1908, when mediation frustrated their plans for escalating, coordinated lockouts. In 1909 there was no effective government intervention during the general strike and the employers won a decisive victory. Westerståhl (1945), pp. 299f, 336; Schiller (1967), pp. 19f., 97, 101ff.
26. Edwards (1991), p. 167; Mörner (1989), pp. 254f.; Rojas (1991), pp. 67f.
27. Westerståhl (1945), p. 289.
28. Bäckström (1977), pp. 81–7; Lindbom (1938), pp. 49–56, 85.
29. This victory did, however, lead to a reaction against socialism and an exodus of non-socialists from the still predominantly Liberal committee. Ideological disagreements within the Social Democratic Club, conflicts surrounding the appointment of the recently converted ex-Liberal Branting as editor of the *Social Democrat* and a burst of repression that led to the imprisonment of Palm then resulted in a temporary shift of the movement's leadership back to Malmö, where it had arrived from Denmark. Bäckström (1977), i.: 159ff.
30. Fulcher (1991), pp. 60–7.
31. This comes out clearly in comparisons with the other main Scandinavian societies. In 1890, 62 per cent of the Swedish working population was employed in the primary sector, as compared with 47 per cent in Denmark and 49 per cent in Norway. Lafferty (1971), p. 43. Similarly, in the same year the proportion of the population living in towns was 19 per cent in Sweden, 33 per cent in Denmark and 24 per cent in Norway. Kuhnle (1975), p. 45.
32. Stephens (1979), p. 143.
33. A Liberal-led national association of suffrage reform societies, which had first emerged in 1887, was founded in 1890 but the SDAP soon

took the initiative with its proposal for a 'people's parliament'. This idea was initially resisted by prominent Liberals but quickly acquired momentum and the people's parliament had its first week-long meeting in 1893. Bäckström (1977), i.: 249–55.

34. Tilton (1991), p. 15.
35. Bäckström (1977), i.: 185.
36. Tilton (1991), p. 20.
37. This was one reason why the party was keen to extend union organisation to Northern Sweden, and in particular to organise railway workers, so that a political general strike would be national and have greater impact. Lindbom (1938), p. 196. Simonson (1985), p. 98.
38. Bäckström (1977), ii.: 65–7.
39. Schiller (1967), pp. 169f.
40. Bäckström (1977), ii.: pp. 146f, 155, 168–71.
41. Rostow (1955), p. 82.
42. This concept was first developed by Kerr and Siegel to explain variations in strike rates. Kerr and Siegel (1954), pp. 191–3.
43. Fulcher (1984), pp. 300–22.
44. An interesting example of this was the LO's ultimatum to the communist dominated miners' union after it concluded a mutual assistance agreement with the Soviet miners' union and formed a Swedish-Russian Cooperation Committee in 1927. A protracted strike/lockout took place in the mines in 1928. The union was told that it had to choose between membership of the committee and membership of the LO; it voted for membership of the LO. Casparsson (1951), ii.: 71–94.
45. Tilton (1991), pp. 248–57.
46. According to this model, the pursuit of a wage solidarity policy would promote economic growth, since inefficient low-wage companies would be forced either to improve productivity or go out of business and allow the transfer of resources to more productive firms. An active labour market policy would transfer labour and prevent the build-up of inflationary bottle-necks where there was a high demand for it. The goals of controlling inflation, increasing equality and maximising economic growth could all be met, and without the need for state wage restraint. Fulcher (1991), p. 191.
47. It was claimed that these would support the wage solidarity policy, redistribute wealth, increase worker influence, provide capital for investment, assist wage restraint and help to finance pensions. Fulcher (1991), p. 282.
48. Wigforss, the leading Social Democrat ideologist who was also, remarkably, Finance Minister between 1932 and 1949, argued that

economic planning was a more effective way of attaining socialist goals. Lewin (1975), p. 286.

49. De Geer (1978), p. 326; Fulcher (1991), pp. 138–49; Söderpalm (1976), pp. 48f, 58, 98.
50. Korpi (1983), p. 49; Scase (1976), p. 307; Esping-Andersen (1985), pp. 22, 31f.
51. Fulcher (1991), pp. 261–96.
52. Fulcher (1987), pp. 233–5.
53. Przeworski (1985), p. 106.
54. Himmelstrand et al. (1981), pp. 185–90; Esping-Andersen (1985), pp. 31–34; Tilton (1991), pp.134–8.
55. Tilton (1991), p. 137.
56. Stephens (1979), p. 132.
57. Rustow (1955), pp. 106–9.
58. Castles (1978), pp. 139–42.
59. Hence the employers' hostility to it, though restrictions were placed on the investments that the fund was allowed to make and the ownership of industry by private capital was not significantly threatened. Fulcher (1991), p. 283. Esping-Andersen (1985), xvf., pp. 30–37, 89; Stephens (1979), pp. 178, 194.
60. Sainsbury (1991), p. 47.
61. Swedish Institute (1992).
62. Sundstrom (1993), p. 140.
63. It is reported that the union density of full-time women workers rose to 87.8 per cent in 1992, as compared with 85.6 per cent for men. Amongst white-collar workers, the corresponding figures are 86.7 per cent for women and 79.9 per cent for men. *Dagens Nyheter*, 19 December 1992.
64. Holmberg and Gilljam (1987), pp. 174f.
65. Edwards (1991) pp. 166–71, 175.
66. Sundstrom (1993), p. 139f.
67. LO (1991), p. 153.
68. Swedish Institute (1993).
69. Thus in 1992 people from other Scandinavian countries comprised 174,000 of the 499,000 foreign residents in Sweden. Swedish Institute (1993).
70. Gould (1993), pp. 179, 208; Swedish Institute (1993).
71. During 1982–1989 labour costs in Sweden rose by 76.5 per cent, compared with a rise of 64.9 per cent in Britain or 36.6 per cent in West Germany. *European Industrial Relations Review* (1992), nos. 219, 221.
72. Fulcher (1991), pp. 204–22.

73. Korpi (1983), pp. 199–204; Holmberg and Gilljam (1987), pp. 264, 316.
74. Sainsbury (1991), pp. 45–9.
75. Duverger (1959), p. 95.
76. Heclo and Madsen (1987), p. 23.
77. Linton (1985), p. 10.
78. Heclo and Madsen (1987), p. 24; Linton (1985), pp. 12f., 21f; Rustow (1955), p. 151.
79. Linton (1985), p. 19.
80. Heclo and Madsen (1987), p. 25.
81. Ibid, pp. 24f.
82. Linton (1985), pp. 18f.
83. Milner (1989), p. 166.
84. Heclo and Madsen (1987), p. 26.
85. Fulcher (1991), pp. 285–289; (1993), pp. 8–10, 14–24.
86. Olsen (1991), p. 130f.
87. Bergström (1991), pp. 14–6; Fulcher (1993), pp. 11f.
88. Heclo and Madsen (1987), pp. 268–78; Åsard (1985), p. 12.

Bibliography

Åmark, K., *Fackligt makt och fackligt medlemskap: de svenska fackförbundens medlemsutveckling 1890–1940*, Lund, 1986

Åsard, E., *Kampen om löntagarfonder*, Stockholm, 1985

Bäckström, K., *Arbetarrörelsen i Sverige*, Stockholm, 1977

Berglund, B., *Industriarbetarklassens formering: arbete och teknisk förändring vid tre svenska fabriker under 1800–talet*, Göteborgs Universitet, 1982

Bergström, H., 'Sweden's politics and party system at the crossroads', *West European Politics*, vol. 14, no. 3, 1991, pp. 8–30

Blake, D. J., 'Swedish trade unions and the Social Democrat party', *Scandinavian Economic History Review*, vol.8, no.1, 1960, pp. 19–44

Casparsson, R., *LO under fem årtionden*, Stockholm, 1951

Castles, F. G., *The Social Democratic Image of Society*, London, 1978

Cederqvist, J., *Arbetare i strejk: studier rörande arbetarnas politiska mobilisering under industrialismens genombrott*, Stockholm, 1980

De Geer, H., *Rationaliseringsrörelsen i Sverige*, Stockholm, 1978

Duverger, M., *Political Parties: Their Organisation and Activity in the Modern State*, London, 1959

Edwards, M. L., 'The Swedish gender model: productivity, pragmatism and paternalism', *West European Politics*, vol. 14, no. 3, 1991, pp. 166–81

Elvander, N., *Skandinavisk arbetarrörelse*, Stockholm, 1980

Esping-Andersen, G., *Politics against Markets*, Princeton, NJ, 1985

Fulcher, J., 'The Institutionalising of Industrial Conflict and Institutional Breakdown: a Case-study of Sweden in Comparative Perspective', unpublished PhD thesis, University of Leicester, 1984

——, 'Labour movement theory versus corporatism: Social Democracy in Sweden', *Sociology*, vol. 21, no. 2, 1987, pp. 231–52

——, *Labour Movements, Employers, and the State: Conflict and Cooperation in Britain and Sweden*, Oxford, 1991

——, 'The transformation of Swedish industrial relations', Leicester University Discussion Papers in Sociology, S93/2, 1993

Gould, A., *Capitalist Welfare Systems: A Comparison of Japan, Britain and Sweden*, London, 1993

Heclo, H. and H. Madsen, *Policy and Politics in Sweden: Principled Pragmatism*, Philadelphia PA, 1987

Himmelstrand, U., G. Ahrne, L. Lundberg, and L. Lundberg, *Beyond Welfare Capitalism*, London, 1981

Holmberg, S. and M. Gilljam, *Väljare och val i Sverige*, Stockholm, 1987

Kerr, C. and A. Siegel, 'The interindustry propensity to strike – an international comparison', in A. Kornhauser, R. Dubin and A.M. Ross (eds), *Industrial Conflict*, New York, 1954

Korpi, W., *The Working Class in Welfare Capitalism*, London, 1978

——, *The Democratic Class Struggle*, London, 1983

Kuhnle, S., *Patterns of Social and Political Mobilisation: A Historical Analysis of the Nordic Countries*, London, 1975

Lafferty, W. M., *Economic Development and the Response of Labor in Scandinavia: a Multi-level Analysis*, Oslo, 1971

Lewin, L., 'The debate on economic planning in Sweden', in S. Koblik (ed.), *Sweden's Development from Poverty to Affluence 1750–1970*, Minneapolis, MA, 1975

Lindbom, T., *Den svenska fackföreningsrörelsens uppkomst och tidiga historia*, Stockholm, 1938

Lindgren, J., *Svenska metallindustriarbetareförbundets historia* I, Stockholm, 1938

——, H. Tingsten and J. Westerståhl, *Svenska metallindustriarbetareförbundets historia* II, Stockholm, 1948

Linton, M., 'The Swedish road to socialism', *Fabian Society*, 503, 1985

LO, *Rättvisa i vägskålen*, Stockholm, 1991

Lohse, L., *Arbetsgivarnas inställning till föreningsrätt, arbetarskydd och arbetstid i statsvetenskaplig belysning*, Stockholm, 1963
Milner, H., *Sweden: Social Democracy in Practice*, Oxford, 1989
Mörner, M., '"The Swedish model": historical perspectives', *Scandinavian Journal of History*, vol. 14, no. 3, 1989, pp. 245–67
Olsen, G., 'Labour mobilisation and the strength of capital: the rise and stall of economic democracy in Sweden', *Studies in Political Economy*, vol. 34, 1991, pp. 109–45
Przeworski, A., *Capitalism and Social Democracy*, Cambridge, 1985
Rojas, M., 'The "Swedish model" in historical perspective', *Scandinavian Economic History Review*, vol. 39, no. 1, 1991, pp. 64–74
Rustow, D. A., *The Politics of Compromise*, Princeton NJ, 1955
Sainsbury, D., 'Swedish social democracy in transition: the party's record in the 1980s and the challenge of the 1990s', *West European Politics*, vol. 14, no. 3, 1991, pp. 31–57
Scase, R., *Readings in the Swedish Class Structure*, Oxford, 1976
Schiller, B., *Storstrejken, 1909*, Göteborg, 1967
Simonson, B., *Socialdemokratin och maktövertagandet: SAP's politiska strategi 1889–1911*, Göteborg, 1985
Söderpalm,S. A., *Direktörsklubben*, Stockholm, 1976
Stephens, J. D., *The Transition from Capitalism to Socialism*, London, 1979
Stråth, B., *Varvsarbetare i två värvsstäder*, Göteborg, 1982
Sundstrom, M., 'The growth in full-time work among Swedish women in the 1980s', *Acta Sociologica*, vol. 36, 1993, pp. 139–50
Svensson, T., *Från ackord till månadslön*, Göteborg, 1983
Swedish Institute, *Equality between men and women in Sweden*, Stockholm, 1992
Swedish Institute, *Immigrants in Sweden*, Stockholm, 1993
Tilton, T., *The Political Theory of Swedish Social Democracy: Through the Welfare State to Socialism*, Oxford, 1991
Westerståhl, J., *Svensk fackföreningsrörelse: organisationsproblem, verksamhetsformer, förhållande till staten*, Stockholm, 1945

–3–

The Netherlands

Lex Heerma van Voss

The twentieth-century history of the Dutch labour movement actually starts in 1894, the year that a coalition of Amsterdam diamond workers' unions won a large strike. In the wake of this success the unions, which until then had organised only in single occupations (for example cutters or polishers) within the diamond industry and then only either Jews or gentiles, merged into the ANDB (*Algemeene Nederlandsche Diamantbewerkersbond*, General Union of Dutch Diamond Workers).

The ANDB went on to become a very successful and exemplary union.[1] In time it organised all Amsterdam diamond workers and became the nucleus around which the Socialist trade union federation NVV (*Nederlands Verbond van Vakverenigingen*, Dutch Federation of Trade Unions) was formed. In the same year, 1894, the SDAP (*Sociaaldemocratische Arbeiderspartij in Nederland*, Social Democratic Labour Party in the Netherlands) was founded by a small group of Socialist activists, who broke away from the older SDB (*Sociaal Democratische Bond*, Social Democratic League). The SDAP and the NVV, are the central concerns of this chapter. We will examine the degree to which the central Socialist organisations were able to unite the Dutch working classes behind them throughout the whole of the twentieth century.[2]

The Dutch Working Classes and the Early Growth of the Labour Movement

The Netherlands began to industrialise only late in the nineteenth century.[3] Traditionally, the service sector had formed an important part of the Dutch economy, and it remained important as can be seen from the figures on the composition of the labour force contained in Table 3.1. In this table, the figures for manufacturing industry together with those for the transport sector give as exact a figure as possible for the group of 'blue collar' workers. This is a somewhat anachronistic label for the first period to be described here, when the strongholds of the labour movement were still to be found among labour aristocrats. Until the 1880s trade unions mainly found adherents among skilled workers in smaller firms in the big cities in the western part of the country; here, workers in crafts like printing, cigar-making and building had organised themselves to defend their way of life from the competition of industrial capitalism. These craft unions were more often active as productive cooperatives or Socialist discussion groups than in trying to improve work conditions through traditional trade union activities.

Table 3.1. Composition of the Dutch labour force, 1899–1991

	Agriculture	Manufacturing	Utilities, transport mining and construction	Services (incl. others, and unknown)	Total
1899	30.8	23.5	13.6	32.1	100
1909	28.4	24.2	15.5	31.9	100
1920	23.5	26.0	17.7	32.8	100
1930	20.6	25.9	18.1	35.4	100
1947	19.3	27.0	16.6	37.1	100
1960	10.7	30.7	18.7	39.9	100
1971	6.1	26.6	17.7	49.6	100
1981	5.3	20.4	16.7	57.6	100
1991	4.5	18.0	13.4	64.1	100

Source: Centraal Bureau voor de Statistiek (CBS)

At the end of the 1880s, however, this situation changed. In Amsterdam, the traditional centre of Dutch working-class militancy, a new generation of workers – many of them recent immigrants to the city – in growing industries, where craft traditions were less important, turned to trade union activity.[4] Other groups which likewise felt the harshness of the new industrial relations system and the economic downturn included agricultural workers in the north, dockers in the port of Rotterdam and textile workers in the Twente region in the east; these also started to organise themselves into trade unions and struck for better working conditions. As a consequence around 1890 the SDB, which functioned both as a political party and as a federation of trade unions, was for a short time organising older craft workers in the cities, less skilled recent immigrants to the cities and agricultural and industrial labourers elsewhere.

This list gives some impression of the variety of soil in which the labour movement tried to take root around the turn of the century. The soil and implantation metaphor can even to some extent be taken literally; the rich clay soils in the northern provinces of Friesland and Groningen had given rise to large-scale agrarian enterprises, where a sharp class distinction existed between farmers and agricultural labourers. In the peat districts in the northeastern provinces of Groningen and Drente, low-paid workers were digging peat in conditions which recall to mind the 'isolated-mass' theory.[5]

In the rich western provinces of The Netherlands wages were relatively high, as they had been for centuries. This meant that some industries moved to the poorer, sandy soils in the eastern and southern parts of the country. Here, members of small peasant families were available as cheap labour for cottage industry or factories. We have seen how the SDB had some following among the Twente textile workers in the east, but in the southern province of Brabant, where the same conditions existed, the position of the Catholic Church was very dominant and the labour movement did not gain a foothold easily.

By the early 1890s, the new SDB adherents in the north were feeling the effects of agricultural crisis. Their first efforts at organisation and their strike activities had not brought the success for which they had hoped. Understandably, they then became more radical. Significantly, it was the northern branch of Hoogezand-Sappemeer which proposed at the 1893 SDB congress a motion which stated that the Socialists would not, not even for purposes of propaganda, take part in parliamentary elections. It was the adoption of this motion which ultimately led to the formation of the SDAP a year later. Although the SDAP tried to keep its distance from the liberal left and stressed its Socialist orthodoxy, it was clearly more reformist and parliamentarian than the SDB.

In its first year, the SDAP was hardly able even to organise meetings in the centre of the Dutch working-class movement, Amsterdam. When it tried to do so in October 1894, some of its leaders were beaten up. The SDAP was not able to attract many members from the SDB; it had to win for itself a new membership. In Amsterdam the SDB had a stronghold among workers in the building trade, for whom working-class solidarity seemed the most realistic strategy. However, the Amsterdam diamond workers had other experiences: their trade union had proven capable of organising the diamond trade and raising their standards of living. To them, the SDAP's relatively moderate stance was plausible and they formed the hard core of its Amsterdam branch.[6] Teachers were also prominent in the SDAP as were other intellectuals, which led to an explanation of its acronym as the 'Schoolmasters', Doctors' and Advocates' Party' by its more militant opponents.

Party life was indeed dominated by intellectuals and middle-class party members – and not only in the early period – even if the members more typically belonged to the working classes.[7] Regionally, the SDAP in its early years depended heavily upon the support in the northern provinces of Friesland and Groningen, but after 1900 the western provinces of North-Holland and South-Holland became more important. The SDAP members tended to live in urban and industrial constituencies, especially in the four biggest cities (Amsterdam, Rotterdam, The Hague and Utrecht), provincial towns, agricultural areas in the northern provinces and industrial areas like Twente or the Zaandam area north of Amsterdam. In the Catholic south the party only took root in a handful of industrial towns.[8]

Although the SDAP was at the time very much a general staff without an army, it won two seats in the first general election in which it participated, that of 1897 (Table 3.2). Apparently the position which the party took appealed to the better-off workers who had the vote at the time. Party leader P. J. Troelstra was even elected in three districts; he could take up only one of the seats and the other two were lost again, but a third seat was won in a by-election in 1899. One of these successes was attained in the Twente textile town of Enschede, but all others were in the northern provinces of Friesland and Groningen. When the number of seats doubled in 1901 they were still all in the north and east; the first seat in one of the big city constituencies was only gained in a by-election in 1902. From then on the proportion of votes from the big cities in the west in the overall composition of the SDAP vote increased. In the general election of 1913 the percentage of SDAP votes in the districts where it had put up candidates grew from 14 per cent to 19 per cent, and it won fifteen seats. The SDAP was offered three (out of a total of nine) seats in a liberal government which would introduce general suffrage, but it turned the offer down.

The first twenty years were years of spectacular growth, not only for the SDAP but also for the trade union movement. As mentioned earlier, the diamond workers' union, the ANDB became the nucleus of the Socialist federation of trade unions, the NVV. This was formed in 1906.

The ANDB had adopted a British model of trade unions with a strong executive, paid officials, disciplined members, high membership dues and consequently a large strike fund. The only national trade union organisation, the NAS (*Nationaal Arbeids Secretariaat*, National Labour Secretariat), had been formed in 1893 as a federation of the SDB and eight trade unions of skilled workmen, the typographers, cigar-makers, carpenters, railwaymen, cabinet-makers, brush-makers, diamond workers and teachers. The NAS itself adopted a federal structure with a weak executive. The NAS developed syndicalist principles, relying on solidarity among the workers to collect funds during conflicts and supporting spontaneous strikes, and it opposed parliamentary activities

Table 3.2. Percentage of Seats Won by the SDAP (1897–1940) and PvdA (1946–1994) and other Socialist Parties at Parliamentary Elections, 1897–1994

	SDAP	Others		PvdA	Others
1897	2	1	1946	29	10
1901	6	1	1948	27	8
1905	6	1	1952	30	6
1909	7	–	1956	33	5
1913	15	–	1959	32	3
1917	15	–	1963	29	5
1918	22	3	1967	25	6
1922	20	2	1971	26	11
1925	24	1	1972	29	10
1929	24	2	1977	35	5
1933	22	5	1981	29	6
1937	23	3	1982	31	5
			1986	35	2
			1989	33	4
			1994	25	5

Other parties include all parties which called themselves Socialist or Communist, and Groen Links in 1989. Until 1917 members of the Dutch lower house (*Tweede Kamer*) were elected in single-member districts. From 1917, when general suffrage for men was introduced, the system of proportional representation was adopted. The number of seats was raised from 100 to 150 in 1956. To make the figures comparable, the results are given as a percentage of the total number of seats.

and social legislation. Although much of this ran against the ideas of the ANDB, it joined the NAS as the only existing umbrella organisation of trade unions.

Within the NAS executive, member trade unions, large or small, had one vote apiece. The NAS consequently became dominated by small and often radical unions. The ANDB and other larger trade unions felt less and less at home within the NAS, and some of them left the organisation. Attempts to reform the NAS failed and matters were driven to a crisis by the railway strikes of 1903.[9] The first railway strike in January of that year surprised the railway management by its size; management recognised the unions and gave in to other demands. The government then introduced a law which forbade public servants and railwaymen to strike and a second strike in April against this law was lost. Temporarily, this meant the destruction of the union of railwaymen.

Both sides within the labour movement, the Syndicalists and the Social

Democrats, saw the other side as the cause of this failure. The Syndicalist NAS called for 'the struggle of autonomous workers against gentlemen which are being followed by workers'. In 1905 the Social Democrats within the trade union movement founded their own national federation, the NVV, based upon the 'modern' principles which the ANDB had embraced.

Even more than the NAS, the NVV found its supporters among skilled workers. At the start almost half of the NVV members were diamond workers. Under the influence of new unionist ideas, however, the NVV started to organise factory workers into a separate union. Undoubtedly it was an important change in that unskilled factory workers felt it useful to organise themselves into unions, but by the outbreak of the First World War this union only numbered some 2,000 members. This meant that it had only slightly contributed to the growth of the NVV, which had grown from its original size of less than 20,000 members to more than 80,000. At that time other federations counted some 50,000 members, while non-affiliated unions numbered almost 130,000 more workers. This growth continued during the war, when the trade union confederations were recognised through their role in the state apparatus set up to alleviate the consequences of unemployment. Strikes in 1911–1913 and 1919–1920 brought new groups into the process of unionisation.[10] Collective contracts symbolised the growing importance of trade unions.

By the end of the decade, the Socialist movement had a following among the Dutch population. In the 1918 elections, the first with universal male suffrage, the SDAP polled 22 per cent of the votes, and union density peaked in 1919 (Figure 3.1). Labour seemed to be on the rise. It remained to be seen whether the Dutch labour movement could cross the threshold it was now confronting.

Pillarisation

For a few days in November 1918 it seemed as if there was no threshold at all. Under the influence of the revolutionary developments in Germany, SDAP leader Troelstra proclaimed a revolution. His revolutionary aspirations were not shared by the majority of the SDAP leadership, nor – probably – by the majority of its members. The SDAP never mobilised its members to instigate the revolution its leader had called for. The Roman Catholic and Protestant trade unions, on the other hand, did mobilise to show their support for their government and the Queen. In a few days it was clear that there would be no revolution in The Netherlands, although the government gave in to some of the workers' demands.

The attitude and even existence of these denominational trade unions were felt by the Socialist labour movement to be the main obstacle to the

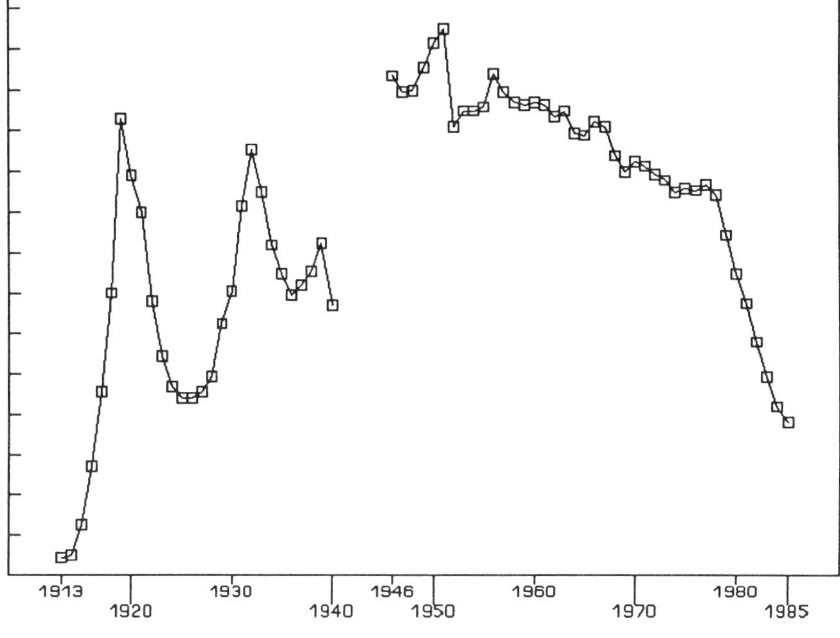

Figure 3.1 Net Union Density Rate. Netherlands 1913–1985.

Source: Adapted from Visser, 'In Search of Inclusive Unionism', [11]

growth of their support among workers. In a way this was precisely why these trade unions had been formed. In the Catholic south the hegemony of the Church seemed threatened if workers organised as workers and not as *Catholic* workers. For some Catholic leaders even this organisation went too far; they propagated other forms of association, which smacked less of unionism. However, experiments with *Standsorganisaties*, of which both small employers and employees would be members, failed. It was clear that the idea of organisation based on their interests as workers appealed to numerous Catholic workers.

As Roman Catholic workers, particularly in the southern town of Maastricht, proved susceptible to Socialist ideas, the advocates of Catholic trade unions prevailed.[12] The bishops forced Catholics out of a mixed Protestant-Catholic union of textile workers which had formed in Twente, and which they could not control on account of its mixed character; only under the threat of excommunication did Catholic workers leave this mixed union. Catholic trade unions were to have a religious advisor, who was appointed by and responsible to the episcopate and who had a say in trade union policy. In 1909 the *Roomsch Katholiek Vakbureau* (Roman Catholic Trade union bureau) was founded and in 1925 the *Vakbureau* was transformed into a real trade union federation, the RKWV (*Roomsch-Katholiek Werkliedenverbond*, Roman Catholic Working Men's Federation).

In the Protestant camp there were no bishops to decisively influence the discussion on the way workers should organise. However, when the Roman Catholics had left the mixed organisations these continued as *de facto* Protestant trade unions. Their federation, the CNV (*Christelijk Nationaal Vakverbond*, Christian National Trade union federation), was formed in 1909.

The organisation of Catholic and Protestant workers into denominational unions formed a key part of the *verzuiling* (pillarisation) of Dutch society.[13] The pillarisation of Dutch society, which was at its height between 1920 and 1960, meant that in most societal areas separate Protestant, Catholic and non-denominational, 'general' organisations existed. A devout Catholic would vote for a Catholic political party, rent a house from a Catholic housing association, read a Catholic newspaper and borrow books from a Catholic library, listen to a Catholic broadcasting corporation, play in a Catholic brass band, belong to a Catholic football club, and – of course – to a Catholic trade union. The trade union would be a small society in itself, with its own publishing house, bank, sanatorium and insurance company catering for many of its members' needs. Each of the pillars would thus be able to lead a life of its own and to minimise the risk of corruption through contacts with others; there were denominational employers' organisations as well as unions.

For Catholic and Protestant workers, the pillarised trade union movement provided a way to organise themselves as workers and still remain within the fold of their religious community and thus within the bounds of respectability. Each community in turn promoted its workers' interests; the Catholic trade union movement, for instance, supported working-class boys who wanted to become priests. The pillars also offered a network which reached to the top of the political and social pyramid; through this network, the denominational trade unions could influence government, in which the confessional parties were always included between 1918 and 1994.

The third, 'general' pillar was less unified than the Protestant and especially the Catholic pillars. Organisations within the third pillar often claimed that they did not belong to any pillar at all, as they excluded nobody on denominational grounds. They often called themselves 'general' to signify exactly this. The general pillar consisted of those who did not belong to the Catholic Church or one of the Protestant denominations, but were mainly latitudinarian followers of the Dutch Reformed Church who preferred general organisations over specifically Protestant ones. As the general pillar had no binding ideology, it often split along class lines into Liberal, upper-class and Socialist working-class segments. In some representations of the system of pillarisation these are treated as separate pillars, bringing the total to four. Naturally, these pillars were not 'complete', as there were for instance no Socialist employers' organisations or Liberal libraries, but both groups had political parties, newspapers and broadcasting corporations. Thus in many ways Dutch society was divided into four inward-looking pillars, whose members needed little contact with those belonging to the other pillars.

Pillarisation has often been described as peculiar to The Netherlands. However, similar developments occurred in other countries where denominational parties won large shares of the popular vote.[14] The Socialist pillar had much in common with other more or less closed cultures of labour, like the proverbial British working-class culture or the 'Lager' of German Social Democracy in the Weimar Republic.[15]

Pillarisation meant that in most trades at least three competing unions existed: a Catholic union, usually called after a patron saint (St. Eloy, who was a smith, for the union of metalworkers; St. Stephanus, who was martyred by stoning, for the union of brick-makers, etc.), a Protestant union and a general union, which belonged to the NVV.

The NVV tried to chart a middle course between being associated with socialism and not. It never called itself socialist, and explicitly invited religious workers to join its 'general' unions. This was, however, seen by all concerned as only a thin veneer; SDAP members were very prominent in the NVV, and NVV-officials were leading members of the Party. The other trade unions pointed out that the NVV was in fact a Social Democratic organisation.

Pillarisation supplied a good breeding ground for developing a specific labour-movement culture, especially in the Socialist pillar. The Roman Catholic labour movement certainly developed ideals about the way Catholic workers should live, but in critical instances these were subordinated to the demands of the Roman Catholic hierarchy.[16] Within the Socialist pillar, the labour movement had more room to develop a culture of its own. Once again, the ANDB took the lead. Among the services it offered its members were the opportunity to visit concerts and plays, a library and books published by the union, a trade union office which still is – years after the demise of the union itself – one of the landmarks of the Amsterdam school in architecture, and even advice on the way to furnish one's living room. The culture thus offered to workers was only marginally different from the one that the left-wing bourgeoisie were suggesting the workers should adopt. Some of the elements of these general 'civilising' efforts, like anti-alcoholism, could be given a special Socialist emphasis quite easily.

The ANDB wanted its members to share bourgeois 'high' culture, it wanted them to become more respectable so they would show they deserved better wages and hours and it wanted to form them into disciplined forces in the class struggle.[17] Many of these initiatives were repeated on a larger scale by the movement as a whole in the inter-war years, when educational courses were offered and a publishing house was set up by the labour movement.[18]

The results of these efforts were mixed. On the one hand, certainly in all three pillars a distinctive culture was developed which determined, for instance, what a militant could read. As the pillars had their own housing associations, whole blocks could be influenced by this culture. On the other hand this culture of militants could alienate workers from less disciplined strands of working-class culture. These remained strong in older neighbourhoods of larger cities, while the workers who had absorbed the culture of the Socialist movement moved to the new blocks of houses being built in the suburbs by Socialist housing associations or by the town (typically on the instigation of Social Democratic politicians).

The inter-war years saw within the Socialist movement attempts to develop a working-class culture which differed much more from bourgeois civilising efforts.[19] The typical example was the youth organisation of the SDAP, the *Arbeiders Jeugd Centrale* (AJC). It developed distinctive rituals, but its culture always remained that of a small elite, even within the Socialist movement itself. Many socialist militants themselves were averse to the AJC uniforms, propaganda for abstinence or Esperanto, which they feared would alienate the movement from the working classes. Nevertheless, the AJC and its culture were influential as a breeding ground for future officials. In the long run, both the majority of workers in all pillars and the traditional working-class culture were influenced more by the mass culture spread by media such as the cinema, the popular press, radio and television, than by the attempts of the pillars to design specific cultures.

The plurality of unions lowered the threshold for others to form separate unions. Many trades knew not only a Catholic, CNV and NVV union, but also one or more representing radical socialist or syndicalist feelings. The NAS remained active until the German occupation of 1940. This organisation objected to the idea that a union should present itself as 'general' or neutral, because it saw the union primarily as a way of educating workers about their class position. On the other wing of the political spectrum, a neutral union would object to the ideological position taken by all the others.

We have seen how the second decade of the twentieth century was a period of growth for the trade unions (Figure 3.1). This holds particularly true for the *RK Vakbureau*, the CNV and the NVV, all three of which in these founding years profited both from the growth of the movement as a whole and from the amalgamation of other unions. In the early 1920s membership of the NVV included nearly 40 per cent of the entire trade union movement, about the level at which it would remain for the rest of the organisation's existence. As Figure 3.2 shows, the Catholic and Protestant trade union federations reached their maximum proportion slightly later. This fragmentation of trade union power hampered the struggle with the employers, who were generally less divided.[20]

The position of the SDAP was in many ways similar to that of the NVV. As Table 3.2 shows, its forward march was halted after the 1918 election; for the rest of the inter-war period the SDAP would remain at about its 1918 level. From 1918 until 1939 the government was based upon a coalition of the Catholic and the two main Protestant parties, in some years with the participation of Liberals. If they were to gain more influence, both the party and the trade union came to feel that they had to gain

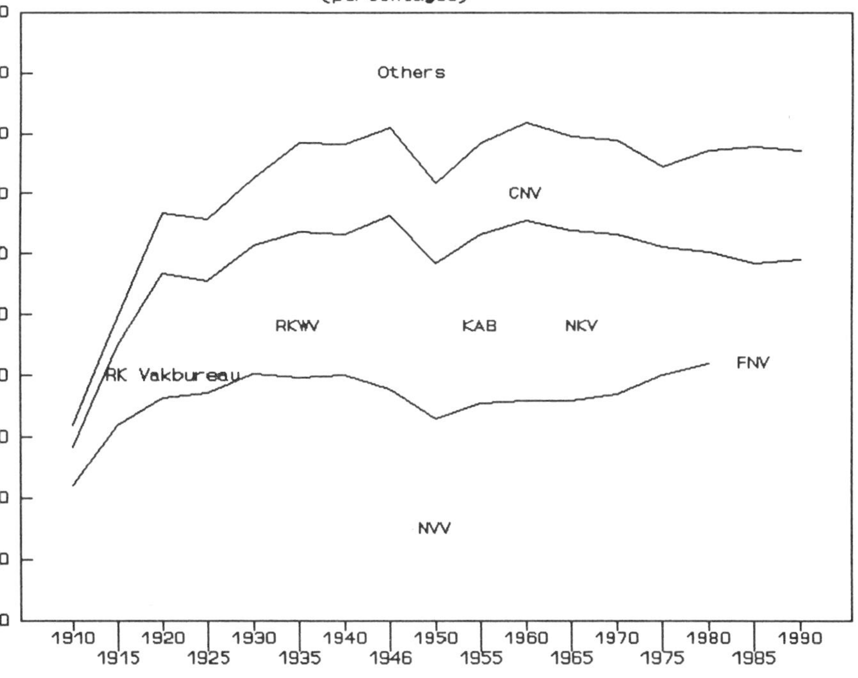

Figure 3.2 Members Trade Unions.

Source: CBS

support among the middle classes and/or among religious workers. 'With 22% or 23% of the population behind one, there simply is no way to take the place of the majority', as one of the SDAP leaders wrote in 1925.[21]

For the parliamentary party, cooperation with progressive Liberals and Catholics seemed the best chance of attaining power in government. The longer the SDAP was kept out of government, the more attractive the posts the party had turned down in 1913 seemed to become. The party came to think of participation in government as a way to win new votes. By this time the SDAP held local government positions in many larger towns; the Socialists had proven to be able administrators, and indeed the prestige of their local leaders probably had gained the SDAP votes. Further, if the Catholics would cooperate with the Socialists, then they could no longer use them as the bogeymen to keep the Catholic workers in line.

The Catholics thought along the same lines. There were crises within the government coalition; in 1923 ten Catholics voted with the opposition to throw out a government proposal for a huge naval building programme, and in 1925 one of the Protestant parties joined the opposition in removing the post of the Dutch delegation at the Holy See from the budget of the Ministry of Foreign Affairs. However, the leader of the Catholic group in parliament, the moderately progressive priest W.H. Nolens, stated that the Catholics would only form a government with the Socialists 'in the last resort'. His successor to be and another representative of 'social Catholicism', P.J.M. Aalberse, once noted in his diary that for the Catholics the coalition with the Protestants was ideal; from time to time a Protestant would become Catholic, but never the other way round. If the Catholics had to form a coalition with the Socialists, the effect would be the opposite: Catholic workers would become Socialist. These were, however, arguments largely for internal use and of internal importance. When the confessional parties needed an excuse for not cooperating with the Socialists, they referred to Troelstra's attempted revolution and declared that the SDAP was not yet to be trusted with the government of the nation.

Traditional Socialist demands such as universal suffrage and the eight-hour day had been attained around 1918. Attempts to formulate new Socialist policies around which the electorate could be mobilised were not very successful. The SDAP developed more or less detailed proposals for the socialisation of important parts of the economy and for worker participation in industrial management, but these failed to fire the imagination like the old issues had done. At the end of the 1920s, however, the SDAP set up a successful and modern press,which appealed to readers from outside the group of party faithful.[22]

NVV leader R. Stenhuis had been the initiator of the campaign against the Navy proposals of 1923. In general he advocated a more aggressive and active party and he tried to find new options for the labour movement. He did this so ambitiously, however, that he accumulated enemies not only in the Party but also within the NVV leadership. When he adopted a plan for developing the party along the lines of the British Labour party, with a large amount of trade union influence over the party, he was sacked in 1928. Still, at least some of the problems were real. The coordination between SDAP and NVV, for instance, which had been very bad, was improved somewhat and the trade union representation in the Parliamentary party was enlarged.[23] If these were improvements, they did not generate significantly more support for the labour movement.

Trade union membership fell and rose with the business cycle in the 1920s, as it did in most other European countries. In absolute numbers membership fell from 680,000 (for all trade unions) at its peak in 1920 to 490,000 in 1926, then climbed again to 620,000 in 1930. As the labour force grew by one sixth in these years, the recovery of union density was slower (Figure 3.1).

During most of the decade the NVV tried to point out to Catholic and Protestant workers that their interests would be better served if they joined the Socialist unions. However, short periods of trade union cooperation, such as during the lock-out in the Twente textile industry in 1923–24, ended in bitter feuds between the unions involved because the Catholic and Protestant workers almost invariably were willing to end conflicts earlier than the Socialist workers. The competition between unions lessened somewhat towards the end of the decade, perhaps because the NVV had realised that it was not gaining a foothold among religious workers, perhaps also because the Catholic trade union movement became more militant after 1925 when the RKWV was formed. In 1926 the RKWV itself had to conclude that working conditions in the south where Catholic workers faced Catholic employers, were worse than in the rest of the country, where Socialist trade unions and Liberal employers' organisations set the tone.[24] All in all, however, trade union power remained much influenced by pillarisation.

If the Socialist labour movement failed to better its position among religious workers, did it fare any better among the middle classes? The Party's new policies, like socialisation, did not seem to be designed to win support among farmers or shopkeepers. In the second half of the 1920s some party members raised the issue of the position of intellectuals and other middle class workers, but these did not get much attention in the party as a whole.[25]

The NVV realised that it was stronger among manual workers than among white-collar workers. It tried in 1921–22 to persuade the ANV, a smaller federation of unions of white-collar workers and civil servants which took a politically neutral position, to merge with it. Although this merger failed, some gains were made (Figure 3.3); the union of office employees which adhered to the NVV became the largest union in its sector around 1925. On the other hand many white-collar workers either remained unorganised or organised elsewhere.[26]

The 1930s added to the already existing problems of the Dutch labour movement. The coalition government of Catholics and Protestants took a classical liberal attitude towards the economic crisis: it tried to keep the Dutch guilder 'sound' by maintaining its convertibility into gold and it tried to lower wage costs in the Dutch economy. This policy led to wage cuts affecting government personnel, and in February 1932 sailors aboard the naval vessel *De Zeven Provinciën* in the Dutch Indies occupied their ship in protest against the cuts. The mutiny was suppressed within a week but the Social Democrats had to some extent supported the sailors. This action was used as fresh proof that the Social Democrats were revolutionary and unfit to govern. Membership of Social Democratic organisations was prohibited for all military personnel. In the general elections a few months after the mutiny the SDAP lost two seats. The party had not been able to use the evident crisis of capitalism to generate more support; the liberal VDB (*Vrijzinnig-Democratische Bond*, Liberal Democratic League), which had been looked upon as a natural third partner in a government of the Catholics and the Socialists, made overtures to the parties of the right and was included in the new government. All in all the SDAP seemed only to get more isolated from new voters and farther away from participation in government.[27]

This forced the Social Democrats to think afresh about some of their traditional policies and a generation of relatively young party intellectuals began pushing through new ideas. They were influenced by the ideals of the AJC and of a small group of 'religious' Socialists who saw Socialism more as a moral choice than as the logical result of a class position. Also influential were the Keynesian economic views of Jan Tinbergen and Hein Vos.[28]

In the years 1933–1935 the SDAP changed some of the policies which appeared to create a gap between it and other political parties or parts of the electorate. The party no longer supported national disarmament and accepted the constitutional monarchy, and the general tone of the opposition became very moderate. Following the example of the Belgian socialists, the SDAP and NVV together developed a plan (*Plan van de Arbeid*, Labour Plan) to combat unemployment through government spending on large infrastructure projects, which would create jobs both directly and indirectly. With this plan, the SDAP addressed itself not only to the working classes but to the Dutch population as a whole, and the expression 'class struggle' was dropped from the 1937 party programme. The propaganda for the *Plan van de Arbeid* was good for the confidence of the SDAP itself, but it was not received very enthusiastically outside the party.[29] The Party did not attract new supporters in the 1937 election (Table 3.2), and it had to wait until 1939 before its moderation brought it the government seats it longed for in order to be accepted by other groups.

The NVV was also severely hampered by the crisis. Trade unions could hardly take a hard line when unemployment was rife. However, trade union membership figures peaked in 1932, three years after the start of the depression, and throughout the 1930s remained above the level of the best years of the 1920s. That the density rate fell after 1932 (Figure 3.1) was partly due to the growth of the labour force, and that membership figures did not fall more can be explained by the role of the unions in unemployment insurance. Trade union members paid for unemployment insurance with their union dues; if they were unemployed for a short period they received benefits from their union and even if they had to fall back on state unemployment benefits later, these were also administered by their union. Benefits were higher and trade union members were treated better than the unemployed who did not belong to a union.[30]

Table 3.3. Dependent Labour Force and Density Rates by Sector, 1920–1985

	Agriculture		Manufacturing, mining, utilities, construction and transport		Services		Total (including unknown)	
	% dlf	dens.	% dlf	dens.	% dlf	dens.	% dlf	dens
1920	19.3	8	46.3	45	33.0	27	100	31
1930	15.6	9	48.0	38	35.1	23	100	28
1947	9.4	32	53.0	53	34.9	28	100	41
1960	4.0	56	57.6	46	37.6	33	100	41
1971	2.0	47	51.3	43	41.6	33	100	37
1979	2.0	27	41.5	42	49.1	31	100	33
1985	1.6	23	32.7	35	50.7	25	100	24

Source: Adapted from Visser 1987

The inter-war period was characterised by a decline in the share of the agricultural labour force (Table 3.1). As trade union density was much lower in agriculture than in other sectors (Table 3.3), this shift contributed to the influence of the trade union movement. The NVV had strengthened its position among non-manual workers, but 90 per cent of its members were still blue-collar workers (Figure 3.3).[31]

A Breakthrough?

We saw that in 1939 the SDAP participated for the first time in government, thus attaining an important goal. However, the time span before The Netherlands was occupied by the Germans in 1940 was too short for the new position of the SDAP to have any important consequences.

The Germans soon appointed a Dutch Nazi as head of the NVV. Individual officials who did not cooperate with the new regime were fired. Locally, in particular in the Twente area, some NVV officials attempted to wind up their organisations; most socialist trade union officials tried to save their organisation as much as possible and asked their members to stay. Only in 1942, when the NVV was changed into the openly fascist NAF (*Nederlands Arbeids Front*, Dutch Labour Front), did most workers leave the organisation. When the Germans tried to force the RKWV and CNV to follow German policies in July 1941, they reacted more strongly than the NVV; the Dutch bishops, for example, forbade Catholics to continue their membership of the RKWV. Membership of both organisations dwindled, but all three trade union confederations continued their existence underground. As early as 1943 talks began with the employers organisations about the form post-war labour relations should take. In the meantime the Germans adopted a system to control wages, which would be maintained after the war.

After the war, all classes of Dutch society craved both re-establishment and renewal of the pre-war order. Many people felt that it was time for a political breakthrough, and an end to the system of pillarisation. In this spirit, the SDAP merged with the VDB and groups of progressive Christians to form the PvdA (*Partij van de Arbeid*, Labour Party). The PvdA was conceived as being a party for the whole population, not only the working class, just as the pre-war innovators had hoped. However, the breakthrough as a whole failed. The pre-war pillars were re-established with their political parties and their trade unions, which won back their old membership. The PvdA had a larger popular appeal than the SDAP (Table 3.2), but it won no more votes than its predecessors together had done before the war. Yet, in one important way, the PvdA was more successful than the SDAP had been in that it was able to participate in government. Together with the Catholics, the Socialists formed the nucleus of all governments in the years 1946–1958, which from 1948 on were headed by the Socialist W. Drees.

The post-war governments had to direct the reconstruction of the Dutch economy. In the first place the production machinery in The Netherlands lay in a shambles after five years of German occupation; the independence of Indonesia which brought the loss of the largest part of the Dutch colonial possessions added to the problem. The Drees governments answered these problems with a policy aimed at the industrialisation of The Netherlands. By 1960 a larger part of the Dutch labour force was employed in industry than ever before or after (Table 3.1). To achieve this result a 'guided' economy was adopted; many consumer goods were rationed until 1949, and wages were kept down to the rate of inflation from 1945 until 1953. Only from 1954 onwards was the growth of the Dutch economy taken into account in wage settlements.[32]

This policy of low wages was accepted by the three reconstituted pre-war trade union federations, the NVV, the CNV and the KAB (*Katholieke Arbeiders Beweging*, Catholic Workers' Movement, the successor of the RKWV). In exchange they were incorporated into the institutions that guided the Dutch economy, such as the Social Economic Council (*Sociaal-Economische Raad*, SER), the central advisory board of the government in social and economic matters. Moreover, the two largest federations had close links with the two leading parties in government, and both hoped that some of their ideals would be realised. For the NVV the building of a welfare state, beginning with old age pensions and unemployment pay, was one of those wishes. The guided economy also led to a growth in collective labour agreements; these had included some 350,000 workers in 1940, but this figure grew to 950,000 in 1951 and to 2,000,000 in 1956. This in turn increased the influence of the 'recognised' trade unions which negotiated these agreements. Strikes seemed unnecessary and anti-social in times when the national economy had to be rebuilt, and the KAB even abolished its strike fund.

Apart from the three 'recognised' federations, one other federation was active after the war. This was the EVC (*Eenheids Vak Centrale*, Unity Trade Federation), which was led by the Dutch Communist Party. This party had split from the SDAP in 1909.[33] It had not managed to acquire a large following before the war, achieving a maximum vote of about 3 per cent of the votes in parliamentary elections in the 1930s, but during the war its prestige had grown because of its prominent role in the resistance against the Germans and because of the improved international standing of the Soviet Union. In the 1946 elections the Communists won 11 per cent of the vote.

In the south of The Netherlands, which had been liberated in 1944 while the northern half of the country was still occupied, a movement towards a breakthrough in trade union relations won much support. This was particularly true among the Limburg coal miners, who had also shown in the 1920s that Catholic control was not complete. When the rest of the country was liberated, the EVC won support in Amsterdam, the Zaan area, Twente and Rotterdam harbour. Some of the centres of Communist-EVC militancy had already been strongholds of the SDB, in which the

Social Democrats had a hard time establishing themselves.[34]

The EVC was more militant than the other three federations. Whereas the three recognised federations accepted the decisions laid down by state mediators, the EVC struck against them. Although the EVC as an unrecognised federation could not be a party in the collective labour agreements, it won a relatively large body of adherents. This growth can be seen in Figure 3.2 in the growth of other trade unions in 1950. In the end, however, its non-recognition and the influence of the Communists (whose postwar popularity was shortlived) within the EVC, meant that the organisation ultimately evaporated. It had lost its importance by 1950 and was discontinued in 1964.

By that time wage restraint had ended. In the early 1950s price control and wage restraint had made Dutch labour cheap and Dutch industry competitive; the Dutch economy boomed and toward the end of the decade employers experienced shortages on the labour market. This made them willing to pay extra wages. Workers found themselves in the paradoxical situation that at times their employers were willing to pay more for their labour than their union was prepared to ask. Understandably, this made workers less willing to pay union dues, and the density rate in industry began to fall (Table 3.3). The trade unions felt that they were alienating their members and began urging relaxation of the system of wage restraint, which happened from 1959 onwards. In 1960 the recognised unions again supported a building workers' strike.

This did not solve the NVV's problems. Compared with both the growth of the non-affiliated unions of higher grade employees and with the growth of CNV and KAB, the growth of the NVV was disappointing. Sociological research showed that the gap between the union leadership and members was widening. In 1964 the NVV union in the metal industry started to organise groups of trade union members within firms as a counterweight against the very centralised activities of the trade unions. These groups, usually more militant than the traditional trade union bodies, were to become a part of the activist climate of the years around 1970, when strike activity flared up and many young people participated in social movements including trade unions and left-wing parties.

Women

Another group that became active in those years were women. Traditionally, the participation of women in the labour force in The Netherlands has been low. In industry, women were well represented only in clothing and textiles, while in the service sector they could be found in nursing, domestic service and education; nursing and domestic service were very hard to unionise.[35] Until 1975 fewer than 20 per cent of women

Table 3.4. Trade Union Density by Sex, Private or Public Sector and Nature of Work

	Female	Male	Private	Public	Manual	Non-manual
1909	2	14				
1920	9	37			28	43
1930	7	34			25	36
1947	8	51	37	57	43	36
1960	15	50	35	67	42	39
1971	13	45	29	60	38	34
1979	17	41	26	52	34	33
1985	13	31	17	46	23	25

Source: Van Eijl and De Groot 1992, Visser 1987

(against about 60 per cent of Dutch men) had jobs.[36] This figure does not take into account many women working intermittently, in the family firm or at home, but even so, trade union density was very low (Table 3.4).

Trade unions often were not interested in organising women. They were expected to work only until they got married, and typically to do unskilled jobs. Trade unions appealed to female workers more as (future) housewives and mothers than as workers; they seldom demanded equal pay or career opportunities for women. If equal pay became an issue, it was usually because male workers felt their position threatened by 'cheap' female labour.[37] Indeed, only a very low percentage of married women in The Netherlands had paid jobs, but the trade union movement which backed this situation was hardly in a position to complain about cheap labour. Around the turn of the century the trade union of office clerks, Mercurius, even forbade women to take its exam, which made it impossible for women to obtain office jobs.[38] The Socialist trade union movement thought that men should earn a family wage; the denominational trade unions even opposed married women working in factories on principle.[39] At several points in time the Catholic party attempted to outlaw factory work for married women, but it did not succeed. However, women in public service were often dismissed upon marriage.

Since the labour shortages, de-pillarisation and the rise of the women's movement in the 1960s, much of this situation has changed. If during the period 1920–1960 it had been 'normal' for women to work only before marriage, in the later period it became more and more common practice for women to continue working after their marriage or at least return to the labour market when their children had grown up.[40] In the early 1970s women struck for equal pay, which was granted by law in 1975. After much hesitation trade unions began to support women's demands, and they began gradually to take women workers' wishes into account. Since 1975, partly through the growth in part-time jobs, The Netherlands has improved its position in Europe in terms of female participation in the labour force.[41] In the past, female participation in the Dutch labour force has been much lower that in other European countries, but this participation has now increased; female participation (as measured by the number of jobs) is now only slightly less than the overall European average. Recently the largest union in industry, the Industriebond FNV, has even positively discriminated in favour of women when appointing union officials.[42] In recent times the difference between male and female unionisation has declined, as Table 3.4 shows.

De-pillarisation

From 1958 until 1973 the PvdA remained in opposition with one exception, the shortlived 1965–66 government in partnership with the Catholics and one of the Protestant parties. This government was brought down by the Catholic party KVP (*Katholieke Volks Partij*, Catholic People's Party) after only one year, which caused a group of progressive Catholics to form the PPR (*Politieke Partij Radicalen*, Political Party of Radicals). This was but one of the signs that the pillars were beginning to crumble.

One of the key changes involved was the secularisation of the Dutch population, which within a generation went from being typically religious to being one of the least believing societies in Europe. The proportion of the population that did not belong to any church tripled from 18 per cent in 1960 to 57 per cent in 1991. As the population became wealthier, travelled more, became better educated and better informed through modern mass media, the confines of the pillar became increasingly less meaningful. The pillars relinquished their hold upon the minds of the people with surprising speed and ease, even if they remained entrenched in the institutions of the Dutch welfare state. Between 1963 and 1972 the share of the vote of the three large denominational parties shrank from one-half to one-third.

In 1973, after a period of radicalisation, PvdA leader J. den Uyl was able to form a left-wing government which included the PPR and individual members of the denominational parties. When this government fell in 1977 the voters rewarded the PvdA with a large election victory, but Den Uyl was not able to form another government. The PvdA remained in opposition again until 1989, with only one unsuccessful short spell in government in 1981–82. At the end of the 1980s its share of the vote began to fall. In a way the PvdA was back at the same position as the SDAP in the 1930s; the economy was in a recession and the only way to win votes seemed to be through participation in government.

Social Democracy was not only threatened by impotence during a recession but also by the changing position and size of its traditional base. The regional basis of the movement, which was discussed earlier, barely changed until the 1980s.[43] The PvdA then had a breakthrough in the Catholic south; however, the confessional parties, which had merged into the CDA (*Christen-Democratisch Appel*, Christian Democratic Appeal), also made a breakthrough among non-denominational voters. Affluence, which was the result of the economic growth since the 1950s, had encroached on all pillars, including the working-class culture which had once been the safe base of social democracy. The voters lost by the confessional parties were at least as prone to find their new place among one of the middle-class liberal parties as within social democracy.

As early as 1945, both the socialist party and the NVV had decided that they should not have close formal relationships as had been the case before the war. Both thought that the association with the other would hinder them from reaching new adherents. The party thought it could more easily attract shopkeepers, small farmers and intellectuals if it had less close ties with the trade union movement; the trade union thought it would be more acceptable to white-collar workers and public servants if it was

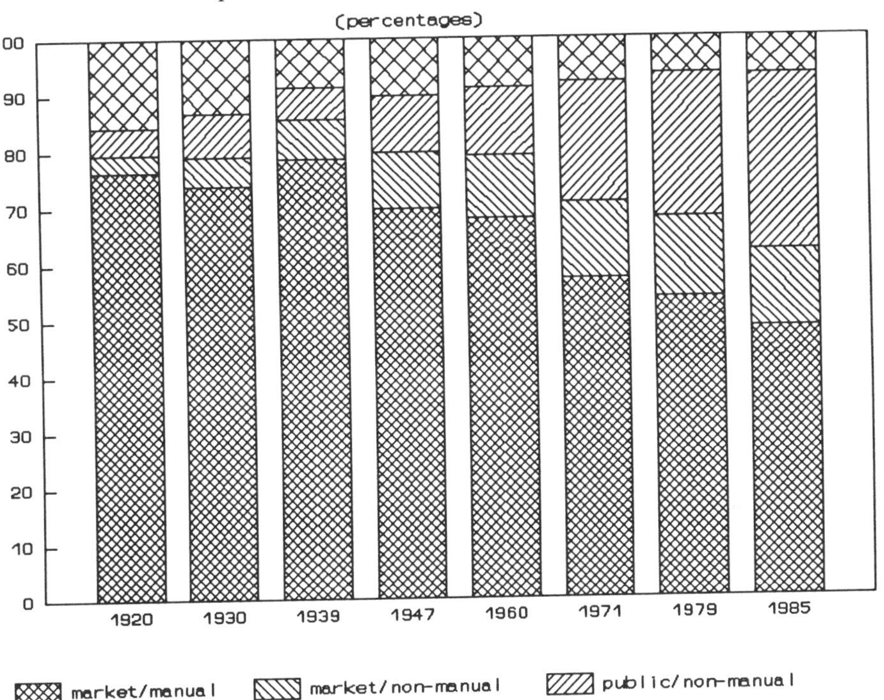

Figure 3.3 Members NVV/FNV.

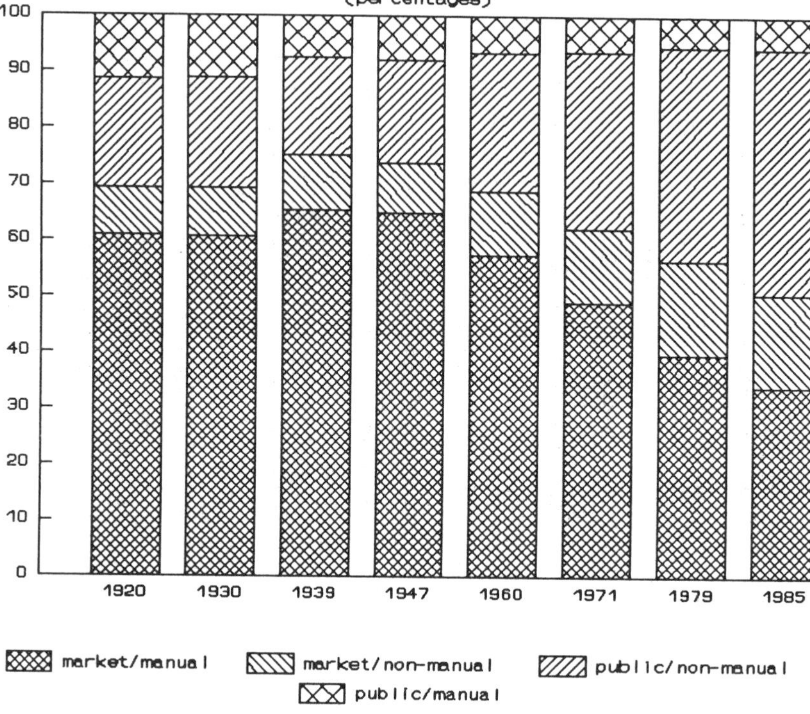

Figure 3.4 Members of All Trade Unions.

not closely bound to one political party.[44] This was all to no avail, because with or without formal ties the PvdA and the NVV nevertheless remained associated with each other as members of the 'red family'. Party and trade union had however rightly surmised that they would want the support of the middle classes or white-collar workers.

In the following years these groups did indeed grow, as Figure 3.5 makes clear. The NVV lagged behind in its share of non-manual workers (Figure 3.3). This did not mean that non-manual workers were not unionised, but, as they had done before the war, they preferred either denominational or non-affiliated unions.

This aversion to unionisation in a social democratic organisation surfaced once again on the occasion of the merger between the NVV and the Catholic trade union federation. After 1963 this organisation called itself NKV (*Nederlands Katholiek Vakverbond*, Dutch Catholic Trade Federation). At the end of the 1960s the NKV loosened the close bonds with the KVP, as the NVV did with the PvdA. Both federations preferred more autonomy over the benefits of pillarisation; the NKV, for instance,

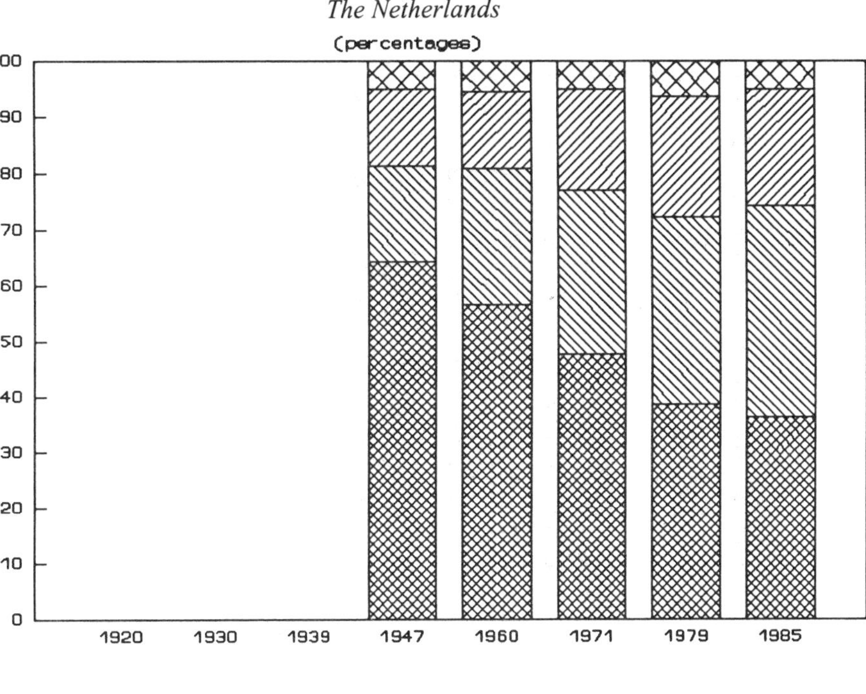

Figure 3.5 Dependent Labour Force.

Source: Adapted from Visser 1987

opposed the KVP ending its coalition government with the PvdA in 1965. De-pillarisation also became apparent when from the end of the 1960s the three trade union federations started talks about closer cooperation. One of the reasons why the NKV supported a merger was that de-pillarisation meant that the NVV was winning members away from NKV and CNV (Figure 3.2). In the end the NVV and the NKV merged into the FNV (*Federatie Nederlandse Vakbeweging*, Federation Dutch Trade Union Movement) in 1981. The Catholic trade union of supervisory staff refused to join the Federation and broke away from the NKV and, along with non-affiliated unions, formed a new trade union federation for middle- and higher-level personnel.

Trade union density was much higher among workers in the public sector than in the private sector (Table 3.4). If we compare Figure 3.4 with Figure 3.5, it becomes clear that this is especially the case for non-manual workers. To some extent the same held true for support for the

PvdA and other left-wing parties in 1982: in all income classes, workers in the public sector were more likely than workers in the private sector to vote for a party of the left.[45]

In the post-war Netherlands, agriculture lost its importance as an employer of labour. That the density rate in agriculture was no longer below that in the rest of the economy no longer mattered. Jobs in industry, the traditional focus of the labour movement where density rates were relatively high, became less important after the peak in 1960 (Table 3.1). The real growth was in the service sector. Here the overall density rate was much lower than average just after the war, but it grew and later it declined less, so that in time it crept up to the overall average (Table 3.3).

With the tight labour market of the 1960s, immigration by workers from other countries grew in importance.[46] The Netherlands had known internal immigration and an inflow of small groups of foreigners, but in 1960 only 1 per cent of the population was of non-Dutch origin. In the 1960s Dutch firms imported workers, first from Italy and Spain, and later mainly from Morocco and Turkey. All of them probably arrived with the intention to return to their countries as soon as they had earned enough to do so, but the economic circumstances in their countries of origin and changes in Dutch immigration policy meant that the latter group especially stayed on. From 1973 on there was also an important influx of Dutch citizens from the former colony of Surinam. Both the immigrants from the Mediterranean and those from the Caribbean had a weak position on the labour market when unemployment rose during the second half of the 1970s.

During the process of radicalisation in the 1970s the unions and their members began asking for fundamental changes in society. The radicalisation of the NKV was especially clear and this contributed to ease the merger with the NVV, even if elements of the separate Catholic and socialist traditions are still discernible within the FNV. The main exponents of radicalisation within the NVV and the FNV, the industrial trade unions, were however also the first to feel the effects of the downturn of the economy and consequently began to point the way back to a policy of defending jobs and pay and keeping a low profile about the reform of society in the early 1980s. When a further international economic crisis weakened the position of the trade union movement, unemployment pay was no longer distributed through the unions as it had been in the 1930s. On the contrary, the Dutch trade union movement became more or less the hostage of the social security system which had been built up since 1945; in exchange for upholding the system, wage restraints were asked of the trade union members with jobs. As the level of benefits was linked to wages, higher wages would make the system unaffordable. Trade unions tried to be reasonable and accepted very modest increases in pay and even decreases in some instances.

In the first half of the 1980s trade union density fell rapidly. However, around 1985 the mood changed.[47] The economy picked up and many new jobs were created, even if the Dutch unemployment figures remained high. From 1988 on the trade union movement became more militant again and the FNV membership, which had dropped from 1,078,000 in 1980 to 893,000 in 1986, rose again to 1,069,000 in 1992. Even trade union density was on the rise again by the early 1990s.[48]

Conclusion

The Socialist labour movement took root in The Netherlands around the turn of the century. As it became a force to be reckoned with it met with opposition, not only from employers but also from the Catholic and Protestant pillars, which were being created with the purpose of protecting workers from the influence of the Socialist labour movement. Pillarisation was at its strongest between 1920 and 1960; in this period, the Socialist labour movement was only successful among certain types of Protestant and non-religious workers. The spatial distribution of religious belief in The Netherlands made pillarisation especially successful in the south, where Catholicism was very dominant. The Dutch Socialist labour movement tried in vain to explain to Protestant and Catholic workers that their class solidarity should override their religious solidarity.

From the late 1960s pillarisation began to erode. By this time, however, the class basis of socialism had also been eroded, partly by the success of the labour movement in bettering the material conditions of the working classes. The local working-class culture and its organisational life, which had made the choice for socialism relatively easy, gave way to a national, even international commercial culture.[49] It not only became possible for the Socialist labour movement to break into the Catholic south, but also for Liberals and Christian Democrats to suggest to groups of workers that their material welfare was best served by others than the Socialists. Both the party and the trade union movement were at risk of becoming exclusively identified with the dwindling group of less-educated and poorly-paid workers in traditional sectors.

The Den Uyl government of 1973–77 was placed at exactly this crossroads when the combination of the decay of the other pillars and the strength of the Socialist pillar provided the strongest support for a left-wing government. In those same years the essential steps were taken for the merger of the NKV and the NVV. The NVV, much the larger of the two federations, set the tone in the new federation, the FNV. We can thus regard this merger as the breakthrough of the NVV to the Catholic worker.

However, we have seen that at the same time the industrial manual worker, the traditional backbone of the NVV, was becoming numerically less important. Since 1981, through the FNV, the Social Democrats have dominated the trade union scene in a way the NVV never was able to, but in the same period the density rate dropped sharply and high unemployment weakened the trade unions. The PvdA shares in the international malaise of socialism, even if it has formed a coalition government with the CDA since 1989.

The fulfilment of the wish to govern has not yet brought the Socialists any breakthrough to new groups within the electorate; on the contrary, cuts in welfare payments, rising unemployment and widespread criticism of the prevalent political culture have brought both coalition parties heavy electoral losses. At the general election of May 1994, the Labour party achieved one of its lowest shares of the vote since 1945.

Notes

1. Van Tijn (1973).
2. Modern histories of the Dutch labour movement which seek to establish systematically why the movement succeeded or failed to win support among different groups are not available. Visser (1987) gives a good analysis of trade union adherence, and his figures have been used extensively here. Overviews include Hueting, De Jong Edz. and Neij (1983) and Harmsen and Reinalda (1975) for the socialist trade union federations, and Harmsen, Perry and Van Gelder (1980) for the trade union in the manufacturing industry and Perry and others (1994) for the party. An overview of the relationship between party and trade union before 1940 is offered by Van Tijn (1986), an overview of the early labour movement by Buiting (1990). The literature on the party is reviewed in Orlow (1995).
3. De Jonge (1976).
4. Knotter (1993).
5. Frieswijk (1989, 1992); Wedman (1992); Kerr and Siegel (1954).
6. Van Horssen and Rietveld (1990).
7. Altena (1994).
8. Buiting (1989); Buiting and Van Schuppen (1992).
9. Rüter (1935).
10. Kuypers and Schrage (1992).
11. Visser (1987) uses several types of density rate. In this figure the net density rate has been chosen, in which corrections have been made

for the number of retired trade union members, which becomes an important factor in the post-1945 period. The labour force used is the total dependent labour force, including unemployed workers. In the tables, even those based on Visser (1987), other figures for the labour force had to be used, which leads to some differences in the trade union density figures.

12. Perry (1983).
13. For pillarisation in relation to the labour movement, see Stuurman (1983); Roes (1985); Righart (1986) and Koppejan (1986). Older accounts of pillarisation in English are Daalder (1966) and Lijphart (1968).
14. Righart (1986).
15. Rabe (1978).
16. Kalb (1991).
17. Adang (1990).
18. Michielse (1980); De Glas (1989).
19. Van Dijk (1990).
20. Heerma van Voss (1988).
21. W. H. Vliegen to P. J. Troelstra, (20.07.1925), quoted in Cohen (1974), p. 60.
22. Van Vree (1989).
23. Cohen (1974).
24. Heerma van Voss (1992).
25. Wijmans (1987); Cohen (1974).
26. Reinalda (1981).
27. Knegtmans (1989).
28. Cohen (1974); Knotter (1989); Knegtmans (1989).
29. Knegtmans (1989).
30. Nijhof and Schrage (1984).
31. As Table 3.4 shows, the overall trade union density rate of non-manual workers was, according to the figures presented by Visser (1987), even higher than that of manual workers. Non-manual workers tended, however, to be members of unions that were not affiliated to the NVV.
32. This account of post-war labour relations is based on Windmuller and De Galan (1977) and Albeda and Dercksen (1989). The economic context can be found in Messing (1981) and Van Zanden and Griffiths (1989).
33. At the time the splinter party was called the SDP (*Sociaal Democratische Partij*, Social Democratic Party), renaming itself after the Russian Revolution.
34. Knotter (1992), p. 161.
35. Bijleveld and Dercksen (1978); Henkes and Oosterhof (1985).

36. Blok (1989); see also Pott-Buter (1993), Plantenga (1993) and van Eijl (1994).
37. Van Eijl and De Groot (1992).
38. De Haan (1992).
39. Roes (1985), p. 63.
40. Plantenga (1993).
41. Schippers and Siegers (1991).
42. Elias (1993).
43. Passchier and Van der Wusten (1990).
44. Hueting, De Jong Edz. and Neij (1983), p. 156.
45. Wijmans (1987), p. 269.
46. Lucassen and Penninx (1985).
47. Vos (1990).
48. According to CBS figures, which differ from Visser's figures used in Figure 3.1, trade union density was 39 in 1980, 24 in 1990 and 25 in 1991–1993.
49. Nijhof and Schrage (1988).

Bibliography

Adang, M., '"Eens zal de dag, opgaand, vinden arbeid en schoonheid vereend." Over socialisme en kunstopvoeding in Nederland aan het begin van de twintigste eeuw' in M. Westen (ed.), *Met den tooverstaf van ware kunst. Cultuurspreiding en cultuuroverdracht in historisch perspectief*, Leiden, 1990, pp. 71–104

Albeda, W. and W. Dercksen, *Arbeidsverhoudingen in Nederland,* 4th edn., Alphen aan den Rijn, 1989

Altena, B., 'Bürger in der Sozialdemokratie. Ihre Bedentung für die Entwicklung der sozialdemokratischen Arbeiterpartei (SDAP) inden Niederlanden, 1894–1914', *Geschichte und Gesellschaft*, 1994, pp. 533–48

Bijleveld, L. and A. Dercksen, 'De roeping van een verpleegster', *Socialisties-Feministiese Teksten*, vol. 1, 1978, pp. 222–38

Bleich, A., *Een partij in de tijd. Veertig jaar Partij van de Arbeid 1946–1986*, Amsterdam 1986

Blok, E., *Werkende vrouwen in de jaren veertig en vijftig*, Amsterdam, 1989

Buiting, M. H. J., *Richtingen en partijstrijd in de SDAP. Het ontstaan van*

de Sociaal-Democratische Partij in Nederland SDP, Amsterdam, 1989
Buiting, H., 'The Netherlands' in M. van der Linden and J. Rojahn (eds), *The Formation of Labour Movements 1870–1914: An International Perspective*, Leiden, vol. I, 1990, pp. 57–84
—— and S. van Schuppen, 'The Implantation of the Social Democratic Labour Party in The Netherlands, 1894–1913', *Tijdschrift voor Sociale Geschiedenis* (TvSG), vol. 18, 1992, pp. 313–332
Cohen, H.F., *Om de vernieuwing van het socialisme. De politieke oriëntatie van de Nederlandse sociaal-democratie 1919–1930*, Leiden, 1974
Daalder, H., 'The Netherlands: Opposition in a Segmented Society' in R. A. Dahl (ed.), *Political Opposition in Western Democracies*, New Haven, 1966, pp. 188–236
Dijk, J. van, *Het socialisme spant zijn gouden net over de wereld. Het kunst- en cultuurbeleid van de SDAP*, Montfoort, Amsterdam, 1990
Eijl, C. van, *Het werkzame verschil. Vrouwen in de slag om arbeid 1890–1940*, Hilversum, 1994
—— and G. de Groot, '"Zij besteden hun geld liever aan een strik in het haar". Vrouwen en vakbonden, 1890–1940', in B. de Vries et al (eds), *De kracht der zwakken*, Amsterdam, 1992, pp. 363–390
Elias, M., *Fabrieksgeheimen. De industriebond FNV en het misverstand der seksen*, Amsterdam, 1993
Frieswijk, J., *Om een beter leven. Strijd en organisatie van de land-, veen- en zuivelarbeiders in het noorden van Nederland, 1850–1914*, Ljouwert, 1989
——, 'The Labour Movement in Friesland, 1880–1918', *TvSG*, vol. 18, 1992, pp. 370–88
Glas, F. de, *Nieuwe lezers voor het goede boek. De Wereldbibliotheek en Ontwikkeling/De Arbeiderspers voor 1940*, Amsterdam, 1989
Haan, F. de, *Sekse op kantoor. Over vrouwelijkheid, mannelijkheid en macht. Nederland 1860–1940*, Hilversum, 1992
Harmsen, G., J. Perry and F. van Gelder, *Mensenwerk. Industriële vakbonden op weg naar eenheid*, Baarn, 1980
—— and B. Reinalda, *Voor de bevrijding van de arbeid. Beknopte geschiedenis van de Nederlandse vakbeweging*, Nijmegen, 1975
Heerma van Voss, L., 'Dutch Shipbuilding Strikes', in L. Heerma van Voss and H. Diederiks (eds), *Industrial Conflict,* Amsterdam, 1988, pp. 49–63
——, 'Om waarheid en recht. Waarom waren de arbeidsvoorwaarden in het Zuiden van Nederland slechter dan in het Noorden?' in B. de Vries et al. (eds), *De kracht der zwakken*, Amsterdam, 1992, pp. 333–62
Henkes, B. and H. Oosterhof, *Kaatje, ben je boven? Leven en werken van Nederlandse dienstbodes 1900–1940*, Nijmegen, 1985

Horssen, P. van and D. Rietveld, 'Socialisten in Amsterdam 1878–1898. Een sociaal profiel van de SDB- en SDAP-aanhang' *TvSG*, vol. 16, 1990, pp. 387–406

Hueting, E., F. de Jong Edz. and R. Neij, *Naar groter eenheid. De geschiedenis van het Nederlands Verbond van Vakverenigingen 1906–1981*, Amsterdam, 1983

Jonge, J. A. de, *De industrialisatie in Nederland tussen 1850 en 1914*, Nijmegen, 1976

Kalb, D., 'Moral Production, Class Capacities and Communal Commotion: an Illustration from Central Brabant Shoemaking, (c.1900–20)', *Social History*, vol. 16, 1991, pp. 279–299

Kerr, C. and A. Siegel, 'The Interindustry Propensity to Strike: An International Comparison' in A. Kornhauser, R. Dubin and A.M. Ross (eds), *Industrial Conflict*, New York, 1954, pp. 189–212

Knegtmans, P. J., *Socialisme en democratie. De SDAP tussen klasse en natie, 1929–1939*, Amsterdam, 1989

Knotter, A., 'Generational Change and the Reorientation of Dutch Social Democratic Economic Policy in the Early 1930s' in A. Blok et al (eds), *Generations in Labour History*, Amsterdam, 1989

——, 'The Historical Geography of Labour in Britain and The Netherlands. Electoral Support and Regional Implantation', *TvSG*, vol. 18, 1992, pp. 148–67

——, 'Van "defensieve standsreflex" tot "verkoopkartel van arbeidskracht". Twee fasen in de ontwikkeling van de Amsterdamse arbeidersvakbeweging, (ca. 1870–ca. 1895)', *TvSG*, vol. 19, 1993, pp. 68–93

Koppejan, J., 'Verzuiling en interconfessionalisme in Nederlands-Limburg 1900–1920', *TvSG*, vol. 12, 1986, pp. 109–34

Kuypers, I. and P. Schrage, '"Als uw machtige arme het wil . . ." De betekenis van de stakingsgolven in de jaren tien voor de ontwikkeling van de Nederlandse arbeidsverhoudingen' in B. de Vries et al (eds), *De kracht der zwakken*, Amsterdam, 1992, pp. 273–308

Lijphart, A. J., *The Politics of Accommodation*, Berkeley, 1968

Lucassen, J. and R. Penninx, *Nieuwkomers, Immigranten en hun nakomelingen in Nederland 1550–1985*, Amsterdam, 1985

Messing, F., *De Nederlandse economie 1945–1980. Herstel groei stagnatie*, Bussum, 1981

Michielse, H. C. M., *Socialistiese vorming. Het Instituut voor Arbeidersontwikkeling (1924–1940), en het vormings- en scholingswerk van de nederlandse sociaal-demokratie sinds 1900*, Nijmegen, 1980

Nijhof, E. and P. Schrage, 'Van bondslokaal tot steunloket: de vakbeweging als sociaal vangnet tijdens de economische crisis in

Nederland', 1929–1935,', *Sociologisch Tijdschrift*, vol. 11, 1984, pp. 260–85

——, 'Behind the Picketline: The Home Front of the Rotterdam Dockers in Times of Social Warfare, 1900–1980', in L. Heerma van Voss and H. Diederiks (eds), *Industrial Conflict*, Amsterdam, 1988, pp. 30–38

Orlow, D., 'The Paradoxes of Success. Dutch Social Democracy and its Historiography', *Bijdragen en Mededelingen betreffende de Geschiedenis der Nederlanden*, vol. 110, 1995, pp. 40–51

Passchier, N. P. and H. H. van der Wusten, 'The Electoral Geography of The Netherlands in the Era of Mass Politics, 1888–1986', in R. J. Johnston, F. M. Shelley and P. J. Taylor (eds), *Developments in Electoral Geography*, London, 1990, pp. 39–59

Perry, J., *Roomsche kinine tegen roode koorts. Arbeidersbeweging en katholieke kerk in Maastricht 1880–1920*, Amsterdam, 1983

—— P.J. Knegtmans, D.P.J. Bosscher, F. Becker and P. Kalma, *Honderd jaar sociaal-democratie in Nederland 1894–1994*, Amsterdam, 1994

Plantenga, J., *Een afwijkend patroon. Honderd jaar vrouwenarbeid in Nederland en (West-) Duitsland*, Amsterdam, 1993

Pott-Buter, H. A., *Facts and Fairy Tales about Female Labor, Family and Fertility*, Amsterdam, 1993

Rabe, B., *Der sozialdemokratische Charakter. Drei Generationen aktiver Parteimitglieder in einem Arbeiterviertel*, Frankfurt New York, 1978

Reinalda, B., *Bedienden georganiseerd. Ontstaan en ontwikkeling van de vakbeweging van handels- en kantoorbedienden van het eerste begin tot in de Tweede Wereldoorlog*, Nijmegen, 1981

Righart, H., *De katholieke zuil in Europa. Een vergelijkend onderzoek naar het ontstaan van verzuiling onder katholieken in Oostenrijk, Zwitserland, België en Nederland*, Meppel, Amsterdam, 1986

Roes, J. (ed.), *Katholieke arbeidersbeweging*, 2 vols, Baarn, 1985–1993

Rüter, A. J. C., *De spoorwegstakingen van 1903. Een spiegel der arbeidersbeweging in Nederland*, Leiden, 1935

Schippers, J.J. and J.J. Siegers, 'Demografie en arbeidsmarkt: gevolgen van ontgroening en vergrijzing in Nederland', *Tijdschrift voor politieke ekonomie*, vol. 14, no. 2, 1991, pp. 9–28

Stuurman, S., *Verzuiling, kapitalisme en patriarchaat. Aspecten van de ontwikkeling van de moderne staat in Nederland*, Nijmegen, 1983

Tijn, Th. van, 'De Algemeene Nederlandsche Diamantbewerkersbond (ANDB),: een succes en zijn verklaring', *Bijdragen en Mededelingen betreffende de Geschiedenis der Nederlanden*, vol. 88, 1973, pp. 403–18

——, 'Partei und Gewerkschaft im sozialistischen Bereich in den Niederlanden, 1869–1940' in H.W. von der Dunk and H. Lademacher (eds), *Auf dem Weg zum modernen Parteienstaat. Zur Entstehung,*

Organisation und Struktur politischer Parteien in Deutschland und den Niederlanden, Kassel, 1986, pp. 129–48

Visser, J., 'In Search of Inclusive Unionism: A Comparative Analysis' unpublished PhD thesis, University of Amsterdam, 1987

Vos, C. J., 'Keertijd of continuïteit? De Nederlandse arbeidsverhoudingen in de jaren tachtig', *Tijdschrift voor Arbeidsvraagstukken*, vol. 6, no. 4, 1990, pp. 60–71

Vree, F. van, *De Nederlandse pers en Duitsland 1930–1939*, Groningen, 1989

Wedman, H., 'The Implantation of the Labour Movement in Groningen before 1918', *TvSG*, vol. 18, 1992, pp. 353–69

Wijmans, L., *Beeld en betekenis van het maatschappelijke midden. Oude en nieuwe middengroepen 1850 tot heden*, Amsterdam, 1987

Windmuller, J. P. and C. de Galan, *Arbeidsverhoudingen in Nederland*, 2nd edn., 2 vols., Utrecht, Antwerpen 1977 (The Dutch edition of J.P. Windmuller, *Labor Relations in The Netherlands*, Ithaca, 1969.)

Zanden, J. L. van and R. T. Griffiths, *Economische geschiedenis van Nederland in de 20e eeuw*, Utrecht, 1989

–4–

Germany

Stefan Berger

Throughout much of the twentieth century the German labour movement has been bedevilled by the contradiction between its organisational strength and its political powerlessness. The Social Democratic Party (SPD) became the strongest working-class party in the world before 1914 without being able either to gain a significant influence on policy-making or to overcome the multiple divisions within the working class. In the Weimar Republic the formation of the strongest communist party in Western Europe (the KPD) left the labour movement divided and decisively weakened in a society where social and economic cleavages translated directly into political ones. National Socialism eclipsed the labour movement for twelve years; Nazi policies towards the working class between 1933 and 1939 and, more importantly, the Second World War undermined the labour movement milieu of pre-fascist Germany.

The re-emergence of Social Democracy in a democratic West Germany after 1945 under the conditions of the 'economic miracle' and the Cold War further contributed towards the erosion of the pre-conditions for a class party. The transformation of the SPD into a catch-all party produced new difficulties when the crisis of 'industrialism' hit Germany in the 1970s and 1980s. In a divided country the communist labour movement had come to power in the GDR, but the response of the working class was less than favourable.

Workers and the Labour Movement in Imperial Germany

In Imperial Germany, workers were second-class citizens. Franchises in most state and local elections as well as the drawing of electoral boundaries in national elections discriminated heavily against them. On the shop floor, workers were often prohibited from joining trade unions and the right to strike was withheld. The policy of employers consciously increased the existing occupational divisions amongst the working class by creating a system of benefits and rewards for *some* workers, whilst simultaneously introducing a rigorous factory discipline for all. Company housing or the silver pocket watch given to workers for long service with the same company are only two examples of a whole array of incentives provided by employers to ensure a docile, disciplined, obedient and above all, non-socialist workforce. Middle-class clubs and societies frequently adopted a patronising attitude towards workers, to whom the very concept of citizenship was denied as they were believed to lack the prime condition for this, namely *Bildung*.[1]

Politically, economically and socially, workers were outcasts. They shared this fate with the labour movement. Between 1878 and 1890 the SPD and the nascent trade union movement were driven into illegality under the Anti-Socialist Law, and the 1890s saw several efforts to renew anti-socialist legislation. Leading Social Democrats remained fearful right up to August 1914 that their elaborate organisational empire could be destroyed yet again by state legislation. The law courts in Imperial Germany sentenced tens of thousands of Social Democrats to prison and hefty fines were imposed for offences ranging from *lèse majesté* to incitement to violence. Middle-class clubs and veterans' organisations did not accept Social Democrats as members.

The isolation of Social Democracy – more notable in Prussia and Saxony than in Baden, Württemberg or Bavaria – led to the SPD developing its own organisational world consisting of party, trade union, cooperative and cultural, educational, sport, youth, women's and other ancillary organisations, which published hundreds of newspapers and journals and provided every possible service for members 'from the cradle to the grave'. 'Organisational patriotism' came to characterise the 'community of solidarity' formed by the labour movement in many proletarian neighbourhoods in Imperial Germany.[2] Far from stifling the vitality of the labour movement by creating a massive bureaucratic apparatus, the labour movement milieu became the central ingredient for many workers' identity and activity.[3] It was reinforced by the wealth of labour symbols, secular rituals and a broad and diffuse sense of ideology.

The adoption of Marxism in the official programmes of the SPD from 1891 to 1959 (with the exception of the short-lived Görlitz programme of 1921) should not overshadow the fact that large sections of the SPD were never influenced strongly by Marxist thought and remained attached to vague communitarian, ethical and humanist convictions.[4] Despite and because of the widespread influence of Kautsky on the party, the Social Democratic community was united not so much by Marxism as by a common millenarian vision.[5] The close *informal* links with the free trade unions were also vital for Social Democracy's organisational strength.[6] The social democratic unions organised 2.5 million workers by 1913, an important potential source of recruits for the SPD. From being treated as 'prep schools for socialism' by SPD leaders in the nineteenth century, the trade unions managed to emancipate themselves to become more independent institutions with the Mannheim agreement of 1906, which made consultation on major policy initiatives mandatory. Already before 1914 the trade unions had gained an important influence over the party, so much so that some observers have spoken of an effective 'trade unionisation' of the SPD.[7] Certainly in major pre-war debates on May Day, the Mass Strike, the youth movement and imperialism, the party always toed the line proposed by the trade unions.

The organisational strength of the social democratic labour movement in Imperial Germany was based on its ability to form a distinct sub-culture in the face of its non-recognition by the state, employers and the middle classes. Just before the outbreak of the First World War the SPD had 1,085,905 members, 80–90 per cent of whom were workers.[8] Already by 1912 the SPD was the largest party in the national parliament; a total of 4.25 million voters, overwhelmingly workers, had elected 110 Social Democratic members of parliament that year. However, organised labour was by no means identical with the working class. The mobilisation levels of the social democratic unions, for example, lagged far behind those of Britain. The SPD never managed to mobilise more than 50 per cent of the working-class vote in elections, and it only brought a distinct minority of workers into its organisational orbit. In fact, the 'typical' Social Democrat was a specific kind of worker: male, skilled, employed, urban, young, Protestant and 'respectable', often the archetypal printer, building or metal worker. Although the German working class was probably at its most homogeneous around the turn of the century, the SPD could not overcome occupational, religious, gender, ethnic and cultural divisions amongst workers.

Wage differentials between the skilled and unskilled and between different occupational groups remained significant. Whereas the average yearly wage for printers in 1900 was 1,317 marks, the average yearly wage for textile workers was 594 marks. Additionally, figures such as these mask regional wage differentials within the same industry, which were significant in the absence of a national bargaining structure in Imperial Germany. By 1913, a skilled worker in the coal mining industry earned 81.1 pfennigs per hour, by contrast an unskilled worker in the same industry by contrast earned 35.9 pfennigs. The gap between male and female wages was also considerable; in the textile industry, male skilled workers earned 44.1 pfennigs per hour, while female skilled workers earned only 30.7 pfennigs.[9]

The type of work experience also remained an important aspect of determining the degree of workers' political awareness. The mechanised and centralised nature of textile work, for example, was not well suited for the development of collective interest organisations. Equally, workers in cottage industries, agricultural labour and women were extremely difficult to organise. By contrast, the strong occupational solidarities in the mining, printing, metalworking and building industries provided fertile ground for trade unionism.

Religious divisions played a major role in workers' rejection of the social democratic labour movement in Imperial Germany and beyond. Catholics accounted for about 35 per cent of the German population before 1918, and Catholic workers formed their own trade unions and supported the Centre Party in elections.[10] Only a minority of workers continued to identify with the Liberals,[11] while some workers were attracted to extremely conservative, monarchic and pro-Imperial institutions like the veterans' associations.[12]

Ethnic divisions also caused problems for the labour movement. In 1907, 6.4 per cent of all workers were foreign, mainly of Polish, Russian and Italian origin. By 1914, approximately 1.4 million foreign workers were resident in Germany. These figures would be significantly higher, of course, if one were to include all those Polish workers who lived and worked within the realm of the German Empire. Foreign workers at best formed their own trade unions; at worst, they served German employers as strike-breakers and cheap labour. Consequently, the labour movement's reaction remained ambivalent. Demands for the protection of German workers stood next to statements calling for international working-class solidarity. The SPD undertook strenuous efforts in parliament to improve the social conditions and legal status of foreign workers, and the free trade unions edited both a Polish and an Italian newspaper in the hope of organising foreign workers – to little avail.[13]

Finally, there remained a gulf between labour-movement culture and working-class culture. While the labour-movement culture contained many elements of genuine proletarian values, collective mentalities and habits, straightforward assumptions about the labour movement as an integral part of a proletarian milieu overestimate the homogeneity of working-class culture and working-class life in Imperial Germany.[14] In fact the working-class culture in specific industrial regions such as the Ruhr were not responsive to the social democratic labour movement until well after the Second World War, despite the fact that they might have shared certain common lifestyles and habits, sentiments and everyday experiences. On the contrary, in assuming a solidaristic proletarian milieu born out of a 'culture of poverty' and supported by a labour movement culture, historians are in danger of idealising and romanticising working-class poverty and, more to the point, over-emphasising politicisation levels amongst German workers.

Working-class life in Imperial Germany remained, on the whole, characterised by insecurity, poverty and high mobility rates. It needed a conscious political decision by workers to become part of a culture of rational recreation based heavily on the idea of self-education, and it always remained only one option amongst many others. It consisted to a considerable extent of adopting middle-class norms and values and striving for a middle class way of life. The *persönliche Ehrenhaftigkeit* of the German worker came to characterise the German labour movement just as the 'respectability' of the British worker characterised the British labour movement. The influence of traditional popular culture and later of mass culture remained more important for the majority of workers.[15]

The ambivalence between a longing for integration into and the self-confident isolation from Imperial German society characterised not only the labour-movement culture. Social Democrats might have preached internationalism, but they felt a deep loyalty to the German nation-state;[16] they might have been anti-imperialist, but at the same time at least some of them revelled in the prospect of a German colonial empire, while many were all too ready to go to war against the Slavs.[17] They might have scorned the churches for their hypocrisy, but at the same time they saw their wives attend church regularly while Social Democratic propaganda was out to claim the essence of Christianity for socialism.[18] They might have been republicans, but at the same time they felt some loyalty and respect for the German monarchy;[19] they might have declared themselves to be in favour of women's liberation, but at home the evidence is that they overwhelmingly accepted oppressive bourgeois models of marriage and family life.[20] At the end of the day the ambivalence of Social Democracy between integration and isolation, which was not altogether of its own making (given the hostile stance of other political parties and social groups towards Social Democracy) contributed to the emergence of an immobile and attentive party which found it increasingly difficult to act politically in the face of growing internal division. As a result, the party found it increasingly difficult to represent the semi-syndicalist radical-aggressive sections of the working class, often composed of younger workers employed in big companies in major industrial areas such as the Ruhr, Saxony, Berlin, Bremen and Stuttgart. Unsurprisingly, it was here that the KPD had some of its most enduring strongholds in the inter-war period.

The free trade unions called for the abolition of capitalism whilst at the same time increasingly functioning within a capitalist framework. Already by 1905, 64 per cent of all successful trade union action was achieved without strike. The printing, beer-brewing and building industries in particular became early models of peaceful negotiation between employers and trade unions. By 1913, 2 million German workers were already covered by collective bargaining agreements, two-thirds of all industrial conflicts were settled peacefully in negotiations between employers and trade unionists, and even amongst the industrialists of the Ruhr heavy industry, a change in attitudes towards trade unionism can be perceived just before the First World War.[21] Certainly the introduction of the eight-hour day by Carl Zeiß in Jena in 1900 was exceptional, and one cannot ignore the fact that many employers, particularly in heavy industry and mining, had set their minds against any cooperation with trade unions. And yet, overall there was a growing recognition amongst an increasing number of employers that cooperation with trade unions, which were perceived as legitimate channels of representation and intermediation of workers' interests, held out the promise of a means of disciplining the workforce and regulating labour conflicts. The change towards more cooperative relations between the interest organisations of employers and employees was reinforced by developments during and after the First World War. The trade union policy of *Burgfrieden* (domestic 'truce' for the duration of the war) brought acceptance by the state, which in turn put pressure on employers (if only for a short time) to accept unions more than in the past.[22]

The First World War was of major importance for the relationship between the working class and the labour movement in other respects. The support of the SPD for war loans ultimately split the party in 1917. Increasingly, the right-wing social democrats (MSPD) seemed threatened with the loss of a significant part of their working-class base, especially when workers became radicalised in the final months of the war. Much of this protest was triggered off by the worsening material conditions of the working class during the First World War, but the great strike waves in the spring of 1917 and again in January 1918 also signalled the longing of many workers for peace and internal political reform.

The working-class unrest was overwhelmingly led by the left-wing social democrats (USPD), whilst the MSPD throughout the revolutionary months of 1918 and 1919 tried to channel working-class protests into calmer waters. Consequently, it looked in 1919–1920 as though the USPD – despite its rampant factionalism – would become the mass party of the working class. Major unions like the metalworkers', textile workers' and shoemakers' unions came under USPD control. Many of those activists involved in the workers' and councils' movement were attracted to the USPD by the failure of the MSPD to use the full democratic potential of the councils. Workers of all ages, skills and wage levels became radicalised and USPD membership rose rapidly from 300,000 in March 1919 to 750,000 in December 1919. In the general election of June 1920 the party received 18 per cent of the vote (up from 7.6 per cent in January 1919), in comparison with 21.6 per cent for the MSPD (down from 37.9 per cent in January 1919). However, the USPD consisted of too many diverse groups to survive and it split apart in October 1920. While its left wing made the Communist Party into a mass organisation, its right wing reunited with the MSPD to reform the old SPD in 1922.

The Aborted Transformation of the Labour Movement in the Weimar Republic

In a political sense, the role of workers as second-class citizens came to an end in 1918. The republic guaranteed them freedom of expression and combination as well as the security of the person. It introduced universal and equal suffrage as well as proportional representation for all parliaments. The Weimar constitution even incorporated a vague commitment to the setting-up of a welfare state. Social Democrats – having been kept at arm's length from political power in Imperial Germany – were now responsible for progressive local government policy in a number of 'red town halls' and the party played a leading role in the state governments of Baden, Hamburg, Hesse and Prussia. Between 1918 and 1922 and again from 1928 to 1930, the SPD participated as senior coalition party in various governments at national level.[23]

Workers also initially achieved substantial recognition in the economic sphere. Many employers cooperated with trade unions in the Central Working Community (*Zentrale Arbeitsgemeinschaft*, ZAG) established in 1918. However, in the face of economic crises of grave proportions, old antagonisms and enmities were given renewed life all too soon and many employers resorted to the old techniques of 'class war from above' practised before 1914. The eight-hour day, which was regarded by many workers as the single most important achievement of the 1918 revolution, was eroded over the course of the 1920s. The Socialisation Law passed in 1919 proved ineffective, as did the provisions made for socialisation and economic democracy in Articles 156 and 165 of the Weimar constitution.

Chronically high levels of unemployment – unheard of before the First World War – continued to frustrate workers. At the height of the Great Slump, in 1933, the number of unemployed stood at 7.89 million. For those in employment, technological innovation in the form of Taylorised, Fordist forms of mass production often meant a stepping up of work rhythms, an increase in work loads and physical toil, a fragmentation of their jobs, a loss of occupational identity and a curtailment of opportunities for workers to pursue individual careers. Productivity was increased, while the relationship between workers and the labour movement was eroded by ideas of national and factory community, the social status of manual work and individual achievement-oriented pay and rewards.[24]

The labour movement's inability in the second half of the 1920s to push through important social reforms (with the exception of the 1927 insurance against unemployment) further alienated workers from the ADGB and SPD. The social democratic labour movement's inertia in the face of the National Socialist onslaught on the Republic, its legalistic tactics against the reactionary putsch in Prussia in April 1932 and its desperate efforts to maintain its organisational empires even after the Nazi take-over in January 1933, further disheartened many activists. The communist tactics of finally bringing about the 'German October' (after several abortive attempts in the early 1920s) through violent street battles against the Nazis and the representatives of the Weimar Republic, may have prevented their followers from falling into the same pessimistic gloom as their Social Democratic counterparts, but ultimately it was an equally futile attempt.[25] The inability of the labour movement to defend working-class interests brought widespread disillusionment to ordinary workers. This is reflected in the dramatic decrease in the number of trade unionists in the 1920s; of 8.14 million members of the socialist union federation (ADGB) in 1920, only 4.1 million remained by 1931. The SPD's inability to repeat its strong electoral performance of 1919 is a further sign of many workers' frustration which occasionally erupted in spontaneous strike movements, for example in the spring of 1919. The formation of the Red Ruhr army after the successful general strike against the right-wing Kapp putsch can also be seen as a rebellion born out of disappointment that the three key demands of organised workers – thorough democratisation of society, a proper welfare state, and socialisation of key industries – were persistently ignored.[26]

The division of society into different social milieux continued in the Weimar Republic. Socially, the events of 1918 and 1919 were of little significance; Weimar society remained attached to class-specific organisational forms and social identities. Inter-class social mobility remained the rare exception. The labour movement continued to serve as a network of solidarity for workers in the absence of an adequate welfare state. Membership of the SPD peaked in 1923 with 1.26 million individual members and the labour movement's cultural and educational organisation reached its widest ever expansion involving well over 2 million workers by 1928, when it split into a communist and a social democratic wing.[27] The percentage of working-class members of the SPD dropped from about 90 per cent before 1914 to 73 per cent in 1926 to 60 per cent in 1930. The party could however claim some success in attracting more middle-class elements. There were serious efforts to extend its working-class base to agricultural workers and small farmers with the adoption of an agrarian programme at the Kiel conference of the SPD in 1927, but decades of prejudice and mistrust could not be overcome in a matter of a few years and the party – with few exceptions – continued to have only limited success in rural areas and amongst middle class voters.[28]

Ultimately, efforts to re-define the SPD as a catch-all party, which were well under way during the period of the Weimar Republic, were unsuccessful.[29] The widespread feeling in the party that the SPD should become more open to non-working-class strata was hampered by the danger of alienating its working-class base in the light of the emergence of the strongest communist party in Western Europe. Every effort of the SPD to achieve a compromise with the liberal, Catholic and conservative parties in the name of stable government was portrayed in the communist press as a betrayal of working-class interests. The young, male, unskilled and often unemployed workers felt attracted by the allegedly more radical postures of the communist party and the communist trade union movement (RGO).[30] They came to perceive the Social Democrats as bossified, ossified and out of touch.[31]

The gulf between the communists and the Social Democrats became unbridgeable when the Social Democrats used the army and right-wing paramilitary groups to put down the Spartacist rising in January 1919. All subsequent efforts of the two parties to work together, as in the governments of Saxony and Thuringia in 1923 or in the plebiscite on the dispossession of the princes in 1926, could not paper over fundamental differences. The KPD's vitriolic campaigns against the SPD as social fascists in the late 1920s finally made a united front against Nazism impossible.

The serious divisions within the working class were more than simple party rivalries. They included generational, occupational, cultural and gender divisions, and not least the gulf separating the employed from the unemployed.[32] Although the internal economic stratification of the working class after 1918 was characterised by decreasing wage differentials between skilled and unskilled workers, skill levels remained of crucial importance.[33] The gap in wages between male and female workers was only slightly reduced for skilled female workers; by 1913 they received 58 per cent of the wage of a skilled male colleague, and by 1930 they received 63 per cent. In the case of unskilled workers, the female average wage hovered around 70 per cent of the wage of male unskilled workers, both in 1913 and 1930. Ever since the 1920s, the share of women workers in employment remained relatively stable in German society at 30 per cent of the workforce. They became increasingly concentrated amongst the rising number of white-collar workers in the rapidly growing tertiary sector of the economy (which had expanded to include 28.1 per cent of the total number of those in work by 1925). By 1925, 44.3 per cent of all white-collar workers in the German economy were women. Their organisation by the social democratic labour movement nevertheless remained problematic.

Nationalist conservatives were far better at organising white-collar workers, who often perceived their white collar as a sign of upward social mobility.[34] The failure of Social Democracy to put the blame for the outbreak of the First World War firmly on the Imperial government and the nationalist right had important consequences for these workers' susceptibility to the political right's claim that the labour movement stabbed the German army in the back and subsequently enslaved Germany by signing the Versailles treaty. This kind of propaganda also attracted Protestant workers in small workshops and in provincial towns or rural areas, who tended to opt for the German National People's Party in the 1920s and for National Socialism rather than Social Democracy in the early 1930s.[35]

The Destruction of the Labour Movement in Nazi Germany

The authoritarian restructuring of social relations in Germany under Nazism had no place for an independent labour movement. After their organisations had been destroyed within weeks of the Nazi assumption of power on 30 January 1933, many trade unionists, social democrats and communists gave their lives resisting Nazism.[36] Some historians have claimed that the working class at large put up what amounted to a class-conscious struggle against Nazi efforts to incorporate them into the people's community (*Volksgemeinschaft*).[37] Others have questioned the invulnerability of the working class to National Socialist advances and even proclaimed the centrality of working class support for the stability of Hitler's regime in the 1930s.[38] Rather than adopt any of the 'maximalist' positions in this debate, the complex variety of possible options should be stressed, from which workers could choose their response to the Nazi regime. These spanned a wide field, from open support to conformity to resistance.

On the one hand, there is a considerable body of evidence which suggests that workers remained wary of National Socialist propaganda. The works councils elections of April 1933 testified to the continued loyalty of the overwhelming majority of workers to their old class organisations, as the social democratic trade unionists gained 73.4 per cent of the vote. Initially, workers had good reason to be dissatisfied with the Nazi government. Their economic situation worsened due to the imposition of a longer working week, the abolition of any independent working-class organisation and the constant intimidation, surveillance and threat of political terror. A spell in the concentration camp for those deemed 'workshy' was only the tip of the iceberg of terrorist measures introduced by the Nazis.

Wage differences according to different industries and occupations increased significantly in the 1930s, which in turn contributed towards growing divisions within the working class. Workers in non-armament related industries in particular continued to receive wages well below their high point of 1928–1929, despite a substantial increase in the number of working hours. In the textile industry, for example, real wages sank even lower than their 1933 low point. Food shortages and the deterioration in the quality of consumer goods also contributed to the feeling of dissatisfaction amongst many workers. By 1938 reports about undisciplined and unruly workers disregarding the tight laws regulating the employment market reached endemic proportions. The appalling conditions in the Reich labour service – poor food and pay in return for long working hours – often repelled young workers.

The resentment of workers found an outlet in spontaneous strikes, acts of defiance against workplace rules, slow-downs in production and absenteeism. Many workers saw through the continuing social inequality and the increased exploitation of workers in Nazi Germany and preserved a memory of their own independent class organisations throughout the twelve years of Nazi rule. Otherwise, the rapid re-emergence of trade unions and working-class parties in 1945 would be extremely difficult to explain.

On the other hand, there is also considerable evidence which suggests that the Nazi regime was becoming popular amongst substantial numbers of workers by the second half of the 1930s. As the Nazis tried to integrate workers into the People's Community under race considerations, the 'racially valuable' workers in particular benefitted from social and economic improvements. The rudimentary welfare state of the Weimar Republic was extended under Nazism, albeit under anti-humanitarian, social darwinist and racist circumstances. Through the surrogate interest organisation for workers, the German Labour Front (DAF) and its sub-organisations, Strength through Joy and Beauty of Labour, the Nazis combined an 'honour of labour' rhetoric with the propagation of holidays for workers and workshop improvement schemes to give workers at least symbolic recognition.[39] Even if many of the facilities introduced under the Beauty of Labour scheme had to be built by workers themselves outside normal working hours and even if the holidays offered were often too expensive for unskilled workers, the integrating effect on some workers cannot be denied. Plans by the DAF for a post-war Germany foresaw an even wider extension of the welfare state as well as the extensive provision of public housing for workers.

The social barriers between white-collar and blue-collar employers were significantly lowered, something which was regarded with satisfaction by many workers.[40] Women workers were pushed out of the few top jobs they had managed to fill in the labour market, due to the Nazis' misogynist policies. By 1939, however, 1.3 million more women were working in Germany than in 1933; as women workers were essential for the rearmament programme, the Nazis even lifted all employment prohibitions for married women (initially introduced in 1933) in 1937. For some young women, membership in the BDM and the *Landjahr* meant a clear dissociation with their traditional place of socialisation in the family. Workers were also particularly impressed by the massive reduction in the number of unemployed by the mid-1930s.

After 1936 wage levels rose from their 1933 low; in armaments-related industries, real wages were higher in 1938–1939 than they had been at their high point in 1928–1929. On average, weekly wages in 1939 were 29 per cent higher than they had been when the Nazis took power in 1933. There was another increase in real earnings between 1939 and 1941, due to the scarcity of labour and the failure of the authorities to implement wage freezes. These were successfully circumvented by employers and workers by means of saving funds, extra paid holidays and other bonuses. Despite the absence of effective and independent trade unions, workers were able to improve their living standards often by individual rather than collective bargaining. Young and healthy workers found the increasing use of piece wages and achievement-based benefits more attractive than older workers.

Rising living standards amongst workers after 1936 helped to discredit the labour movement's earlier predictions about the workers' fate under National Socialism. The promise of upward social mobility combined with the vision of a mass consumer society in which individual achievement would reap rich rewards to contain the working-class politically. Few workers, however, became ardent supporters of the regime. Indifference to politics, atomisation and the withdrawal into the private sphere of the family were more common reactions.

The Second World War was far more important than Nazism in weakening the close ties between the labour movement and the working class. The social and political identities of German workers were affected by the army of slave labour[41] which enabled many German workers to experience a previously unknown upward social mobility as they were suddenly catapulted into positions of responsibility such as foremen and forewomen. While acts of international class solidarity remained the exception, German workers seemed to accustom themselves quickly to their newly acquired status. Furthermore, the Nazi regime was careful to placate working-class dissatisfaction over the deterioration of living standards in the initial years of the war; weekly real wages continued to rise until 1942, and the availability of consumer goods remained at a high level until 1941.

After 1943, however, social class became less and less important as a criteria for distinguishing people in a country which underwent unparalleled physical destruction. Other factors, such as where one lived, whether one was a soldier (39.9 per cent of all industrial German workers were soldiers in 1944) or a refugee, whether one's house was destroyed by bombs and whether one could deal on the black market came more and more to shape people's lives.[42]

Amidst the smouldering ruins of National Socialist Germany, the labour movement began to be rebuilt from below. In the spring of 1945 anti-fascist councils were set up over most of Germany.[43] There was much hope for a united labour movement and much willingness to overcome the ideological divisions which had so weakened the movement in the final years of the Weimar Republic. However, the Cold War, personality clashes and the ultimately unbridgeable gulf between the basic values of social democrats and communists were soon to rekindle the old antagonisms. With the separation into two German states, the division of the labour movement into communist and social democratic wings was effectively translated into a division between two German states. The communists soon controlled the state apparatus in the Soviet zone of occupation and for forty years the GDR was – in name at least – a socialist state. By contrast, in the Western zones of occupation the communists were reduced to a sectarian minority group, desperately out of touch with the bulk of workers in the anti-communist hysteria of the Cold War. The majority of industrial workers in the West opted for the SPD.

The Labour Movement under Transformation in the Federal Republic

In the western zones of occupation the SPD was quickly reconstructed on the lines of the Weimar party. It was in the destroyed German cities that organisational success was most rapid and it was also here – in Hamburg, Bremen and Berlin – that the party did best in the elections of 1946–1947. By the end of 1946, 8,000 local SPD branches had been founded and party membership stood at just over 700,000.[44] Organisational levels in a strict party political sense could reach unprecedented heights in the Federal Republic due to the fact that the party was no longer self-financing but was financed by the state. However, what was not rebuilt was the socialist cooperative movement and, above all, the extensive network of cultural, educational and social ancillary organisations of the SPD which had stood at the centre of the blossoming labour movement culture in the Weimar Republic. Such a politicised culture would have been difficult to recreate as National Socialism did have a depoliticising effect on many workers; in fact, much of the Hitler

Youth generation retained an extremely conservative political outlook in the 1950s. In so far as a minority found its way into the SPD, it was either through the trade unions or the protest movements against re-militarisation and nuclear armaments.[45]

Many of the traditional working-class neighbourhoods, like Hammerbrook in Hamburg, where social ties had been extremely strong before 1933 were destroyed by Allied bombing in the Second World War. After 1945 town planning in German cities aimed at producing socially heterogeneous neighbourhoods to avoid the re-creation of purely working-class neighbourhoods. Americanised forms of mass culture and the widening scope of the mass media further eroded the foundations for a labour-movement culture in the 1950s. Ultimately though, the decision not to revive the labour movement culture was made consciously by the social democratic leadership. The working class should not withdraw into a ghetto of its own making again; the SPD's ambition was to integrate workers as citizens into a socialist German society. For some historians, it was this decision which signified the end of the old labour movement.

The German trade unions also ceased to be part of any wider labour movement culture. Their party-political neutrality was the price which had to be paid for a united movement. The German Trade Union Federation (DGB) overcame the various ideological and religious divisions of pre-Nazi trade unions, and membership in the DGB's sixteen industrial unions quickly rose after the war to six million in 1951.[46] Between 1950 and 1989, union density rates in West Germany remained remarkably stable at between 36 and 40 per cent of the whole dependent labour force. The DGB's major aim was to achieve economic democracy by means of co-determination in the factories.[47] Full parity between employers and trade unions, however, could only be achieved in the coal and steel industry. The works council law of 1952 was an important defeat for the trade unions in that it not only denied full parity of workers' representatives in the management of companies, it also virtually excluded the trade unions from the shop floor. The DGB's decision to operate within the framework of capitalist restoration after 1955 and the success of the economic miracle avoided serious social conflict, however, and in the 1950s and 1960s trade unions could increase the wages of all workers substantially and erode wage differentials successfully.

The SPD saw itself as the only political force in post-fascist Germany with the moral credibility to rebuild the nation, yet it lost the general elections of 1949 and 1953. Despite the SPD's impeccable nationalist and anti-communist credentials under the leadership of Kurt Schumacher, the party could neither break into the traditionally anti-socialist white-collar workers and middle classes nor could it win much support amongst

Catholic workers, agricultural workers and workers in provincial small-scale companies.[48]

Various explanations for this failure have been put forward. The SPD's leading officials were men who had their roots in the Weimar labour movement; the overwhelming majority had spent the years between 1933 and 1945 in a concentration camp or in exile. Few had experienced the massive changes in the everyday lives of workers under National Socialism and in the Second World War. Consequently, a deep generational gap appeared in the post-war years between many Labour leaders and their working-class bases. Furthermore, the SPD's emphasis on economic planning and socialisation proved unpopular, not only with the Western occupation forces but also with the wider public as it was linked to the misery of the immediate post-war years and the GDR's economic system.

Also, the success of the social market economy could not be adequately explained by the SPD. The economic miracle enabled the governing centre-right parties to build up a welfare state in the 1950s and 1960s. The welfare state in turn contributed further to the weakening of the traditional links between labour movement and working class. The state took on more and more of those functions which had previously been provided by the self-help organisations of the labour movement. Under the special economic circumstances of the economic miracle more than six million refugees – 25-30 per cent of all workers in the 1950s – were quickly integrated into West German society. As they experienced their upward social mobility in the 1950s largely as individual success, former collective identities and values were weakened. Finally, the party suffered from the effects of the Cold War, which in Germany built on the traditionally strong potential of anti-communism.

The forms of daily working-class living began to change in the 1950s and 1960s in such a way as to undermine the relationship between the labour movement and the working class. Working class homes became bigger, and by 1978, 30-35 per cent of workers owned their own home. There was more scope for privacy and contemporary observers noted that workers increasingly spent their time with their families rather than in the pub. The meteoric rise in real wages, the reduction in the number of working hours and the increase in paid holidays all facilitated the adoption of a middle-class lifestyle which had not lost any of its earlier attractions for workers. Whereas 49 per cent of workers referred to themselves as working class in 1955, only 35 per cent did so in 1980.[49] The affluent worker who was stepping out of his class and adopting bourgeois forms of behaviour became a fashionable interpretative model in the 1960s.

However, despite much talk about Helmut Schelsky's concept of the 'levelled middle-class society' (*nivellierte Mittelstandsgesellschaft*) workers remained a distinct social class. Marriage patterns, for example, reveal that contacts with other classes were the exception throughout the 1950s and 1960s. Workers remained amongst themselves at work and in their free time more than any other social group in West Germany. The social mobility of workers was within rather than between classes in the two decades following the foundation of the FRG.[50] The number of workers decreased from 45 per cent of the population in 1945 to 33 per cent in the mid-1970s. With the decline in numbers of the German working class and with the additional incentive of the 1953 electoral defeat of the SPD, demands for a transformation of the party into a catch-all party culminated in the 1959 Bad Godesberg conference. Programmatic renewal in which Marxism was repudiated as the official party philosophy stood next to various symbolic changes to the traditional party image. SPD members did not address each other as 'comrade' nor did they automatically use the familiar form of address. The red flag was no longer displayed so prominently as a party symbol. The party also opened itself up to other social classes; this readiness was underlined by the foundation of the Association of the Self Employed in the SPD in 1959, the adoption of a new agrarian programme in 1960, the organisation of a much-noted conference in 1961 which wooed white-collar workers and the demands made in 1962 for an immediate programme to improve the situation of the middle classes in the FRG.[51]

Paradoxically, the Bad Godesberg changes led primarily to an extension of the party's working-class base. For the first time in the party's history, Catholic workers turned to the SPD; predominantly Catholic regions in which the SPD remained the minority party before 1933, like the Ruhr or the Saar regions, became Social Democratic strongholds after 1959. In national elections the SPD achieved a short-lived breakthrough in 1972, but already in 1976 many Catholic workers had returned to the CDU/CSU. By the early 1990s Catholics were keeping their distance from the SPD, which is still a thoroughly Protestant party.

The Catholic milieu, however – just like its social democratic counterpart – was decisively weakened after 1945. The Catholic church hierarchy decided to give their backing to the newly established catch-all party, the CDU/CSU, without making systematic efforts to revive the profusion of Catholic ancillary organisations. Efforts by the Catholic labour movement (the KAB, which still organised an impressive 300,000 workers in the 1950s) to revive separate Catholic trade unions had the support of some Catholic bishops in the 1950s but a breakaway union, founded in 1955, was unsuccessful in recruiting substantial numbers of workers.

The SPD was even less successful in achieving any lasting breakthrough into the middle classes, which formed 55 per cent of the population in 1987. Substantial support in the 1972 general election proved short-lived and support for the SPD in the 1980 election had more to do with the unpopularity of the CDU/CSU's candidate for the chancellorship, Franz-Josef Strauß, than with any genuine conversion to the SPD. Where middle-class voters did not return to the Christian Democrats or the liberal FDP in the 1980s, they were more likely to opt for the Greens than for the SPD, particularly if they were young and well-educated.

If Bad Godesberg did not achieve any direct or long-term widening of the SPD's social base of support, it did contribute towards a public perception that the party was fit to govern. After entering into the Great Coalition with the CDU/CSU in 1966, the SPD benefited from a widespread longing for political renewal and reform after almost two decades of Christian Democratic rule. From 1969 to 1982, it became the senior partner in an SPD/FDP coalition government.[52] The party's traditional belief in the regulatory power of the state became one of the key notions underpinning that coalition.

The first half of the 1970s was the high tide of corporatist experiments in West Germany. 'Concerted Action' between government, employers' federations and trade unions, which began in February 1967 with the aim of planning macroeconomic policies, created problems for the unions when a wave of spontaneous strikes between 1969 and 1973 showed the dangers of becoming involved in corporatist economic management. The DGB pulled out of these talks in 1977 in protest over the employers' and the government's unwillingness to substantially widen the parity co-determination laws. Since the 1970s, the trade unions' emphasis has been not on higher wages but on quality of work issues, such as more breaks and holidays and better education and training, particularly for young workers.[53] In the late 1970s the DGB became increasingly disillusioned with the economic crisis management policies adopted by the SPD in government, and in 1981 it organised massive protest rallies against a government budget which was perceived as a direct attack on the working-class standard of living.

Relations between the DGB and the SPD improved after the fall of the SPD government in 1982. In November 1982 the Kiel declaration of the SPD re-emphasised that the working class and its trade unions continued to be the basis of social democracy. Indeed, 10 per cent of SPD members served as works councillors in 1982. In 1987 every fourth potential SPD voter was a trade unionist and nine out of ten SPD officials were trade unionists. The Association for Questions Concerning Employees (AfA), founded in 1973 in response to the party's growing internal heterogeneity, remains an intra-party trade union pressure group of crucial importance.

Nevertheless, working-class interests have become just one among many interests vying for influence within the SPD since the 1970s: other include professional white-collar workers, civil servants, ecologists, environmentalists and feminists. In 1958, 55 per cent of SPD members were still working class. However, between 1966 and 1972 this figure dropped from 49.4 per cent to 27.6 per cent. By 1982 it had plummeted further to 21.5 per cent. The decline of the working-class element within the SPD was mirrored by the rapid growth of white-collar employees and civil servants as members from the early 1970s onwards.[54] Although these were overwhelmingly sons and daughters of working-class parents – beneficiaries of the educational policies of the 1960s which brought greater social mobility for workers – by 1977, workers were under-represented in all leadership positions at all levels of the party.[55] The influx of new, mostly non-working class members brought membership levels to a new height, from about 700,000 in the early 1970s to just over one million in the mid-1970s. The party was not only getting less working class, it was also getting younger: 75.2 per cent of those who joined the SPD in 1972 were below 40 years of age and almost 20 per cent were under 21 years of age.

An important generational change connected with the change in the party's social structure took place when the '1968 generation' moved into the SPD in the early 1970s. Under their catchword 'modernisation', the party increasingly acquired a 'greener' image. The SPD soon found itself locked into squabbles between the modernisers represented by Oskar Lafontaine and the traditionalists represented by Wolfgang Roth. Whereas the former argue for severing the party's ties with the trade unions in favour of attracting the post-materialist middle-class vote, the latter continue to view the SPD as a party primarily for, if no longer of, industrial workers. There was a widespread perception of the necessity for programmatic renewal of a party which had lost direction.

In the party's 1989 Berlin programme which replaced the Bad Godesberg programme, the 'greening' of social democratic policies is most visible. In its ability to integrate various post-war protest movements from the anti-nuclear movement of the 1950s to the student movement of the 1960s and possibly even to the environmental movement of the 1980s, the SPD (especially in opposition) has revealed its continued character as a protest party and a social movement, however much it has on the other hand tilted towards integration and governmental responsibility.[56] With re-unification, however, a patriotic gloss reminiscent of the Schumacher years has returned to the party, which puts a question mark over the greening of the SPD.[57] Whether the election of Rudolf Scharping as party leader at the 1993 SPD party conference means a return to a more traditional SPD policy remains to be seen.

The influx of new party members in the early 1970s also meant that for the first time in a party which from its inception had argued for the emancipation of women, womens' interests began to be important. In 1948 only 19 per cent of all SPD party members were women, and in the 1950s and 1960s the party remained by and large a male-dominated organisation. Female voters, including a majority of working-class women were far more likely to opt for the CDU/CSU than for the SPD between 1949 and 1969. Only in the 1970s did the huge gender gap in West German politics begin to close.[58] The SPD responded to these changes; in 1973, an Association of Social Democratic Women (ASF) was founded as an intra-party pressure group. By the mid-1980s one in three new members was female and one-third of middle-ranking office holders in the SPD were women. The party is committed to the goal that from 1994, 40 per cent of all party positions will have to be held by women.

If the influx of middle-class party members invigorated and partially transformed party life, it also created a serious problem of communication between the labour movement and its erstwhile most important clientele – the working class. Labour leaders speaking of workers as 'the socially weak' betray the fact that their position as academically-trained members of the post-materialist German middle classes is far removed from the everyday reality of workers. Nowhere is this cleavage more apparent than in the SPD's failure to come to grips with the issue of working-class racism. Foreign workers recruited by the government and employers in the 1960s to serve as a kind of sub-proletariat became direct competitors for German workers in the narrowing job and housing markets of the 1980s.[59] The SPD's adoption of notions of integration or multi-culturalism – vague and badly thought through – are rejected by substantial numbers of blue-collar workers who are increasingly turning to extreme right-wing parties instead.[60]

The popularity of labour leaders amongst workers also plummeted due to the involvement of the leaders in a long list of political scandals. The *Neue Heimat* scandal of 1982 in particular discredited the DGB in the eyes of many workers; it transpired that directors of the trade union-owned housing association *Neue Heimat* had enriched themselves for years whilst at the same time treating their tenants in a worse fashion than nineteenth century capitalists had done. The latest scandals in 1993 involve three top labour leaders: Franz Steinkühler, the leader of the most powerful trade union in the world, IG Metall, had to resign after being accused of insider dealing; Oskar Lafontaine had to defend himself against charges of widespread corruption involving Social Democrats in his state government of the Saarland; and Björn Engholm, the party's chairman and designated candidate as chancellor for the 1994 Federal election, resigned after he admitted deceiving the public over what he knew about the Barschel affair in 1986.[61]

The crisis of the SPD in the 1980s found a parallel in the crisis of the DGB. In the post-Fordist advanced capitalist economies of the 1980s, new forms of production often described as 'flexible specialisation' have led to a growing diversification of the labour force which has in turn made the representation of workers' interests through industrial unions more difficult. In 1993 alone the DGB lost 690,000 members. The unions have tried to find solutions which would protect the core membership, but this has had serious consequences for other workers, notably the young, women, older workers and the unemployed. All of these groups have found it increasingly difficult to find representation within the DGB. By the beginning of the 1990s, the very concept of trade unionism has been called into question.[62] At the same time the core membership of trade unions is increasingly abandoning the SPD at the ballot box, which further undermines the relationship between the SPD and the DGB.

The Labour Movement in Power: The GDR 1949–1989

In the Soviet zone of occupation the political divisions of the labour movement were overcome by force in April 1946. Against the will of the majority of its functionaries, the SPD was merged with the KPD to create the Socialist Unity Party of Germany, the SED. In the new party the KPD retained the upper hand, and many old Social Democrats were purged from party offices in the period 1949–1952.[63] With the help of the Soviet occupiers, the leaders of the SED managed to control virtually all important offices in state and society without creating a one-party state.[64] The membership of the SED after April 1946 increased rapidly to 1.8 million in 1947, and after 1948 the party transformed itself into a Leninist 'party of a new type', building up an all-encompassing organisation in the following years. This was a mirror image of the state administration, with the party functionaries having the right to intervene with the administration at all levels.

The SED organised an extensive network of party organisations and ancillary cultural and educational organisations, which had its traditions in the pre-Nazi labour movement culture. Its party groups (96,104 groups of three or more party members in the mid-1980s), residential, departmental and enterprise organisations reached right down into the workplace and the neighbourhood.[65] The Free German Trade Union Association (FDGB), founded in 1946, quickly became a highly centralist umbrella organisation of comprehensive industrial unions. It acknowledged the primacy of the SED, and its main function as a Leninist trade union movement was to implement the SED's social and economic policies on the shop floor.

The last free elections in the territory of the GDR were the state elections of October 1946. In those elections there was a clear correspondence between the strongholds of the working-class parties, the SPD and the KPD before 1933 and the SED in 1946. Less than forty-four years later, in the elections for the GDR parliament in March 1990, this was no longer the case; in the old industrial heartland of Saxony, in Chemnitz – a labour stronghold from the late nineteenth century to 1933 – only 15 per cent of voters opted for the SPD.[66] Over the course of forty years, the labour movement in power had severed much of its traditionally close links with the working class.

Initially, there had been broad support amongst workers, small farmers, agricultural labourers and refugees from the east for the socialist transformation in the Soviet zone of occupation, begun by land reform in the autumn of 1945. The referendum held in Saxony on the transfer to people's ownership of enterprises owned by Nazi and war criminals won overwhelming support for expropriation (77.7 per cent) in May 1946.[67] The abolition of private ownership of the means of production did not guarantee workers a significant say in the production and the management of companies.[68] However, there were many other benefits for workers. They enjoyed considerable protection against arbitrary dismissals. Trade unions were given substantial rights over workers' training, leisure activities, sick pay and the allocation of holiday places. Enterprises offered a wide range of educational and social amenities from libraries to creche facilities, and workers were particularly encouraged to use the new educational opportunities available to them. Selection criteria for university studies discriminated positively in favour of working-class children until the early 1960s. Workers' and Farmers' Faculties were set up at every university to help workers achieve high social mobility rates in the GDR. Therefore, the possibilities for workers to achieve upward social mobility in the early years of the GDR should have contributed towards an acceptance of the socialist state amongst workers.

However, from the very foundation of the GDR the state put a heavy emphasis on the need for sacrifices from the working class in particular. In 1948 the government started a movement aimed at producing activists in every factory who would be shining models of productivity (the Hennecke movement). Unsurprisingly, workers reacted negatively towards such an intensification of work norms. Throughout the history of the GDR there were conflicts between the state and workers over the increase of work norms. The most serious of these incidents led to the workers' rising against the regime on 17 June 1953 when, according to GDR estimates, there were strikes in 272 towns and cities involving 300,000 workers calling for higher living standards, more and better provision of food and housing and the resignation of the government.[69] The protest largely involved industrial workers in the construction, mining, machine-building, chemical and iron-ore extraction industries.

The proportion of working-class members in the SED plummeted after June 1953 to a mere 34 per cent by the end of the 1950s.[70] The 'scientific-technological revolution' which the GDR embarked upon from the 1960s onwards increased demands on workers: the automation of enterprises – often equivalent to the introduction of monotonous monitoring functions – increased boredom and exhaustion, while also putting greater nervous strain on workers. There was also more night-shift work in order to use the machines to their full economic efficiency. The workers did not have any effective representation through independent unions. Working-class protests included occasional unofficial strikes; high levels of absenteeism, the theft of materials from factories and shopping during work hours can be interpreted as other forms of protest, indicating a considerable degree of job dissatisfaction among GDR workers. The emphasis attached to new technologies contributed to the emergence of new social hierarchies according to leadership functions and technical know-how, wage differentials, ways of spending free time and degrees of alienation from work. A new elitism surfaced, which led to serious divisions between the intelligentsia and the working class despite the SED's official claim that the leadership cadres in party and state represented an *avant-garde* who would rule in the interest of and in close contact with the workers.

The economic miracle, which had been so vital for the integration of the working class into the system of the Federal Republic, remained conspicuously absent in the GDR. The absence of an 'economic miracle' also meant that the SED could not deliver on promises of rising living standards. Indexes showed decreasing social inequality and wage differentials as well as rising real wages but the continuing 'equality of misery' tempted workers to look westwards to compare their situation with that of their fellow Germans. Economic pressures also made it difficult to establish a functioning welfare state in the GDR; for a long time the SED argued that any social policy was unnecessary in a socialist state and only after the eighth SED party conference in 1971 did the state embark on a comprehensive social welfare programme. Old age pensions were increased by 20 per cent in 1971–1972, but they still remained so low as to make work after retirement age a necessity for many pensioners in the GDR. The minimum wage levels for workers were raised in 1972 and again in 1976 but they still compared badly with those of West German workers.

The introduction of the new Labour Code in 1978 saw further social improvements. Resources were put into the improvement of housing and medical care in the GDR, but workers were still dissatisfied with the monotony, anonymity and social isolation prevalent in the vast dormitory towns created by the GDR housing programmes. Medical facilities remained inadequate, in particular in rural areas and in certain specialist areas such as cancer treatment, where not enough hard currency was available to pay for the import of the necessary equipment. Food and rents were heavily subsidised by the state but the quality of most consumer goods was far below West German standards.[71] The burden on the state finances created by subsidies also prevented key investment in other areas of the economy.

If workers had grievances enough against 'their' state, certainly women had several more to add. On the one hand, the labour movement in power placed strong emphasis on women's emancipation: 35.5 per cent of all SED members, 30 per cent of all city mayors and 50 per cent of all trade union functionaries in 1985 were women. By the mid-1980s, it has been estimated that about one-third of all leadership positions in the GDR society were held by women. The SED-controlled mass organisation for women, the Democratic Women's Association of Germany (DFD), furthered educational and occupational opportunities for women and by the mid-1980s, 87 per cent of all women were in employment. In view of the constant severe labour shortage, the state actively encouraged women to take up employment and took great care that women could combine motherhood with a career. In particular, when the party realised that the birth rate in the GDR was declining, it introduced a series of measures in 1971 aimed at helping working mothers.[72]

On the other hand, women remained under-represented in all top positions in the state, the economy and the party. No woman was ever to become a full member of the SED politburo; none of the first secretaries of the party at district level in the mid-1980s was female. The widespread existence of sexist jokes and advertising as well as gender-typed education in schools pointed to the continued existence of gender stereotypes in the GDR. No independent women's movement was allowed to grow in the GDR. The labour force remained largely segregated according to gender, with women working particularly in the lower-paid sectors of the economy or in traditional women's jobs such as education and social services. Consequently, many women remained dissatisfied about being left with the double burden of household and career.[73]

Party membership topped the 2 million mark in 1976 by which time every sixth citizen of the GDR above 18 years of age was a party member. Although the average age of party members reflected roughly the age structure of the population at large, the SED in the 1980s was ruled by a small group of gerontocrats who proved inflexible in the light of the reforms in the Soviet Union under Gorbachev and pressure from younger SED cadres who were urging reform on their party elders. The SED continued the labour movement tradition of very long service by its leading personnel; a position in the party was usually a position for life. If the young inside the party were frustrated by the party gerontocracy, the youth which were not integrated into the state via the labour movement organisations like the Free German Youth (FDJ) became seriously alienated. Even before 1989, a neo-Nazi youth sub-culture flourished in some East German cities.[74] The churches could also provide a shelter for an alternative dissenting youth culture. Active Catholic and Protestant workers also remained permanently alienated from the labour movement in the GDR following their persecution in the 1950s and 1960s, despite the *rapprochement* between the Lutheran church and the state in the 1970s and 1980s.[75]

The SED dictatorship sought legitimation by referring to the 'historic mission' of the working class. SED elites accepted that workers had to be educated to realise that they lived in a workers' state. Especially after June 1953, which gave the SED leadership a fright from which it never really recovered, government tended to limit conflicts with workers. Subsequently workers retained considerable leverage to indirectly push through their economic demands, often against economic reason. The production brigades (founded in 1950 after the Soviet model and put at the centre of the factory's production process in the late 1950s) in particular functioned on the one hand as means of social control of the government but on the other hand also ensured that workers could and did find an effective channel to represent their social interests. A socially engineered, artificial peace between the SED government and the workers (with the trade unions as mediators) characterised the relationship between the two from 1953 to 1989. It failed, however, to create a social and political order which was superior to the capitalist alternative in the West.

Instead of achieving equal opportunities for workers, a new bureaucratically-organised socialist '*Ordo* society' was established.[76] This was based on new social hierarchies and created new conflicts of interest. The labour movement in the reunited Germany was to pay for this legacy with the loss of much of its traditional working-class vote in the territory of the former GDR to the CDU/CSU. The total membership of the SPD in the territory of the former GDR did not exceed 25,000 in June 1993 (compared with over 900,000 in the old *Länder* at the same time). Dominant amongst the present membership are Protestant university-trained professionals; workers remain a small minority. The prospect of a long-term east-west divide in support for the SPD is a very real threat to the party.[77] The fortunes of the PDS, the former SED, are still somewhat uncertain, but it has been unable to win much support in the West, while its continuing high support amongst certain social groups in the East (especially former civil servants, the intelligentsia and women, three groups which have lost out in the unification process) and certain geographical locations (e.g. East Berlin) are notable, the odds still have to be on the slow disappearance of that remnant of the former state labour movement of the GDR from the political scene.

Certainly, massive new social problems await Germany in the 1990s and beyond. In February 1994 the country officially had 4.04 million unemployed, but unofficial figures were much higher. Almost five million people lived on social benefits of some form or another. Glaring social inequalities exist not only between East and West but also within the two territories. New social vision and a revitalisation of the solidaristic values which were once at the very heart of the labour movement are desperately needed, but can the left provide them? In the reunified Germany the labour movement remains split, without clear direction; so far it has been just as powerless to have a decisive influence on the shape of the new Germany now emerging (despite a current SPD majority in the *Bundesrat*) as it was after 1949. Its inability to enforce a change of government in the October 1994 general election has condemned the SPD to four more years on the opposition benches. Organisationally and financially, the SPD and the DGB remain possibly the strongest and most resourceful labour movement in the world,[78] but to translate such strength into political power remains *the* central dilemma for German labour at the end of the twentieth century.

Notes

1. There exists no adequate translation of *Bildung* in English. It means roughly self-perfection through education.
2. On the labour movement in Imperial Germany see especially: Guttsman (1981); Lidtke (1985); Ruppert (1986); Evans (1990). Amongst the wealth of well-researched local studies see for example Nolan (1981).
3. Tenfelde (1990), p. 263 points out that the number of paid district party agents of the SPD before 1914 numbered only 157. The seemingly endless debates on a political labour aristocracy have become rather stale by now. For good summaries, see Linder (1985) and Breuilly (1992), Chapter Two.
4. Steinberg (1979); Berger (1994a), Chapter Five.

5. Hölscher (1989); Pierson (1993).
6. Moses (1982); Fricke (1987), pp. 910–1009; Borsdorf (1987).
7. Schorske (1955).
8. Fricke (1987), p. 334.
9. For the development of wages in Imperial Germany, see Ritter and Tenfelde (1992), p. 470 ff.
10. Blackbourn (1987), pp. 188–216; Patch (1985).
11. On the failure of the German liberals to accommodate working-class interests in comparative perspective, see Breuilly (1992), pp. 115–159.
12. Ritter and Tenfelde (1992), p. 738.
13. Herbert (1986), pp. 68–70.
14. Rosenbaum (1992), p. 288 f.
15. Abrams (1992). Compare also the interesting notion of *Eigensinn* of the German worker which not necessarily led to social democratic politics in Lüdtke (1986).
16. Wehler (1962); van der Linden (1988); Groh and Brandt (1992).
17. Fletcher (1984).
18. Berger (1994a), Chapter Five.
19. Blessing (1979).
20. Evans (1987); Rosenbaum (1992).
21. Glovka Spencer (1984), also Grebing (1985), p. 124 f.
22. Feldmann (1966); Miller (1974); Kocka (1983); Kruse (1994).
23. See Breitmann (1981) and Maehl (1986) for the close identification of the SPD with the Weimar Republic.
24. Trieba/Mentrup (1983).
25. There is, however, a rather convincing argument that the SPD had few realistic alternatives to their policy of toleration and inertia after 1930. See Pyta (1989). For the hyper-active communists see Rosenhaft (1983).
26. Braunthal (1978).
27. Wunderer (1987); Guttsmann (1990).
28. Winkler (1990), p. 585.
29. Lösche, Walter (1992), pp. 1–76.
30. Fowkes (1983); Winkler (1988), pp. 445–9.
31. Indeed, if we consider the average of its members, the SPD became increasingly an old party. In 1930, only 8 per cent of its members were below 25 years of age. The SPD parliamentary party during the final years of the Republic had the highest average age of all the parliamentary parties represented in the *Reichstag*. For the ossified and immobilising structures of the SPD in the Weimar Republic see also Hunt (1970).
32. Peukert (1991). In contrast to Imperial Germany, ethnic divisions

remained unimportant in the Weimar Republic. The number of foreign workers was quantitatively irrelevant and the labour movement was strong enough to ensure the juridification of all aspects of foreign labour. This made the use of foreign labour as blacklegs impossible. See Herbert (1986), pp. 114–9.

33. Winkler (1988), p. 47. By 1928, the wages of skilled workers were on average 50 per cent higher than they had been before the war. By contrast, the wages of unskilled workers were 74 per cent higher.
34. In so far as the social democratic trade union movement made any progress towards mobilising white-collar workers, it was often those white-collar workers who came from blue-collar working-class homes.
35. Falter (1987). Only 30 per cent of workers lived in urban areas in the Weimar Republic.
36. Peukert (1983); Peukert (1989).
37. Mason (1993, first German edition in 1975); Domarus (1977).
38. Fischer (1983); Falter (1987); Ruck (1988); Mallmann and Paul (1991).
39. Smelser (1991); Lüdtke (1991).
40. Prinz (1986).
41. In the autumn of 1944, 7.7 million foreign workers worked in Germany, about 30 per cent of the whole industrial workforce. See Herbert (1986).
42. Herbert (1989), p. 356.
43. Niethammer, Borsdorf, Brandt (1976).
44. Kaden (1980).
45. Boll (1993).
46. M. Fichter (1990).
47. Thum (1991).
48. By the mid-1980s, almost 50 per cent of workers lived in provincial towns and regions, whilst only 28 per cent of workers worked in major companies with more than 1,000 employees.
49. Klingemann (1984), p. 617. West Germany revealed exceptionally low levels of working-class consciousness in the post-war period. In the mid-1970s, 68 per cent of British workers and 63 per cent of Finnish workers regarded themselves as working class.
50. Mooser (1984), particularly Chapters Two and Three.
51. Klotzbach (1982).
52. Braunthal (1983).
53. Markovits (1986); Thelen (1991).
54. Paterson and Padgett (1991), p. 93.
55. Bretschneider (1978), p. 59.
56. For the relationship between SPD and the post-1945 extra-

parliamentary protest movements see Dowe (1993).

57. For the new nationalism amongst SPD functionaries see T. Fichter (1993). For a criticism of Fichter, see Berger (1994 b).
58. Rusciano (1992).
59. Herbert (1986), pp. 179–236. By 1980, about 2 million foreign workers and their families, 4.5 million people in total, lived in Germany.
60. Betz (1993), p. 422.
61. The then minister-president of Schleswig-Holstein, Uwe Barschel, had instigated a 'dirty tricks' campaign against his SPD opponent in the 1987 *Landtag* elections. Engholm knew of this even prior to the disclosure of the affair by *Der Spiegel* magazine, but played the role of the innocent, unknowing victim in public.
62. Regini (1992).
63. Bouvier and Schulz (1991).
64. Moraw (1973).
65. Förtsch (1969).
66. Schmitt (1992).
67. McCauley (1979), pp. 1–46 on the early years of the SED in the Soviet zone of occupation. Invaluable for working-class experiences in the GDR is Niethammer, von Plato, and Wierling (1991). See also Philipsen (1993), Chapter Six, 'Workers in the "Workers' State"', and Hübner (1993).
68. Bust-Bartels (1980).
69. The increase in work norms was the most important reason for the rising. Contributing further to it were the supply problems with food and the anger over the inner-German border.
70. The membership structure of the SED was quite different to the old pre-Nazi working-class parties right from the start. Industrial workers were in the minority, 47.8 per cent in 1947. The 1960s saw a conscious effort by the party leadership to make the working-class element the biggest faction within the party and indeed, by 1978, 56.1 per cent of the party members were classified as workers. This was only achieved by means of a statistical 'trick'. GDR statistics after 1963 simply abolished any differences between white-collar employees and industrial workers. Additionally, children of party officials, ministers, army officers and the whole social elite of the country were classified as of working-class origin, provided their parents had been workers before their meteoric rise in the institutions of the GDR.
71. McCauley (1979), pp. 189–91.
72. Creches and kindergardens were made readily available, there was a reduction of working hours for women with two or more children,

a monthly household day was introduced, paid leave was given to women to take care of sick children, pregnancy and post-natal leave was extended to a full year with a return to a job with the same or similar qualification level guaranteed, there was a generous loan scheme to help young families and an afternoon day care service was introduced for schoolchildren.

73. For the situation of women in the GDR see Lemke (1985); Alsop (1992), pp. 185–200.
74. Little is known about ethnic divisions of the working class and their relevance for the decline in working-class support for the labour movement in the GDR. The GDR imported foreign labour, particularly from Vietnam, so as to cope with its persistent labour shortage. Impressionistic evidence would point towards the assumption that a stale rhetoric of internationalism could not prevent the emergence of high degrees of anti-Polish and anti-Vietnamese feeling amongst workers in the GDR.
75. The high points of this *rapprochement* were marked by the church-state summits of 1978 and 1985 and by the Luther anniversary in 1983.
76. Meier (1990); Meuschel (1992).
77. Silvia (1993).
78. All DGB unions successfully expanded their organisations to East Germany where union density rates are substantially above West German figures. See M. Fichter (1993).

Bibliography

Abrams, Lynn, *Workers' Culture in Imperial Germany: Leisure and Recreation in the Rhineland and Westphalia*, London/New York, 1992

Alsop, Rachel, 'The Experience of Women in Eastern Germany', in Jonathan Osmond, *German Reunification: A Reference Guide and Commentary* London, 1992, pp. 185–200

Berger, Stefan, *The British Labour Party and the German Social Democrats, 1900–1931*, Oxford, 1994

——, 'The British and German Labour Movements Before the Second World War: The *Sonderweg* Revisited', *Twentieth Century British History*, vol. 3, 1992, pp. 219–48

——, 'Nationalism and the German Left', *New Left Review*, no. 206, 1994b, pp. 55–70

Betz, Hans-George, 'The New Politics of Resentment. Radical Right-Wing Populist Parties in Western Europe', *Comparative Politics*, vol. 25, 1993, pp. 413–27

Blackbourn, David, *Populists and Patricians: Essays in Modern German History*, London, 1987

Blessing, W. K., 'Der monarchische Kult, politische Loyalität und die Arbeiterbewegung', in G. A. Ritter (ed.), *Arbeiterkultur*, Königstein i.T., 1979, pp. 185–208

Boll, Friedhelm, 'Hitlerjugend und "skeptische Generation". Sozialdemokratie und Jugend nach 1945', in Dieter Dowe (ed.) , *Partei und soziale Bewegung. Kritische Beiträge zur Entwicklung der SPD seit 1945*, Bonn, 1993, pp. 33–57

Borsdorf, Ulrich (ed.), *Geschichte der deutschen Gewerkschaften. Von den Anfängen bis 1945*, Köln, 1987

Bouvier, Beatrix and Schulz, Horst Peter, '*. . . die SPD aber aufgehört hat zu existieren'. Sozialdemokraten unter sowjetischer Besatzung,* Bonn, 1991

Braunthal, Gerard, *Socialist Labor and Politics in Weimar Germany: The General Federation of German Trade Unions*, Hamden CN, 1978

——, *The West German Social Democrats 1969–1982: Profile of a Party in Power*, Boulder, 1983

Breitman, Richard, *German Socialism and Weimar Democracy*, Chapel Hill, 1981

Bretschneider, Michael, *Mitgliederzahlen der Parteien und ihre räumliche Verteilung 1977*, Berlin, 1978

Breuilly, John, *Labour and Liberalism in Nineteenth Century Europe: Essays in Comparative History*, Manchester, 1992

Bust-Bartels, A., *Herrschaft und Widerstand in den DDR Betrieben*, Frankfurt a.M., 1980

Domarus, W., *Nationalsozialismus, Krieg und Bevölkerung. Untersuchungen zur Lage, Volksstimmung und Struktur während des Dritten Reiches*, Munich, 1977

Dowe, Dieter (ed.), *Partei und soziale Bewegung. Kritische Beiträge zur Entwicklung der SPD seit 1945*, Bonn, 1993

Evans, Richard J., *Comrades and Sisters: Feminism, Socialism and Pacifism in Europe, 1870–1945*, Sussex New York, 1987

——, *Proletarians and Politics: Socialism, Protest and the Working Class in Germany Before the First World War*, New York/London, 1990

——, *The German Working Class, 1888–1933: The Politics of Everyday Life*, London, 1982

Falter, Jürgen, 'Warum die deutschen Arbeiter während des "Dritten Reiches" zu Hitler standen', *Geschichte und Gesellschaft*, vol. 13, 1987, pp. 217–31

Feldman, Gerald, *Army, Industry and Labor in Germany 1914–1918*, Princeton, 1966

Fichter, Michael, *Einheit und Organisation. Der Deutsche Gewerkschaftsbund im Aufbau 1945–1949*, Köln, 1990

——, 'A House Divided: A View of German Unification as it has Affected Organised Labour', *German Politics*, vol. 2, 1993, pp. 21–39

Fichter, Tilman, *Die SPD und die Nation. Vier sozialdemokratische Generationen zwischen nationaler Selbstbestimmung und Zweistaatlichkeit*, Berlin, 1993

Fischer, Conan, *Stormtroopers: A Social, Economic and Ideological Analysis, 1929–1935*, London, 1983

Fletcher, Roger, *Revisionism and Empire: Socialist Imperialism in Germany 1897–1914*, London, 1984

Förtsch, Eckart, *Die SED*, Stuttgart, 1969

Fricke, Dieter, *Handbuch zur Geschichte der deutschen Arbeiterbewegung 1869–1917*, 2 vols, Berlin, 1987

Geary, Dick, 'Socialism and the German Labour Movement Before 1914', in Geary (ed.), *Labour and Socialist Movements in Europe Before 1914*, Oxford/New York/Munich, 1989, pp. 101–36

——, 'The failure of German Labour in the Weimar Republic', in Michael Dobkowski (ed.), *Towards the Holocaust: Social and Economic Collapse of the Weimar Republic*, London, 1983

——, *European Labour Politics From 1900 to the Depression*, London, 1991

Glovka Spencer, Elaine, *Management and Labour in Imperial Germany: Ruhr Industrialists as Employers 1896–1914*, New Brunswick NJ, 1984

Grebing, Helga, *Arbeiterbewegung. Sozialer Protest und kollektive Interessenvertretung bis 1914*, Munich, 1985

Groh, Dieter, and Brandt, Peter, '*Vaterlandslose Gesellen'. Sozialdemokratie und Nation 1860–1990*, Munich, 1992

Guttsman, W. L., *The German Social Democratic Party, 1875–1933: From Ghetto to Government*, London, 1981

——, *Workers' Culture in Weimar Germany. Between Tradition and Commitment*, New York/Oxford/Munich, 1990

Herbert, Ulrich, *Geschichte der Ausländerbeschäftigung in Deutschland 1880–1980*, Berlin, 1986

——, 'Arbeiterschaft im "Dritten Reich". Zwischenbilanz und offene Fragen', *Geschichte und Gesellschaft*, vol. 15, 1989, pp. 320–60

Hölscher, Lucian, *Weltgericht oder Revolution. Protestantische und sozialistische Zukunftsvorstellungen im deutschen Kaiserreich*, Stuttgart, 1989

Hübner, Peter, 'Balance des Ungleichgewichtes. Zum Verhältnis von

Arbeiterinteressen und SED-Herrschaft', *Geschichte und Gesellschaft*, vol. 19, 1993, pp. 15–28

Hunt, Richard N., *German Social Democracy, 1919–1933*, New Haven CN, 1964

Kaden, Albrecht, *Einheit oder Freiheit. Die Wiedergründung der SPD 1945–1946*, 2nd edn., Berlin Bonn, 1980

Klingemann, H. D., 'Soziale Lagerung, Schichtbewußtsein und politisches Verhalten. Die Arbeiterschaft der Bundesrepublik im historischen und internationalen Vergleich', in Rolf Ebbighausen and Friedrich Tiemann (eds), *Das Ende der Arbeiterbewegung in Deutschland?*, Opladen, 1984

Klotzbach, Kurt, *Der Weg zur Staatspartei. Programmatik, praktische Politik und Organisation der deutschen Sozialdemokratie, 1945–1965*, Berlin Bonn, 1982

Kocka, Jürgen, *Facing Total War: German Society 1914–1918*, Leamington Spa, 1984

Kruse, Wolfgang, *Krieg und nationale Integration*, Essen, 1994

Lemke, Christiane, 'Women and Politics in East Germany', *Socialist Review*, vol. 15, 1985

Lidtke, Vernon, *The Alternative Culture: Socialist Labor in Imperial Germany*, New York/Oxford, 1985

Linder, Marc, *European Labor Aristocracies: Trade Unionism, the Hierarchy of Skill and the Stratification of the Manual Working Class Before the First World War*, Frankfurt a.M. New York, 1985

Lösche, Peter and Walter, Franz, *Die SPD: Klassenpartei-Volkspartei-Quotenpartei*, Darmstadt, 1992

Lüdtke, Alf, 'Cash, Coffee-Breaks, Horseplay: Eigensinn and Politics among the Factory Workers in Germany circa 1900', in Michael Hannagan and Charles Stephenson (eds), *Confrontation, Class Consciousness and the Labour Process*, New York, 1986, pp. 65–95

——, '"Ehre der Arbeit": Industriearbeiter und Macht der Symbole. Zur Reichweite symbolischer Orientierungen im Nationalsozialismus', in Klaus Tenfelde (ed.), *Arbeiter im 20. Jahrhundert*, Stuttgart, 1991

Maehl, W. H., *The German Socialist Party: Champion of the First Republic, 1918–1933*, Philadelphia, 1986

Mallmann, Klaus-Michael and Paul, Gerhard, *Herrschaft und Alltag. Ein Industrierevier im Dritten Reich*, Bonn, 1991

Markovits, Andrei, *The Politics of the West German Trade Unions: Strategies of Class and Interest Representation in Growth and Crisis*, Cambridge, 1986

Mason, T. W., *Social Policy in the Third Reich: The Working Class and the 'National Community'*, Oxford, 1993. First German edition: *Arbeiterklasse und Volksgemeinschaft. Dokumente und Materialien zur*

deutschen Arbeiterpolitik 1933–1945, Opladen, 1975
McCauley, Martin, *Marxism-Leninism in the German Democratic Republic: The Socialist Unity Party SED*, London, 1979
Meier, Artur, '1990: Abschied von der sozialistischen Ständegesellschaft', *Aus Politik und Zeitgeschichte*, no. 40, B16/17, 1990, pp. 3–14
Meuschel, Sigrid, *Legitimation und Parteiherrschaft in der DDR*, Frankfurt a.M., 1992
Miller, Susanne and Potthoff, Heinrich, *A History of German Social Democracy from 1848 to the Present*, Leamington Spa/Hamburg/New York, 1986
——, *Burgfrieden und Klassenkampf*, Düsseldorf, 1974
Mooser, Josef, *Arbeiterleben in Deutschland 1900–1970*, Frankfurt a.M., 1984
Moraw, Frank, *Die Parole der 'Einheit' und die Sozialdemokratie*, Bonn, 1973
Moses, John A., *Trade Unionism in Germany from Bismarck to Hitler*, 2 vols, London, 1982
Niethammer, L. et al (eds), *Arbeiterinitiative 1945*, Wuppertal, 1976
——, *Die volkseigene Erfahrung. Eine Archäologie des Lebens in der Industrieprovinz der DDR*, Berlin, 1991
Nolan, Mary, *Social Democracy and Society: Working Class Radicalism in Düsseldorf 1890–1920*, Cambridge, 1981
Padgett, Stephen, 'The German Social Democrats: A Redefinition of Social Democracy or Bad Godesberg Mark II', *West European Politics*, vol. 16, 1993, pp. 20–38
Patch, W. L., *Christian Trade Unions in the Weimar Republic, 1918–1933*, New Haven, 1985
Patterson, William E. and Padgett, Stephen, *A History of Social Democracy in Postwar Europe*, London, 1991
Peukert, Detlev, *Inside Nazi Germany: Conformity, Opposition and Racism in Everyday Life*, Harmondsworth, 1989
——, 'Der deutsche Arbeiterwiderstand 1933–1945', in K. D. Bracher, M. Funke and H. A. Jacobsen, *Nationalsozialistische Diktatur 1933–1945. Eine Bilanz*, Bonn, 1983, pp. 633–54
——, *The Weimar Republic: The Crisis of Classical Modernity*, London, 1991
Philipson, Dirk, *We Were the People*, London, 1993
Pierson, Stanley, *Marxist Intellectuals and the Working-Class Mentality in Germany 1887–1912*, Cambridge MA, 1993
Prinz, Michael, *Vom neuen Mittelstand zum Volksgenossen*, Munich, 1986
Pyta, W., *Gegen Hitler und für die Republik. Die Auseinandersetzung der deutschen Sozialdemokratie mit der NSDAP in der Weimarer Republik*, Düsseldorf, 1989

Regini, Marino (ed.), *The Future of Labour Movements*, London, 1992
Ritter, Gerhard A. and Tenfelde, Klaus, *Arbeiter im Deutschen Kaiserreich 1871–1914*, Bonn, 1992
Rosenbaum, Heidi, *Proletarische Familien. Arbeiterfamilien und Arbeiterväter im frühen 20. Jahrhundert zwischen traditioneller, sozialdemokratischer und kleinbürgerlicher Orientierung*, Frankfurt a.M., 1992
Rosenhaft, Eve, *Beating the Fascists? The German Communists and Political Violence 1929–1933*, London, 1983
Ruck, Michael, *Bollwerk gegen Hitler? Arbeiterschaft, Arbeiterbewegung und die Anfänge des Nationalsozialismus*, Köln, 1988
Ruppert, Wolfgang (ed.), *Die Arbeiter. Lebensformen, Alltag und Kultur von der Frühindustrialisierung bis zum Wirtschaftswunder*, Munich, 1986
Rusciano, Frank Louis, 'Rethinking the Gender Gap: The Case of West German Elections 1949–1987', *Comparative Politics*, vol. 24, 1992, pp. 335–57
Salter, Stephen, 'Germany', in idem and John Stevenson (eds) *The Working Class and Politics in Europe and America, 1929–1945*, London New York, 1990, pp.99–124
Schmitt, Karl, 'Politische Landschaften im Umbruch: Das Gebiet der ehemaligen DDR 1928–1990', in O. W. Gabriel and K. G. Troitzsch (eds), *Wahlen in Zeiten des Umbruchs*, Frankfurt a.M., 1992, pp. 403–41
Schorske, Carl E., *German Social Democracy 1905–1917: The Development of the Great Schism*, Cambridge MA, 1955
Silvia, Stephen J., 'Left Behind: The Social Democratic Party in Eastern Germany', *West European Politics*, vol. 16, 1993, pp. 24–48
Smelser, Ronald, 'Die Sozialplanung der deutschen Arbeitsfront', in R. Zitelmann and M. Prinz, *Nationalsozialismus und Modernisierung*, Darmstadt, 1991
Stachura, Peter (ed.), *Unemployment and the Great Depression in Weimar Germany*, London, 1986
Steinberg, H. J., *Sozialismus und deutsche Sozialdemokratie. Zur Ideologie der Partei vor dem ersten Weltkrieg*, 5th edn., Berlin/Bonn, 1979
Tenfelde, Klaus, 'Germany', in Marcel van der Linden and Jürgen Rojahn (eds), *The Formation of Labour Movements 1870–1914: An International Perspective*, 2 vols, Leiden, 1990
Thelen, Kathleen, *Union of Parts: Labor Politics in Postwar Germany*, Ithaca, 1991
Thum, Horst, *Wirtschaftsdemokratie und Mitbestimmung. Von den Anfängen 1916 bis zum Mitbestimmungsgesetz 1976*, Köln, 1991

Trieba, V. and Mentrup, U., *Entwicklung der Arbeitswissenschaft in Deutschland. Rationalisierungspolitik der deutschen Wirtschaft bis zum Faschismus*, Munich, 1983

van der Linden, Marcel, 'The National Integration of European Working Classes 1871–1914', *International Review of Social History*, vol. 33, 1988, pp. 285–311

Wehler, Hans Ulrich, *Sozialdemokratie und Nationalstaat. Die deutsche Sozialdemokratie und die Nationalitätenfragen in Deutschland von Karl Marx bis zum Ausbruch des ersten Weltkrieges*, Würzburg, 1962

Winkler, Heinrich August, *Von der Revolution zur Stabilisierung. Arbeiter und Arbeiterbewegung in der Weimarer Republik 1918–1924* Berlin Bonn, 1984

——, *Der Schein der Normalität. Arbeiter und Arbeiterbewegung in der Weimarer Republik 1924–1930*, 2nd edn., Berlin Bonn, 1988

——, *Der Weg in die Katastrophe. Arbeiter und Arbeiterbewegung in der Weimarer Republik 1930–1933*, 2nd edn., Berlin Bonn, 1990

Wunderer, Hartmut, *Arbeitervereine und Arbeiterparteien. Kultur- und Massenorganisationen in der Arbeiterbewegung, 1890–1933*, Frankfurt a.M., 1987

–5–

Britain

Chris Williams

> [T]he labour movement . . . has a tendency towards the comforting simplicities of an evocative and sentimental nostalgia: in its current uncertainty, it does tend in its radicalism to fall back on the vanished solidarities of a time when a coherent and unified working class may seem to have been properly resistant, conscious and oppressed . . .[1]

From the foundation of the Labour Representation Committee in 1900 to the present day, Britain's 'socialist' labour movement has been built upon the strength of its trade unions.[2] In 1914, 4.1 million British workers were members of trade unions (representing 23 per cent of the total workforce); by 1920, the movement had doubled in size to 8.3 million (45.2 per cent). The combined forces of economic depression, unemployment, the restructuring of British industry and some hostility from both employers and the state reduced trade unionism to a trough of 4.4 million (22.6 per cent) by 1933. However, the stability of the British economy after the Second World War, the increased affluence of the manual working class, the absence of large-scale unemployment and the integration of the labour movement and particularly its leadership into the circles of government, facilitated British trade unionism's expansion to 9 million members (roughly 44 per cent of the workforce) from the late 1940s to the early 1960s. The 1960s and 1970s saw an expansion of trade unionism amongst white-collar workers, and by the late 1970s British trade unionism reached its apogee with nearly 13.5 million members (55.4 per cent). However, since the industrial relations disturbances of the 1978–1989 'Winter of Discontent' and the Conservative Party's victory under Margaret Thatcher in the 1979 general election, trade unionism has declined both in numbers and in influence upon both government and industry. By 1990, there were 9.9 million trade unionists in Britain, representing only 37.7 per cent of the workforce.

If trade unionism has been in a state of crisis since the late 1970s, there is a substantial body of opinion that holds that the political half of British socialism, the Labour Party, has been in decline since the early 1950s.

Taking the title 'Labour Party' in 1906, six years after its foundation, the party was able to form minority administrations under Ramsay MacDonald in 1924 and 1929–1931. Despite its collapse at the general election of 1931 the party remained the major opposition to the Conservatives throughout the 1930s, having effectively replaced the divided Liberal Party in that role in the 1920s. Winning a sweeping victory in the general election of 1945, the governments of Clement Attlee (1945–1951) implemented a series of radical changes in British welfare provision and economic organisation, establishing the National Health Service and nationalising a number of key industries including coal, the railways and iron and steel.

The party lost the general election of 1951 but could take satisfaction in its legislative achievements and in having attained its highest-ever vote of just under 14 million at the polls. However, with the Conservatives taking the initiative and winning two more general elections, Labour remained out of office until 1964, although the consolidation of two-party competition with the eclipse of the Liberal Party and the consensual 'Butskellite' nature of British government during the 1950s still allowed Labour to share in the political limelight. Its electoral successes of 1964, 1966 and 1974 under Harold Wilson meant that in the period 1964–1979 Labour was in office for over eleven years. Credence was therefore lent to Wilson's claim that Labour was set to replace the Conservatives by becoming the 'natural party of government'.

However, successive electoral defeats in 1979, 1983, 1987 and 1992 have cast considerable doubt upon the future relevance of the party and its policies. The total vote polled in 1983 was the lowest since the General Election of 1935, when the electorate was considerably smaller. Although the secession of the Social Democrats (SDP) in 1981 ultimately did not present the threat to the party's electoral position that was predicted at the time, nevertheless in the wake of the 1992 defeat Labour has continued the seemingly endless search for both a coherent identity and a programme that would seem attractive and viable to the electorate. The abandonment of Clause IV of the party's constitution (which specified public ownership as the party's objective) was joined by proposals for the diminution of the influence of the trade unions within the party, and with the already diluted language of socialism being increasingly marginalised in favour of the languages of equality and (more significantly) market efficiency, it became possible for even sympathetic observers to feel that Britain's 'socialist era' was at an end.[3] Others had predicted as much some years earlier; for the Marxist historian Eric Hobsbawm, the 'Forward March of Labour' had been halted in the early 1950s.[4] The aim of the first part of this chapter is to consider the historical roots of 'the crisis of British socialism' in so far as they are reflected in the internal structures and external relations of the British working class. Although traditional works on 'labour history' provide much of the material for this examination, its more sterile debates and narrow perspectives must be avoided. To understand the place of the 'socialist' labour movement within British working-class life, a broader survey of more recent and more original works of 'social history' is necessary.[5]

The Roots of Labour Movement Strength

At the beginning of the twentieth century, Britain was an industrial and urban society par excellence. Fully 78 per cent of the population of England and Wales, and 74 per cent of the population of Scotland lived in urban settlements. Of a total working population of 16.7 million recorded by the 1901 census, only 1.5 million were engaged in agriculture, forestry and fishing. Manual workers, who filled the ranks of the trade unions and who were thus the Labour Party's most immediate constituency, accounted for approximately three-quarters of the population.

This nominal 'working class' came to terms with the 'permanency' of capitalism from the third quarter of the nineteenth century onwards, and largely eschewed revolutionary philosophies and insurrectionary strategies thereafter.[6] Simultaneously, it is believed to have developed a relatively homogeneous and autonomous associational culture which, although not highly politicised, was very class conscious. As Eric Hobsbawm put it, this was the time of 'the working class of cup finals, fish and chip shops, palais de danse and Labour with a capital L'.[7] This 'working-class culture' has been regarded as being both the bedrock of the British labour movement and its limitation, having provided its bearers with at one and the same time an independent, largely impermeable sense of identity, and a deeply cautious, socially conservative and strategically reactive set of political attributes.[8] Partly, although not exclusively, as a result of this culture, British socialism's more exotic strains have had a marginal place within working-class politics viewed on a national scale. Before the Great War, syndicalism and industrial unionism flourished only amongst small groups of enthusiasts and autodidacts. Their influence upon individual trade-union leaders (particularly on miners such as Arthur Cook and Arthur Horner) was significant, and the authorities were paranoiacally over-sensitive to the spread of what were regarded as 'alien' ideas, but the industrial disorders of 1910–1914 labelled 'The Great Unrest' had far more to do with economic pressures than with the popularity of revolutionary ideologies.[9] Contemporaries were too swift in attributing the heightened consciousness of a labour-capital divide which marks the period 1910–1920 to the spread of syndicalism and later

'Bolshevism'. The latter inspired and instructed the formation in 1920 of the Communist Party of Great Britain from a variety of Marxist sects and societies. The Communist Party operated (albeit sometimes spectacularly) throughout the inter-war years on the fringes of the Labour Party, but its total membership in that period never exceeded 20,000; although until 1927 it could claim, often through trade-union delegates and local-constituency parties, to be putting pressure upon the Labour Party to change its policies, the purging of Communists after 1926 and the erosion of 'Poplarism' amongst local-government authorities by means of increased central state interference led to the Communist Party's frustration.[10] Its attempt during the so-called 'Third Period' (1928–1933), when the Communist International adopted the 'Class Against Class' policy, to forge a separate trade-union movement barely got off the ground, and it was with some relief that its leaders were able to make an ideological return to the fold with the coming of the doctrine of the United Front.[11] The largely non-socialist origins of the Labour Party in the 1900 Labour Representation Committee and the overwhelming attachment to moderate-left politics account for the predominant strains of gradualism and a generalised, non-theoretical 'Labourism'. This has largely excluded revolutionary sentiment, and even ambitious thinking about the restructuring of British society. As Ferdynand Zweig put it, 'Labour means a slow progress in the spirit of socialism, but not socialism as an all-embracing principle of life'.[12]

Two other factors account for the success of the Labour Party in monopolising the allegiances of left-leaning members of the working class. First, the existing constitutional framework and the attitude of the British state towards the labour movement were relatively unproblematic. Although Aneurin Bevan was later to suggest that British democracy was first tried only at the general election of 1929, most male socialists entered the twentieth century confident that the electoral system would not work greatly to their disadvantage: electoral reform for men was not a major issue, whatever the retrospective discoveries of historians as to the distortion of the Labour Party's potential constituency.[13] As for the enfranchisement of women, Labour's leaders were hesitant about too great a commitment to a change whose dimensions they could not control, whilst most trade-union officials worried about the implications the vote might have for female competition in the labour market. Although neither of these fears were substantially realised, the fortuitous provision for women in the 1918 Representation of the People Act did not produce any rolling demand for complete enfranchisement, least of all from within the labour movement. When it finally arrived in 1928, it was precisely because it was not an issue over which politicians greatly worried.[14]

Overall, the British labour movement's interest in constitutional matters may be characterised as one of idle curiosity, occasionally stimulated by controversial (and mainly theoretical) prescription. Proposals for re-ordering the British constitution, and particularly for tinkering with the roles of the royal family, the House of Lords and the civil service, have been seen either as provocative interventions in internal party squabbles or as misleading diversions from the real business of winning elections.

A major reason for this lack of interest in constitutional change is that working-class politics had developed, from the mid-nineteenth century onwards, within a liberal constitutional framework. Trade unions had been able to operate with a large measure of legal freedom since 1875, whilst socialist societies and political parties organised without hindrance. Thus it was possible for trade unionists and socialists to believe that the state was, in the best liberal tradition, class-neutral. It was precisely because of the confidence of the labour movement in the flexibility of the state that the legal offensive against trade unions by certain employers in the 1890s gave rise to the emergence of the Labour Party.[15] The Great War drew the state and labour movement closer together, conferring legitimacy and responsibility upon the latter in return for a willingness to moderate its challenge to the authority of the former. The Second World War repeated this process, and in addition, the subsequent creation of a large public sector forged an alliance between state and trade unions that was only to be broken in the 1980s.[16] The complicity of the British working-class with the structures of the state has, therefore, been due not to coercion, but mainly to hegemonically-derived consent, and also to direct material self-interest.[17]

The second factor working in favour of a moderate, democratic and constitutionalist labour movement in Britain has been the nature of employer-employee relations. It may be granted that certain industries such as engineering and transport acquired deserved reputations for employer intransigence and hostility towards trade unions. In addition, industrial disputes from the lockout of the slate quarrymen at Penrhyn in North Wales (1900–1903) to the violent struggles at Grunwick in 1977 and at Wapping in 1986 have passed into labour movement folklore as representations of the rapacious and brutal nature of British capitalism, both historical and contemporary. Perhaps the one industry where the images of confrontation and violence have been starkest is coal: these images range from the shooting of miners at Featherstone in 1893, the intervention of the military in the Cambrian Combine dispute in the Rhondda and Gilfach valleys in 1910–1911, the victimisation of union activists after the General Strike defeat of 1926 and the rise of the threat of company unionism, particularly in Nottinghamshire, all the way to the bitter death-throes of the deep-mined industry in the 1984–1985 dispute. But, however emblematic of conflict, the coal industry was also an area where there were long-established negotiation and arbitration procedures, and where there were lengthy periods of industrial quiescence (notably from the late 1940s through to the 1960s).

More generally, from 1900 until the late 1970s at least, most employers signalled their willingness to work with trade unions and to establish permanent collective bargaining structures.[18] Furthermore, the state was prepared to intervene to act as a brake upon employer counter-offensives, even at times when the labour movement was severely weakened. One example was in the aftermath of the defeat of the 1926 General Strike, when the final form taken by the 1927 Trade Disputes Act was a much watered-down (and therefore more conciliatory) version of the proposals advanced by the National Confederation of Employers' Organisations.[19] Moreover, it is not clear that trade unions, for all their official hostility towards capitalism, were unrelentingly intransigent in their dealings with employers, and in fact they were at times extremely reluctant to remove themselves from the context of a market in which they felt they had strength. This was particularly apparent in the late 1960s and late 1970s when the trade unions proved highly resistant to Labour governments' attempts to regularise industrial relations and wages through programmes such as 'In Place of Strife' and the 'Social Contract'.[20] A readiness to accommodate with capitalism was also marked in the pragmatic, centrist reaction of the Ernest Bevin-dominated TUC to the defeat of 1926, which was to engage the employers in the Mond-Turner talks of 1928–1929. Although the naive and politically anachronistic current of trade-union behaviour labelled 'Lib-Labism' was replaced in the years before the Great War by more confrontational industrial strategies, conciliation and compromise continued to be vital tools in the hands of even the most publicly radical and politically committed trade unionists, at least until the advent of Arthur Scargill as leader of the National Union of Mineworkers in 1981.[21]

The Forward March of Labour Halted?

The above section has attempted to explain the strength of the British labour movement, particularly in the period from 1900 up to 1979. Since the Conservative Party's victory at the General Election of 1979 there have been changes in the relationships between the movement and both state and employers, which have displaced the movement from its central position in British society and cast serious doubt upon its future. By the early 1970s, the Conservative Party was attempting to face down the power of the trade unions, and although its timing was poor and its leadership inept, allowing the NUM in particular to score (immediately exaggerated) victories, there was a groundswell of public opinion which considered that the power of the unions had to be curbed.[22] Supported by the public sector industrial relations breakdown of the late 1970s, the Thatcher administrations were able to emasculate the power of the most aggressive trade unions with a series of industrial confrontations and changes in public-sector management. Like-minded employers followed this lead enthusiastically.

However, it would be unwise to place too great an emphasis upon these recent developments as solely responsible for the declining relevance of the labour movement in British public life. As already remarked, some commentators have seen the roots of decline as located in social trends or as rooted in historic failures by the movement to address particular segments of society, and it is with these arguments that this section is concerned.

Manual workers have been the major reservoir of Labour Party and trade-union support. The changing occupational structure of twentieth-century British society has led to a shrinkage in potential support of this nature. The proportion of the British workforce that can be classed as manual has fallen from 74.6 per cent in 1911 to 64.2 per cent in 1951, and to 47.7 per cent in 1981.[23] With the continued contraction of the coal industry in particular in the last decade, a further substantial decrease by the end of the century may be expected. Furthermore, the gradually declining importance of muscle power in the modern economy has ensured that the manual workforce is no longer seen as being so central to Britain's economic future.

Alongside these changes has come the expansion of white-collar occupations. By the time of the 1981 census, these jobs outnumbered blue-collar jobs.[24] Although unionisation is not insignificant in many white-collar occupations (34.3 per cent were unionised in 1971, for instance), it is considerably lower than that of blue-collar workers (52 per cent in 1971).[25] Furthermore, it has become a commonplace of modern sociology that clerical workers in particular have a far weaker self-image as working class than workers in traditional heavy industries, or even than workers in light but still factory-based industries.

To compound both these developments, the electoral allegiance of both manual and non-manual workers, as well as that of trade unionists to the Labour Party, has slipped considerably in recent years.[26] Although debates over the rise of the 'affluent worker' or the process of 'embourgeoisement' have become increasingly unfashionable, there seems little doubt that the British working class, manual or non-manual, has defined itself as much by its practices as consumers as by its common identity as producers. For consumers, it is the Conservative Party that has proved attractive, particularly in recent elections. According to recent estimates Labour's hold amongst the 'manual working class' slipped from a high of 69.5 per cent in 1966 to 42.6 per cent at the General Election of 1983. The Conservatives, on the other hand, have risen from 24.9 per cent to 34.5 per cent amongst this group over the same period. What is worse for Labour is that its attraction to 'intermediate and routine non-manual classes' (which have been growing both in absolute numbers and as a proportion of the British workforce/electorate) has declined: from 33.4 per cent in 1966 falling to 19.4 per cent in 1983, whilst the Tories have found fairly consistent support amongst this category (53.9 per cent in 1966, 52.8 per cent in 1983).[27]

Of course working-class support for the Conservative Party is not an original development: Tory influence among this section of society dates back to the development of a mass electorate in the late nineteenth century. It has been sustained both by the persistence of 'deferential' attitudes amongst some voters and, perhaps what is more important, by a more 'secular' identification with the policies and record of the Conservatives. Whereas working-class Conservatism could, in the first half of this century at least, clearly be identified with socio-economic characteristics such as rurality, non-membership of trade unions and work in small units of production, such connections have become increasingly difficult to sustain as the appeal of the Conservative Party to even 'class-conscious' workers has grown.[28]

Another feature of electoral allegiance that is worrying for the Labour Party is that its residual support, whether in the 1931 general election or in those of 1979–1992, has often been highest in areas of high unemployment. Unemployment, underemployment and poverty are all drains on the potential support for the labour movement in that although they (through proof of capitalism's failure) may provide the justification for a socialist solution, they simultaneously undermine the chances of its achievement. Those areas currently with the lowest proportion of economically-active males (between the ages of sixteen and sixty-four) in employment read as a list of Labour bastions: Merseyside, Mid Glamorgan, West Glamorgan, Tyne and Wear and Cleveland.[29] While high unemployment may scar the collective memory, and while the experience of the depressed areas of the 1930s might have contributed in no small measure to the reconstructionist mood capitalised upon by the Labour Party in its general election campaign of 1945, no political party can build its future upon those marginalised by the working of the modern economy.

The British labour movement's greatest failure, however, and one that applies to the whole of the twentieth century, may have been its inability to build more secure institutional foundations amongst working women. Nineteenth-century British trade unionism was grounded in a gender division of labour that sought to exclude or marginalise female workers. The struggle for female trade unions began late, and although, given the difficulties faced by women trade unionists, it may be unfair to accuse them of being unsuccessful in their efforts, the proportion of working women in trade unions never came close to matching that of men.[30] In 1920, 23.9 per cent of female workers were unionised, compared with 54.5 per cent of men; by 1980 the gap had scarcely closed, with 37.2 per cent of women workers being in trade unions against 63.4 per cent of men.[31]

For much of the twentieth century gender relations have been regionally specific, and where the labour market was dominated by men, women were not just marginalised in terms of employment, but very often politically marginalised as well. The best example of such areas would be mining communities where few women found an outlet in paid employment, and where the workplace as well as political and social cultures were dominated by male concerns and male sociability. Dennis, Henriques and Slaughter in their classic sociological study of a mining community, *Coal is Our Life*, commented that 'the interest and activities of the women in the Labour Party in Ashton are "social" rather than political in character and in addition are often typically "feminine" in Ashton terms'.[32]

Not all areas found their economies and political structures to be so male-dominated. In the textile industries of northeast Lancashire there was a much greater degree of cross-gender solidarity, and this area provided one of the national 'voices' for women's concerns.[33] Indeed it was the industrial north that proved (along with London) to be the most successful terrain for the Women's Labour League before 1918, although under the Labour Party's new constitution and with the scattering of the broader feminist movement, that distinctive voice was heard less and less in the inter-war years.[34] Most areas saw women in some form of paid employment, increasingly after the Second World War, but their work continued to be segregated from that of men and confined to a secondary labour market with low wages and inferior status: their 'industrial' and 'political' concerns frequently suffered as a result. British trade unionism was under a double handicap in the area of greatest expansion amongst women workers, clerical work, where traditions of trade-union organisation were nascent rather than well-established. Whereas in 1911 179,000 women were engaged in such employment (3.3 per cent of all occupied females), by 1981 this figure had risen to 2,874,000 (29.1 per cent of all occupied females).[35] Having comprised 29.8 per cent of the non-manual workforce in 1911, by 1981 women made up 42.8 per cent of this occupational sector.[36]

Overall, it is fair to judge the British labour movement as having been negligent in the attention it has paid to and the priority it has placed upon women workers. This has largely been due to its readiness to protect the more privileged position of those male, and usually 'skilled', workers who were dominant within the trade unions and the broader labour movement. This absence of concern has ultimately rendered the links between a majority of working-class women and the movement tenuous and fragile, and attempts to integrate women through an approach to some sort of 'rainbow' coalition have generated their own strategic tensions and have achieved only very limited success.

The decline in the significance of manual labour, the rise of white-collar work, the spread of mass unemployment and the expansion of female employment have all weakened British trade unionism. These trends have been apparent since the 1950s, but have been particularly acute since the 1970s. The political impact of these social and economic trends, the last of which in particular has gone largely unmediated by an often inert and blinkered trade-union movement, has been to cast the Labour Party in the image of a 'regional class party', representative of the council estates, the public sector, industrial Scotland and the rest of the metaphoric 'North'.[37] Escaping from that historical cul-de-sac without losing either its identity or its purpose (however understood) has become Labour's most pressing dilemma.

No 'Classic' Working Class?

The first two sections of this chapter have largely concentrated upon the fall from grace of Britain's labour movement, and in so doing have introduced themes of vital importance to an understanding of the place of labour within contemporary British society. However, there is also a need to accommodate recent advances in social history which together have provided a more sophisticated understanding of the British working class and its industrial and political concerns.

The cumulative impact of such 'revisionism' in both political and social histories of that class has been recognised even by academics closely allied to the labour movement. David Howell, for instance, has posed the question 'When was "The Forward March of Labour"?' and given the answer that it was nothing but a historical illusion. Howell suggests that a reconstructed labour history can still be informed by socialist values, but that it has to be intellectually sceptical of any notion of a 'Forward March'. Political history is full of contingency: no determinism or logical progression can any longer be presumed.[38] In the field of social history, the collective weight of recent scholarship has operated to question the assumed or asserted homogeneity of the working class, even in its 'classic' formulation (between about 1900 and 1950).

Some of the focus upon division and difference within the working class has essentially reworked familiar themes. This is particularly the case with the analysis of skill differentials and other occupational gradations. Analyses of the British working class of the nineteenth century have consistently stressed the exclusionary nature of the 'craft unions' and the privileges accorded to artisans and craftsmen and their prominence within supposedly working-class institutions.[39] There continues to be some mileage in the notion of a 'labour aristocracy' in the late nineteenth century economy.[40] Nevertheless, a canon of labour history orthodoxy was that the significance of such divisions was reduced as the rise of new technologies led to 'deskilling' (and the consequent 'homogenisation' of the working class), and as the rise of new forms of trade union organisation overcame barriers internal to the industrial workforce.

Such a view can no longer be sustained, even by the most sympathetic labour historian. Although the first two decades of the twentieth century saw the consolidation of industrial and general forms of trade union organisation (the formation of the Amalgamated Engineering Union in 1920 is an example of the former, the formation of the Transport and General Workers' Union in 1922 and the National Union of General and Municipal Workers in 1924 are examples of the latter), serious divisions between workers in single industries continued and were occasionally reinforced by trade union practice.[41] Thus in the motor car industry, both the AEU and the National Union of Vehicle Builders resisted the recruitment of semi-skilled workers, while in the cotton industry the Spinners' Union effectively marginalised piecers.[42]

Nor can the notion of 'deskilling' be upheld, implying as it does the notion of there being a certain 'essential' and ahistorical skill content to any particular task. Skill was constantly in the process of construction and reconstruction and 'remained a central axis of occupational organisation within the working class'.[43] To David Lloyd George it was quite clear: '"Labour" means skilled Labour and there is quite as great a gulf between skilled and unskilled Labour as between the propertied class and Labour generally.'[44]

Thus, even where trade unionism was prevalent such as in leading sector industries as coal, cotton and engineering, organisation did not of itself lead without complication to labour movement unity. What is equally significant is that in the newer industries of the inter-war period (such as the motor industry, chemicals and rubber), trade unionism was slow to grow, whilst in the low-wage sectors of the economy (such as food manufacturing), non-unionism was widespread well into the 1970s.[45] Part of the explanation lies in existing trade union discrimination against workers who were considered to present a threat to the privileged position of skilled (and unionised workers).

Also significant were employer intolerance and hostility, and the absence in many sectors of units of production large enough to make union organisation practical.[46] Levels of under-employment and unemployment (in the 1930s and from the early 1980s) must also figure in any explanation of trade-union weakness. Finally, an often overlooked point is that the self-image of Britain's labour movement was overwhelmingly urban, and levels of trade unionism amongst agricultural workers have consistently been low: from only 0.7 per cent in 1911, they rose to 23.5 per cent by 1921 only to collapse to 4.6 per cent by 1931. Bringing these different points together, whatever the movement's rhetoric, throughout the last two centuries British labour has relied most not upon poor workers engaged in a constant struggle to find and retain employment, but upon relatively well-off workers in stable occupations. Put simply, trade unionism has not been relevant to all, or perhaps even most, members of the British working class.

There has been further refinement of the notion of working-class consciousness as largely production (and work) determined. For whilst 'workface' history has commanded a great deal of worthy attention in recent years, the sphere of consumption has been seen as one in which the internal differences and status obsessions of the working class were played out.[47] Although manual workers in the late nineteenth and early twentieth centuries often sank their funds into communal institutions, this has been seen as an expression not so much of class consciousness as of direct material interest, appealing to each status- and security-conscious working-class 'member' on an individualist basis.[48] There is more than an echo in such work of Robert Roberts's view that his *Classic Slum* was populated by individuals obsessed with their relative position only within the limited social hierarchy of their own neighbourhood.[49]

More recent histories have revealed the extent to which apparently homogeneous working-class communities were in fact riven by social and behavioural differences, of which the labels 'rough' and 'respectable' are inadequate reflections.[50] It would be a mistake to accuse the residents of inter-war and post-1945 council housing estates of somehow losing the variety of associational life and even the intermeshing of community needs and interdependencies that characterised older working-class neighbourhoods. The new estates did however weaken the geographical and sociological links between home and workplace, and created a forum within which workers could place a greater emphasis upon their individual and family needs, processes that drew some of the sting from a sense of working-class solidarity as a basis for class action. In an extreme case, such as the developing Dukeries coalfield of Nottinghamshire between the wars, such tendencies were reinforced by the degree of employer influence exerted in 'model villages'.[51]

Studies of the religious beliefs, attitudes and loyalties of the working class have deepened this picture of internal differentiation. Divisions between Catholics and Protestants were of primary significance amongst workers in Liverpool and Glasgow but were not unknown outside these cities, particularly where Irish Catholics were concerned.[52] Even amongst Protestant denominations, loyalties and prejudices could influence patterns of trade-union development.[53] The labour movement had its secular side, even its atheists, but its 'militant' heartlands such as Scotland and South Wales were long dominated by socialists as 'ethical' as anywhere else in Britain.[54]

Refinement of the notion of a homogeneous, class-conscious British proletariat has proceeded further through the study of working-class nationalism and chauvinism. The first half of 1919 witnessed a rash of race riots in South Shields, Glasgow, Liverpool, London and Cardiff in which lives, both black and white, were lost. Economic tensions and divisions within the workforce were at the root of this violence. In the Cardiff riots an older immigrant community, the Irish, was at the forefront of the assault upon the black seamen of Butetown.[55] After the Second World War racism amongst Midlands car workers and East End dockers occasionally received press attention.

Even where an immigrant presence was not regarded as a 'problem' British workers long retained a self-image that relied for its confidence, pride, and sense of superiority upon the grandeur of (and later the memory of) Empire. Frequently the labour movement operated (out of choice as much as of necessity) in an imperial, even jingoistic framework.[56] Indeed, it was pointed out in the 1970s and 1980s that both 'Little Englandist' and 'imperialist' attitudes could be observed in the British Left's rejection of the European Community on the one hand and the inflated claims made for the Campaign for Nuclear Disarmament on the other.[57]

Nevertheless, it would be mistaken to accord too strong a place to manifestations of nationalism; Oswald Mosley's British Union of Fascists made gains in Lancashire and the East End of London in the 1930s (in the latter case based on explicit anti-Semitism). However, the movement was highly dependent upon the oscillations of the local economy and upon the existing ideological traditions of the local working class for its success. Targeting of the working class on the basis of occupational interests and unemployment failed to have much impact outside such areas.[58] There was more than an element of parochialism and simple xenophobia about British fascism. By the late 1930s its working-class base had shrunk, and it was far more reliant upon the disgruntled middle classes of the Home Counties and the south-east of England.[59] As for the post-war manifestations of British fascism, the National Front, the British Movement and the British National Party, their derisory showings have attracted only sporadic attention.

Nationalism in Scotland and in Wales has generally been of a more progressive character, particularly since 1945.[60] Although there has been, since the 1960s in particular, a rise in support for ostensibly separatist nationalist parties in Scotland and Wales, neither nationalist movement has attempted to undermine the existing trade-union movement, suggesting a working-class resistance to anything more than the instrumental gains offered by the nationalist parties.

In summary, much of the recent social history of the British working class has combined to provide an impression of class disunity, even during the classic period of its existence (between 1900 and 1950). The strength of the labour movement in those decades is thus revealed as more contingent and precarious, certainly more temporary, than the movement and its historians have been prepared to believe in the past. Ironically, historians of the British working class and British labour movement in the twentieth century may have to now take comfort, rather than inspiration, from Edward Thompson's clarion call to remember 'the blind alleys, the lost causes, and the losers themselves'; to undertake to rescue 'even the deluded followers of' all Labour leaders from Ramsay MacDonald to Tony Blair 'from the enormous condescension of posterity'.[61]

Shared Visions and Unities

It is however possible to carry such microscopic dissection of the working class too far. For while historians must be prepared to shed the celebratory myths of labour-movement historiography, they also need to be alert to the very real salience of the unities and loyalties (sometimes political) of the class and movement, however fragile their social foundations. James Cronin has argued that ' . . . the critical question for historians is how the persistence of divisions within the working class coexisted with a popular image of a solidary class'.[62] What is evident, however, is that a simple opposition between socio-economic 'divisions' and solidaristic 'images' does an injustice to the creation of shared visions, purposes and unities by at the very least a dominant majority of the British working class.

Historians of working-class culture in the inter-war years have resisted the temptation to disaggregate completely workers' experiences outside the workplace.[63] Such experiences did not need to be explicitly political in order to carry a class charge. However interesting experiments such as the British Workers' Sports Federation (Communist Party) and the National Workers' Sports Association (Labour Party) were in their own right, such bodies pale into insignificance when their combined membership (approximately 15,000 in the early 1930s) is set against that of, for instance, the Youth Hostels Association (37,285 in 1935), or the 750,000 players linked to the Football Association. The same holds true for youth organisations such as the Woodcraft Folk, the Labour Party League of Youth and the Young Communist League in comparison with the Boy Scouts and Girl Guides.[64] The British labour movement was occasionally, in certain regional or local settings, able to provide its own 'hegemonic' culture for its adherents, but far more frequently the higher echelons of the movement held what workers did in their leisure time at arm's length.[65] The vast majority of workers devoted themselves not to the cultural institutions of the labour movement but to the everyday forms of commercialised leisure. Nevertheless, historians of leisure have shown how the experience and discourses of organised sport, for example, provided the (generally male) working class with 'an area of free expression and cultural independence'.[66]

Women were not wholly excluded from this culture. Going to the cinema was the most popular form of entertainment for the inter-war working class, and one in which women participated.[67] Despite the individualism of the Hollywood message, 'going to the movies was very much a communal activity and indeed much of the pleasure came from the shared experience . . .'.[68] If historians are prepared to shed anachronistic pre-suppositions about the ways in which 'class-conscious' workers should have behaved, it is apparent that, whatever the cultural conservatism of the working class in this period, they 'colonised' and gave (necessarily varied) meanings to their leisure pursuits which were not shared by other sections of British society.

This cultural impermeability on the part of the British working class only strengthened the long-held beliefs of opponents of the labour movement that they were confronting a largely homogeneous and organised working class that sought to manipulate government and economy in its own 'sectional' interests. The first half of the twentieth century saw the consolidation of middle-class and lower middle-class hostility towards the movement, and saw also the failure of the Labour Party, despite the rhetoric of 'classlessness' on the part of its leaders, to create effective alliances with groups outside the manual working class (possibly with the exception of some 'economically disinterested' professionals). The 'rise of Labour' represented a political and economic threat to the actual or aspiring wealthy, and the Conservative Party founded its success between the wars upon a mobilisation of 'public spirit' against such a challenge to the established order.

To some degree, therefore, the 1920s and 1930s saw the exogenous creation of a working-class solidarity.[69] When the degradation and humiliation of the experiences of the Depression were added to this stereotyped public hostility, an admittedly defensive but nevertheless resilient and burning collective consciousness of difference and of political purpose could result. 'Miner writer' Bert Coombes commented thus upon the inter-war years, in 1944:

> That period has been one of deceit after deceit, frustration after frustration, mounting into a crescendo of bitterness that may slacken with the passing years, but will never be forgotten. The children in mining areas knew that their fathers were real men, their mothers equal to any women in the land, and yet they saw them treated as if they encumbered the earth. They have decided that the agony they saw in the lives of their parents shall never be their lot. If ever the official mind has shown itself brutal and inefficient it is in the handling of the miners and their problems. In some ways I blame the public for what has happened; because in this democratic country the workers have the power to control if they would stir themselves . . .[70]

It would be a mistake, however to imagine that working-class consciousness was simply enlivened by a desire for revenge or redress. Coombes was writing from inside an industrial workforce that had done more than most to generate its own solidarity through collective struggle. The participation of whole generations of young men and women in industrial battles that seemed to be about the future of their way of lives served only to consolidate a sense of unity and purpose. In analysing the longer term structures of sectionalism, historians can easily overlook the revelatory significance of the historical 'moment'.

A fascinating illustration, albeit one distance removed, of the radicalising impact of the brief mobilisation of the 1926 General Strike is provided by Raymond Williams's autobiographical novel *Border Country*, which has as its centrepiece the solidarity of the railwaymen of the village of 'Glynmawr' with the Mineworkers' Federation of Great Britain. What is, at length, apparent as important in the novel is what Williams himself, in a separate commentary, considered to be the political 'inheritance' he received from his father's experiences of 1926:

> A child of five, as I was then, can gain from a father who had experienced that complex struggle for consciousness a spirit and a perspective that have lasted, often under pressure, in the radically different places where I have since lived and worked.[71]

The understanding of the importance of generational experiences to the traditions and solidarity of the British labour movement is admittedly in its infancy.[72] While work on this theme is necessarily tentative, it may be suggested that the impact of the pre-war Great Unrest, the First World War, the Russian Revolution, the rise of International Communism and the contemporaneous 'post-war emergency' gave rise to a process of generational socialisation qualitatively distinct from anything that had gone before.[73]

Given the strong regional bases of the labour movement, the inter-war years in particular saw the emergence of a set of localised but vibrant, even aggressive working-class identities, resting upon local occupational structures.[74] Indeed, it is possible to argue that in certain critical respects there was no British labour movement, but that there were a series of projections from the localities and regions onto an ostensibly national stage of the principles, priorities and preferred policies of the movement, which had been determined at the local level. These competed with each other in a national framework that was not stable and unchanging, but which was at various times dominated by regional or group priorities.[75] In the inter-war period, South Wales, Clydeside, Lancashire, Yorkshire and the northeast of England thus came, in many respects, to constitute not only Labour's economic bedrock but also its wider identity. In the longer term the strong, regionally-generated class consciousnesses have outlived the erosion of their economic foundations and the passing of the historical 'moments' of their creation, and have continued to exercise an influence upon the labour movement.[76]

The significance of regional traditions of labour-movement involvement and loyalty is also revealed by the experience of workers in the motor car industry in Oxford in the 1930s. While there can be no automatic assumption that migrant workers from older, established regions with traditions of trade unionism would necessarily bring such traditions with them and establish them in all centres of the 'new' industries, in Oxford at least the contribution made by ex-miners from the South Wales coalfield was substantial. These workers dominated the local branch of the TGWU and provided an important stimulus to the growth of the local Labour Party.[77] In doing so, they were learning from and adapting the experiences and patterns of the mining community, where the centrality of the trade-union branch or 'lodge' has become a commonplace historical observation, and where the representation of intense occupational consciousness in Labour voting could be equally umbilical.[78]

In Coventry, the Welsh played a lesser role alongside incomers from both Scotland and the northeast of England. It seems that the very process of participation in the institutions of the labour movement created its own loyalties, and not just in areas of strong occupational consciousness such as the coalfields, where the correspondence between socio-economic identity and political allegiance was relatively direct. In some areas where social, economic, even ethnic divisions were widespread amongst the working class, the existence and success of the Labour Party could be critical to a sense of class consciousness: this could be the level at which such consciousness was constructed. Thus in Poplar in London, 'the use of borough councils and boards of guardians to advance the interests of Labour's constituency provided the basis of political unity, not any sense of class unity engendered by the workplace'.[79]

In Glasgow the impact of the religious divide was gradually muted by the accommodation found between the Labour Party and local Catholicism.[80] More generally Mike Savage has suggested that ' . . . as Labour gained control of municipal authorities and so had greater ability to make the city in the image of the working class, so they could also facilitate working-class formation'.[81] Deeper understandings of the permanence of sectionalism and difference amongst the British working class in the period of its 'classic' formation should not be permitted to obscure the real unity and achievements of that class's labour movement, understood in the necessarily less-deterministic terms of ideological creation and political agency.

Conclusion

There was, then, no 'Forward March of Labour'. Nor was there, between 1900 and 1950 or at any other time, a homogeneity about the working class which 'naturally' gave rise to the British labour movement. The watchwords of the new social history are unevenness in class formation and difference in social consciousness. Instead of an objectively united working class, Britain possessed one of a multi-form character. As Patrick Joyce has written, 'tendencies to unity are always offset by tendencies to fragmentation; economic changes are always creating new sources of division among wage earners even as they undermine others'.[82]

Nevertheless, political or 'labour' unities were possible, even in coexistence with workplace sectionalism, ethnic difference, or cultural differentiation. Whilst one is loath to overstress the 'autonomy of the political', it is undeniable that such unities were frequently created in the ideological and political domains, and were manufactured with languages of class, justice and assertions of common identity which need to be taken seriously, rather than being seen as relating to a deeper socio-economic 'reality'.[83] The challenge for historians of the British labour movement must be to probe more deeply into working-class mentalities in order to disentangle the competing claims of individual, family, class and other identities. This will involve coming to terms with the new vistas of discourse analysis, already beginning to stir controversy in nineteenth-century historiography, with profound implications for that of the current century.[84] David Gilbert's comparative study of mining communities in South Wales and Nottinghamshire in 1926 has shown how languages of unity, whilst providing the resources or 'capacities' for collective action in the face of overwhelming odds, could also lead to a distorted understanding of what was possible at the time, as well as bequeathing an analytical framework for understanding subsequent confrontations whose utility might be doubted.[85] Locked into the myths of Patrick Wright's 'vanished solidarities', and passively bemoaning the social and economic trends that have supposedly loaded the political dice in favour of its opponents, the British labour movement has increasingly failed to reproduce sufficiently persuasive or relevant languages as the century has proceeded, and this failure has left vast swathes of British society both voiceless and undefended.

Acknowledgments

I would like to thank Andy Croll, Sara Spalding and Harri Williams for their help in the writing of this chapter.

Notes

1. Wright (1985), p. 157.
2. For the purposes of this chapter the assumption is made that both the Labour Party and its affiliated trade unions comprise the majority of the 'socialist' labour movement. This is not to disavow what is at times a genuine argument over the meaning of that 'socialism'.
3. Jenkins (1987); Minkin (1991). One dimension of recent history which has received relatively little attention has been the impact of the collapse of the Communist bloc in Eastern Europe upon the perceptions of Western European socialists. However much the latter distanced themselves from the failures and perversions of the former, the end of Soviet-led socialism has brought with it an irreversible sense of closure to the Marxist project.
4. Hobsbawm (1981).
5. Naturally the aridity of labour history is connected to the bleak predicament of the Labour movement, the latter casting grave doubt upon the guiding assumptions of the former.
6. Thompson (1978); McKibbin (1990). There is, of course, a substantial debate on how widespread 'revolutionary strategies' were amongst the working class before the mid-Victorian period. See Phillips (1989) for a survey.

7. Hobsbawm (1984).
8. This characterisation is particularly associated with the work of McKibbin (1990), pp. 294–7.
9. Holton (1976); Davies (1991).
10. Branson (1979); Ryan (1978).
11. Branson (1985); Martin (1969).
12. Zweig (1952), p. 189.
13. Bevan (1976), p. 27. The debates over the 'franchise factor' remain substantial. For an important recent contribution to the literature, see the work of Duncan Tanner (1990).
14. Pugh (1991).
15. Saville (1960).
16. Harris (1990).
17. Macintyre (1980), pp. 47–65. It is all too easy for left-inclined historians to ignore the real attachments between the working class and the state. Bernard Waites has observed that 'The sacrifices made on behalf of the working-class movement and of socialism in Britain have been as nothing compared with those her citizens have made, more or less willingly, for the nation-state.' Waites (1987), p. 275.
18. Clegg, Fox and Thompson (1964); Clegg (1985); Gospel (1987).
19. Lowe (1987). Although the replacement of 'contracting out' of Labour Party affiliation by trade unions with 'contracting in' had a serious impact upon the former, in 1927 65.8 per cent of all trade unionists were affiliated to the Labour Party, but by 1946 the figure had fallen to 29.9 per cent. Bain and Price (1989), pp. 190–2. In absolute numbers there had been 3.2 million trade unionists affiliated in 1927, falling by 1928 to 2 million. Pelling (1982), pp. 187–9.
20. Barnes and Reid (1980).
21. For a similar theme in a broader context see Joyce (1991), pp. 93–140.
22. Crewe, Day and Fox (1991), p. 251. Even as late as 1985 a majority still believed that the trade unions had too much power. Milward (1990), pp. 27–50.
23. Bain and Price (1989), pp. 162–5.
24. Bain and Price (1989) estimate that over the period 1911–1981 the number of non-manual workers increased by 287 per cent whilst the number of manual workers declined by 11 per cent.
25. Bain and Price (1980), pp. 41–2.
26. It is important to distinguish between electoral allegiance (expressed in Labour voting) and levels of trade-union affiliation to the Labour Party, which have remained largely stable (between 48 and 57 per cent of all trade unionists) since the repeal of the 1927 Trade Disputes Act in 1946. Bain and Price (1989), pp. 190–2.

27. Crewe, Day and Fox (1991). In 1987 the 'manual working class' voted 43.7 per cent for Labour, 34 per cent for the Conservatives; the 'intermediate and routine non-manual classes' voted 21.4 per cent for Labour, and 54.3 per cent for the Conservatives. For 1992 the categorisations have changed but the message is essentially similar. Labour managed to poll 40 per cent of the vote amongst the 'skilled manual' class and 51 per cent amongst the 'unskilled manual' class, with the Conservatives managing 39 per cent and 30 per cent respectively. For the 'routine nonmanual' class the Conservatives attracted 49 per cent of the vote, Labour 28 per cent. Sanders (1993), pp. 171–222.
28. McKenzie and Silver (1968); Jessop (1974); Lee (1979).
29. OPCS (1992). For women there is little variation: Mid Glamorgan, Dyfed, Cleveland, Merseyside, West Glamorgan.
30. Drake (1984).
31. Bain and Price (1980), pp. 186–8.
32. Dennis, Henriques and Slaughter (1969), p. 167. Interestingly the book is dedicated 'To The Yorkshire Mineworker'. The study's methods and conclusions have been recently reviewed: Warwick and Littlejohn (1992), pp. 32–3.
33. Savage (1987), pp. 171–9.
34. Collette (1989).
35. Routh (1987), p. 74.
36. Bain and Price (1980), pp. 165–8.
37. To paraphrase the political scientist Ivor Crewe. Cited in Laybourn (1988), pp. 139–40.
38. Howell (1990).
39. Zeitlin (1989). Zeitlin writes: 'The very notion of craft control implied the formulation of a set of rules which reached beyond the individual workplace to regulate the labour market as a whole. Craft unions sought to protect the market value of their members' skills by controlling access to the trade, establishing rights over a particular job territory, and standardising wage rates and working conditions across as wide an area as possible.'
40. Hobsbawm (1984).
41. Coates and Topham (1991).
42. Tolliday (1987).
43. Penn (1983).
44. Cited in Harrison (1981), p. 206. Or, as Joyce (1991), p. 93, puts it, '. . . the figure of class derived most fully from the craft-based trade model – that of the skilled, male, head-of-household – was one predicated upon powerful elements of animosity and division within the ranks of workers.'

45. Thus, in 1931, whereas 51.4 per cent of coal miners and 52.3 per cent of workers in cotton, flax and man-made fibres were unionised, and only 13.9 per cent of workers in chemicals and allied industries, 14.8 per cent of workers in food and drink, and 26.8 per cent of workers in metals and engineering were similarly organised. Bain and Price (1980), pp. 43–78.
46. In the coal industry the considerable fluctuations in union density are largely related to employer hostility and to the state of the industry in the inter-war period. Thus, whereas by 1921, 76.6 per cent of the workforce was unionised, this figure had fallen by 1928 to 51.8 per cent, reached a low of 51.3 per cent in 1932, but rose to 97.3 per cent by 1955. Bain and Price (1980), p. 45.
47. Price (1986).
48. Johnson (1985).
49. Roberts (1973), pp. 13–28.
50. Davies and Fielding (1992).
51. Waller (1983).
52. Waller (1981); Smith (1984).
53. Gilbert (1992), p. 161.
54. Knox (1988).
55. Evans (1980, 1991, 1994).
56. For the historical perspective see the work of Lunn (1990) and Lunn and Thomas (1988). The legacy of such attitudes for the 1970s is identified by Lawrence (1982).
57. G. L. Williams and A. L. Williams (1989).
58. Lewis (1987).
59. Thurlow (1987). Explanations of the relative absence of Celtic fascism, identified by Lunn and Thurlow (1980), p. 16, as desirable, remain in their infancy.
60. For fascistic tendencies within the early Plaid Cymru see the work of Davies (1983).
61. Thompson (1968), p. 13.
62. Cronin (1984), p. 150.
63. For a spirited defence of Hobsbawm's position on working-class culture, see the work of Kirk (1991).
64. Jones (1988), p. 197.
65. Clark (1981); Waters (1990).
66. Holt (1989), p. 165; Jones (1988), p. 66; Hargreaves (1986), p. 67.
67. Cunningham (1990), pp. 311–2; Jones (1987).
68. Stead (1989), p. 245; Jones (1987), pp. 10–12.
69. McKibbin (1990), 'Class and Conventional Wisdom: The Conservative Party and the "Public" in Inter-war Britain.
70. Coombes (1944). Coombes, certainly no militant, dedicated his book

'To The World's Workers'.
71. R. Williams (1977), p. 8.
72. van Voss (1989).
73. Campbell (1989).
74. For the emergence of 'Labour Wales', see the work of Jones (1992). For the Yorkshire equivalent see that of Reynolds and Laybourn (1987). The most aggressive and extreme manifestations of working class identities in this period are examined by Macintyre (1981).
75. Howell (1983) has ably demonstrated the value of a regional perspective to an understanding of the 'rise of Labour', and this needs extension into the twentieth century. What such a perspective may eventually reveal is that the nation is not the best framework for any analysis of European (one might say European and American) labour movements: that there may be equivalent or greater mileage in trans-continental and trans-Atlantic regional and local comparisons.
76. Witness the passionate debates over the legacy of Clydeside: Foster (1992); Brotherstone (1992). In South Wales the memories are more distant, but still revealing: G.A. Williams (1978); C. Williams (1992).
77. Whiting (1983); Chandler (1989); R. Williams (1964). Chandler's work should correct the misunderstandings of both Zeitlin and Lyddon: Zeitlin (1980, 1983); Lyddon (1983, 1993).
78. C. Williams (1990, 1991).
79. Gillespie (1989), p. 164.
80. McCaffrey (1991).
81. Savage (1993), p. 76.
82. Joyce (1990), p. 180.
83. Biagini and Reid (1991) provide an interesting, if uneven, introduction to the continuities in languages of radical politics, and assert that, 'whatever underlying economic and social changes are assumed, reductionist explanations of political events will always be inadequate, and that the form eventually taken by popular politics will depend on the relative success of appeals from rival parties and programmes'.
84. See the vigorous debate over 'post-structuralist' approaches to nineteenth- and twentieth-century British history: Joyce (1991, 1993); Jones (1983); Mayfield and Thorne (1992, 1993); Lawrence and Taylor (1993).
85. Gilbert (1992).

Bibliography

Bain, G. S., and Price, R., *Profiles of Union Growth: A Comparative Statistical Portrait of Eight Countries*, Oxford, 1980

——, 'The Labour Force', in A. H. Halsey (ed.), *British Social Trends since 1900: A Guide to the Changing Social Structure of Britain*, Basingstoke, 1989

Barnes, Denis and Reid, Eileen, *Governments and Trade Unions: The British Experience, 1964–79*, London, 1980

Bevan, Aneurin, *In Place of Fear*, Wakefield, 1976

Biagini, Eugenio F., and Reid, Alastair J. (eds), *Currents of Radicalism: Popular Radicalism, Organised Labour and Party Politics in Britain, 1850–1914*, Cambridge, 1991

Branson, Noreen, *Poplarism 1919–1925: George Lansbury and the Councillors' Revolt*, London, 1979

——, *History of the Communist Party of Great Britain, 1927–1941*, London, 1985

Brotherstone, Terry , 'Does Red Clydeside Really Matter Any More?', in Robert Duncan and Arthur McIvor (eds), *Militant Workers: Labour and Class Conflict on the Clyde 1900–1950: Essays in Honour of Harry McShane (1891–1988)*, Edinburgh, 1992

Campbell, Alan, 'Tradition and Generational Change in the Scots Miners' Unions, 1874–1929', in Aad Blok, Dirk Damsma, Hermain Diederiks and Lex Heerma Van Voss (eds), *Generations in Labour History: Papers presented to the Sixth British-Dutch Conference on Labour History*, Amsterdam, 1989

Chandler, A. D., 'The Re-Making of a Working Class', PhD thesis, University of Wales, Cardiff, 1989

Clark, David, *Colne Valley: Radicalism to Socialism*, London, 1981

Clegg, H. A., Fox, A. and Thompson, A. F., *A History of British Trade Unions since 1889, Volume I, 1889–1910*, Oxford, 1964

——, *A History of British Trade Unions since 1889, Volume II, 1911–1933*, Oxford, 1985

Coates, Ken and Topham, Tony, *The Making of the Transport and General Workers' Union, Volume I*, Oxford, 1991

Collette, Christine, *For Labour and For Women: The Women's Labour League, 1906–18*, Manchester, 1989

Coombes, B. L., *Those Clouded Hills*, London, 1944

Crewe, Ivor, Day, Neil and Fox, Anthony, *The British Electorate 1963–1987: A Compendium of Data from the British Election Studies*, Cambridge, 1991

Cronin, James E., *Labour and Society in Britain 1918–1979*, London, 1984

Cunningham, Hugh, 'Leisure and Culture' in F. M. L. Thompson (ed.), *The Cambridge Social History of Britain 1750–1950, Volume 2: People and their Environment*, Cambridge, 1990

Davies, Andrew, and Fielding, Steven (eds), *Workers' Worlds: Culture and Communities in Manchester and Salford, 1880–1939*, Manchester, 1992

Davies, D. Hywel, *A Call To Nationhood: The Welsh Nationalist Party, 1925–1945*, Cardiff, 1983

Davies, D. K., 'The Influence of Syndicalism and Industrial Unionism in the South Wales Coalfield, 1898–1921: A Study in Ideology and Practice', PhD thesis, University of Wales, Cardiff, 1991

Dennis, Norman, Henriques, Fernando and Slaughter, Clifford, *Coal is Our Life: An Analysis of a Yorkshire Mining Community*, London, 1969

Drake, Barbara, *Women in Trade Unions*, London, 1984

Evans, Neil, 'The South Wales Race Riots of 1919', *Llafur: Journal of Welsh Labour History*, Vol. 3, No. 1, 1980

——, 'Immigrants and Minorities in Wales, 1840–1990: A Comparative Perspective', *Llafur: Journal of Welsh Labour History*, Vol. 5, No. 4, 1991

——, 'Across the Universe: Racial Violence and the Post-War Crisis in Imperial Britain, 1919–1925', *Immigrants and Minorities*, forthcoming.

Foster, John, 'Red Clyde, Red Scotland', in Ian Donnachie and Christopher Whatley (eds), *The Manufacture of Scottish History*, Edinburgh, 1992

Gilbert, David, Class, *Community and Collective Action: Social Change in Two British Coalfields, 1850–1926*, Oxford, 1992

Gillespie, James, 'Poplarism and Proletarianism: Unemployment and Labour Politics in London, 1918–34', in David Feldman and Gareth Stedman Jones (eds), *Metropolis London: Histories and Representations since 1800*, London, 1989

Gospel, Howard F., 'Employers and Managers: Organisation and Strategy, 1914–39', in Chris Wrigley (ed.), *A History of British Industrial Relations Volume II: 1914–1939*, Brighton, 1987

Hargreaves, J., *Sport, Power and Culture: A Social and Historical Analysis of Sports in Britain*, London, 1966

Harris, Jose, 'Society and the state in twentieth-century Britain', in F. M. L. Thompson (ed.), *The Cambridge Social History of Britain 1750–1950 Volume 3: Social Agencies and Institutions*, Cambridge, 1990

Harrison, Brian, *Peaceable Kingdom*, Oxford, 1991

Heerma van Voss, Lex, 'Introduction', in Aad Blok, Dirk Damsma, and Lex Heerma van Voss (eds), *Generations in Labour History: Papers*

Presented to the Sixth British-Dutch Conference on Labour History, Amsterdam, 1989

Hobsbawm, Eric, *The Forward March of Labour Halted?*, London, 1981

——, *Worlds of Labour: Further Studies in the History of Labour*, London, 1984

Holt, Richard, *Sport and the British: A Modern History*, Oxford, 1989

Holton, Bob, *British Syndicalism, 1900–1914*, London, 1976

Howell, David, *British Workers and the Independent Labour Party, 1888–1906*, Manchester, 1983

——, 'When was "The Forward March of Labour?"', *Llafur: Journal of Welsh Labour History*, Vol. 5, No. 3, 1990

Jenkins, Peter, *Mrs. Thatcher's Revolution: The Ending of the Socialist Era*, London, 1987

Jessop, Bob, *Traditionalism, Conservatism and British Political Culture*, London, 1974

Johnson, Paul, *Saving and Spending: The Working-class Economy in Britain 1870–1939*, Oxford, 1985

Jones, R. Merfyn, 'Beyond Identity: The Reconstruction of the Welsh', *Journal of British Studies*, Vol. 31, 1992

Jones, Stephen G., *The British Labour Movement and Film, 1918–1939*, London, 1987

——, *Sport, Politics and the Working Class: Organised Labour and Sport in Inter-war Britain*, Manchester, 1988

Joyce, Patrick, 'Work', in F. M. L. Thompson (ed.), *The Cambridge Social History of Britain 1750–1950 Volume 2: People and Their Environment*, Cambridge, 1990

——, *Visions of the People: Industrial England and the Question of Class 1848–1914*, Cambridge, 1991

——, 'The Imaginary Discontents of Social History: a Note of Response to Mayfield and Thorne, and Lawrence and Taylor', *Social History*, Vol. 18, No. 1, 1993

Kirk, Neville, '"Traditional" Working-Class Culture and "the Rise of Labour": Some Preliminary Questions and Observations', *Social History*, Vol. 16, No. 2, 1991

Knox, W. W., 'Religion and the Scottish Labour Movement c.1900–39', *Journal of Contemporary History*, Vol. 23, 1988

Lawrence, Errol, 'Just Plain Common Sense: the "Roots" of Racism', in Centre for Contemporary Cultural Studies (ed.) *The Empire Strikes Back: Race and Racism in 70s Britain*, Birmingham, 1982

Lawrence, Jon and Taylor, Miles, 'The Poverty of Protest: Gareth Stedman Jones and the Politics of Language – a Reply', *Social History*, Vol. 18, No. 1, 1993

Laybourn, Keith, *The Rise of Labour: The British Labour Party*

1890–1979, London, 1988

Lee, Alan J., 'Conservatism, Traditionalism and the British Working Class, 1880–1918', in David E. Martin and David Rubinstein (eds), *Ideology and the Labour Movement: Essays Presented to John Saville*, London, 1979

Lewis, D. S., *Illusions of Grandeur: Mosley, Fascism and British Society, 1931–81*, Manchester, 1987

Lowe, Rodney, 'The Government and Industrial Relations, 1919–39', in Chris Wrigley (ed.), *A History of British Industrial Relations Volume II: 1914–1939*, Brighton, 1987

Lunn, Kenneth and Thurlow, Richard, *British Fascism: Essays on the Radical Right in Inter-war Britain*, London, 1980

—— and Thomas, R., 'Naval Imperialism in Portsmouth, 1905–1914', *Southern History*, Vol. 10, 1988

——, 'Labour Culture in Dockyard Towns: A Study of Portsmouth, Plymouth and Chatham, 1900–1950', *Tijdschrift voor sociale Geschiedenis*, Vol. 18, 1990

Lyddon, Dave, 'Workplace Organisation in the British Car Industry: A Critique of Jonathan Zeitlin', *History Workshop Journal*, Vol. 15, 1983

——, '"Trade Union Traditions", The Oxford Welsh, and the 1934 Pressed Steel Strike', *Llafur: Journal of Welsh Labour History*, Vol. 6, No. 2, 1993

McCaffrey, John F., 'Irish Issues in the Nineteenth and Twentieth Century: Radicalism in a Scottish Context?, in T. M. Devine (ed.), *Irish Immigrants and Scottish Society in the Nineteenth and Twentieth Centuries*, Edinburgh, 1991

Macintyre, Stuart, *A Proletarian Science: Marxism in Britain, 1917–1933*, Cambridge, 1980

——, *Little Moscows*, London, 1981

McKenzie, Robert and Silver, Allan, *Angels in Marble: Working Class Conservatives in Urban England*, London, 1968

McKibbin, Ross, *The Ideologies of Class: Social Relations in Britain 1880–1950*, Oxford, 1990

Martin, Roderick, *Communism and British Trade Unions 1924–1933: A Study of the National Minority Movement*, Oxford, 1969

Mayfield, David, and Thorne, Susan, 'Social history and its Discontents: Gareth Stedman Jones and the Politics of Language', *Social History*, Vol. 17, No. 2, 1992

Mayfield, David, and Thorne, Susan, 'Reply to "The Poverty of Protest" and "The Imaginary Discontents"', *Social History*, Vol. 18, No. 2, 1993

Millward, Neil, 'The State of the Unions', in Roger Jowell et al (eds), *British Social Attitudes: the 7th Report*, Social and Community Planning Research, Aldershot, 1990

Minkin, Lewis, *The Contentious Alliance: Trade Unions and the Labour Party*, Edinburgh, 1991
Pelling, Henry, *A Short History of the Labour Party*, London, 1982
Penn, Roger, 'Trade Union Organisation and Skill in the Cotton and Engineering Industries in Britain, 1850–1960', *Social History*, Vol. 8, No. 1, 1983
Phillips, Gordon, 'The British Labour Movement before 1914', in Dick Geary (ed.), *Labour and Socialist Movements in Europe before 1914*, Oxford, 1989
Price, Richard, *Labour in British Society*, London, 1986
Pugh, Martin, *Women and the Women's Movement in Britain, 1914–1959*, Basingstoke, 1991
OPCS, *1991 Census: Outline Statistics for England and Wales*, CEN 91, CM 58, 1992
Reynolds, Jack and Laybourn, Keith, *Labour Heartland: A History of the Labour Party in West Yorkshire during the Inter-war Years, 1918–1939*, Bradford, 1987
Roberts, Robert, *The Classic Slum: Salford Life in the First Quarter of the Century*, Harmondsworth, 1973
Routh, Guy, *Occupations of the People of Great Britain, 1801–1981*, Basingstoke, 1987
Ryan, P. A., '"Poplarism" 1894–1930', in Pat Thane (ed.), *The Origins of British Social Policy*, London, 1978
Sanders, David, 'Why the Conservative Party Won – Again', in Anthony King et al (eds), *Britain at the Polls, 1992*, Chatham NJ, 1993
Savage, Michael, *The Dynamics of Working-Class Politics: The Labour Movement in Preston 1880–1940*, Cambridge, 1987
Savage, Mike, 'Urban History and Social Class: Two Paradigms', *Urban History*, Vol. 20, No. 1, 1993
Saville, John, 'Trade Unions and Free Labour: the Background to the Taff Vale Decision', in Asa Briggs and John Saville (eds), *Essays in Labour History*, London, 1960
Smith, Joan, 'Labour Tradition in Glasgow and Liverpool', *History Workshop Journal*, Vol. 17, 1984
Stead, Peter, *Film and the Working Class: The Feature Film in British and American Society*, London, 1989
Stedman Jones, Gareth, *Languages of Class: Studies in English Working Class History 1832–1982*, Cambridge, 1983
Tanner, Duncan, *Political Change and the Labour Party 1900–1918*, Cambridge, 1990
Thompson, E. P, *The Making of the English Working Class*, Harmondsworth, 1968
——, 'The Peculiarities of the English', in: idem *The Poverty of Theory*,

London, 1978
Tolliday, Steven, 'The Failure of Mass-Production Unionism in the Motor Industry, 1914–39', in Chris Wrigley (ed.), *A History of British Industrial Relations Volume II: 1914–1939*, Brighton, 1987
Thurlow, Richard, *Fascism in Britain: A History, 1918–1985*, Oxford, 1987
Waites, Bernard, *A Class Society at War: England 1914–1918*, Leamington Spa, 1987
Waller, P. J., *Democracy and Sectarianism: A Political and Social History of Liverpool 1868–1939*, Liverpool, 1981
Waller, Robert J., *The Dukeries Transformed: The Social and Political Development of a Twentieth Century Coalfield*, Oxford, 1983
Warwick, Dennis and Littlejohn, Gary, *Coal, Capital and Culture: A Sociological Analysis of Mining Communities in West Yorkshire*, London, 1992
Waters, Chris, *British Socialists and the Politics of Popular Culture, 1884–1914*, Manchester, 1990
Whiting, R. C., *The View From Cowley: The Impact of Industrialization upon Oxford, 1918–1939*, Oxford, 1983
Williams, Chris, 'The South Wales Miners' Federation', *Llafur: Journal of Welsh Labour History*, Vol. 5, No. 3, 1990
——, 'Democratic Rhondda: Politics and Society, 1885–1951', PhD thesis, University of Wales, Cardiff, 1991
——, 'History, Heritage and Commemoration: Newport 1839–1989', *Llafur: Journal of Welsh Labour History*, Vol. 6, No. 1. 1992
Williams, Geoffrey Lee and Williams, Alan Lee, *Labour's Decline and the Social Democrats' Fall*, Basingstoke, 1989
Williams, Gwyn A., 'Dic Penderyn, the Making of a Welsh Working Class Martyr', *Llafur: Journal of Welsh Labour History*, Vol. 2, No. 3, 1978
Williams, Raymond, Border Country, London, 1960
——, *Second Generation*, London, 1964
——, 'The Social Significance of 1926', *Llafur: Journal of Welsh Labour History*, Vol. 2, No. 2, 1977
Wright, Patrick, *On Living in an Old Country*, London, 1985
Zeitlin, Jonathan, 'The Emergence of Shop Steward Organisation and Job Control in the British Car Industry: A Review Essay', *History Workshop Journal*, Vol. 10, 1980
Zeitlin, Jonathan, 'Workplace Militancy: A Rejoinder', *History Workshop Journal*, Vol. 16, 1983
Zeitlin, Jonathan, '"Rank and Filism" in British Labour History: A Critique', *International Review of Social History*, Vol. 34, No. 1, 1989
Zweig, Ferdynand, *The British Worker*, Harmondsworth, 1952

–6–

Italy

Tobias Abse

Introduction

Italy is an idiosyncratic country with an idiosyncratic labour movement. The most startling illustration of this is the fact that the Italian Communist Party's greatest electoral triumph (34.4 per cent of the vote) came not in 1946 but in 1976, a result which was totally at variance with the general Western European pattern. Therefore, it is hardly surprising that there are problems fitting Italian reality into any analytical framework devised with German or French circumstances in mind.

This chapter will attempt to make sense of the complex relationship between the Italian labour movement and the Italian working class by exploring the broad economic, social and cultural trends that shaped it, rather than by recounting all the minutiae of splits, fusions and personality clashes within the ever-shifting kaleidoscope of organisations that have claimed to represent the Italian working class during the twentieth century. The issues to be explored will include the timing and extent of Italian industrialisation and urbanisation and the structural divisions within the working class, with some emphasis on the unusual importance of regionalism. Other foci of the chapter will include the relationship of workers and their political organisations with other classes and the influence of other social institutions, especially the Catholic Church, in shaping the labour movement. Furthermore the workers' relationship with employers, the changing legal structure of industrial relations which regulated this relationship, and the way in which Italian workers' relations with and perceptions of the state were coloured by both the authoritarian character of the unification process and the traumatic experience of fascism will be examined. Finally, the extent to which Italian labour movement culture remained permeated by a rebellious and potentially violent working-class culture, referred to as *sovversivismo*, despite all the efforts of its more respectable leaders to eradicate it, will be explored.

Urbanisation and Industrialisation

Urbanisation and industrialisation have been crucial factors in shaping the development of European working classes and in influencing the degree of support they have given to labour movements. In the Italian case, urbanisation and industrialisation have not always been synonymous even in the twentieth century. Italy, or at least northern and central Italy, became a relatively urban society much earlier than most Western European countries, as the city-states of the later medieval and Renaissance periods demonstrate. Industrialisation occurred much later than urbanisation, and some of the main traditional urban conglomerations of pre-unification Italy such as Rome, Naples and Palermo have never been predominantly industrial cities. Italy's manufacturing base has been heavily, though by no means exclusively, concentrated in the northwestern industrial triangle of Turin, Milan and Genoa. Most historians (with the prominent exception of Stefano Merli,[1] who argues for the existence of a fully-fledged industrial proletariat largely made up of textile workers by 1900) see Italian industrialisation as a twentieth century rather than a nineteenth century phenomenon. From Gershenkron onwards, most economic historians have agreed in placing the starting point of Italian industrialisation in 1896.[2]

The 1896–1914 era, the 1896–1907 period in particular, saw extremely rapid economic growth with manufacturing production increasing by 60 per cent between 1900 and 1913. The First World War saw a breakneck expansion of Italian heavy industry, with the shipbuilding and engineering firm Ansaldo increasing its workforce from 6,000 in 1915 to 111,000 in 1918 and FIAT's workforce, increasingly employed on military rather than civilian projects, leaping from 4,000 to 40,000 over the same period.[3] Even the fascist period was not as stagnant as some more traditional accounts used to assert. The switch from peacetime to wartime production in Italy began to a large extent in 1936 with Abyssinia, and not in 1940 with the fall of France; in the years 1935–1939, 11.8 per cent of Italy's national income was spent on war preparations, compared with Nazi Germany's 12.9 per cent and a mere 6.9 per cent in France and 5.5 per cent in Britain. Although Italy pushed this share up to 18.4 per cent of national income in 1939–40, such a level of mobilisation was not sustainable. The agreement between Agnelli and Mussolini to plan the development of war production, reached on 24 October 1940, achieved its targets only in 1942.

Italy's war economy proved less successful in the Second World War than in the First. If the 1938 figure for industrial production is represented as 100, 1940 saw Italy achieve 110 before falling back disastrously to 89 in 1942 and 70 in 1943. The most conspicuous phenomenon associated with the outbreak of war was not a switch from car production to tank production at FIAT, which had already started in 1936, but the entrance of women into a labour market from which the fascists had quite consciously sought to exclude them during the inter-war years. It is no accident that on 5 June 1940 previous fascist legislation discriminating against women was rescinded and replaced by a decree allowing the substitution of female for male personnel in public administration. This had effects in a wide variety of sectors: women were seen driving trams as well as staffing the post offices. Even in large factories like FIAT in Turin or Pirelli and Falk in Milan, where at least some of the male workforce were protected from the call-up, the lower grades included an increasing number of women, generally the wives and daughters of men who had been sent to the front. Women were the most mobile and marginal segment of the labour force and they could be taken on and sacked with equal rapidity. The increased female participation in the labour force was not confined to either white-collar or industrial employment; as had already occurred in the First World War, women had to substitute for men in agricultural labour as the army made its habitual demands on the peasantry.[4]

Nonetheless, even if the entire century is characterised by growing industrialisation and urbanisation, the great transformation of Italy from a predominantly rural and peasant society to a predominantly urban and industrial one really occurred after the Second World War, during the 'economic miracle' of the 1950s and early 1960s. Nearly one million southerners left the *Mezzogiorno* for other regions of Italy during the critical years between 1958 and 1963, but to present the great migration purely in terms of a move from north to south would be to distort a more complex phenomenon. Around ten times this number of Italians – 9,140,000 – were involved in some form of inter-regional migration, including migration from rural areas of the north and centre, between 1955 and 1971. Milan's population grew from 1,274,245 in 1951 to 1,681,045 in 1967, while Turin surged from 719,300 inhabitants in 1951 to 1,124,714 in 1967. These new immigrants to Turin, unlike their Piedmontese predecessors in the first quarter of the century, came overwhelmingly from the three southern provinces of Foggia, Bari and Reggio Calabria.[5]

The overall strength of the Italian workers' movement in the twentieth century has been limited by the size of the industrial working class itself, particularly in the first half of the century, although it would be wrong to assume that all Italian peasants and agricultural labourers have necessarily been conservative or reactionary. The Italian labour movement has always had considerable support in the countryside and some syndicalist mobilisations of rural labourers on the large estates of Apulia in the first quarter of the century were reminiscent of the rural radicalism of Andalusia.[6] Rapid industrialisation, often in combination with internal migration from one part of Italy to another, has had an enormous effect on the development of the Italian working class and its degree of attachment to working-class movements. Many have argued that it was the southern migrants from peasant backgrounds, especially Apulians and Calabrians, who triggered the industrial militancy of Turin in the 'Hot Autumn' of 1969. There can be no doubt that the very rapid expansion of the industrial workforce during the First World War played a very important role in generating the labour militancy of the *biennio rosso* in 1919–1920, although the exact balance between the peasant or artisan new to industrial production and the second generation factory worker varied between one city and another.[7]

It must be underlined that the traumatic experiences of rapid industrialisation and urbanisation do not necessarily lead workers towards an attachment to what are conventionally regarded as the modern forms of the labour movement. In the early twentieth century the Tuscan steel town of Piombino and the Ligurian shipbuilding and engineering centres, La Spezia and Sestri Ponente, became strongholds of anarchism and anarcho-syndicalism rather than of orthodox socialism or reformist trade unionism.[8] Despite the role of migrant workers in both the *biennio rosso* and the Hot Autumn, it would be wrong to look for mechanical links between every wave of labour militancy to sweep twentieth-century Italy and the long-term structural processes of industrialisation and urbanisation. The mass strikes of 1943 and 1944, and subsequent developments between 1945 and 1948, had very little connection with such processes and will therefore be examined in later sections of this chapter in the context of the working-class experience of fascism and of working-class political traditions. At a local level it is also worth emphasising that what remained in electoral terms, the reddest industrial city in Italy in April 1992, Livorno, has, despite the thoroughly mixed ethnic origin of its early inhabitants, had one of the most settled working-class communities over the last nine decades, with nearly all migration in the twentieth century coming from its own rural hinterland, whose inhabitants had been politically radicalised by agrarian struggles prior to their arrival in the city.

Most generalisations about the politically radicalising effects of urbanisation and industrialisation only really apply to northern and central Italy. Increased urbanisation and, to some extent, industrialisation in southern Italy have done comparatively little to strengthen the labour movement – or indeed to strengthen faith in collective action of any kind. It is even arguable that the shift away from agriculture destroyed such residual radicalism as arose from the agitation over agrarian reform in the late 1940s, in which peasant communists played a role, and hastened the trend towards corruption and clientelism in regions like Calabria and Apulia. The large masses of urban poor in both Naples and Palermo have shown no persistent inclination to vote for parties of the left, even if one must acknowledge that these masses in Palermo, and to a large extent in Naples, are really made up of *sottoproletari* without any stable source of legal employment and easy prey for the Mafia and Camorra, rather than classical industrial proletarians.[9]

In Italy, as in other Western European countries, the industrial working class has started to contract in size, while the number of those employed in the tertiary sector has increased. However, these developments began rather later than in Britain or France; the Italian industrial working class grew steadily from 3,410,000 in 1951 to 4,190,000 in 1961 and 4,800,000 in 1971. Thereafter, the working class declined from 47.1 per cent of the active population in 1971 to 42.7 per cent in 1983, while the urban middle class rose from 38.5 percent in 1971 to 46.4 per cent in 1983.[10] Although these changes have clearly not strengthened the labour movement, it would be simplistic to draw a direct correlation with voting patterns.

Structural Divisions Within the Working Class

Sectionalism arising out of occupational divisions within the working class has been a problem for the Italian labour movement throughout its existence. Much emphasis must be placed upon regional divisions within the Italian working class, which have on occasions played as important a role as the conventional divisions between skilled and unskilled or blue-collar and white-collar workers. The regional division has sometimes been the primary one during crucial phases such as the *biennio rosso*, when the isolation of the Piedmontese movement in April 1920 or the failure to synchronise risings in places like Ancona, La Spezia, Piombino and Viareggio in the summer of 1920, as well as the cultural, economic and political gap between northern and southern Italy, was at least as important to the outcome as the more straightforward and intellectually-rooted political divisions of the left.[11] The regional division between north and south also played an important part in the failure of the left to emerge victorious from the political struggles between 1943 and 1948, when the Wind from the North, as the Resistance legacy was popularly described, had little resonance in most areas of the South. The dramatic political events since 1989 have once again given a new prominence to the old regional divisions within Italy, with regionalist sentiment making some inroads into segments of the northern working-class electorate after the dissolution of the PCI.[12]

In the early days of the labour movement, in the last decade of the nineteenth century and the first two decades of the twentieth century, it was often far easier to rally all the workers of a given city or province behind the local *camera del lavoro*, or chamber of labour, formed on the model of the French *bourse du travail*, than it was to unite all the workers in a given trade or industrial sector into a nationwide trade union. The first *camera del lavoro* was founded in Milan in 1890 and fifty-seven such institutions existed by 1900, while the first national trade union confederation, the *Confederazione Generale del Lavoro* (CGL) was not founded until 1906. In 1910 the local, territorially-based *camere del lavoro* had a total of 504,841 adherents, although the national, centrally-organised CGL had only managed to recruit 165,192 members.[13]

In so far as nationwide trade unions were formed in this period, they tended to find it easier to recruit the more highly-paid skilled workers than to sign up poorly-paid unskilled workers. It was far simpler to organise printers or railwaymen than to unionise female textile workers. The only major exception to this general rule about the different degrees of response amongst skilled and unskilled workers was the high degree of unionisation amongst farm labourers in certain regions of Italy, particularly the Po Valley provinces; in 1907, 32 per cent of the CGL's membership came from farm labourers, and by 1913, 48 per cent of its members were drawn from the agricultural sector.

It has been argued by some historians, following in the footsteps of Gaetano Salvemini, that the reformist-dominated Socialist Party of the Giolittian era (1900–1915) represented the sectional interests of the more skilled, more literate and better-paid northern working class and offered very little to the southern masses, particularly the southern peasantry. In other words, in the years before the franchise extension of 1912, the party was acting as the party of the labour aristocracy rather than the party of labour in general.[14]

Sectionalism can to a large extent be linked to the ebbs and flows of the Italian labour movement over the course of the twentieth century. Sectionalism of the more conventional, occupational sort has often been transcended in the great potentially revolutionary upsurges of the Italian labour movement. Both the *biennio rosso* of 1919–20 and the Hot Autumn of 1969 saw a deliberate erosion of differences within the working class, with demands for flat rate, across-the-board wage increases – or even ones that were inversely proportional to current salaries – being raised, and often won, in the more politicised and militant factories.[15] The *biennio rosso* temporarily swept away even the distinction between manual workers and white-collar workers, which was generally even more deeply rooted than the distinction between skilled and unskilled manual workers. White-collar workers sometimes took the lead in the struggle against the employers, most notably in the Orlando shipyard in Livorno in the first half of 1920.[16]

The most famous instance of sectionalism in recent times was what has become known as the March of the 40,000, in which 30,000–40,000 FIAT foremen, managers, white-collar workers and blue-collar workers marched through Turin on 14 October 1980 demanding the right to return to work on the thirty-fourth day of the FIAT strike.[17] Various theories have been advanced to explain the event. Some have claimed minimal involvement amongst genuine production workers, occasionally alleging that FIAT also drew on middle-class sympathisers not employed in any of its plants. Others have claimed that the participants were an inter-class alliance of Piedmontese united by quasi-racial prejudice against militant southern immigrant workers. Nonetheless, whether the sectionalism was occupationally or regionally-based, it served its purpose of first breaking class solidarity and then the strike itself.

Sectionalism did not always favour the employers, even in cases where it hindered the achievement of working-class unity. In the 1980s, as the strength of the traditional labour movement waned in the wake of the defeats at FIAT and in the Wage Indexation Referendum of 1984, the new rank and file movements opposing the trade union leadership, the COBAS (*comitati di base*), often took on a pronounced sectionalist colour, placing the immediate interests of the strongest sections of the working class or employed labour more generally (i.e. teachers and air traffic controllers as well as railwaymen) before those of class unity. One should nevertheless be very wary of some of the allegations about fascist sympathies made by the bureaucrats from the three major trade union confederations; if the COBAS leaders had any politics at all, these were more likely to be on the extreme left than the extreme right.

In some famous instances of Italian twentieth-century labour militancy the lead came from the skilled workers. This was the case in 1919–1920 when skilled shipbuilding and engineering workers played roles not too far removed from their Scottish counterparts on Clydeside, and much of the productivist ideology current amongst the members of Torinese factory councils in 1919–20 was a direct expression of the craft pride of skilled workers. However, the general consensus about 1968–1969 seems to place the emphasis on the unskilled worker, the *operaio massa*, often a young southerner, as the central protagonist of the Hot Autumn in the northern factories.

Some groups of Italian workers, such as the dockers, have had an extremely sectionalist outlook throughout the twentieth century. However, the extent to which this prevented them from uniting behind the demands of the labour movement more generally has varied from locality to locality and decade to decade, with the Livornesi and Genovesi showing a much greater degree of politicisation than the Neapolitans, and dockers showing more political enthusiasm during the *biennio rosso* than in more settled times.

No discussion of sectionalism can completely ignore the weakening of the labour movement by religious divisions which often reinforced existing divisions based on gender and occupation, as was exemplified by the success of the Catholic *Confederazione Italiana del Lavoro* (CIL) in recruiting female textile workers in 1919–1920. The Italian trade union movement has rarely been grouped into one confederation for any length of time during the twentieth century, if one ignores its conscription into fascist unions during Mussolini's dictatorship. Whatever importance might be placed on divisions between the socialists of the CGL and the syndicalists of the *Unione Sindacale Italiana* (USI) before 1922, or the communists of the *Confederazione Generale Italiana di Lavoratori* (CGIL) and social democrats of the *Unione Italiana del Lavoro* (UIL) after 1948, the primary fissure has always been that between the Catholics and the secular left. Even the Hot Autumn only bridged this gulf for a handful of years, despite the presence of New Left activists within the *Confederazione Italiana di Sindacati Liberi* (CISL).

The Relationship of the Working Class and Labour Movement with Other Classes in Italian Society

No labour movement or working class has ever existed in isolation from other classes, and societies completely polarised between a tiny capitalist class and an enormous factory proletariat could not in reality be found anywhere in Europe this century. It is essential, therefore, to address the numerous problems raised by the relationship of the working class, and particularly of its political and economic representatives, the Socialist and Communist Parties and the various trade union confederations, to other classes. In this section the primary emphasis will not be on relations with industrial capitalists as employers, which will be dealt with in the fifth section, but on relations with the bourgeoisie in a more general sense, as well as with the petty bourgeoisie and the peasantry.

Before discussing the degree of class cooperation and whether, or when, this benefited the organised working class or its opponents, it is necessary to focus on the complex question of the role of class barriers in Italian society in the twentieth century. For most of the twentieth century there was a huge gulf between the labouring poor and the educated and wealthy elite from the nobility and upper bourgeoisie, a gulf that was reinforced by the illiteracy or semi-literacy of large sections of the population, many of whom spoke dialect as their first, or sometimes only, language. Moreover until recently, and to some extent even now in the regions where the communist tradition lingers on, there was a strong sense of class pride amongst large sections of the industrial working class, an automatic and spontaneous use of the word *operaio* (worker) rather than, say, building worker or steel worker, when identifying their own social position.

Yet, although there have been various trends within the Italian labour movement that have adopted an *operaista* (workerist) rhetoric, they have generally been minority trends. Moreover, while the earliest *operaisti*, Lazzari's followers, who joined the Socialist Party in 1892, after some years of militancy in the Lombard *Partito Operaio Italiano*, were authentic expressions of the working class, many later *operaista* groups, from the syndicalists of the early twentieth century to *Potere Operaio* in 1969–1973, were in fact led by middle-class intellectuals.[18]

From Turati to Occhetto, most of the leaders of Italian left-wing parties have been from the educated middle classes rather than the working class and the peasantry. Berlinguer himself was a Sardinian noble. Even trade union leaders like Trentin have university degrees. The majority of the Italian socialist deputies of the Giolittian period came from the educated middle class, a phenomenon which Robert Michels remarked on at the time and which has recently been confirmed by the statistical evidence of James Miller. Only two out of thirty-three PSI deputies in 1900 were of working-class origin, and the proportion had changed very little by 1913 when the figure was five out of fifty-two. Conversely, twenty-one out of thirty-three deputies in 1900 had a degree; the figure in 1913 was forty out of fifty-two.[19]

From the very beginning, the PSI was a multi-class party in which the proletariat composed the largest of minorities rather than a predominantly proletarian party with a small minority of middle-class intellectuals. In 1903 workers constituted approximately 42.3 per cent of the party's 42,451 members. Agricultural labourers made up another 21 per cent of the membership, while artisans provided about 15 per cent and the middle classes 10.5 per cent.[20] Although this multi-class constituency may not have necessarily been devoted to intransigent class politics under all circumstances, such a mixture of workers, artisans and landless labourers periodically came into conflict with the middle-class intellectuals of the Socialist Parliamentary Group (GPS).

Given the class composition of the GPS, it is hardly surprising that its favoured strategy during the Giolittian period was one of an alliance with the more progressive wing of the bourgeoisie, represented by Giolitti, in order to achieve social reforms. This strategy led to conflicts with the party's membership in the country, which periodically demanded a more intransigent posture and prevented the socialist parliamentarians from accepting office in any bourgeois coalition government. The popularity of a more radical line amongst the party's supporters in the country can be demonstrated by the rise in *Avanti*'s circulation under Mussolini's editorship between 1912–1914, when sales averaged 60,000 a day and reached 100,000 on occasions – in marked contrast to the paper's nadir of 20,000 a day during Bissolati's ultra-reformist editorship in 1910. PSI membership, which had fallen during the period of reformist dominance, rose – along with *Avanti*'s sales – from 28,689 in July 1912 to 47,724 in April 1914, demonstrating that a verbal commitment to revolution rather than reform was the easiest way to build a mass party.

The limited cooperation with the middle-class reformers in the Giolittian period enabled the workers to obtain better welfare legislation and trade union rights as well as more political liberty than they had enjoyed in the 1890s. Giolitti adopted a much more tolerant attitude towards strikes than his predecessors Crispi, Pelloux and di Rudini had shown, provided that strikes had economic and not political goals and were in the private and not the public sector. The left-wing press was subjected to far less censorship than had been customary before 1900. Limited accident and disability insurance was introduced, and restrictions were placed on female and child labour. A state monopoly on insurance was introduced in 1911 and virtually universal male suffrage was gained in 1912. In 1910 only 2.9 million men had had voting rights, roughly a quarter of the adult male population of about 12 million; after the 1912 reform, only illiterate men under the age of thirty who had not done military service remained excluded from the franchise. However, it should be noted that only about half the potential electorate voted in 1913.

Despite the limited gains of the reformist strategy, it is equally obvious that this class cooperation was to the advantage of the middle-class Giolittian liberals who bought a large measure of social peace without making profound alterations in the structure of Italian society, and that cooperation between the representatives of the northern workers and the northern middle class did little for the southern peasantry. Indeed, some commentators have argued that class cooperation may not have been in the best interests of the industrial working class.[21]

The Italian labour movement's relationship with the peasantry has been as significant to its success or failure as its relationship with the middle classes. The Giolittian period saw the socialists making inroads into sections of the northern peasantry, the landless labourers of Emilia-Romagna in particular. Many socialist deputies in the years before 1914 were elected by rural rather than urban constituencies; fifteen of the PSI's fifty-two seats in 1913 were in Emilia-Romagna, a region devoid of large industrial centres. The high proportion of farm labourers amongst the CGL's membership is a further indication of the semi-rural character of Italian socialism before 1914.

The *biennio rosso* was characterised by the prevalence of a more intransigent maximalist line towards the middle-class liberals, despite the reformist and class collaborationist tendencies of many deputies on the right of the PSI. It must be underlined that much of the growth in the Socialist vote in the 1919 election, compared with the 1913 election, came from the peasants, especially the sharecroppers, with a breakthrough in rural Umbria and considerable gains in rural Tuscany.[22] While the left made some errors in failing to coordinate working class and peasant struggles,[23] and to appreciate the full significance of the complex sub-divisions within the rural population, the oft-repeated assertion that socialist opposition to the First World War totally alienated peasant war veterans is highly debatable.

To talk of class cooperation during the fascist period has little meaning; the working class, insofar as it maintained a left-wing political identity in the face of state repression, did so by retreating into a wary isolation. The Resistance of 1943–1945 recruited anti-fascists from a variety of social backgrounds and involved workers, peasants and middle-class intellectuals alike, even if the rank and file of many partisan bands was largely recruited from the peasantry of the areas in which they operated.

An alliance with sections of the peasantry and, to some extent, the small entrepreneurs of northern and central Italy played an important part in the labour movement's control of local and regional government in the Red Regions as well as in the vote for the left in general elections between 1946 and 1992. The continuation of such an alliance outside Tuscany, Umbria and the Marche has now been called into question by the rise of the Lega Nord, which has clearly won a considerable measure of peasant support in a number of Emilian provinces, particularly Parma and Piacenza.

Finally, it might be argued that it was an excessive reliance on electoral and financial support from the middle classes rather than the labour movement that eventually led the Italian Socialists to the disaster of 1992–1994. The PSI's once substantial working-class base had been shrinking since the 1964 split; the left-wing splinter, the PSIUP, took 30 per cent of the party's membership but a much larger proportion of its union activists. However, this long-term trend gathered pace after Craxi became party leader in 1976. In the 1980s the party made a self-conscious appeal to the northern urban middle class and generated a growing harvest of clientelist votes in the South, engaging in conflict with the trade unions over wage indexation while forming close financial ties with Berlusconi and others in the run-up to *Tangentopoli*.

The Role of Other Social Institutions in the Shaping of the Italian Labour Movement

The army and the school systems have had a far less significant role in transmitting nationalist and, implicitly or explicitly, anti-socialist ideas in Italy than they have had in France or Germany. The Italian masses were never nationalised nor were peasants turned into Italians.[24] Although it would be foolish to underestimate the influence of family and gender on the Italian labour movement, such influences were often subtle and indirect.

The discussion of the role of external social institutions in shaping the Italian labour movement must start with the Catholic Church. The Catholic Church has been the only church in twentieth-century Italy to have had any political influence whatsoever. It has played an enormous role in shaping, not just working-class movements, but every aspect of political and social life in twentieth-century Italy.

Throughout the twentieth century the Catholic Church has been hostile to the growth of first socialism and then communism, and thus to any working-class organisation whether political, economic or cultural, which was influenced by such ideologies. Italy's proximity to the Vatican has ensured that theoretical hostility has been translated into political practice. The strategies adopted by the Church over the century to combat the threat from the left have varied from giving discreet support to right-wing liberals or making a marriage of convenience with the fascist dictatorship,[25] to blessing or tolerating the formation of Catholic political parties and trade unions.

Italian unification had resulted in the loss of the papacy's temporal power, and Pope Pius IX refused to have any official dealings with the new state. The Italian prime minister Crispi still suspected the Church of aiming at the dismemberment of the Italian kingdom at the time of the Sicilian *Fasci* in 1894, and the repression after the Milan riots of 1898 was directed at Catholic as well as at socialist, anarchist and republican activists. In the Giolittian period the Church began to relax its *Non Expedit*, a total ban on Catholic participation as either voters or candidates in the parliamentary elections of the liberal and initially very anti-clerical Italian state, not because of a growth of papal tolerance towards secularising liberalism but because of a fear of socialism. From 1904 onwards, Catholics were urged to vote in certain constituencies for right-wing liberals in order to prevent the election of socialists and other anti-clericals.

The *Non Expedit* was further relaxed in 1909 as the socialist threat showed no sign of diminishing. Initially this policy paid some dividends, since the socialists had been able to elect more deputies with 12.9 per cent of the vote in 1900 than with 21.3 per cent in 1904, even if their parliamentary strength rose again in 1909, despite a fall in their share of the poll to 19 per cent.[26] The 1913 election which followed the extension of the franchise to most adult males saw a much greater degree of Catholic participation, with twenty-nine right-wing Catholic deputies being elected and many liberal deputies relying on Catholic votes for their majorities. Despite the growing subterranean influence of the Catholic lobby demonstrated by the Gentiloni Pact, Pius X remained opposed to the founding of a formal Catholic political party.

In 1919, things changed. The new pope, Benedict XV, gave his blessing to the foundation of both a Catholic political party, the *Partito Popolare Italiano*, and a Catholic trade union confederation, the CIL.[27] The *Popolari* was a deeply divided but multi-class party well to the left of the pre-war clerico-moderates and competed with the socialists for peasant votes, while the CIL recruited large numbers of female textile workers as well as sharecroppers, small leaseholders and, in certain places, landless labourers, although its challenge to the socialist CGL amongst male industrial workers was less effective. The *Popolari* obtained 100 seats in the November 1919 general election and 107 seats in the election of May 1921, clearly establishing themselves as a mass party with about 20 per cent of the vote, second only to the socialists. Even if the CIL had only roughly half the socialist CGL's membership at the peak of unionisation in 1920, it clearly out-numbered the anarcho-syndicalist USI.

Despite the relative popularity of the party and the trade union confederation, the Church made another policy switch under Pope Pius XI to a policy of an alliance with fascism, sacrificing the *Popolari* and the CIL because of a fear of Bolshevism and a belief that the fascists would be the best partners. The Church's withdrawal of support from Don Sturzo and his *Popolari* made a considerable contribution to the destruction of the organised labour movement in Italy between 1922 and 1926. The settlement of the 60-year old dispute between Church and State by the Concordat of 1929 played a key role in legitimising the fascist regime in the eyes of the more religious and less politicised sections of both the working class and the peasantry, particularly women and southerners, who were influenced by the Pope's description of Mussolini as the man sent by Providence. The Church also gave its blessing to Mussolini's war in Abyssinia, gaining further consensus for the regime, and very naturally endorsed the Italian fascist decision to intervene in Spain in support of Franco against the anti-clerical republic.

After the Second World War, the Church made the greatest single contribution to splitting the trade union movement by giving its backing to the influential CISL, which was a far more serious rival to the communist-socialist CGIL than the small American-backed, social democratic breakaway UIL was ever likely to be. Pius XII's intervention in the April 1948 election, in which he instructed the clergy to warn voters of the hell-fire that awaited those who placed their crosses against the candidates of the communist-socialist alliance, stands in stark contrast to his notorious failure to condemn the Holocaust during the Second World War.

The Church's continued backing for the Christian Democratic Party must have had its effect on a portion of the working class and the peasantry in every subsequent election. This was particularly the case in the areas of Lombardy and Venetia which were dominated by a white sub-culture, centred around regular church-going, Catholic youth organisations, Catholic cooperatives, Catholic savings banks and a wide variety of other economic, social and cultural institutions linked to the clergy. However, the rapid secularisation over the last twenty-five years has clearly led to some diminution in the Church's influence over electoral behaviour. Although the unifying effects of the Hot Autumn of 1969 and the working-class struggles of the early 1970s brought the CISL much closer to the CGIL,[28] the late 1980s saw a resurgence of the split in the trade union movement in which confessional factors played at least some part. The disintegration of the Christian Democrat monolith since April 1992 may have led to some loosening of the papal insistence on the political unity of Italian Catholics, preached for nearly half a century, but the Pope and the lower-ranking northern clergy seem to be backing the Lega Nord as the best available bulwark against the left.

Gender differences have had an important effect on the working-class movement, in part because of a failure by a male-dominated labour movement, especially the Communist Party of Togliatti and Berlinguer, to address issues that were of central importance to women. Togliatti's decision to abandon the long-standing anti-clericalism of the Italian socialist and anarchist tradition meant that the major party of the left was in an extremely weak position to appeal to younger women once they had begun to free themselves from Catholic ideology with its stress on large families and total hostility to contraception, abortion and divorce.[29]

The period between 1976 and 1978 saw a deepening chasm emerge between the Italian women's movement and the Italian Communist Party as a result of the PCI's desperate desire to ingratiate itself with the Catholic Church over the abortion issue. Occhetto's adoption of gender-based quota systems within the leadership group of the PCI/PDS from 1989 onwards may well have had less resonance with the female electorate than with the party's own female membership; the trend towards the one-child family and the lowest birthrate in the European Union has been one of the most significant social changes in Italy over the last twenty-five years, while the growth in female political and trade union activism has been relatively slow to emerge.

Family traditions have also played an important role in shaping the working-class movement, particularly under the fascist dictatorship when memories of working-class struggles and adherence to a generic left-wing ideology of *sovversivismo* were passed from one generation to the next. Despite recent attempts to explain the militancy of Turin and Milan in 1943–1944 solely in terms of war-time food shortages, bombing raids and factory conditions unmediated by any ideological heritage, the sudden reappearance of mass strikes after twenty years of fascist dictatorship may well point to the memory of the *biennio rosso* being passed on from father to son within the working-class family. The continuity of political traditions in some Red Regions like Tuscany, where socio-economic conditions have been transformed out of all recognition in the course of the twentieth century, cannot be explained without examining the considerable degree of political socialisation within the family; the dramatic shift away from *mezzadria* (sharecropping) at the end of the 1950s makes it impossible to explain the century-long continuity in Siena province from PSI to PCI to PDS in terms of workplace traditions or geographical patterns of settlement.

Whatever the intentions of Italian governments in general, and the fascist regime in particular, it is doubtful whether either the Italian army or the Italian school system have functioned as particularly effective agencies of social control or seriously undermined the influence of the labour movement. The Italian army has never imbued its conscripts with militarist enthusiasm; even the fervour about the war in Abyssinia was far greater amongst the civilian population, reliant on edited newsreels and radio commentaries, than amongst the troops in the field. Large sections of the population, particularly in the south and in the countryside, received little education before 1945. While Catholic values within the school system might have reinforced clerical inclinations amongst children of Catholic families participating in a white sub-culture, they probably had the reverse effect on adolescents from anti-clerical backgrounds.

The Role of Employers' Actions in the Formation of Working-Class Economic and Political Attitudes

In Italy, as in other European countries, employers' actions have had a significant role in the formation of working-class economic and political attitudes. Repressive regimes within the factory, shipyard or mine may have ensured short-term quiescence but they have generally provoked suppressed rage against the whole economic, social and political order, which was vented the moment the situation changed in the workers' favour. In the Giolittian period some employers tried to ban unions altogether. The case of the Orlandos, Livorno's major employers who owned both the main shipyard and the leading engineering factory in the city, demonstrates that such conduct did not necessarily ensure conservative political attitudes amongst the employees, if the political culture of the surrounding community was dominated by the radical left – as it was in that rebellious port city.[30] It might seem plausible to argue that the Orlandos' repressive strategy was a dangerous one in a cosmopolitan trading city whose artisans and dockers had played such a significant role in the Revolution of 1848, but a similar strategy might have been more effective in remoter and less politicised areas. However, if one looks closely at one case of industrial development outside major urban areas, the evidence in the case of the Tuscan extractive industries (iron mining on Elba and in the province of Arezzo and marble-quarrying in the province of Massa Carrara) suggests isolation could not protect the employer indefinitely.[31]

The FIAT car plants of Turin have been subjected to a greater degree of historical and sociological investigation than any other Italian factory, and every period of repressive internal conditions within the FIAT plants has in the long run given rise to another outbreak of labour militancy, sometimes in the plant itself and sometimes on the streets of Turin.[32] The effective militarisation of labour in Turin during the First World War produced the August 1917 insurrection during the war itself and the epic industrial struggles of 1920, which included two rounds of factory occupations and another full-blown insurrection in April 1920. The repressive factory regime of the fascist years, characterised by the introduction of the Bedaux system with its associated de-skilling, wage cuts and a very close relationship between Agnelli and Mussolini that deprived even the Torinese fascist trade unions of any real capacity to intervene inside FIAT's empire, played a role in the great strikes of 1943 and 1944 as well as in the intermittent militancy between 1945 and 1948.[33]

The Cold War atmosphere of the 1950s, with its sackings and blacklisting of communist militants and the systematic isolation of trouble-makers by exiling them to particularly unpleasant departments within the plant, seemed at first to have the desired taming effect on the FIAT workforce. In 1959 none of eleven different strikes called in the various FIAT plants succeeded. On 13 June 1962, 93,000 FIAT workers clocked on as usual, despite a chorus of insults from the 100,000 workers on strike at all the other major Torinese factories. However, on 23 June 1962 the majority of the FIAT workforce finally involved itself in a strike once more, and in July 1962 thousands of FIAT workers were involved in days of rioting in Piazza Statuto, whose primary target was the offices of the UIL, a union that had enjoyed a privileged relationship with the FIAT management.[34]

The Hot Autumn of 1969 allowed the FIAT workforce to enjoy revenge against the management. The first sign of the management's determination to end what had become institutionalised insubordination came in the sacking of sixty-one carefully selected shop stewards in the autumn of 1979. The success of this operation opened the way for mass sackings the following year, provoking the unsuccessful 35-day strike from which the unions at FIAT have never recovered.

The daily experience of repression in the factory, whilst it might often deter workers from joining unions or starting strikes, generally tended to reinforce commitment to radical ideologies based on violent class conflict rather than more moderate reformist brands of socialism. This may explain why some factory workers in a white (Catholic) area like the Veneto, with relatively little experience of conventional left-wing parties or trade unions, were briefly won over to the politics of the ultra-leftist group *Potere Operaio* in the late 1960s.[35]

Some of the differences in temper between the Torinese and Milanese working class may have been determined by the fact that Milan had a multiplicity of employers, in contrast to Turin where FIAT's domination sharpened the association between industrial and political struggle. While the long tradition of moderate reformist socialism that started with the Milanese intellectual Turati may well have come to an inglorious end with the deep involvement of Craxi's Milanese associates in *Tangentopoli*, such a tradition of moderation and class alliances had been the product of a more complex and articulated social structure in which even the largest employer, Pirelli, never played the dominant role in the life of the city that FIAT did in Turin.

The legitimacy of strikes in Italy was frequently determined by the state as well as, or instead of, the employers. After the Milanese riots of 1898 it looked as if the Italian state was determined to strangle the trade unions at birth, but this repressive phase proved to be relatively short-lived. Giolitti moderated working-class attitudes and behaviour to some extent by removing the state from many industrial disputes, as long as these were of an economic and not a political nature and did not threaten public services such as the railways. Giolittian tolerance was much more evident in the northern regions than in southern Italy, where old traditions of collusion between *carabinieri* and *agrari* continued more or less unchecked.

The *biennio rosso* was marked by an unparalleled wave of industrial and agricultural strikes, and the employers and landowners of northern and central Italy had little choice but to yield to the bulk of the strikers' demands. This period culminated in the nationwide Occupation of the

Factories in September 1920, against which Giolitti refused to make use of military force.

From September 1920 to October 1922 the employers were increasingly able to make use of fascist squads for strike-breaking purposes, with a large measure of collusion from the local representatives of the police, *carabinieri* and army. After the fascists completed their takeover in 1925 they forced the working class into fascist trade unions which either failed to defend workers' interests at all, or attempted to do so not by strikes but by more informal pressure on employers or the state. The fascists banned strikes altogether; this ban was formally included in the penal code of 1930. Some strikes occurred during the economic crisis of the early 1930s despite their manifest illegality, but these were short, localised, and scattered. The mass strikes of 1943 and 1944 were completely illegal and the second wave involved a confrontation not just with the Italian fascists but with the more formidable forces of the Third Reich.

Italy's liberation in April 1945 once again shifted the balance of forces in favour of the workers and strikes became more widespread. After the Christian Democrat victory in the April 1948 general election the apparatus of the state was once again used to assert the power of the employer, with Interior Minister Scelba becoming notorious for the frequency with which he used police violence to repress strikers.

Over the last two decades, industrial relations in Italy have been regulated by the *Statuto dei Lavoratori* (May 1970), passed through Parliament in the wake of the Hot Autumn of 1969. This gave the unions far more rights than their counterparts in most other Western European countries enjoyed over the same period. The provisions of the *Statuto* effectively guaranteed workers job security, obliged employers to assign workers to jobs in line with their formal qualifications, and permitted mobility from job to job within the plant only if it did not involve downgrading. Workers were allowed to hold assemblies and referenda in the plant and union officials were permitted to collect union dues in the factory. Blacklists, discrimination and the victimisation of union activists were prohibited.[36] The very protection granted to workers under the *Statuto* encouraged the expansion of a parallel unofficial labour market based on *lavoro nero*.[37]

Whatever the legal framework, the legitimacy of various kinds of industrial action tends to vary with changing circumstances and this trend has been exacerbated by the relatively low level of general respect for legality in modern Italy. For instance, it is worth noting that many forms of struggle developed at FIAT's Turin plants between 1969 and 1979 were retrospectively labelled as terrorism, not just by the employer but even by such a prominent communist spokesman as Amendola. On a somewhat lighter note, not all the forms of struggle devised during the Hot Autumn were threatening or violent. The Italians pioneered a wide variety of rolling and partial strikes – ingenious practices, many of which have no British, French or German equivalent and all of which were designed to maximise both confusion and production losses, while minimising loss of pay for the participants.

Relations Between the State and the Working-Class Movement

The role of the state in shaping working-class political attitudes is always a significant one, as Dick Geary has recently reminded us in his comparative study of European labour politics.[38] A repressive state, provided it does not succeed in crushing the working-class movement altogether, as the Nazis did in Germany and some would say Franco did in Spain, is bound to radicalise it, while a liberal and constitutional state may well win the workers' movement over to the moderate politics of reformism, to a strategy based on compromise rather than confrontation. The role of the Italian state in the twentieth century was particularly significant, firstly because Italy's unification from above had left a marked residue of anti-statist sentiment amongst Italian workers that stretched far beyond the ranks of committed anarchists and anarcho-syndicalists; and secondly, because Italy was a fascist dictatorship for more than twenty years during the period, an experience which not only perpetuated but in fact further magnified every existing element of working-class distrust of or diffidence towards the police, army, *carabinieri*, law and criminal justice system.

Italy had been unified from above, not below, with the institutions of the Piedmontese state being imposed on the other regions. The 1860s were for all practical purposes a decade of civil war on the southern Italian mainland, even if the northern-dominated government chose to label the phenomenon the *brigantaggio* (brigandage). The Sicilian hostility towards the Piedmontese state was one of the factors behind the growth of the Mafia. The narrow liberal elite was distrustful of the Italian masses, who were suspected of being far more attached to the Catholic Church or their locality than to the nation-state, and in late nineteenth-century Italy an elected assembly based on universal male suffrage was never contemplated, not even for cosmetic purposes. In 1870 only 1.98 per cent of the population had the right to vote under a very narrow franchise based on property and literacy qualifications. Depretis's extension of the franchise in 1882 was relatively narrow, only increasing the electorate to 6.9 per cent of the population. The upper house of the Italian Parliament, the Senate, was nominated rather than elected and authority over military and foreign affairs effectively remained in the hands of the king rather than Parliament.[39]

The turbulence of the 1890s – particularly the Sicilian Fasci of 1894 and the riots of 1898, centred on but not confined to Milan – was met with increased repression against the labour movement, and by the turn of the century, it looked as if parliamentary liberalism would be discarded in favour of a regime based on the monarchy and the army.

Instead, however, the shift from Crispian repression to Giolittian tolerance began around 1900. This shift was probably not altogether unconnected with the assassination of the increasingly autocratic King Umberto by an anarchist during the course of the year, and had an enormous impact on the Italian working-class movement. Without this shift, the reformist approach favoured by the Socialist Parliamentary Group and the leadership of the CGL would have had absolutely no credibility.

However, despite Giolitti's limited social reforms, genuine commitment to parliamentary rule and willingness to tolerate the existence of trade unions, every conflict between strikers and demonstrators on the one hand and troops or police on the other in which workers or peasants lost their lives provided instant propaganda for the revolutionary left both inside and outside the Socialist Party. Such 'proletarian massacres' were likely to trigger general strikes, the most widespread of which was that of 1904. The syndicalists' greater degree of hostility towards the bourgeois state personified by Giolitti was one of the factors that led them to leave the Socialist Party in 1908 and to found their own *Camere del Lavoro*, which were eventually brought under the umbrella of the USI in 1912.

The years immediately before the First World War saw another deterioration in the relationship between the state and the working-class movement. Giolitti's invasion of Libya in 1911 discredited the pro-Giolittian reformists within the Socialist Party and revived the anti-militarist and hence anti-statist sentiment within the wider working-class movement. Giolitti's extension of the franchise in 1912 failed to integrate the masses into the nation. By the time he granted near-universal male suffrage, raising the potential electorate to 24 per cent of the population, the Socialist Party had moved markedly to the left. In order to block the electoral progress of the now revolutionary socialists Giolitti had to resort to an alliance with the Catholics, which not only deepened the socialists' alienation but lost him the support of his most reliable allies, the anti-clerical radicals.

The Giolittian system was now on the verge of complete breakdown and the 'old fox' was in no position to guide the transition from élite politics to mass politics. The outbreak of the *Settimana Rossa* (Red Week) in June 1914, as a result of troops shooting down anti-militarist demonstrators in Ancona, showed quite clearly the extent of Italian working-class alienation from the state; rioting was widespread throughout the country and turned into full-blown insurrections in Romagna and the Marche. Socialists, republicans, anarchists and syndicalists found themselves in alliance, however briefly, against the forces of the state, and the Italian government realised that there was no hope of the monarchy rallying the people to fight in any war on the side of Austria-Hungary.[40]

Increased state intervention in the economy during the First World War had a paradoxical effect on the labour movement. On the one hand, the involvement of some major trade union leaders from the CGL in a tripartite partnership of state, employers and unions increased the reformist inclinations of men like d'Aragona and Rigola, who felt that government ministers and major industrialists were at last treating them as equals. On the other hand, the effective militarisation of the factories, where any male striker was liable to be sent to the front line, increased discontent amongst ordinary workers whose hours and pace of work were vastly increased at a time of food shortages and rising prices. These workers were pushed in a revolutionary rather than reformist direction in the aftermath of the war or in the case of the Torinese workers who participated in the insurrection of August 1917, during the war itself.[41]

The *biennio rosso* of 1919–1920 demonstrated that the moderate leadership of the PSI and the CGL could no longer control the anti-statist inclinations of their radicalised memberships; riots like the *Caroviveri* riots over the cost of living in July 1919 or insurrections like those in Ancona and Piombino in the summer of 1920 were as common as the peaceful demonstrations or orderly strikes favoured by the recognised leaders of the movement. While it is certainly true that Giolitti adopted his customary non-interventionist 'wait and see' approach, rather than risk aggravating the situation by sending in the troops, the notion that the state apparatus reacted to the *biennio rosso* with complete passivity, particularly in rural areas, is grossly exaggerated to say the least.[42]

Differing views of the state within the workers' movement played a great role in determining responses to the rise of fascism. Those sections of the movement which had supported Giolitti, exemplified by Turati, instructed the masses not to meet violence with violence and vainly sought a solution in parliamentary coalitions with the liberals or the *Popolari*. Those who had already committed themselves to the overthrow of the existing state, whether anarchists, maximalist socialists, communists, republicans or syndicalists, were far more likely to support the *Arditi del Popolo*, a united front organisation which attempted to organise mass violent resistance to fascism.[43]

Bordiga's attempts to push the communists down a sectarian blind alley, coupling solitary and isolated violent resistance to fascism with total hostility to all other working-class organisations targeted by the fascists, proved less successful than many historians have imagined. Giolitti's inclusion of the fascists in the *Blocco Nazionale* list for the May 1921 general election rapidly increased the favouritism of the security forces towards fascist groups in their violent clashes with the left. Cesare Mori's attempt to mobilise the forces of the state against fascism during his period as Prefect of Bologna was a remarkable exception to the general rule of collusion and complicity during 1921–1922, when soldiers, *carabinieri* and policemen often went beyond turning a blind eye to fascist aggression.[44]

The experience of a fascist regime with close links to the industrialists and a deep-rooted hostility to any form of working-class self-organisation radicalised working-class attitudes in those instances where it did not reduce workers to apathy and despair. Indeed, it was the experience of the fascist regime which created a mass Communist Party in Italy.[45] Before the march on Rome in October 1922, the socialists far outnumbered the communists who had become a separate party in January 1921, precisely when the revolutionary tide of the *biennio rosso* had started to ebb. The communists' unique capacity to sustain some sort of clandestine organisation inside Italy throughout the years of the dictatorship enabled them to win over many working-class militants who had previously backed the socialists or anarchists.[46]

The experience of the armed resistance to the Germans and their Italian fascist allies during 1943–1945 also played a role in shaping working-class attitudes towards both the legitimacy of the post-war state and the use of political violence for decades to come. Many workers who had nurtured hopes of the Resistance leading to a socialist revolution obstinately clung to a belief in an insurrectionary path to socialism, no matter how often the communist leadership repudiated such notions; the depth of this belief was shown by the spontaneous attempt at insurrection on 14–16 July 1948 in response to the assassination attempt on Togliatti.[47] A fear that the Italian state was moving in a fascist direction during Tambroni's premiership led to a wave of working-class riots in July 1960[48] and the belief, to some extent justified by various unsuccessful coup attempts, that a right-wing dictatorship might be round the corner influenced the initially ambiguous response of the working class to the left-wing terrorism of the 1970s.

Labour-Movement Culture, Popular Culture and *Sovversivismo*

The general European distinctions between working-class culture, labour-movement culture and popular culture are further complicated in the

Italian case by the existence of a culture, or sub-culture, based on the Catholic Church, which is frequently referred to in the social science literature as the white sub-culture. This sub-culture is discussed, albeit briefly, in the fourth section of this chapter. This particular section will concentrate on variants of the red sub-culture and on popular culture in the more general sense.

The most noticeable feature of the early twentieth century is the considerable gap between working-class culture and the official labour-movement culture propagated by Turati's Socialist Party. The official labour movement culture of early twentieth-century Italy bore at least some resemblance to that of German social democracy. Socialists, trade unionists and even anarchists promoted and encouraged libraries, evening classes and other forms of working-class self-education. Bands and choral groups were an integral part of mutual aid societies and other labour movement organisations; it is worth emphasising that the famous workers' anthem *Inno dei Lavoratori* was written in 1886 by Filippo Turati himself.[49] The unofficial working-class culture which drew on earlier artisan or peasant traditions was a much more rebellious and violent culture; this was the culture of *sovversivismo*, characterised by anti-statism, anti-militarism, anti-clericalism and a belief in the legitimacy of violence in the winning of economic disputes or the struggle for political power.[50]

Unless one grasps the significance of the overlap between the official and unofficial culture of the labour movement, it is impossible to understand why anarchists, syndicalists and anarcho-syndicalists, who were minority components of the labour movement in the first quarter of the twentieth century, were repeatedly able to win over substantial elements of the working classes, who in calmer times associated themselves with the Socialist Party, to their goal of violent and spontaneous revolution.[51] Without the existence of this unofficial second culture, both the *Settimana Rossa* of June 1914, led by the anarchist Malatesta but drawing in a much wider range of left-wing forces, and the *biennio rosso* of 1919–1920 would be very hard to explain, given the great stress the Socialist Party and its associated trade union confederation, the CGL, laid on discipline and deference to the leadership.[52]

The culture of *sovversivismo* was not totally destroyed by the fascist regime and remained an integral part of the world view of large sections of the communist rank and file for decades after the war, despite the condemnation of Gramsci and, to an even greater extent, Togliatti. The earlier layer of *sovversivismo* with its semi-anarchist roots became overlaid by what one might call a popular Stalinism, something which persisted amongst elements of the PCI's base long after the leadership's turn to Eurocommunism in the mid to late 1970s. The war years saw the emergence of a myth of the Soviet Union and the Red Army embodied in a vision of Stalin as a popular avenger, who would arrive in Italy at the head of the Red Army to liberate all the oppressed from the tyranny of the bosses and the fascists.[53]

This mixture of *sovversivismo* and popular Stalinism led large numbers of rank and file communists to believe that the leadership's talk of parliamentary roads and pacific methods was only a tactical ploy, and that one day the Party would put itself at the head of the masses and give the order for revolution.[54] The events of July 1948 were an attempt to turn this myth into reality.[55]

As the previous section emphasised, resistance veterans who had actually been involved in armed struggle against the Germans and their fascist collaborators were particularly prone to this set of beliefs and they may well have passed these ideas on to their children; this might explain both the mentality of some founding members of the Red Brigades, particularly Franceschini and the other Emilians, and the degree of sympathy that they initially enjoyed amongst some sections of the working class.[56] More spontaneous variants of *sovversivismo* fed into other revolutionary groups founded in the aftermath of 1968, and it is no accident that the original Tuscan *Potere Operaio*, most of whose members joined *Lotta Continua*, gained its following along a coastline which had contained many of the anarchist strongholds of 1919–1920.[57]

Popular culture of the kind that arouses such enthusiasm amongst cultural studies theorists arrived in Italy during the fascist regime, when state-sponsored football first became a mass sport, replacing old games that the fascists associated with *sovversivismo*, though Gribaudi overstates his case about the younger generation of Torinese workers rejecting *sovversivismo* in favour of consumerist individualism, leaving himself with very little capacity to explain the mass strikes of 1943–1944 in Turin without resorting to economic determinism.[58] Because American culture first arrived in Italy during the bleak years of the fascist regime, the initial impact was sometimes radicalising rather than demobilising in its political effects; Americanising trends were identified with political opposition to the regime's own cultural nationalism. However, the post-war era demonstrated all too clearly that while Americanisation aroused all the anathemas that the traditional Catholic proponents of the white subculture were able to hurl at it, in the longer run in Italy, as in the rest of Europe, Americanisation posed a major threat to the older solidarity and community-based values of both the official labour movement culture and *sovversivismo*.[59]

The student movements of the 1960s and 1970s were, of course, influenced by an increasingly Americanised popular culture with a particular appeal to youth. But while the Italian student movement of

1967–1968 drew on American models at a superficial level, it also incorporated many motifs from the old *sovversivismo* and it was not until 1977 that all of the worst features of the American model gained the upper hand over the outgrowths of an authentically Italian revolutionary tradition. The 'Metropolitan Indians' were a belated copy of the American hippies, and the violence of *Autonomia*'s rank and file probably owed more to American gangster films than the more abstruse theorising of its guru, Professor Antonio Negri.

The future of *sovversivismo*, represented by *Rifondazione Comunista*, and of the official labour movement culture represented by the PDS remains open. The April 1992 general election, in which for the very first time the most extreme left-wing force in Italian politics, *Rifondazione Comunista*, gained a lower percentage of the vote amongst the under-25s than amongst the over-25s, may well be an indication that both the official labour movement culture and *sovversivismo* are no longer able to reproduce themselves. On the other hand, the June 1993 local elections revealed *Rifondazione Comunista* to be the second party in Turin and Milan, after the Lega Nord, and indicated a substantial PDS revival was in progress in cities dominated by the official labour movement culture of the Red Regions, such as Siena, Grosseto, Ancona and Ravenna.

Conclusion

Italian politics has been thrown into a state of flux since 1989 as the divisions fostered by the Cold War have lost much of the meaning they had for nearly half a century. Although neo-liberal policies of privatisation and attacks on the welfare state are gaining ground, the Italian labour movement has retained a greater capacity to mobilise its followers for general strikes and political demonstrations than most of its European counterparts, as the general strike of 14 October 1994 proved. Militant networks based on factory councils and beyond the control of any political party are as much a feature of the Italian working-class movement in the early 1990s as they were in the early 1970s or in 1919–1920; *Rifondazione Comunista* was the strongest left-wing force in the municipal elections of 1993 in both Turin and Milan, whilst the PDS has inherited the bulk of the PCI's traditional following in Tuscany, Umbria and the Marche.

Italy has not yet followed the French or Spanish path towards an ever more moderate social democracy; Craxi's Socialist Party, which once imagined it would become the hegemonic force on the left, is fighting for its very survival. The strongholds of the Lega Nord lie in areas where the white, rather than red sub-culture was dominant and workers never voted for the socialist and communist left in significant numbers. The inroads made by Forza Italia into the Milanese and Torinese working classes in the general election of March 1994 may yet be reversed by the massive unpopularity of the recent pension reforms and the failure of Berlusconi to fulfil his promise of a million new jobs; the 61 per cent for the left candidate in a two-horse race with the right in the Pistoia by-election of September 1994 shows the regional limits of Forza Italia's appeal.

Given the massive social, economic and cultural changes that have occurred in the second half of the twentieth century, changes such as mass migration from south to north and from country to city, secularisation, a dramatic decrease in family size and the Americanisation of popular culture, the degree of political continuity is quite remarkable. However, the recent history of both Italy and other European countries in the twentieth century demonstrates how rapidly mass unemployment can erode trade unions' membership and bargaining power, so it would be rash to assume the Italian labour movement can necessarily hold out against a hostile European tide.

Notes

1. Merli (1972).
2. Gershenkron (1962).
3. Corner (1990), p. 155. Camarda and Peli (1980), Musso (1980) and Procacci (1983) are probably the most important works on the Italian working class and the First World War.
4. Castronovo (1988), pp. 237–56, Mafai (1989), pp. 43–72 and Abse (1992).
5. Ginsborg (1990), pp. 210–53, provides the best concise account of these processes available in English.
6. Snowden (1986) is the best account in English.
7. These questions are discussed by Camarda and Peli (1980), Musso (1980), Procacci (1983) and Tognarini and Varni (1990).
8. For Piombino, see Bianconi (1970), Favilli (1974) and Tognarini (1980). For La Spezia, see Bianchi (1981). Levy (1989) discusses the general issues very lucidly.
9. Allum (1973) remains an incomparable source on Naples and Chubb (1982) is a very good introduction to Palermo.
10. Ginsborg (1990), p. 238 and pp. 410–1.
11. See Abse (1991) and Williams (1975) for more detailed discussion of these events.

12. For some discussion of very recent developments, see Abse (1993), (1994).
13. Figures taken from Davis (1989), p. 214; like most Italian statistics for this period, they must be treated as approximations only.
14. This view of the PSI as a sectionalist rather than more genuinely class party can be found in del Carria (1979) vol. 2, p. 144 and in Miller (1990), p. 38.
15. For Livornese and Torinese examples from the *biennio rosso*, see Abse (1991) and Maione (1975); Abse (1985), Barkan (1984) and, especially, del Carria (1979) demonstrate the recurrence of this egalitarian phenomenon in the Hot Autumn of 1969.
16. Abse (1991), pp. 59–65.
17. Ginsborg (1990), p. 404.
18. Riosa (1976) and Furiozzi (1977). Roberts (1979) concentrates on the syndicalist intelligentsia, particularly Panunzio and Olivetti. The most famous Italian *operaista* intellectual of recent times, Professor Antonio Negri, makes Panunzio and Olivetti seem models of rectitude.
19. Figures taken from Miller (1990), p. 101.
20. Miller (1990), p. 38.
21. It is not just del Carria (1979) who condemns the PSI's strategy. Miller (1990), p. 113, says of the GPS: 'The success of Giolitti's *trasformismo* was so complete that the group was powerless', and de Grand (1989), p. 37, argues: 'The relationship between Giolitti and Turati never became one of true equality.'
22. For Umbria see Bogliari (1980), and for Tuscany see Abse (1991). Umbria and Tuscany were regions dominated by sharecroppers rather than landless labourers, so this breakthrough represented a broadening of the socialist constituency among the peasantry and played a crucial role in turning these areas into the 'red regions' of the post- Second World War era. Abse (1986) contains more general observations about the peasant shift to socialism after 1918.
23. Williams (1975).
24. Mosse (1975) and Weber (1977) deal with related issues in the German and French context.
25. Pollard (1985), Binchy (1940).
26. Miller (1990), p. 37.
27. Molony (1977).
28. For a detailed discussion of these developments, see Barkan (1984).
29. Abse (1985) and (1987).
30. For further details about Livornese industrial relations and their effect on the city's politics, see Abse (1991), Spadoni (1979) and Tognarini and Varni (1990).

31. By 1920, the miners and quarrymen of Tuscany were some of the most fervent anarcho-syndicalists in the country. For Elban iron miners' attitudes during the *biennio rosso*, see Abse (1991), pp. 31–3, pp. 91–2 and pp. 174–7, and for the earlier history of Elban iron mining, see Spadoni (1979). Biagianti's (1984) account of iron mining and iron miners in the Valdarno reveals many notable similarities with Elba. For the hostility between quarry owners and quarry men in the marble quarries of Massa Carrara, see Gestri (1976) and Bernieri (1971). These repressive mine owners and quarry owners had no hesitation in giving direct support to fascist squads in 1921–1922; the quarry owners bankrolled Carrarese fascism and Biagianti has demonstrated that iron masters, and not *agrari*, were the paymasters of fascism in Arezzo province.
32. The pattern has not been broken by the defeat of autumn 1980; both the violent incidents during trade union demonstrations in autumn 1992 and the high communist, rather than PDS, vote in the first round of the June 1993 local elections indicated that, contrary to Barkan's (1984) forecasts, mass sackings and robotisation on the assembly line have not changed the underlying attitude of the workforce; the one district of the city where the communist-backed Novelli defeated the FIAT-backed Castellani in the second round of the June 1993 mayoral contest was Mirafiori itself, the site of the biggest and most famous FIAT plant.
33. Maione (1975), Musso (1980) and Sapelli (1975) are the best sources for events at the FIAT plants between 1900 and 1935.
34. Ginsborg (1990), pp. 250–3 provides a succinct but effective account of the turning of the tide; most of the illustrations for the general points made by Barkan (1984) are taken from the vicissitudes of the FIAT workforce.
35. For further details about the struggles at the Montedison chemical factories at Porto Marghera, see del Carria (1979), vol. 5, pp. 131–4.
36. Contini (1985) offers the best summary of the *Statuto* in English.
37. Translated literally, this means 'black work' but in many instances it amounted to sweated labour in which escaping taxes did not compensate the workforce for longer hours, lower wages, no national insurance and worse conditions. Much of the fashionable literature on flexible specialisation in Italy should be treated with scepticism; it frequently involves glamorising these forms of exploitation and practices in the Veneto and in the south have often been much harsher than in the frequently cited small enterprises of Emilia-Romagna.
38. Geary (1991).
39. Mack Smith (1989) is the most thorough investigation of the role played by the monarchy in the politics of unified Italy.

40. Lotti (1972) remains the classic account of the *Settimana Rossa.*
41. Hertner and Mori (1983) contains some interesting material on the attitude of the trade union leaders; Camarda and Peli (1980), Musso (1980) and Procacci (1983) provide the best general introduction to the relationship between workers and the state in 1915–1918 and challenge the old nationalist and fascist myth that the industrial working class enjoyed a very comfortable existence during the war. There is a wide variety of more specialised monographs and articles exploring the working-class experience of war in various other localities, of which Tomassini's chapter in Tognarini and Varni (1990) is one of the best, but most of the major points made by Musso about Turin or Camerda and Peli about Lombardy are valid for the other industrial centres.
42. Detailed refutation would require the citation of a massive list of local studies. The easiest bibliographical starting-point in English is probably my survey of local studies, Abse (1984).
43. The most detailed account of the nature and activities of the *Arditi del Popolo* can be found in del Carria (1979), vol. 3, pp. 213–60, although Natoli (1982), pp. 135–70, is a useful corrective on certain points. Abse (1991), pp. 169–92 analyses the *Arditi del Popolo*'s role in Livorno. For an English-language summary, see Abse (1986).
44. Abse (1991) analyses the collusion between the security forces and the fascists in the Livornese context, highlighting the significance of the prefect at local level and arguing that the key factor in the fascist conquest of Livorno was the replacement of the old-fashioned Giolittian prefect Gasperini by the pro-fascist prefect Verdinois in the summer of 1921. A brief summary in English is offered in Abse (1986).
45. See Spriano (1976), especially volumes 4 and 5 dealing with 1940–1945, for a well-documented analysis of this process.
46. Spriano (1976), volumes 2 and 3, chronicles the years of clandestinity.
47. Di Loreto (1991), del Carria (1979), vol. 4, pp. 199–213, Moscato (1983), pp. 149–64; also Tobagi (1978) and Orlandini (1976).
48. See Ginsborg (1990), pp. 256–8 and del Carria (1979), vol. 5, pp. 11–23, for further details about this important episode.
49. Bell (1986) devotes much attention to these questions; however, it must be remembered that Sesto San Giovanni provides a rather extreme instance of a virtually self-sufficient workers' culture.
50. There is relatively little material about *sovversivismo* available in English, perhaps because of Gramsci's famous negative observations about it and perhaps because of the many continuities between the official labour movement culture of Turati's reformist PSI and that of Berlinguer's Eurocommunist PCI; for introductions to the

concept see Andreucci (1981), Abse (1986) and Levy (1989). In Abse (1991), *sovversivismo* is central to the explanation for the *biennio rosso* and the rise of fascism. Two important articles, Mannari (1981) and Mannari (1990), see it as central to Livornese anti-fascism under the regime and Santomassimo (1980) sees it as an important component of anti-fascism elsewhere in Tuscany. Sapelli (1977) believes it was equally significant in Turin. Franzina (1987) argues that it was also of great importance in what has traditionally been seen as the very 'white' city of Vicenza.

51. Levy (1989) develops this general argument at much greater length.
52. For the *Settimana Rossa*, see Lotti (1972) and for the *biennio rosso*, see Abse (1986), Abse (1991), Maione (1975), Spriano (1975) and Williams (1975).
53. A popular anti-fascist wall slogan during the last years of the Second World War was 'Baffone viene' which translated literally means 'The man with the big moustache is coming', demonstrating the extent to which Stalin had become a popular hero amongst a working class and peasantry with no real knowledge of conditions in the USSR.
54. See di Loreto (1991) for an analysis of the ambiguous position of the PCI in the 1940s and an explanation about why a thoroughly reformist leader like Togliatti was in no position to totally repudiate the revolutionary yearnings of his own base.
55. It is worth noting the former Resistance leader Pietro Secchia, Togliatti's arch-rival within the PCI until his disgrace in 1954, spent his life believing in the myths of popular Stalinism and, according to Mafai (1984), only refrained from giving his official sanction to the spontaneous insurrection of July 1948 because of specific instructions given to his brother by the Soviet embassy.
56. Pitkin (1985) is merely one of the more academically respectable sources which bear witness to a phenomenon whose existence the PCI leaders went to extraordinary lengths to deny.
57. Tarrow (1989), pp. 242–63 gives the best account of the Tuscan *Potere Operaio* available in English, assisted by his access to Adriano Sofri's personal archive.
58. Gribaudi (1987).
59. For more material about the Americanisation of everyday life from the 1950s onwards, see Gundle (1986).

Bibliography

Abse, Tobias, 'A Survey of Local Studies of the Rise of Italian Fascism', *ATI Journal*, Spring 1984, pp. 19–33

——, 'Judging the PCI', *New Left Review*, no. 153, 1985, pp. 5–40

——, 'The Rise of Fascism in Industrial Cities: the Case of Livorno 1918–1922', in David Forgacs (ed.), *Rethinking Italian Fascism*, London, 1986, pp. 52–82

——, 'A Reply to Gundle', *New Left Review*, no. 163, 1987, pp. 36–9

——, *Sovversivi e fascisti a Livorno: Lotta politica e sociale, 1918–1922*, Milan, 1991

——, 'Italy', in Jeremy Noakes (ed.), *The Civilian in War: The Home Front in World War II*, Exeter, 1992, pp. 104–25

——, 'The Triumph of the Leopard', *New Left Review*, no. 199, 1993, pp. 3–28

——, 'Italy: A New Agenda', in Perry Anderson and Patrick Camiller (eds), *Mapping the West European Left*, London, 1994, pp. 189–232

Allum, Percy, *Politics and Society in Post-War Naples*, Cambridge, 1973

Andreucci, Franco '"Subversiveness" and anti-fascism in Italy', in Raphael Samuel (ed.), *People's History and Socialist Theory*, London, 1981, pp. 199–204

Barkan, Joanne, *Visions of Emancipation: the Italian Workers' Movement since 1945*, New York, 1984

Bell, Donald Howard, *Sesto San Giovanni: Workers, Culture and Politics in an Italian Town 1880–1922*, New Brunswick and London, 1986

Bernieri, Antonio, 'La nascita del fascismo a Carrara', *La Toscana nel regime fascista*, Florence, 1971, pp. 677–703

Biagianti, Ivo, *Sviluppo industriale e lotte sociali nel Valdarno superiore (1860–1922)*, Florence, 1984

Bianchi, Antonio, *Lotte sociali e dittatura in Lunigiana storica e in Versilia (1919–1930)*, Florence, 1981

Bianconi, Pietro, *Il movimento operaio a Piombino*, Florence, 1970

Binchy, D. A., *Church and State in Fascist Italy*, London, 1940

Bogliari, Francesco, *Il movimento contadino in Umbria dal 1900 al fascismo*, Milan, 1979

Camarda, A. and Peli, S., *L'altro esercito*, Milan, 1980

Castronovo, Valerio, 'L'industria di guerra 1940–1943', in Francesca Ferrantini Tosi, Gaetano Grassi and Massimo Legnani (eds), *L'Italia nella seconda guerra mondiale e nella resistenza*, Milan, 1989

Chubb, Judith, *Patronage, Power and Poverty in Southern Italy*, Cambridge, 1982

Clark, Martin, *Modern Italy 1871–1982*, London, 1984

Contini, Giovanni, 'Politics, Law and Shop Floor Bargaining in Post-war

Italy' in S. Tolliday and J. Zeitlin (eds), *Shop Floor Bargaining and the State: Historical and Comparative Perspectives*, Cambridge, 1985

Corner, Paul, 'Italy', in S. Salter and J. Stevenson (eds), *The Working-Class and Politics in Europe and America 1929–1945*, London and New York, 1990, pp.154–71

Davis, John A., 'Socialism and the Working-classes in Italy before 1914', in Dick Geary (ed.), *Labour and Socialist Movements in Europe before 1914*, Oxford/New York/Munich, 1989

de Grand, Alexander, *The Italian Left in the Twentieth Century: A History of the Socialist and Communist Parties*, Bloomington Indianopolis, 1989

del Carria, Renzo, *Proletari senza rivoluzione: storia delle classi subalterne in Italia*, 5 vols, Rome, 1979

di Loreto, Pietro, *Togliatti e la 'doppiezza': il PCI tra democrazia e insurrezione 1944–49*, Bologna, 1991

Favilli, Paolo, *Capitalismo e classe operaia a Piombino 1861–1918*, Rome, 1974

Franzina, Emilio, *Bandiera rossa ritornerà, nel cristianesimo la libertà: Storia di Vicenza popolare sotto il fascimo (1922–1944)*, Verona, 1987

Furiozzi, Gian Biagio, *Il sindacalismo rivoluzionario italiano*, Milan, 1977

Geary, Dick, *European Labour Protest from 1900 to the Depression*, London, 1991

Gershenkron, Alexander, *Economic Backwardness in Historical Perspective*, Cambridge Mass., 1962

Gestri, Lorenzo, *Capitalismo e classe operaia in provincia di Massa-Carrara: dall' unità d'Italia all' età giolittiana*, Florence, 1976

Ginsborg, Paul, *A History of Contemporary Italy: Society and Politics 1943–1988*, Harmondsworth, 1990

Gribaudi, Maurizio, *Mondo operaio e mito operaio: spazi e percorsi sociali a Torino nel primo novecento*, Turin, 1987

Gundle, Stephen, 'L'americanizzazione del quotidiano: Televisione e consumismo nell Italia degli anni Cinquanta', *Quaderni Storici*, vol. XXI, no. 62, 1986, pp. 561–94

Hertner, P., and Mori, G. (eds), *La transizione dall' economia di guerra all' economia di pace in Italia e Germania dopo la prima guerra mondiale*, Bologna, 1983

Levy, Carl (ed.), *Socialism and the Intelligentsia, 1880–1914*, London, 1987

——, 'Italian Anarchism 1870–1926' in David Goodway (ed.), *For Anarchism: History, Theory and Practice*, London, 1989, pp. 25–78

Lotti, Luigi, *La settimana rossa*, Florence, 1972

Mack Smith, Denis, *Italy and its Monarchy*, New Haven and London,

1989

Mafai, Miriam, *L'uomo che sognava la lotta armata*, Milan, 1984

——, *Pane nero: Donne e vita quotidiana nella seconda guerra mondiale*, Milan, 1989

Maione, Giuseppe, *Il biennio rosso: autonomia e spontaneità operaia nel 1919–20*, Bologna, 1975

Mannari, Enrico, 'Tradizione sovversiva e comunismo durante il regime fascista (1926–1943): Il caso di Livorno', *Annali della Fondazione Feltrinelli XX (1979–80)*, Milan, 1981, pp. 837–74

——, 'Una città "sovversiva": La protesta operaia negli anni del fascismo' in Ivan Tognarini and Angelo Varni (eds), *Le voci del lavoro: novant'anni di organizzazione e di lotta della camera del lavoro di Livorno*, Naples, 1990, pp. 465–96

Merli, Stefano, *Proletariato di fabbrica e capitalismo industriale: il caso italiano 1880–1900*, Florence, 1972

Miller, James Edward, *From Elite to Mass Politics: Italian Socialism in the Giolittian Era 1900–1914*, Kent Ohio, 1990

Molony, J. N., *The Emergence of Political Catholicism in Italy*, London, 1977

Moscato, Antonio, *Sinistra e potere: L'esperienza italiana 1944–1981*, Rome, 1983

Mosse, George L., *The Nationalisation of the Masses: Political Symbolism and Mass Movements in Germany from the Napoleonic Wars through the Third Reich*, New York, 1975

Musso, Stefano, *Gli operai di Torino 1900–1920*, Milan, 1980

Natoli, Claudio, *La Terza Internazionale e il fascismo (1919–1923): Proletariato di fabbrica e reazione industriale nel primo dopoguerra*, Rome, 1982

Orlandini, Sandro, *Luglio 1948: L'insurrezione proletaria nella provincia di Siena in risposta all'attentato a Togliatti*, Florence, 1976

Pitkin, Donald, *The House that Giacomo Built*, Cambridge, 1985

Pollard, John, *The Vatican and Italian Fascism, 1929–1932: A Study in Conflict*, Cambridge, 1985

Procacci, Giovanna (ed.), *Stato e classe operaia in Italia durante la prima guerra mondiale*, Milan, 1983

Procacci, Giuliano, *La lotta di classe in Italia agli inizi del secolo XX*, Rome, 1970

Riosa, Alceo, *Il sindacalismo rivoluzionario in Italia e la lotta politica nel partito socialista dell' età giolittiana*, Bari, 1976

Roberts, David D., *The Syndicalist Tradition and Italian Fascism*, Chapel Hill North Carolina, 1979

Santomassimo, Gianpasquale, 'Antifascismo popolare', *Italia Contemporanea*, no. 40, 1980

Sapelli, Giulio, *Fascismo, grande industria e sindacato: il caso di Torino 1929–1935*, Milan, 1975

——, 'Machina repressiva, "sovversivismo" e tradizione politica durante il fascismo', *Mezzosecolo: Annali del Centro Studi Gobetti 1976–77*, no. 2, 1977, pp. 107–60

Snowden, Frank M., *Violence and Great Estates in the South of Italy: Apulia 1900–1922*, Cambridge, 1986

Spriano, Paolo, *The Occupation of the Factories: Italy 1920*, London, 1975

——, *Storia del partito comunista italiano*, 5 vols, Turin, 1976

Tarrow, Sidney, *Democracy and Disorder: Protest and Politics in Italy 1965–1975*, Oxford, 1989

Tobagi, Walter, *La rivoluzione impossible: L'attentato a Togliatti: Violenza politica e reazione popolare*, Milan, 1978

Tognarini, Ivan, *Fascismo, antifascismo, resistenza in una città operaia:* vol.I *Piombino dalla guerra al crollo del fascismo 1918–1943*, Florence, 1980

——, and Varni, Angelo (eds), *Le voci del lavoro: novant' anni di organizzazione e di lotta della camera del lavoro di Livorno*, Naples, 1990

Weber, Eugen, *Peasants into Frenchmen: The Modernization of Rural France 1870–1914*, London, 1977

Williams, Gwyn A., *Proletarian Order: Antonio Gramsci, Factory Councils and the Origins of Communism in Italy 1911–1921*, London, 1975

–7–

Spain

Angel Smith

Introduction

During the twentieth century, Spanish history has been closely linked to that of its European neighbours. This can particularly be seen in the case of the Spanish labour movement. It was, after all, Bakunin's Italian emissary Giuseppe Fanelli who introduced anarchism to Spain in 1868–1969, and Marx's son-in-law Paul Lafargue who two years later stimulated the formation of an opposition Marxist current of thought.

Yet each national history is specific and, in the case of Spain, the great socio-economic and cultural variations between regions makes it difficult to generalise about the country as a whole. Overall, in economic terms Spain was differentiated from its large Western European neighbours by the great preponderance of agriculture within the national economy right through to the 1960s; even as late as 1930, 45 per cent of the active population still worked on the land. Institutionally and culturally Spain also had its own peculiarities; at the turn of the century the Catholic Church still played a key role in national life; the army had been a powerful force since the *Reconquista*, particularly in Castilian and Andalusian society; and clientelist relations were an essential element in public life.

The crystallisation of working-class identities and beliefs can only be understood within this broad economic, cultural and institutional context, and it is therefore in these terms that we will begin by analysing the process of class formation in Spain in the first section of this chapter. This makes it possible to look in more detail at labour culture, and the development of the labour movement.

Labour organisation grew rapidly in the period between 1914 and 1936, and quickly became divided between a socialist and syndicalist/anarchist wing. To a degree there were similarities here with the experience of other continental European labour movements. Nevertheless, both the profundity of the class divisions which cut across Spanish society and the buoyancy of the anarchist tradition seem to place

Spain apart. These will be some of the major questions dealt with in sections two and three.

The defeat of the Republican forces at the hands of General Franco in 1939 signified the end of an era for the labour movement. Fierce repression was followed by rapid industrialisation in the 1960s. Working-class identities therefore had to be reconstructed, and the 'new working class' operated in a very different institutional context. The ways in which new identities were forged and how the labour movement was re-built within an authoritarian political regime are examined in section four.

Spain finally emerged from dictatorship in 1976 a much changed society. With the rapid economic development of the 1960s and 1970s Spain had, at least in part, 'caught up' with her more industrialised Western neighbours. Parliamentary institutions were consolidated over the next decade. Many of the structural and cultural changes which affected the working class, and which from the 1970s were to loosen the bonds of affinity within the working-class community were therefore part of a trend seen across much of Europe. At the same time the 'terciarisation' of the economy and the imposition of a more homogeneous set of cultural values was to lead to a debate within the left regarding the social classes to which it should appeal for support, as well as the relationship between party and unions. It is the effects of these structural and cultural changes, and the policies, debates and divisions the new realities have provoked on the left, that are addressed in sections five and six of this chapter.

Class Formation, the State and Social Elites 1875–1923

As we have already suggested, agriculture remained the dominant source of employment in the early twentieth century. Over four million people lived off the land in 1900. Smallholder and tenant farmers tended to predominate in northern Spain, while in the south a land-hungry peasantry (*braceros* or *jornaleros*) worked on the great estates (*latifundia*) of a small landowning elite. In 1900 there were over one and a half million waged agrarian labourers in the country, while the number of urban workers was around the one million mark. Of these last, about one-third were concentrated in Catalonia, the only region of Spain which had experienced an industrial revolution in the early nineteenth century. The leading sector was the cotton textile industry, and by the turn of the century textile workers represented nearly one-half the region's entire labour force. The late nineteenth century also saw industrial growth in Vizcaya, and the development of a modern coal mining industry in Asturias.[1] However concentration on the most obvious manifestations of industrial growth tends to obscure the continued preponderance of artisanal work structures in much of manufacturing. For example, building workers made up one-third of the entire urban workforce in 1900, and this was an industry in which the most demanding tasks were typically undertaken by skilled artisans (*oficiales*). The importance of the skilled worker was most evident in Madrid, the country's second largest manufacturing centre, but even in Barcelona (in part because much of the cotton textile industry was to be found concentrated along the river banks in the north-east of the region), up to 50 per cent of adult male workers had undertaken some form of apprenticeship.[2]

The Spanish working class was therefore characterised by its diversity. The great distances and poor transport system ensured that urban and rural areas were in large measure isolated from one another. Nevertheless, in the larger urban centres a degree of similarity could be discerned; in cities such as Barcelona, Valencia, Bilbao and Madrid in the late nineteenth century, the weight of skilled artisanal workers within the labour force combined with the existence of a large petit bourgeoisie of shop keepers and small-scale employers, resulted in the emergence of a popular, inter-class, republican tradition which was socially moderate (though more radical currents later emerged, especially from the 1890s) and which laid emphasis on the attainment of civil liberties and parliamentary democratic rights. Both the workers and middle classes felt excluded from political power, and in these circumstances the major political battle lines were drawn between the 'people' and the 'oligarchy'.

In these areas a specifically working-class culture developed only slowly. In the mid-nineteenth century popular residential districts in the major towns were inhabited by both the lower middle class and working classes. Spatial segregation only developed from the end of the century with the construction of middle- and upper-class neighbourhoods outside the old centres and proletarian dwelling quarters on the periphery. Work structures were also transformed during these years with the advance of capitalist methods of production. This happened not only in the most obviously industrial sectors of the economy; given the slow pace of Spanish industrialisation, artisanal methods of production tended to remain in place longer than in more advanced capitalist states, but nevertheless, as elsewhere, the imposition of market criteria led to an erosion of artisans' position within the labour process. The result was a widening gulf between masters and men within the skilled sector of the economy. This process probably first manifested itself in Barcelona, but even in Madrid, which contained a bloated service sector and a large class of functionaries combined with a relative scarcity of core industrial activities, a new proletarian city grew up around the populist centre between 1890 and 1930.[3]

As in other parts of Europe, skilled artisanal workers were in the strongest position to form trade unions; thus in cities such as Barcelona and Valencia there was a long tradition of trade union organisation. In other sectors of the economy the power of the local employers, divisions within the labour force and/or the lack of class consciousness made unionisation far more difficult. Employers' strategies in rural areas included the formation of company towns in order to ensure a captive labour force; this could be seen in the Catalan cotton textile industry for example.[4] Even in an urban environment, large-scale employers were able to set up paternalistic-authoritarian regimes and – at least until the years 1910–1914 – keep trade unions at bay. This was the case, for example, with the Vizcayan steel magnates.[5] The rural labourers of the south were also highly dependent on the landowners.

It was on the great estates that revolutionary ideologies found fertile soil, but even so protest by the peasantry was sporadic until the Second Republic (1931–1936). The reasons were partly a result of working conditions. Landless labourers were usually employed on a daily basis, and were therefore particularly vulnerable to victimisation. In addition work was unskilled, and in conditions of almost permanent underemployment substitute labour could usually be found.[6] Finally, the Spanish working classes were marked out by their low incomes, which were further affected by high food prices, a consequence of the imposition of tariff barriers on imported wheat, and heavy indirect taxes. At the turn of the century the southern labourers lived in dire poverty, but in cities such as Barcelona and Madrid even most artisanal workers lived near the poverty line.[7] Conditions were to improve little until the 1930s.

The organisations of the working class also had to contend with the Spanish state. As has often been stressed, the dominant tradition within Spanish liberalism was highly authoritarian. The Cánovas Restoration (1875–1923) strongly defended the interests of Spain's social elites. The military continued to play an important role in public life, and the legality and legitimacy of trade unions was insecure. The state was also slow to introduce social reforms, and was then unable effectively to enforce the provisions of these reforms. In part this was a consequence of the proverbial penury of the Spanish state. Not only was the country relatively poor in European terms, but the government was also reluctant to significantly tax social elites. In these circumstances, it is not surprising that the state barely tried to establish cultural hegemony through the development of a programme of elementary education which might instill a sense of common national identity, or to integrate the working classes into public life. Instead, elites continued to rely on the teaching of the reactionary Catholic Church to maintain social control.[8]

Furthermore, where possible the lower classes were deliberately excluded from the political process by the operation of *caciquismo*. The so-called *caciques* were local political bosses who in return for favours would get the government's preferred candidate elected. As a result, even though universal male suffrage was theoretically reinstated in 1890 (it had operated briefly between 1868–1873), the government of the day was ensured a large parliamentary majority. *Caciquismo* worked most effectively in rural areas, where landowners and their agents had a great deal of power over the local population.[9] In the south at the same time, landowners rejected any interference in their 'right' to run their estates as they saw fit. Their aversion to labour unions was accentuated by the fact that the profitability of the *latifundia* system was based on the payment of breadline wages.[10] However, such practices were not only to be found in rural Spain; a combination of the authoritarian liberal tradition and the economic difficulties faced by industrialists who were to a large extent dependent on the underdeveloped home market made many little disposed to tolerate trade unions. This attitude could for example be seen in Barcelona where, especially after a rash of strikes in 1902, larger manufacturers in particular accused the Restoration governments of being too soft on strikers and adopted a corporatist ideology.[11]

The combined result of these factors was, not surprisingly, a high degree of alienation of workers from society and its institutions. Nineteenth-century urban Spain was punctuated by popular riots against the authorities. The prime target of the crowds' hatred was often the ultra-conservative Catholic Church.[12] Nor, as in many western countries, could the state rely on imperial adventures and colonial conquest to generate a sense of national pride and identity with the regime; the Spanish military were singularly unsuccessful in their overseas adventures, leading to the development of a strong popular aversion to colonial wars.[13]

The Rise of Organised Labour, 1900–1923

It has often been stated that before 1914 the Spanish labour movement was characterised by its weakness. If by this it is meant that it had been extremely difficult because of state and employer opposition to develop powerful, stable union organisations, then this appreciation is correct. But this does not mean there was little opposition to the system; in the late nineteenth and early twentieth centuries, as has been suggested, much of this opposition was canalised through republicanism. In urban areas republicans were often involved in the formation of workers' cooperatives, mutual aid societies and recreational bodies; from the turn of the century in Barcelona and Valencia, radical, proletarianised republican parties made great efforts to tie workers to their organisations through ancillary cultural institutions.[14] The result was that, despite its inter-class ideology, republicanism played a key role in building a working-class sense of identity.

Purely working-class organisations did however develop from the 1870s onward. Anarchists or anarcho-syncialists as they should more properly be called, were during brief periods able to affiliate large numbers of workers from industrial Catalonia and in the western Andalusian provinces of Seville, Cádiz, Málaga and Córdoba. In Catalonia the anarcho-syndicalists gained the support of both industrial and skilled workers.[15] In Andalusia the landless and land-hungry labourers affiliated to anarcho-syndicalist unions, though the movement also gained the backing of industrial and skilled workers in the provincial capitals along with impoverished tenants, sharecroppers and even small-scale producers in more rural areas.[16] Meanwhile from the 1880s the Socialists, whose leadership was largely drawn from the Madrid printers, slowly began to establish a base first amongst the skilled workers of Madrid (which was to be the centre of Socialist organisation until the 1930s) and then amongst the workers of Bilbao, the iron ore miners of Vizcaya and the coal miners of Asturias.[17] Until 1936 these two very different groups would ferociously compete for working-class patronage.

The Socialist leadership had by the turn of the century adopted the Guesdist model of reformist union and political practice combined with revolutionary rhetoric, and looked slowly to build up the strength of their party and union within society. Hence they followed a moderate trade union strategy which aimed at limiting the use of the strike as a weapon, and they competed in municipal and national elections. In sharp contrast the anarcho-syndicalists combined militant direct action strike tactics aimed at provoking general strikes – with the view to eventually provoking a revolutionary general strike which would overthrow capitalism – with virulent anti-politicism and a total rejection of the possibility of ameliorative reforms within the framework of capitalism.

Despite these antecedents, union membership only began to grow rapidly as the economic climate improved after 1910 and then took off in the boom conditions of the First World War, when Spain was able to take advantage of her neutral position to supply the warring nations. By 1920 around half the workers in Spain's major cities were unionised.[18] This mobilisation was accompanied by a massive upsurge in strike activity, the flames of which were fanned by workers' attempts to maintain their living standards in the face of rapidly rising prices (see Table 7.1). These strikes first hit the larger industrial centres, but from 1919 in Andalusia, which had been quiescent since the early years of the century, there was a great burst of labour protest known as the Bolshevik Triennium.

The anarcho-syndicalists and socialists were able to incorporate most of this growth into their own labour federations. The surge in membership came not only in already established areas; the anarcho-syndicalists made rapid advances in Valencia and also established themselves strongly in the capital of Aragón, Zaragoza, and to a lesser extent in the region's rural areas.[19] The socialists also gained an important presence in southern Spain, particularly in the mining enclaves and in the provinces of Jaén and to a lesser extent Granada and Córdoba (where they competed for peasant support with the anarcho-syndicalists).[20] Indeed by the 1930s the socialists were stronger than the anarchists in rural Andalusia.

As a result of this growth by 1920 the Socialist Party (*Partido Socialista Obrero Español*-PSOE) had over 54,000 members, and its trade union wing the General Worker's Union (*Unión General de Trabajadores*-UGT) had over 200,000 affiliates. More spectacular was the expansion of the anarcho-syndicalist National Labour Confederation (*Confederación Nacional del Trabajo*-CNT) which at the end on 1919 had about 700,000 workers in its orbit.

Table 7.1. Strikes, Strikers and Working Days Lost in Spain, 1905–1934.

Year	Strikes	Strikers	Working Days Lost
1905–1907	370	112,596	
1908–1910	356	55,897	
1911–1913	490	142,776	3,678,218
1914–1916	409	176,740	3,816,078
1917–1919	835	359,104	7,605,111
1920–1922	1086	447,792	12,736,628
1923–1925	730	209,432	4,471,472
1926–1928	287	162,491	2,330,327
1929–1931	1232	539,153	7,901,685
1932–1934	2402	1,853,407	29,145,460

Sources: Instituto de Reformas Sociales, *Estadística de Huelgas, 1905–1922* (Madrid, 1906–1923); Ministerio de Trabajo, Comercio e Industria, *Estadística de Huelgas, 1923–1929* (Madrid, 1924–1930); Ministerio de Trabajo y Previsión Social, *Estadística de Huelgas, 1930–1934* (Madrid, 1934–1936); Josep Lluís Martín Ramos, "Anàlisi del moviment vaguístic a Barcelona (1914–1923)", in *Recerques*, No. 20, (1988), p. 110.

In order to improve the statistics the official figures for Barcelona city for the years 1914–1923 have been replaced by those elaborated by Martín Ramos (1988), which are the result of an exhaustive study of newspapers of the period.

From 1910 and particularly during the war years, faced with this unprecedented mobilisation of labour, employers looked to form regional or even national organisations in order to defend their interests. Hence, the populist political tradition, still dominant in the 1900s, increasingly gave way to the politics of class, with the result that the republican parties were to a large extent eclipsed by purely working-class organisations. Yet under the impact of growing labour agitation and given the favourable economic conditions, some groups of employers previously reluctant to recognise labour unions were now obliged to negotiate. The UGT was able to take advantage of this fact; in 1913 the Asturian coal companies accepted the socialist miners' union (*Sindicato Minero Asturiano*-SMA) as labour's bargaining agent,[21] similarly, from 1910 the socialists moved into the Vizcaya steel mills where they also established collective bargaining procedures.[22] This growth naturally led to a change in the structure of the UGT. A paid union bureaucracy had began to emerge during the first decade of the century and this was consolidated during the war years; in mining and metallurgy, centralised industrial labour federations were built.[23]

This tendency towards negotiation was even visible within the dominant Catalan branch of the CNT. This seems at first sight a surprising development for since the 1890s the anarcho-syndicalists had followed a policy of general strikes at all costs. The reason for this change is to be found in the rapid growth of the organisation from 1916, which made even committed anarcho-syndicalist union activists proud of the edifice they had built and consequently wary of putting the organisation in jeopardy through rash strikes. As part of this push to develop the union and conduct strikes more efficiently the anarchists formed their own industrial federations (the so-called *Sindicatos Unicos*), though unlike the UGT these only operated at a local level. At the same time at the 1918 Sants congress the Catalan leadership, whose principal figure was Salvador Seguí, toned down the movement's anarchist credentials in order to maximise support.[24] Nevertheless, union organisers in general remained more militant than their UGT counterparts, and it proved almost impossible to control a body that was growing at breakneck speed and being flooded by the previously non-unionised.[25]

The context was to change drastically when, with the end of the wartime bonanza, employers struck back by attempting to both cut costs and undermine the unions. Strikes became bitter and protracted. In Asturias employers reacted to the post-war recession by undermining established work practices;[26] Barcelona was shaken by the great Canadiense strike in the electricity generating industry at the beginning of 1919, and thereafter employers launched an all out offensive co-opting the regional military hierarchy in order to annihilate the CNT.[27] In Madrid, the city's leading industry, construction, had already been badly affected by the rise in price of raw materials during the war, and between 1917 and 1919 there were general strikes in printing and the food industry and a lock-out in construction.[28] In Andalusia from the spring of 1919 the central state resolutely backed the local bourgeoisie, declaring states of emergency and closing down union headquarters.[29]

As both socialists and anarchists developed the organised labour movement they also tried to tie workers more effectively to their organisations by structuring their own labour culture. Like their colleagues in the Second International (and the Barcelona and Valencian republicans), from the first decade of the century the Socialists founded so-called *Casas del Pueblo* (Houses of the People) which encompassed consumer cooperatives, offices for affiliated unions, a small library and space for recreational activities, and at the same time began providing mutual benefits through their unions.[30] Unfortunately, detailed studies of Socialist sub-culture in Spain are missing. What evidence there is suggests that the party's Madrid leadership laid stress on sobriety and prudence, with the 'grandfather' of Spanish Socialism, Pablo Iglesias – president of both the PSOE and UGT from 1899 until his death in 1925 – held out as the example to be followed.

This culture was reproduced in all Western social democratic parties from the turn of the century. It seems to have been an extension of the culture of the skilled worker (on which all these movement's were originally based) with its emphasis on respectability, though exaggerated by the sacrifice and dedication which the union and party activist had to endure in order first to become educated and then build the organisation, and refracted through the reformist trade union strategy which the Socialists pursued. This could make sense in an area like Madrid, where until the Second Republic the PSOE-UGT was largely based on artisans, though even here frequent Socialist complaints against drinking indicate that the base often did not live up to the leadership's ideal.[31] In Madrid this culture of respectability, combined with relatively high union dues, ensured that the socialist milieu would be very much centred on the male breadwinner in fixed employ. Yet, as we have seen, the Socialists also recruited in very different worlds such as the rural south, amongst workers who could have little sympathy with or understanding of this culture, and who were, as we shall see, frequently to be out of tune with the Madrid leadership.

Anarchist culture was far more diffuse. The anarcho-syndicalists opposed union actions such as opening cooperatives or offering benefits because they argued such practices would only serve to blunt the revolutionary impetus of the workers; they therefore limited themselves to setting up 'rationalist schools' and libertarian athenaeums which in fact educated relatively few workers.[32] Instead, they relied for support on the presence of militants at work and in the neighbourhood, backed by the press and pamphlets, and their ability to galvanise the support of the community around strike demands and, particularly by the 1930s, wider issues such as the level of rents.[33] In urban Spain this was linked to a difference in the space occupied by both movements, for while the Socialist leadership looked to negotiate, the anarchists' major field of operations was the street, where workers were to be mobilised against the bourgeoisie.[34] The result would be, as will be seen, that at least in urban Spain anarchists often recruited workers in the sectors of the economy where there was most conflict and, by the Second Republic, especially amongst unskilled immigrant labour.

Despite these divergences both socialist and anarchist cultures were male-dominated. As in other European countries, working-class women mostly worked as domestics, homeworkers and as unskilled factory hands (particularly in cotton textiles). The socialist and anarchist labour federations argued that in order to maintain their independence women should work, yet at a grass roots level men had largely adopted the bourgeois ideal of the woman as housewife and mother. Women, it was conceded, could work while young in order to help their parents, but once they were married it was hoped they would retire to the domestic sphere, though it was grudgingly conceded they might have to work because of low male incomes.[35] In these circumstances it was not surprising that few women were unionised. The UGT unions were probably the worst in this respect. Anarcho-syndicalist trade unionists could be more open, but they still generally believed that women should not be employed if there was unemployment amongst male workers. Nor was this perspective generally rejected by the women themselves.

This is not to say, however, that women played no role in social protest. In strikes in the cotton textile industry they showed themselves to be at least as radical as their male colleagues. In Catalonia they also actively participated in anti-militaristic and anti-clerical rioting during Tragic Week in 1909. However, it is probably true to say that women were most involved in protests which centred on the sphere of consumption and which therefore fitted most closely with what they saw as their primary role as providers for the family. Hence throughout urban Spain between 1916–1919 women were at the forefront of actions against the rising cost of living, and were prominent in attacks on bakeries.[36] The urban working class woman does not therefore appear – as some male labour leaders claimed – to have been more religious or conservative than her male counterpart. She shared the popular and working-class radical culture, yet at the same time largely accepted man's primacy at work.

The evolution of the labour movement during this period raises two major questions. First, how was it that the left was able to incorporate almost the entire union movement into its fold? Second, what were the reasons behind the continued division of the left, and in particular for the buoyancy of the anarchist tradition?

The first question clearly needs to be related to the high degree of alienation from state and society mentioned previously. Both the low standard of living and the narrowness of the political system made it difficult for well-organised strata of workers to emerge who were willing to operate within the confines of the established order. The only union of these characteristics to exist in Spain was the Three Steam Classes (*Tres Classes de Vapor*, TCV) a large textile federation that was at its height in Catalonia between 1868–1891. The TCV was very much reformist in nature, being inspired by the English 'New Model' unions and Broussist Possibilism, but this did not prevent it from being all but destroyed in a joint state-employer offensive in the early 1890s.[37]

The relative weakness of trade federations before 1914 also meant that skill divisions were often not formally institutionalised; hence there was relatively little opposition to UGT and CNT attempts to integrate workers within industrial unions. At a cultural and ideological level, moreover, the work of the left was facilitated because the wider working-class community generally shared its world view, regarding the state with suspicion and the Church as the enemy, and increasingly taking for granted the inevitable conflict of interests between labour and capital. Hence, while there were of course great differences between the skilled and unskilled, and between rural and urban workers, the general hostility of the employers and state, along with the low standard of living, meant that most workers could be integrated within leftist organisations at an economic and political level.

The reverse of this coin was the limited efforts made by elites to integrate labour. One important consequence of this was the almost total failure of Catholic unions. By the time these began to operate from the 1900s the atmosphere was already adverse; but things were made much worse by the fact that the Catholic hierarchy blocked the operation of independent Catholic unions which might have genuinely defended workers' interests. On the contrary, the unions favoured by the hierarchy were subordinate to employers and stressed religious rather than social activities. There could therefore be no repetition of events in Germany and Belgium, where large Catholic parties with a strong union base could divide the labour movement.[38]

The reasons behind the continued strength of anarchism in working-class circles is a complex question. One interpretation which gained significant currency was the argument that anarchism was particularly well suited to the 'millenarian' Andalusian peasantry, and that Andalusian immigrants then spread the message to Catalonia.[39] However, the very diversity of the working-class base of socialism and anarchism would seem to explode any such explanations. In fact anarchism took root in Catalonia before there was significant immigration from the south while, as we have noted, the Socialists were able to affiliate growing numbers of southern peasants from 1918–1919. In addition, more recent research has emphasised that Andalusian labourers did not in semi-religious fashion simply down tools in anticipation of the 'great day', but, like industrial workers, mobilised behind specific demands.

Certainly chance played a part in the spatial distribution of anarchism and socialism. Anarcho-syndicalists were the first to establish a trade union base in Catalonia and Andalusia. On the other hand, before the arrival of the Socialists the skilled workers of Madrid and the mine workers in Vizcaya and Asturias were practically unorganised. Hence, the Socialists rapidly came to be seen as the representatives of the entire working class.[40]

Nevertheless, it would be difficult to accept this simple explanation only. Recent explanations of patterns of militancy within a particular nation-state have tended to emphasise the overall economic and institutional setting, and this seems a fruitful way of approaching the Spanish case. Here a key factor limiting the Socialist's advance was probably the difficulties the socialist faced in promoting their social democratic political and union practice in the context of the Restoration. As a consequence of their policies, the Socialists often appealed to what may be termed the labourist wing of the movement: workers in relatively strong unions who had developed collective bargaining practices with their employers, or in sectors of the economy where class conflict was not particularly severe. Thus between 1899 and 1911 the heart of the Madrid UGT, the bricklayers' union *El Trabajo*, organised most of the workers in the trade and operated a closed shop.[41] More generally, the reformist strategy of the Madrid Socialists operated effectively in a context in which class divisions were still somewhat muted.[42] Similarly in Barcelona from the late nineteenth century the Socialists became linked with more moderate sectors of the labour movement, and during the Second Republic, workers in both banking and commerce joined the UGT.[43]

Between 1914 and 1918 socialist practice also seemed well suited to the Asturian mining and Basque steel industries. In these industries, as has been seen, employers were willing to negotiate. Moreover, the Socialists were able to appeal to the state to enforce agreements reached in those sectors of the economy in which working conditions were relatively homogeneous.[44] This was made possible by the contradictory policies pursued by the Restoration state; it dealt with revolutionary threats ruthlessly yet, because of the growing crisis of the Restoration after the Spanish-American War of 1898, governments made concessions to labour in order to maintain social peace. They were particularly to do so in the case of the Socialists, who were seen as a more responsible opposition force.[45]

However, in areas where unions were weak, working conditions were localised and/or social conflict was severe, the UGT's union practice could appear as inappropriate. In these areas it was often only through the mobilisation of the entire labour force of a trade, industry or even locality that employers could be intimidated into making concessions, and in these circumstances anarchist direct action tactics might make more sense. This pattern was apparent in rural Andalusia before the Second Republic, where short bursts of union activity were followed by employer and state counter-attacks which totally broke the back of the unions.[46] In industrial Catalonia before 1914 a quite similar pattern of boom followed by bust can be perceived, with anarchists gaining strongest support from workers in conflict-ridden industries such as metallurgy and construction.[47]

This picture is however complicated by two closely related factors. First, the intensification of class conflict in an industry dominated by the UGT could lead to a radicalisation of the trade union base and put the leadership's tactics in question. As we shall see, this actually happened in the Asturian mining and Madrid construction industries. Second, socialist militants, who were essentially union organisers, were to a degree willing to adapt to local patterns of labour agitation even if this meant reworking official UGT policy. The result could also be tension between militant local unions and the UGT hierarchy; before 1914 this was most notably the case in the socialist-dominated iron ore mining unions of Vizcaya where violent, generalised protest action was resorted to in order to wring out concessions.[48] A similar pattern was subsequently repeated in the rural south.

The PSOE was to face a number of similar problems at a political level. In the early years Socialists had to face strong republican opposition. In Madrid, where they built up a powerful union base, this could finally be overcome,[49] but where the anarchists maintained a strong union presence, the socialists found it difficult to compete. Antagonism was however much attenuated from 1910 when the party leadership abandoned its former isolationism and signed an alliance (*conjunción*) with various republican groupings, with the result that the socialists were able to use their higher profile to extend their influence.

From 1916 the growing strength of labour and the crisis of the Restoration held out the hope of real political change. In many localities it seemed possible for the first time to break the power of the *caciques*. Workers therefore had a positive reason to vote. Nevertheless the results were modest: in 1918 the PSOE still had only 7 MPs. The immobilism of the Spanish state could still generate support for the more unambiguously revolutionary alternative provided by the anarchists, whilst the paucity of social legislation could make believable the anarchist claim that the bourgeois state was not reformable. Furthermore, given the operation of *caciquismo* and the lack of reform, there was still much scepticism regarding the utility of elections, which could also be exploited by the anarchists.

This difficulty in reforming the system also created pressure for the PSOE to radicalise its stance. This was seen in August 1917 when, despite its better judgement, the PSOE-UGT leadership, along with the CNT, felt it had little choice but to call a general strike to try and overthrow the Restoration. The bloody consequences made the Socialist leaders shy away from further revolutionary action. On the other hand, the repression produced extreme bitterness amongst working-class militants and stimulated the development of a current of leftist opposition within the organisation.[50] This opposition grew in strength during 1918–1920 as the climate throughout Central and Western Europe became increasingly revolutionary, and was further stimulated by the escalation of social conflict in Spain.

The left's battle cry was the dissolution of the *conjunción* and adherence to the Bolshevik Third International. The PSOE-UGT hierarchy was however able to ensure the organisation remained in their hands and so in 1921 these leftists formed their own Communist Party (*Partido Comunista Español*, PCE). The party's union base was essentially made up of the militant Vizcayan iron ore miners, a radicalised sector of the Asturian SMA and groups of largely young workers from a number of Madrid trades. However, the deepening recession ensured that workers in unions less well organised than the SMA generally accepted the UGT's strategy of containment. At the same time, with the prospect of revolution ever more distant, enthusiasm waned, especially given the authorities harsh response to the appearance of communism. Therefore when in 1923 General Miguel Primo de Rivera carried out his *coup d'etat* the communists had hardly had time to establish a solid presence.[51] Similarly within the Catalan CNT, spiralling social conflict also produced a radicalisation of the organisation and in this case put paid to any timid step towards reformism. The offensive launched by employers and the local military against the Catalan CNT led men like Seguí to lose control of the confederation. From the summer of 1919 a dirty war was conducted against the CNT; gunmen were recruited from the rightist Free Syndicates to eliminate leading *Cenetistas*, and Seguí was himself to fall victim in March 1923. Gone as a result was the possibility that the CNT might evolve in a more purely trade-unionist direction; on the contrary, anarchist gunmen and hard-liners were to become more prominent.[52]

Dictatorship, Democracy and Revolution, 1923–1939

The key to the success of the Primo coup was the growing belief amongst social elites that their interests were not sufficiently well protected under the Restoration system. Hence the anarchists and Communists were banned. Nevertheless, an attempt was made to secure social stability by coopting the socialists into a system of parity committees composed of representatives of labour, capital and the government.[53]

The deal was rejected by the republican-democratic wing of the PSOE but was supported by the UGT leadership, who saw it as a way of conserving the organisation and stealing a march on its working-class opponents. It was these *ugetistas* who were to get their way. Their success reflected the growing power of the trade unions within the socialist movement given the limited role the PSOE could play within the Spanish state. In practical terms the *ugetistas* were justified in this, for while the anarchists and communists were decimated the socialists were able to maintain their strength, with the result that when the monarchy entered into crisis in 1930 the socialists were the only highly developed organisation in Spain.[54]

The socialists were only to abandon tacit collaboration in the late 1920s when the dictatorship entered into crisis. The subsequent proclamation of a reforming Republic in which the state would play a positive role in improving workers' living conditions served enormously to enhance the socialists' prestige. Hence when general elections were held in June 1931 the PSOE became the largest party in the new parliament with 113 seats, and UGT membership shot up to over 1 million by 1932.[55] Throughout the Second Republic, the socialists were the leading labour organisation in the country.

From 1930 the republicans and socialists entered into a new alliance, and they now took over the reigns of government together. The socialists believed it was the task of the republicans to carry through a bourgeois democratic revolution and so gave them the lion's share of the ministries.[56] The UGT, however, demanded that the Ministry of Labour should be in its hands, and from this vantage point it looked to spearhead the integration of labour into the fabric of state and society. Hence the parity committees (now called *jurados mixtos*) were strengthened and extended into rural areas and welfare provisions were enhanced.[57] Particular emphasis was given to altering the balance of power in the rural South. This reflected both the continued importance of the land in Spain's social structure and the growing number of landworkers within the UGT itself.[58] The new government therefore immediately set out to improve the lot of the landless workers. Most importantly, after the June election victory an agrarian reform bill was drawn up which would redistribute part of the estates of the *latifundistas* to the peasantry. In this way the alliance between the petty bourgeoisie and working class, which had in the past served to win elections in Madrid and Bilbao, now began to operate on a national scale. As in the case of the *conjunción*, it was to be the escalation of class conflict which was to tear this alliance apart.

Class divisions ran deep, and much of the right was still opposed to the operation of free trade unions and, increasingly, to parliamentary democracy. These tensions were exacerbated by the depression which had spread throughout the Western world from 1929. By 1933 unemployment affected about 15 per cent of the urban and rural labour force. Additionally, workers had benefited little from the economic boom under the dictatorship. As in the past therefore, when the lid was taken off the social cauldron in 1930–1931 a wave of strikes ensued. The recession continued to deepen and by 1933 employers, their profit margins under threat, began to put up stiff resistance leading strikes to become increasingly intractable.[59]

It was in this context that the CNT was reborn, as hard-line militants were able to capitalise on the discontent in urban Catalonia, Aragon, and parts of Andalusia. The coming of the Republic, it should be stressed, served seriously to question basic anarchist tenets. It was now difficult to argue that elections were useless and all bourgeois regimes alike; furthermore, the scope provided for unions to operate might call into question the insurrectionary tradition. These problems were at the root of a division which opened up in the CNT between so-called *treintistas* and *faístas*. The *treintistas* were men of Salvador Seguí's generation, who put emphasis on the need to build up the unions; they also began to edge away from the anarchist heritage by extending benevolence to the Republic and not actively opposing worker participation in elections. The *faístas* on the other hand were often younger men forged in the bloody labour wars at the end of the Restoration. These young firebrands were in the anarchist tradition able to take advantage of the frustrations of a working class subject to repression and dictatorship in order to pursue their radical goals. The socialists and republicans, afraid that the unrest would discredit the Republic and interested in undermining the CNT, responded in a heavy-handed way; this weakened anarchist organisation, but also allowed militants to rehearse their argument that all bourgeois governments were basically alike. The result was that by 1933 the *faístas* had taken over the CNT and the *treintistas* were forced to set up their own opposition Unions (Sindicatos de Oposición).[60]

Within Catalonia, the break between *treintistas* and *faístas* also mirrored emerging ethno-skill divisions within the labour force. Since 1914 Catalonia had experienced considerable industrial development, leading to an influx of immigrants from outside the region. These immigrants inhabited the overcrowded flats and shanty towns that grew up on the edge of Barcelona, and worked as unskilled hands in construction, metallurgy and textiles. It was to the poorer sectors of the working class, which included a high proportion of immigrants, that the *faístas* largely appealed. During the 1930s the condition of these workers improved little; they were particularly affected by heavy unemployment, and with the republican governments pursuing traditional deflationary policies they continued to receive no unemployment benefits.[61] Other labour unions recruited to a greater degree amongst skilled Catalan workers. Within the more favourable context of the Republic skilled workers were now looking to work through the state and establish more stable bargaining relations with employers. Class conflict in the largely unskilled trades, however, remained raw and bitter.[62] This new pattern of spacial segregation and skill differential also found expression at a cultural level with *faístas* rejecting 'bourgeois morality' and supporting criminal activity – often a necessity in the poorest neighbourhoods – as a legitimate revolutionary weapon.[63]

It was not only anarchist-dominated areas that saw a radicalisation of parts of the labour movement. In Socialist-controlled areas the leadership also had difficulty keeping the rank-and-file in check, and in the rural south there was anger at the old oligarchy's ability to block reform legislation. Frustration was exacerbated by the slow passage of the agrarian reform bill through the house, and when it was finally approved in September 1932 the legislation proved slow and cumbersome to put into effect.[64] In Asturias, unrest was intensified by the fact that the coal industry was in European terms unproductive and had entered into a profound crisis; the SMA had been able to re-establish its dominance in the coalfield, but faced with the mine owners' determination to cut costs there were calls for more aggressive action.[65] In Madrid class conflict also escalated. As in many cities, the construction industry in Madrid became the focus of an often violent confrontation between newly-mobilised unskilled workers and the large companies which had grown up since the 1920s. In this atmosphere in 1933, the CNT was able to make inroads into the Spanish capital on the back of an aggressive campaign against lay-offs.[66]

This discontent soon fed into national politics, calling the continuance of the socialist-republican alliance into question. The UGT's Largo Caballero, along with the majority wing of the union's leadership responded to this pressure; unable – as before in 1921 – to keep rank-and-file militancy in check and afraid of being displaced within the labour movement, they simply radicalised their rhetoric, voicing their doubts as to the possibility of 'carrying out the work of socialism within the framework of bourgeois democracy'. In the aftermath of the left's electoral defeat of November 1933, comparisons were drawn with Russia in 1917 and there was talk of the need to 'take power'. The *Caballerista* wing of the Socialist Party maintained this revolutionary rhetoric until 1936.

The right's assault on the social reforms of 1931–1933 aggravated social tensions. Meanwhile, the rise of the fascist and authoritarian right in Europe served further to polarise society and politics. For a younger generation of workers who had become politically conscious in the 1930s, this seemed to invalidate social democratic party and union strategies, while at the same time because of the Western economic crisis the Soviet Union became a beacon of hope for many socialists.[67] This formed the background to the decision taken by the PSOE-UGT in October 1934 to call for a uprising against the government. There was no chance of success; even the precise objectives were unclear. However in Asturias, where the various working-class organisations were united, the uprising turned into a full-blown insurrection.[68]

Society was now so polarised that it would be difficult to avoid a civil war fought primarily on class lines. Once the war had begun, the radicalised working-class base of the CNT and much of the UGT pressed home a social revolution. Local organs of worker power were established, and most industry in Catalonia and agriculture in Aragon, Andalusia and Extremadura (until retaken by the Nationalists) was collectivised. This was essentially a trade union revolution, a reflection of the great power of the unions within the Spanish left.

This does not mean that the republican masses totally identified with the trade union leadership; in Barcelona there is some evidence that workers resisted union demands for higher productivity to satisfy the war effort, and there was opposition to collectivisation by smallholding peasants and sharecroppers in rural areas and the petty bourgeoisie in the cities.[69] These divisions fed into the debate on the place of war and revolution in the republican camp.

Because of the Republic's reliance on Soviet military supplies the PCE grew rapidly during the war. Following Stalin's lead, the PCE argued that the war had to be won before a social revolution could be carried through, and along with republicans and moderate socialists it began from 1937 to roll back the union revolution.[70] It has often been argued that for this reason during the war the PCE became a refuge for bourgeois afraid of social revolution. While there is some truth in this it was also the case that the Communists built up a strong working-class base made up of white-collar and other workers who during the Second Republic had been linked to more moderate sectors of the labour movement. This was clearest in Catalonia where a combination of depression, the anarchists' revolutionary adventurism, and support given by the regional Esquerra government to non-CNT unions ensured that on the eve of war affiliation to the Catalan CNT had dropped to under 150,000, while that of the UGT had grown to 80,000. These UGT unions were inherited by the Catalan Communist party, the PSUC, during the war.[71] It was on this base that the Communists would attempt to become the dominant opposition force under Franco.

Out of the Ashes: The Rebirth of Spanish Labour, 1939–1976

The defeat of the left was followed by massive repression. Following the Italian fascist model, independent unions were outlawed and replaced by a state union, the Spanish Syndical Organisation (*Organización Sindical Española*, OSE), which was staffed by bureaucrats belonging to the regime's single party, the FET de las JONS (or *Movimiento* as it was increasingly called). The OSE was hierarchically organised. At plant level both workers and employers had to affiliate, and working conditions were determined by the Ministry of Labour.

In the 1940s and the first half of the 1950s the Ministry ensured wage increases were kept well below the rate of inflation. On the other hand, in supposed compensation for the loss of bargaining rights, the Ministry introduced a number of benefits, in particular a level of job security unparalleled in the democratic Western world. In the rural south the regime ruthlessly imposed social control.[72] Urban workers put up more resistance, but by the late 1940s both the UGT and CNT had been almost totally dismantled.[73]

Yet the Franco regime did not become the haven of social peace that its supporters had assumed it would be. The following two and a half decades were to see a slow revival of labour unrest – sporadic and discontinuous at first – which by the early 1970s was to prove the greatest challenge with which the regime had to contend. Underlying this rebirth was the industrial growth of the Spanish economy in the 1960s. This growth followed the progressive abandonment of the regime's disastrous autarkic economic policies from the early 1950s, thereby allowing Spain to become part of the western economic boom. Rapid economic growth of course also brought in its wake massive structural and social change; first, there was a rapid transfer of people and resources from countryside to town, and second, Spain witnessed startling rates of urban growth with much of the country's population concentrated into a small number of industrial and commercial centres. There were also fundamental shifts in Spain's industrial structure. Most Spanish enterprises remained small-scale, but for the first time major concerns employing in excess of 1,000 workers and often linked to multi-national capital were superimposed.[74]

Economic development brought with it higher incomes. Working-class living standards rose by an average of 232 per cent between 1950–1975, and workers were increasingly drawn into the new consumer society. Yet these improvements were bought at the cost of long working hours and a substantial intensification of work. Moreover, in the tradition of its authoritarian predecessors, the regime did little to extend the tax base and government spending as a percentage of GDP remained extremely low in European terms. This was reflected in the social wage; when in the 1940s and 1950s immigrants flooded into the cities, many had to live in shanty towns on the periphery. In the 1960s these were increasingly replaced by massive, often poorly constructed, tenement blocks, but the residents of these satellite cities lacked urban, social and recreational facilities. In 1970 Spanish workers were therefore still considerably worse off than most of their Western counterparts.[75]

The industrial transformation of Spain ensured that in the future social conflict would take a very different path from that of the 1930s. As the importance of agriculture in the national economy declined and the southern wheat lands became mechanised they were emptied of landless labourers. Hence the titanic struggle between the *braceros* and *señoritos* became a thing of the past, with the result that Spanish society itself became far less radically polarised; this made it easier to build a consensus in favour of democratic reform. In urban areas industrial growth had the effect of slowly altering the balance of power within society. Strike waves in Barcelona and Vizcaya in 1951 were protests against the poverty and drudgery of post-war Spain; workers in 1956 and 1957 were more assertive when strikes were called in the main industrial centres for wage increases to cover the rising cost of living.

Yet protest was still only sporadic. It was of course hampered by fear of persecution: participation in strikes could and often did result in dismissal. In addition, the *Movimiento* bureaucracy tried to tie workers to the OSE through welfare benefits, recreational facilities and a system of labour lawyers to help pursue claims with the Ministry of Labour. In the major cities, divisions between the large immigrant labour force and natives also retarded action; in Greater Barcelona, as in the 1930s, in metallurgy and chemicals, Catalans tended to work in a supervisory capacity or in skilled posts while immigrants were employed in the unskilled jobs on the shop floor. These newly arrived masses were usually too concerned simply with survival to worry about collective action.[76]

It was only in the 1960s, and particularly from 1967, that labour protest became more sustained. From 1973–1976 Spain experienced a strike wave almost unparalleled in Europe (see Table 7.2). Unrest was at first largely based in the traditional industrial centres of Asturias, Vizcaya and Barcelona, but from the second half of the decade Madrid became more active along with the smaller industrial nuclei. In Asturias unrest amongst

Table 7.2. Strikes, Strikers and Working Days Lost in Spain, 1966–1992.[77]

Years	Disputes	Strikers	Working Days Lost
1966–68	1097	–	661,381
1969–71	2702	889,073	2,511,648
1972–74	4074	1,320,449	3,416,468
1975–77	–	6,512,354	26,706,631
1978–80	–	11,846,369	51,053,899
1981–83	–	–	12,304,300[a]
1984–86	3504	4,561,300	11,860,700[b]
1987–89	3739	9,955,540	20,351,500[c]
1990–92	3993	7,694,922	12,516,200

Sources: Sebastian Balfour, *Dictatorship, Workers and the City: Labour in Greater Barcelona since 1939*, Oxford, 1989, p. 143; J.A. Sargadoy and D. León Blanco *El Poder Sindical en España*, Barcelona, 1982; *El País*, 23 May 1993

[a] Figures do not include Catalonia.
[b] Figures for 1984 and 1985 do not include Catalonia, figures for 1986 do not include the Basque Country.
[c] Figures do not include the Basque Country.

the miners was largely a response to the continuance of the economic crisis in the industry, which led to several waves of cost-cutting and redundancies. In other areas, however, strikes tended to reflect the rising expectations of an increasingly self-confident working class, composed to a large extent of a new generation of workers who had not experienced the horrors of Civil War or the privations of the 1940s. These were most widespread in the steel and metallurgy industry which accounted for nearly 50 per cent of the strikes in the country between 1963 and 1974.[78]

The social upheavals of these years destroyed old communities and ways of life, but they also laid the basis for a reforging of working-class identity. On the periphery of cities like Barcelona and Madrid, vast new industrial areas sprang up where before there had only been small towns or even agricultural and waste land. It was in these 'red belts' that a new working-class culture was forged, aided in the 1960s by the crystallisation of a more homogeneous semi-skilled labour force in the large industrial concerns, which went some way to overcoming divisions between the skilled and the unskilled.

New immigrants had also adapted to their surroundings by the end of the decade; many had found factory employment and were now entering *en masse* into collective disputes. This helps explain the explosion of militancy amongst unskilled construction workers from 1971. These workers were joined by other categories of unskilled labour, and by white-collar workers such as bank employees and teachers, who began to unionise and take action for the first time since the Second Republic. Corporatist tendencies were by no means absent. For example, in the large Barcelona metallurgical enterprises, workers' efforts centred on securing favourable plant agreements with their employers, and little energy was expended on bringing the wage levels of workers in smaller enterprises up to their level.

There were nevertheless several countervailing influences. In the first place, struggles not only centred on the place of work; urban deprivation often led to the formation of vociferous neighbourhood associations which campaigned for improved services. Secondly, the impact of repression and demands for the legalisation of independent unions united workers in a common cause. It was in the predominantly blue-collar urban environments of areas like Baracaldo, Getafe and the Baix Llobregat that this cooperation would be greatest.[79]

The emerging labour movement remained strongly male-oriented. The Franco regime was steeped in conservative Catholic family values, and actively strove to exclude married women from the labour force. This simply reinforced the gender division of labour as well as patriarchal family structures. A growing number of women entered the labour market in the 1960s, but they continued to work in low-paid, unskilled sectors, which union organisers found difficult (and in general made little effort) to reach. Moreover women, if possible, still left work upon getting married. As a result, in 1970 women only represented 19.6 per cent of the economically active population.

Nevertheless, the 1960s did see working-class women beginning to play a more active role in the public sphere. They were in the vanguard of the protest by the neighbourhood associations. These years also saw the re-emergence of feminism in Spain, and these ideas were taken up in left-wing circles. Women drawn into leftist politics at this time were far less likely to accept their assigned role as wife and mother. It seems significant in this respect that a study of 324 shop stewards from Madrid and Barcelona by Robert Fishman in 1981 should reveal that 11 per cent of the (generally younger) communist-leaning *Comisiones Obreras* shop stewards were women, compared to only 1 per cent of UGT shop stewards. Overall, however, new attitudes were slow to penetrate the working-class household, and during the transition to democracy the labour movement was still to a large extent a male preserve.[80]

In order to understand how sustained protest became possible within an authoritarian political framework, we need to look in more detail at the industrial relations system. The OSE was, as we have seen, controlled by the *Movimiento*. To build up a power base within the working class, and thereby shore up their position against other elements within the regime who wished to downgrade their status, the *Movimiento* functionaries tried to develop networks of patronage by co-opting labour leaders. They were also prepared to make some concessions to labour and introduce reforms allowing a degree of worker representation.

The big change came in 1958 with the approval of the Law of Collective Agreements, which for the first time allowed for local collective bargaining between workers' representatives and management. Additionally, from 1962, 'economic' strikes were no longer regarded as criminal actions. The change was, it seems, approved at the highest level because it was felt that in the new more liberal economic climate wages should be determined locally rather than by the state. Many employers were at first opposed and hence ironically, as during the Primo de Rivera dictatorship, found themselves reluctantly negotiating with labour in a right-wing authoritarian regime. As the economic boom intensified, employers in the more dynamic industries came to accept plant and local negotiations as long as wage increases were accompanied by productivity agreements. This was the background to the great proliferation of collective agreements in the 1960s.[81]

These reforms provided the workers with real opportunities to influence working conditions, but the *Movimiento*'s dream of building a strong working-class base soon proved to be an illusion. The *Movimiento*'s lukewarm support for workers' demands allowed independents and even members of the clandestine opposition to be elected onto the factories works committees. Moreover, given the strict limits applied to collective bargaining (if an agreement was not reached a settlement could still be imposed by the Ministry of Labour), some workers began to mobilise outside the structures of the OSE. It was in this context that the Workers' Commissions (*Comisiones Obreras*, CC.00) were to make their appearance. These had their origin in factory committees set up spontaneously during strikes in 1962, and from 1964 they took on a more permanent form. Affiliates and sympathisers combined work within the OSE with the organisation of semi-clandestine local industry-wide committees and area commissions. Finally, in 1967, a national leadership emerged.

Between 1962–1966 as a consequence of the regime's policy of *apertura* (opening) designed to promote a positive image to the outside world, the Workers' Commissions were able to operate relatively openly, and had considerable success, both in channelling worker discontent (though by no means all labour protest took place within the bounds of the *Comisiones*) and colonising the lower echelons of the OSE (at the higher levels the *Movimiento* bureaucrats were protected by a complex system of indirect elections). However, by 1967 it had become clear that they could present a serious threat to the regime. This led to a crackdown, and the leadership had to move underground. In addition, a wage freeze declared in November undermined the organisation's negotiating role.

Yet with the massive upsurge in labour protest from 1969, CC.OO were rapidly to revive. From this date, they cleverly combined economic demands with political calls for the legalisation of free trade unions. These were demands to which workers could relate and which at the same time called into question the whole system. From 1973–1976 labour agitation escalated further with the frequent declaration of 'area general strikes' which brought out the entire working population of clusters of towns or whole cities. These strikes often began as economic disputes but were aggravated by police repression and/or the sacking or arrest of union delegates.[82]

By this time the whole industrial relations system was breaking down. In the Baix Llobregat in the Greater Metropolitan Area of Barcelona, for example, workers were actually declaring strikes from within the official union headquarters. The workers' movement now formed the spearhead of a broad opposition front of progressive Catholics, students and nationalists who were paralysing the Francoist system. Employers also found their profit margins squeezed, particularly after the oil price rises of 1973/74, and they were thereafter confronted by a gathering economic recession. The job security provisions enshrined in the regime's labour laws already contradicted capitalist rationality, and if the system could not protect the employers from widespread labour unrest then it was worse than useless.

By 1974 the Franco regime was patently unable to do this. It was on the defensive and had no popular credibility. The government was, therefore, hardly likely to make an incomes policy stick, and it feared the social consequences of adopting an overtly deflationary economic strategy. The left certainly had no reason to rein in its working-class supporters unless political concessions were forthcoming. A further massive increase in strikes in 1976 in response to inflationary pressures along with an attempt to impose a pay freeze apparently convinced many in the social elite that their best interests would be served by sweeping the whole Francoist system aside. This made possible for the first time in Spanish history a broad inter-class alliance in favour of democratic reform.[83]

The Left from Dictatorship to Democracy

Both the major labour organisations of the Second Republic, the CNT and PSOE-UGT, found it difficult to come to terms with the new conditions imposed by the Nationalist victory. The Socialists, given their experience of Stalinism during the Civil War, adopted a virulently anti-communist stance and pinned their hopes on an Allied intervention to oust Franco. Yet by the mid-1950s this was patently an illusion. The lot of the anarchists was no happier. Already during the Civil War they had been rent asunder by the contradiction between the need to collaborate with the Republican authorities, and their anti-statist ideology. Under Franco they divided between anti-political purists and syndicalists willing to cooperate with the rest of the opposition. Furthermore, with little political (and therefore monetary) support outside Spain, they were very much isolated in a world which largely saw their beliefs as an anachronism.

The two organisations' labour strategy fared little better. Following the failure of their attempt to rebuild their organisations inside Spain in the 1940s, they retreated into their shell. Traumatised by the Civil War defeat, they refused to operate within the OSE, arguing that participation would only serve to legitimise the regime.[84]

It was this isolationism which gave the Communists the opportunity to extend their influence. From 1948 the PCE had adopted the policy of infiltrating the OSE. After the approval of the Law of Collective Agreements and the growth of *Comisiones* this strategy was to prove effective, particularly when combined with the party's attempt to throw off its Stalinist past by adopting Eurocommunism.[85]

Comisiones were in their origin a pluralist force. From the mid-1960s, however, communist influence became more pronounced. In some respects, *Comisiones* took up the heritage of the CNT (indeed they were largely dominant in the same areas as the CNT in the 1930s). They combined a weak central organisation with the power to mobilise whole factories or even regions. Yet the Communists were far better equipped to lead the movement in the context of Francoism than the anarchists could ever be; they were prepared to operate within the OSE (ideological anathema to the anarchists), and had a hard core of clandestine militants hierarchically organised, thereby making it difficult for the regime totally to dismember the movement. These organisational considerations along with the ideological factors mentioned previously explain why the PCE emerged in the 1970s as the most powerful opposition force, solidly implanted in the working class, while the CNT remained only a pale shadow of its former self.

Nevertheless, the control exercised by the PCE should not be over-estimated. Again like the CNT in many ways, the CC.OO remained a movement with a core of militant activists and a large diffuse pool of sympathisers. These participated to a greater or lesser extent in the CC.OO because they felt it was the only organisation to defend their interests effectively. However, this by no means indicated that they were committed communists.

This could be seen during the transition to democracy. From the mid-

1950s the communists hoped to use the *Comisiones* to organise a general strike in order to bring down the regime, yet they were never able effectively to organise a nationwide political strike. This was perhaps not surprising; many workers were still outside the reach of the opposition. More importantly perhaps, most were unwilling to risk a cataclysmic confrontation with the state. This was not after all the downtrodden proletariat of the rural south active in the 1930s; a significant proportion of heads of household by the late 1960s were home owners and had experienced a rapid improvement in living standards. Furthermore, after the death of Franco in November 1975 it quickly became apparent that under pressure the political elites were prepared to introduce far-reaching democratic reforms.[86]

It was in this context that the Socialist Party was able to re-emerge rapidly as a major force on the Spanish left. Between 1970 and 1974 the Socialist old guard was ousted and replaced by a younger, more dynamic team, under the leadership of the Sevilian labour lawyer Felipe González. At first, verbally at least, this group seemed highly radical, but as the decade progressed their practice became increasingly moderate. In 1979, the PSOE dropped Marxism and adopted a clearly social democratic programme.

When from July 1976, under prime minister Adolfo Suárez, the regime showed itself willing to negotiate a transition to democracy, both Socialists and Communists agreed in return to drop their demands for a total dismantling of the Francoist state and the formation of a provisional government, and allow the elites' economic and social power base to remain largely intact.[87] This was in part a consequence of the balance of power within society; Francoists could still, after all, call on the army if the need arose. It was also the result of thirty years of stable democratic institutions in Western Europe. Though a diffuse anti-capitalist sentiment could be perceived in working-class circles, throughout most of society Western political institutions (allied to Western lifestyles) were seen as the ideal.

The shift was, however, easier to make for the Socialists than for the Communists. By dropping its militant republicanism and accepting (at least in the short term) the continuance not only of the capitalist system but, with the October 1977 Moncloa Pacts, an austerity package to restore the profitability of Spanish industry, the PCE lost its revolutionary image and purpose. Disillusioned militants left the party in droves. This was coupled with discontent over the authoritarian style of leadership of the General Secretary, Santiago Carrillo, and the team he brought back with him from exile, especially amongst younger activists. The combined result of these tensions was that in 1981–1982 the party split into three groups.[88]

The new Socialist leadership was also ruthless with dissent, but its centralisation of decision-making was put at the service of a seemingly coherent policy whose major objective was to bring Spain into line with the other Western liberal democracies. Given the weakness of the UGT in the mid-1970s, the reorganisation of the Socialist movement fell on the shoulders of party men. As a result, the senior leadership became dominated by professionals who often had little experience of union affairs. This in fact gave the party executive great scope in elaborating a policy it felt would maximise electoral support.

In the second half of the 1970s the party became anxious to reorganise the UGT as a counter-balance to the Communist leaning CC.OO and to provide a channel of dialogue with organised labour. This policy was to a large degree successful; the UGT benefited from the positive image of the party, and as economic recession deepened it gained support amongst those sections of the working class fearful of CC.OO's more militant stance. By the early 1980s, judged by the results of workplace elections, the UGT was as strong as the *Comisiones*. Yet, unlike the situation within the PCE where a symbiotic relationship between party and union developed, the new UGT was never to exercise much influence over party policy. There was to be no equivalent to Largo Caballero in the Spain of the 1980s.[89]

This allowed the party to adapt to the realities of what it saw as the 'new Spain'. From the late 1970s it continued to stress the need for social reforms but coupled this with a programme of economic modernisation rather than socialist transformation. This was linked to the Socialists' belief that in order to attain power it would need to break with the politics of class and appeal to the entire electorate. The message was backed up by sociologists and political scientists – often close to the party – who argued that Spain was now an 'advanced' capitalist society in which class boundaries were becoming more blurred, and in which the economy was undergoing a process of terciarisation with the rapid growth of a 'new middle class' of technicians and professionals whose vote the Socialists would need if they were to attain power.

Certainly, the PSOE's victory in the October 1982 elections, with 44 per cent of the votes cast, and its ability to remain in power ever since, demonstrates that the message of modernisation and social progress struck a chord with the Spanish electorate. The bedrock of the Socialist vote has, however, been the poorer south and the industrial working class.[90]

Party, Union and Class in the 1980s

Spanish trade unions appeared to enter the transition on the crest of a wave, yet the links between the new labour movement and the working class did not become as strong as shop stewards in the 1970s had hoped.

By 1978 the unions claimed over five million members (though most never paid dues), more than 50 per cent of the workforce, but from 1979 they began to weaken.[91] By the mid-1980s union membership was down to about one-quarter million.

This meant that on paper the Spanish union movement was the weakest in Europe. In part the reasons were institutional. It was not the same to have paper membership as to build a labour confederation, and it seems that the unions were hampered by the legacy of the OSE, which in some quarters produced an expectation that problems would be solved from above.[92]

More important was the effect of the economic recession, which had first struck in 1973 and was seriously aggravated during 1979 by the second oil price rise. This was reflected in the decline of the number of strikes from 1980 (see Table 7.2). But the crisis not only reduced worker militancy; it also destroyed much of the heavy industry on which the new working-class was forged. At the same time, as socialist theorists had emphasised, working-class culture was becoming more diffuse. The expansion of the role of the state in education and social services from the 1960s had reduced the role of the organisations of the left, which was reflected in the lack of services offered by the union movement. In parallel fashion new forms of mass entertainment replaced leftist social functions. The PCE in particular tried to keep alive a sense of working-class identity with the annual May Day demonstrations and the week long festivals (*fiestas*) organised by regional parties, but television and film served to create a more homogeneous set of values.

The PSOE, indeed, never tried to recreate the role it had played before the Franco regime. Instead it became a largely elitist party, staffed in its upper echelons by middle-class professionals. The working class continued to vote left (especially for the PSOE); association of the right with the Franco regime ensured that the phenomenon of the working-class conservative would hardly make its appearance in Spain. Voting for the Socialists in the 1980s required far less ideological commitment than voting for the left in the 1930s.

Finally, the unions still found it difficult to break out of their base in the world of the male blue-collar worker and effectively organise office employees and women. This was particularly the case of the *Comisiones*, which in 1984 still had 46.2 per cent of its affiliates in metallurgy, construction and transport, and only 5.6 per cent in banking, commerce, teaching and the health services.[93] This was at a time when the numbers of workers in the service sector was rapidly outstripping those in industry and women were increasingly being incorporated into the labour market. Hence by 1988 47 per cent of the active population worked in services, and by 1992 33 per cent of the employed labour force was female.[94]

This tends to overstate reality. The new industrial relations system created between 1978–1980 allowed for workers (irrespective of whether they were unionised or not) in each plant to conduct workplace elections every four years to elect union representatives. These representatives were then empowered to negotiate with management. During the 1980s well over 6 million workers were covered by collective agreements; thus, many workers could be union sympathisers without actually affiliating. A long Spanish tradition was thereby perpetuated. As would become clear during the economic upturn between 1986 and 1990, unions seemingly weak on paper could still mobilise large numbers into taking strike action.[95]

The fact that labour unions remained anchored within the world of labour while the PSOE had broken free from its ideological moorings led to growing tensions as the decade progressed. After the Socialists came to power in 1982 they moved further to the right and adopted an orthodox monetary policy aimed at bringing down wage costs and inflation, thereby restoring the profitability of Spanish industry. This was immediately denounced by the *Comisiones*, which tried to mobilise against government policy.[96] The UGT, on the other hand, remained wedded for a time to its Socialist partner, and backed a government call for tripartite discussions between themselves, unions and employers. The result was a series of pacts signed between 1982 and 1986 whereby the UGT essentially agreed to reductions in job security and to keep wage increases within a certain range in return for improved social provision. These pacts had statutory backing, leading some authors to talk of the Spanish industrial relations system as a version of the neo-corporatist model practised in central and northern Europe.

The Spanish variant proved however to be very unstable. There was worker discontent over the government's economic policy, which was seen as fomenting unemployment; by 1985 the unemployment rate stood at 21.9 per cent of the active work force. The UGT was also increasingly dissatisfied with the meagre social return for its sacrifices, and was afraid that if it became too identified with government policies it could lose support to the *Comisiones*. The union first expressed discontent in 1985, and in the more favourable economic climate of 1986–1988 relations deteriorated further. As industrial unrest grew, the UGT leadership saw it would be impossible to impose new sacrifices on a restless rank-and-file, and in any case it was dismayed that the government continued to give priority to the control over wage costs and fiercely opposed any attempt to reduce employment through the use of temporary contracts.[97]

In these circumstances, no further pacts were signed after 1985. Relations between the PSOE and UGT finally reached breaking point in 1988 when the UGT and the *Comisiones* agreed jointly to call a one-day general strike for 14 December. At the same time the UGT leaders, Nicolás

Redondo and Antón Saracibar, resigned the Socialist whip in parliament. The long association of party and union, therefore, seemed to be at an end. The government had calculated that the unions would be too weak to attempt such drastic action. It was mistaken; the strike proved to be a great success with seven million workers staying at home.[98] It showed that the unions were still able to reach out to the mass of salaried workers, and it also became clear that a dilution of class consciousness did not mean that workers were unwilling to strike in defence of their perceived interests.

Indeed, in December 1988 an identity of interests crystallised between blue- and white-collar workers. Juan José Linz has argued that in Spain a clearly differentiated middle-class consciousness has not developed to the same extent as in Central Europe.[99] Certainly the events of 1988 indicated that amongst the salaried classes a feeling existed that they had borne the brunt of the modernisation of Spanish state and society, and they were clearly dissatisfied that inequalities of wealth had not been significantly reduced.

Tensions within the Socialist party also developed during the 1980s. These were considerably exacerbated by the result of the 1989 general election in which, although the Socialists retained power, their share of the vote fell to 39.9 per cent, and they suffered a significant haemorrhage of working-class support. Tensions centred on the neo-liberal government ministers and the followers of the government's vice-president, Alfonso Guerra. While the neo-liberals tended to have Felipe Gonzalez's ear, Alfonso Guerra largely controlled the party's apparatus. Both these sections of the party agreed that the party should appeal to all social classes and not specifically to organised labour. It was only the weak left-wing tendency *Izquierda Socialista* which wished to retain a strong organic link with the unions. However, while the neo-liberals put the competitiveness of the economy before all else, the *Guerristas* believed in the need to remain within the social democratic tradition and make concessions to organised labour in order to shore up the party's working-class base.[100]

These differences were patched up in time for the June 1993 general election. This was held at an inauspicious time for the party; externally, socialist parties seemed to be on the retreat throughout Europe, while internally the party had over the previous two years been rocked by a series of corruption scandals, and had to fight the campaign in the teeth of a dramatic economic downturn. Yet to the surprise of many, the party was able to buck the trend, and although it lost its overall majority, with 38.7 per cent of the vote the Socialists still remained the largest party in parliament.

Several factors explain this turn of events. Firstly, the young leader of the *Partido Popular* (PP), José María Aznar, could never match Felipe

González's standing as a major statesman and the man who had consolidated democracy in Spain. Just as important, the right had not fully thrown off the stigma of the Franco years. Despite the PP's attempt to promote itself as a party of the centre-right, there was still a fear that should they return to power the social conquests and civil liberties won over the previous fifteen years might be imperilled, a fact which was skilfully exploited by the PSOE during the election campaign. For this reason many working-class voters unhappy at the Socialists' policies finally voted for them in order to keep out the right.[101]

Despite what tasted like victory, however, the PSOE's task in government will not be an easy one. Quite apart from the need to form a minority government and reach agreements with opposition parties in the context of an economic recession, clear differences remain regarding the identity of the party. During the election campaign the government seemed to move to the left, offering the possibility of an entente with the UGT, but this has since dissipated with the UGT and CC.OO calling another one-day general strike for 27 January 1994. This has been accompanied by the eruption of the dispute between neo-liberals and *Guerristas* into open conflict. With the party in power this is unlikely to lead to a outright split; in opposition, it may well prove far more difficult to preserve this relationship intact.

Notes

1. Tuñón de Lara (1977), vol. 2, pp. 11–4; Martin (1990), pp. 41–43.
2. Smith (1992), p. 350.
3. Garciá Delgado (ed) (1992), Ralle (1989), pp. 164–8; Smith (1992), pp. 349–356; Byrne (1992), pp. 115–42. Friás Fernández (1992), pp. 143–72; Fesefelt (1993), pp. 49–83.
4. Smith (1991), pp. 340–6.
5. Fusi (1975), pp. 76–9.
6. Calero (1973), pp. 288–389; Calero (1976), p. 51.
7. Castillo (1990), p. 215; Smith (1992), p. 352.
8. Shubert (1990), pp. 168–90; Martin (1990), pp. 237–62; Castillo (1991–1992), pp. 149–76.
9. Varela Ortega (1977).
10. Fontana (1973), pp. 189–190.
11. Bengoechea (1994), pp. 37–101.

12. Connelly Ullman (1972); Romero Maura (1975).
13. This was well brought out in accounts by labour activists of the time. For Catalonia, see in particular Salud (1936) and Bueso (1976).
14. Romero Maura (1975); Reig (1982); Culla (1986); Duarte (1987); Alvarez Junco (1990); Townson (ed) (1994).
15. Termes (1973); Smith (1991), pp. 153–91.
16. Lida (1972); Calero (1976) pp. 30–3; Kaplan (1977), p. 80.
17. Castillo (1986), pp. 9–34; Heywood (1989), pp. 231–65.
18. Tuñón de Lara (1977), vol. 2, pp. 280–81; Gabriel (1981), pp. 259, 275–285.
19. Casanova (1985), pp. 9–22.
20. Calero (1976), pp. 33–7.
21. Shubert (1987), pp. 110–6.
22. Fusi (1975), pp. 397–428.
23. Tuñón de Lara (1977), vol.2, pp. 275–385.
24. Lladonosa (1975); Gabriel (1981), pp. 672–708.
25. Balcells (1965), pp. 67–82.
26. Shubert (1987), pp. 121–8.
27. Balcells (1965), pp. 125–59; Bengoechea (1994), pp. 173–283.
28. Elorza (1981), pp. 241–58; Sánchez Pérez (1991), p. 537.
29. Díaz del Moral (1973), pp. 318–22.
30. Guereña (1991), pp. 645–92.
31. Aviva and Isaac Aviv (1981), pp. 499–500.
32. Boyd (1976), pp. 125–70.
33. Salud (1936), pp. 47–49; Rider (1989), pp. 87–91.
34. Juliá (1984), pp. 150–71.
35. Nash (1983), pp. 40–52.
36. Elorza (1981), pp. 245–55; Kaplan (1992), pp. 106–25; Nash (1983), pp. 55–6; Smith (1991), pp. 344–71.
37. Smith (1991), pp. 346–50.
38. Martin (1990), pp. 147–73.
39. Díaz del Moral (1973); Brenan (1950); Hobsbawm (1958).
40. Morato (1972), pp. 296–332; Fusi (1975), p. 73, pp. 484–5; Shubert (1987), pp. 104–16.
41. Byrne (1992), pp. 124–6.
42. Aviva and Isaac Aviv (1981), p. 490.
43. Smith (1989), pp. 27–37; Gabriel (1990), pp. 47–72.
44. Gabriel (1981), pp. 522–3.
45. Shubert (1987), p. 118; Martin (1990), pp. 249–62.
46. Calero (1976), p. 75.
47. Smith (1990), pp. 153–272.
48. Fusi (1975), pp. 233–42.
49. Elorza (1981), pp. 256–8.

50. Meaker (1974), pp. 62–99; Heywood (1990), pp. 29–58.
51. Fusi (1975), pp. 429–78.
52. Meaker (1974), pp. 442–80; Martin (1990), pp. 211–36.
53. Martin (1990), pp. 263–79.
54. Contreras (1981), p. 60; Martin (1990), pp. 279–86.
55. Contreras (1981), pp. 88–9.
56. Preston (1982), pp. 51–9.
57. Juliá (1983), pp. 41–53; Martin (1990), pp. 297–310.
58. Preston (1984), p. 166.
59. Balcells (1971); Cabrera (1983), pp. 196–250; Martin (1990), pp. 305–9, 348.
60. Brademas (1974), pp. 58–104.
61. Rider (1989), pp. 80–6; Ealham, (1995), pp. 140–3.
62. Balcells (1974), pp. 181–306; Durgan (1990), pp. 29–45; Martin (1990), pp. 310–25.
63. Ealham (1995), pp. 133–47.
64. Malefakis (1970), pp. 207–65, 289–307; Preston (1982), pp. 51–91.
65. Shubert (1987), pp. 141–50.
66. Juliá (1984), pp. 191–323.
67. Biscarrondo (1975); Preston (1982), pp. 92–119.
68. G. Jackson et al (1985).
69. Seidman (1991); Casanovas (1985), pp. 177–219.
70. An excellent analysis of the politics of the republican zone is to be found in Graham (1991).
71. Durgan (1990), p. 44; Gabriel (1990), p. 64.
72. Sevilla-Guzman (1979), pp. 125–56.
73. Tuñón de Lara and Biescas (1980), pp. 242–7.
74. Tezanos (1989a), pp. 80–90.
75. Balfour (1989), pp. 6–8, 41–8.
76. Molinero and Ysàs (1989), pp. 37–43; Balfour (1989), pp. 22–40.
77. Data for the years 1966 to 1980 is taken from the books by Balfour and Sargadoy and León Blanco. For post-1980, we have relied on the data collected by the Ministry of Labour. Unfortunately, for much of this period Catalonia and the Basque Country were not included in the figures. This means that the drop in conflict from 1980 is no doubt exaggerated. For example, the employers' organisation, the CEOE, which from 1980 also compiled its own figures, calculated that during the period 1981 to 1983 261.6 million working days were lost. See *Papeles de Economía Española*, (1985), p. 242.
78. Maravall (1978), pp. 44–64; Molinero and Ysàs (1989), pp. 52–76.
79. Balfour (1989), pp. 41–109; Juliá (1991), pp. 29–36.
80. Nash (1991), pp. 160–77; Calvo Poyato (1990), pp. 551–67; Fishman (1990) pp. 73–5.

81. Maravall (1978), pp. 26–9; Balfour (1989), pp. 14–20, 34–8, 62–5; Fishman (1990), pp. 93–94. As against the stress on the Falange in promoting the changes, Maravall maintained that collective bargaining was established in order to ensure worker acquiesence to productivity increases. The main problems with this argument are that, as pointed out, many employers were opposed to collective bargaining, and that in the past they had felt no compunction in imposing settlements on their workforce.
82. Balfour (1989), pp. 62–98; Fishman (1990), pp. 110–29.
83. Balfour (1989), pp. 142–235; Preston (1986), pp. 53–90; Molinero and Ysàs (1989), pp. 65–80; García Delgado and María Sanz (1991), pp. 212–5.
84. Heine (1983); Gillespie (1989), pp. 53–218.
85. Preston (1981), pp. 36–65.
86. Balfour (1989), pp. 185–223; Fishman (1990), pp. 97–8.
87. Gilespie (1989), pp. 219–376; Fishman (1990), p. 185.
88. Heywood (1985), pp. 167–170; Juliá (1991), pp. 140–5.
89. Julía (1988), pp. 139–148; Gillespie (1989), pp. 402–12; Fishman (1990), p. 168.
90. Tezanos (1989b), pp. 433–93; Gillespie (1989), pp. 367–419; Juliá (1991), pp. 29–49, 151–9.
91. Péréz Díaz (1987), p. 234.
92. Fishman (1990), pp. 11, 135, 187–246; Balfour (1989), pp. 231, 241–58.
93. Gillespie (1990), pp. 60–1; Soto Carmona (1993), pp. 511–2.
94. Tezanos (1990), p. 122; *El País* 14 May 1993.
95. *El País* 2 May 1993, p. 44; 23 May 1993, pp. 20–1.
96. Soto Carmona (1993), pp. 476–88.
97. Péréz Díaz (1987), pp. 95–123; Gillespie (1990), pp. 50–2.
98. Juliá (1988); Fishman (1990), pp. 256–8.
99. Linz (1984), pp. 59–95.
100. Gillespie (1993), pp. 78–96.
101. *El País*, 8 June 1993, pp. 20–1.

Bibliography

Alvarez Junco, José, *El Emperador del Paralelo. Lerroux y la Demagogia Populista*, Madrid, 1990

Aviv, Aviva and Isaac, 'Ideology and Political Patronage: Workers and

Working Class Movements in Republican Madrid, 1931–1934', *European Studies Review*, vol. 11, 1981, pp. 487–515

Balcells, Albert, *El Sindicalisme a Barcelona, 1916–1923*, Barcelona, 1965

——, *Crisis Económica y Agitación Social en Cataluña, 1931–36*, Barcelona, 1971

——, 'La crisis del anarco-sindicalismo y el movimiento obrero en Sabadell entre 1930 y 1936', in Balcells, *Trabajo Industrial y Organización Obrera en la Cataluña Contemporánea (1900–1936)*, Barcelona, 1974

Balfour, Sebastian, *Dictatorship, Workers and the City: Labour in Greater Barcelona since 1939*, Oxford, 1989

Bengoechea, *Soledad, Organització Patronal i Conflictivitat Social a Catalunya. Tradició i Corporativisme entre Finals de Segle i La Dictadura de Primo de Rivera*, Barcelona, 1994

Bizcarrondo, Marta, *Araquistáin y la Crisis Socialista en la Segunda República: Leviatán, 1934–1936*, Madrid, 1975

Boyd, Carolyn P., 'The anarchists and education in Spain, 1868–1909', *The Journal of Modern History*, vol. 48, no. 4, 1976, pp. 125–72

Brademas, John, *Anarcosindicalismo y Revolución en España, 1931–1937*, Barcelona, 1974

Brenan, Gerald, *The Spanish Labyrinth: An Account of the Social and Political Background of the Spanish Civil War*, 2nd edn., Cambridge, 1950

Bueso, Adolfo, *Recuerdos de un Cenetista*, vol. 1, Barcelona, 1976

Byrne, Justin, 'Trabajo y conflictividad en el sector de la construcción de Madrid, 1900–1914', *Sociología del Trabajo*, no. 15, 1992, pp. 115–42

Cabrera, Mercedes, *La Patronal ante la Segunda República. Organizaciones y Estrategia, 1931–1936*, Madrid, 1983

Calero, Antonio M., *Historia del Movimiento Obrero en Granada (1909–1923)*, Madrid, 1973

——, *Movimientos Sociales en Andalucía,(1820–1936)*, Madrid, 1976

Calvo Poyato, Carmen, 'La mujer en España', in Salvador Giner (ed.), *España: Sociedad y Política*, Madrid, 1990, pp. 551–67

Casanova, Julian, *Anarquismo y Revolucion en la Sociadad Rural Aragonesa, 1936–1938*, Madrid, 1985

Castillo, Santiago, 'Organización y acción del PSOE hasta 1900', in Santos Juliá (ed.), *El Socialismo en España*, Madrid, 1986, pp. 9–34

——, 'Spain', in Marcel Van Der Linden and Jürgen Rojahn (eds), *The Formation of Labour Movements, 1870–1914: An International Perspective*, Leiden, 1990, pp. 209–40.

——, 'Todos iguales ante la ley . . . del más fuerte', *Sociología del*

Trabajo, nueva época, no. 14, invierno, 1991–1992, pp. 149–76

Connelly Ullman, Joan, *La Semana Trágica*, Barcelona, 1972

Contreras, Manuel, *El PSOE en la Segunda República: Organización e Ideología*, Madrid, 1981

Culla i Clarà, Joan B, *El Republicanisme Lerrouxista a Catalunya, (1901–1923)*, Barcelona, 1986

Díaz del Moral, Juan, *Historia de las Agitaciones Campesinas Andaluzas-Córdoba*, Madrid, 1973

Duarte, Angel, *El Republicanisme Català a la Fi del Segle XIX*, Vic, 1987

Durgan, Andrew, 'Sindicalismo y Marxismo en Cataluña 1931–36: Hacia la Fundación de la Federación Obrera de Unidad Sindical', *Historia Social*, vol. 8, Autumn, 1990, pp. 29–45

Ealham, Christopher, 'Anarchism and Illegality in Barcelona, 1931–1937', *Contemporary European History*, vol. 4, 1995, pp. 133–51

Elorza, Antonio, 'Socialismo y agitación popular en Madrid (1908–1920)', *Estudios de Historia Social*, nos 15–9, 1981, pp. 229–61

Fesefelt, Henrike, 'Condiciones de trabajo, Formación de clases y organización sindical: Los sindicatos de Tipógrafos y Albañiles' *en Madrid, 1888–1923*', Spagna Contemporanea, No. 4, 1993, pp. 49–83

Fishman, Robert, *Working-Class Organization and the Return of Democracy in Spain*, Ithaca and London, 1990

Fontana, Josep, 'Transformaciones agrarias y crecimiento económico en la España contemporánea', in Fontana (ed.), *Cambio Económico y Actitudes Políticas en al España del Siglo XIX*, Barcelona, 1973, pp. 147–213

Friás Fernandez, Juan Carlos, 'Niveles de Vida, Mentalidades Colechives y Socialismo: Los Típografos Madrileños a Finales del Siglo XIX', *Hispania*, no. 180, 1992, pp. 143–72

Fusi, Juan Pablo, *Política Obrera en el País Vasco, 1880–1923,* Madrid, 1975

Gabriel, Pere, 'Classe obrera i Sindicats a Catalunya, 1903–1920', unpublished PhD thesis, Barcelona Central University, 1981

——, 'Sindicalismo y sindicatos socialistas en Cataluña: La UGT, 1888–1939', *Historia Social*, vol. 8, 1990, pp. 47–72

Garciá Delgado, José Luis (ed), *Las Ciudades en la Modernización de España. Los Decenios Interseculares*, Madrid, 1992

——, José Luis and José María Serrano Sanz, 'Economía', in Manuel Tuñón de Lara (ed), *Historia de España X. Segunda Parte*, Madrid, 1991, pp. 189–314

Gillespie, Richard, *The Spanish Socialist Party: A History of Factionalism*, Oxford, 1989

——, 'The break-up of the "Socialist family": party-union relations in

Spain, 1982–89', *West European Politics*, vol. 13, no. 1, January, 1990, pp. 47–62

——, 'Programa 2000: the appearance and reality of socialist renewal in Spain', *West European Politics*, vol. 16, no. 1, January, 1993, pp. 78–96

Graham, Helen, *Socialism and War: The Spanish Socialist Party in Power and Crisis*, Cambridge, 1991

Guereña, Jean-Louis, 'Las casas del pueblo y la educación obrera a principios del siglo XX', *Hispania*, LI\2, 178, 1991, pp. 229–61

Heine, Helmut, *La Oposición Política al Franquismo*, Barcelona, 1983

Heywood, Paul, 'Spanish Communists in crisis', *Journal of Contemporary Communist Studies*, vol. 1, nos. 3–4, 1985, pp. 167–70.

——, 'The labour movement in Spain before 1914', in Richard Geary (ed.), *Labour and Socialist Movements in Europe before 1914*, London, 1989, pp. 231–65

——, *Marxism and the Failure of Organised Socialism in Spain, 1879–1936*, Cambridge, 1990

Hobsbawm, Eric, *Primitive Rebels: Studies in Archaic Forms of Social Protest in the Nineteenth and Twentieth Centuries,* Manchester, 1958

Jackson, Gabriel, et al. *Octubre 1934. Cinquenta años para la Reflexión*, Madrid, 1985

Juliá, Santos, 'Corporativistas obreros y reformadores políticos: crisis y escisión del PSOE en al II República', *Studio Histórica*, vol. 1, no. 4, 1983, pp. 41–52

——, *Madrid, 1931–1934: De la Fiesta Popular a la Lucha de Clases*, Madrid, 1984

——, (ed.), *La Desavenencia. Partido, Sindicato y Huelga General*, Madrid, 1988

——, 'Sociedad y política', in Tuñón de Lara (ed.), *Historia de España X. Segunda Parte. Transición y Democracia*, Barcelona, 1991, pp. 29–186.

Kaplan, Temma, *Anarchists of Andalusia, 1868–1903*, Princeton, 1977

——, *Red City, Blue Period: Social Movements in Picasso's Barcelona*, Berkeley, 1992

Lida, Clara E, *Anarquismo y Revolución en la España del Siglo XIX*, Madrid, 1972

Linz, Juan José, 'La sociedad española, presente, pasado y futuro', in Linz (ed.), *España: un presente para un futuro. 1 La Sociedad*, Madrid, 1984, pp. 59–95

Lladonosa, Manuel, *El Congrés de Sants*, Barcelona, 1975

Malefakis, Eduard, *Agrarian Reform and Peasant Revolution in Spain*, New Haven, 1970

Maravall, José María, *Dictatorship and Political Dissent: Workers and Students in Franco's Spain*, Cambridge, 1978

Martin, Benjamin, *The Agony of Industrialization: Labour and Industrialization in Spain*, Ithaca, 1990
Meaker, Gerald, *The Revolutionary Left in Spain, 1914–1923*, Stanford, 1974
Molinero, Carme, and Pere Ysàs, 'Comissions Obreres', in Pere Gabriel et al., *Comissions Obreres de Catalunya, 1964–1989*, Barcelona, 1989, pp. 29–80
Morato, Juan José, *Líderes del Movimiento Obrero Español*, Madrid, 1972
Nash, Mary, *Mujer, Familia y Trabajo en España 1875–1936* Barcelona, 1983
——, 'Pronatalism and motherhood in Franco's Spain', in Gisela Bock and Pat Thane (eds), *Maternity and Gender Politics: Women and the Rise of the Welfare States*, London, 1991, pp. 160–77
Pérez Díaz, Víctor, *El Retorno de la Sociedad Civil*, Madrid, 1987
Preston, Paul, 'The PCE's long road to democracy 1954–1977', in Richard Kindersley (ed.), *In Search of Eurocommunism,* London, 1981, pp. 36–65
——, *The Coming of the Spanish Civil War*, 2nd ed, London, 1982
——, 'The agrarian war in the South', in Preston (ed.), *Revolution and War in Spain, 1931–1939*, London, 1984, pp. 159–81
——, *The Triumph of Democracy in Spain*, London, 1986
Ralle, Michel, 'La sociabilidad obrera en la sociedad de la Restauración', *Estudios de Historia Social*, nos 50–51, 1989, pp. 161–99
Martín Ramos, Josep Lluís, 'Anàlisi del Moviment Vaguístic a Barcelona (1914–1923)', *Recerques*, no. 20, 1988, pp. 93–114
Reig, Ramir, *Obrers i Ciutadans. Blasquisme i Moviment Obrer*, Valencia, 1982
Rider, Nick, 'The practice of direct action: the Barcelona rent strike of 1931', in David Goodway (ed.), *For Anarchism: History, Theory and Practice*, London, 1989, pp. 79–103
Romero Maura, Joaquín, *La Rosa del Fuego. El Obrerismo Barcelonés de 1899 a 1909*, Barcelona, 1975
Salud, Emili, *Vivers de Revolucionaris. Apunts Històrics sobre el Districte Cinquè*, Barcelona, 1936
Sargadoy. J. A., and D. León Blanco, *El Poder Sindical en España*, Barcelona, 1982
Seidman, Michael, *Workers Against Work: Labor in Paris and Barcelona during the Popular Fronts*, Berkeley, 1991
Sevilla-Guzman, Eduardo, *La Evolución del Campesinado en España*, Barcelona, 1979
Shubert, Adrian, *The Road to Revolution in Spain: The Coal Miners of Asturias 1860–1934*, Urbana and Chicago, 1987
——, *A Social History of Modern Spain*, London, 1990

Smith, Angel, 'The failure of the UGT and PSOE in Catalonia, 1888–1915', *Journal of the Association for Contemporary Iberian Studies*, vol. 2, no. 2, Autumn, 1989, pp. 27–38

——, 'Industry, Labour and Politics in Catalonia, 1897–1914', unpublished PhD thesis, University of London, 1990

——, 'Social conflict and trade union organisation in the Catalan cotton textile industry, 1880–1914', *International Review of Social History*, vol. XXXVI, no. 3, 1991, pp. 331–76

——, 'Oficis i formació de classe a Barcelona, 1899–1914', *Congrés Internacional d'Història Catalunya i la Restauració*, Manresa, 1992, pp. 349–56

Soto Carmona, Alvaro, 'Comisiones Obreras en la transición y consolidación democrática. De la asamblea de Barcelona a la huelga general del 14-D, 1976–1988') in David Ruíz (ed.), *Historia de Comisiones Obreras*, (1958–1988), Madrid, 1993, pp. 451–523

Termes, Josep, *Anarquismo y Sindicalismo en España. La Primera Internacional 1864–1881*, Barcelona, 1972

Tezanos, José Félix, 'Modernización y cambio social en España', and 'Continuidad y cambio en el socialismo español', in Tezanos et al (eds), *La Transición Democrática Española,* Madrid, 1989, pp. 63–115, 433–493

——, 'Clases sociales', in Salvador Giner (ed.), *España. Sociedad y Política*, Madrid, 1990, pp. 109–41

Townson, Nigel (ed.), *El Republicanismo en España, 1830–1977*, Madrid, 1994

Tuñon de Lara, Manuel, *El Movimiento Obrero en la Historia de España*, 3 vols, 2nd Edition, Madrid, 1977

——, Manuel and José María Biescas, *España bajo la Dictadura Franquista, 1939–1975*, Barcelona, 1980

Varela Ortega, José, *Los Amigos Políticos. Partidos, Elecciones y Caciquismo en la Restauración, (1875–1900)*, Madrid, 1977

—8—

France

Susan Milner

On 31 March 1992, many political commentators in France pronounced a solemn farewell to the French working class.[1] The historic occasion which caused this rather premature valediction was the closure of Renault's Billancourt plant, which over the course of the twentieth century had seen over a million blue-collar workers pass through its gates. Since the end of the Second World War, Billancourt had acted as the showcase for France's economic and social policy and a laboratory for experiments in work organisation. For many, it alone symbolised France's true working class; when the rebellious students of May 1968 decided to make contact with France's workers they went to Billancourt, where workers constituted the spearhead of the strike movement and where, on 27 May 1968, the strikers' decision to reject the negotiated settlement effectively prolonged the strike movement throughout France.

The closure of the factory seemed to symbolise the fate of France's working class as a whole, which in the late 1980s appeared to be undergoing profound changes in composition and identity. Whereas workers formed a majority of the waged workforce in the mid-1970s, in 1993 unskilled workers represented only 14.5 per cent of the workforce, and skilled workers 30.5 per cent.[2] The relative decline of the working class has accompanied changes in trade union and party political allegiances. In June 1991 the *Confédération Générale du Travail* (CGT), close to the French Communist Party and strongly identified as a 'class and mass' union, lost control of Billancourt's works council for the first time in forty-three years, mirroring the nationwide decline of a fragmented French trade unionism but particularly that of the traditionally dominant CGT. The French Communist Party, throughout the period of the Fourth Republic (1946–1958) the biggest single party on the French political scene, was the first casualty of these changes. Since 1981 it has commanded only around 10 per cent of the vote. More generally the political link between the working class and the left appears to have been broken: in March 1993 the left suffered its biggest defeat of the post-war period, as workers formed the bulk of the growing abstentionist electorate.

However, whilst it is true that in the last quarter of the twentieth century the French working class and labour movement are undergoing dramatic changes within the context of economic upheavals, the idea that the economic crisis of the 1970s has brought about a break with a tradition of a homogeneous and class-conscious working class typified by the skilled metalworker of Renault's factories does not bear closer inspection. Sociologists have already called into question both the homogeneity of the working class and the myth of the 'heroic' worker as a central actor in French society,[3] which was fostered notably by the Popular Front but also in the post-war years of reconstruction when labour power helped to produce France's economic miracle (the 'thirty glorious years'). As for the French labour movement, it has always been weak and, throughout most of the twentieth century, divided between Christian and 'independent' trade unionism, the latter itself split between revolutionary and reformist wings even when they were organisationally united in the CGT at the start of the century.

In the first decade of the twentieth century, the CGT (then the sole national confederation) numbered between 350,000 and 500,000 members. Even counting the local Catholic or autonomous unions, the total number of organised workers was less than 10 per cent of the workforce (around 700,000). In the final decade of the twentieth century, less than 10 per cent of the French workforce is unionised. No less than four general confederations plus a white-collar union (the *Confédération Générale des Cadres*) and a teachers' union (the *Fédération de l'Education Nationale*, set up to avoid having rival ideological groups competing in negotiations and composed of smaller unions also associated with the major confederations) and a number of small autonomous unions share this meagre group. The differences arise partly from the development of Catholic trade unionism from the end of the nineteenth century (the *Confédération Française des Travailleurs Chrétiens* was set up in 1919, and the *Confédération Française Démocratique du Travail* grew out of it in 1964), but also from ideological splits in which communism and opposition to it play a pivotal role (as in *Force Ouvrière*'s split from the CGT in 1947).

Table 8.1. Trade Union Membership Figures[4]
(Approximate figures in thousands)

	CGT	CFTC	CFDT	FO	CGC	FEN	Total
1950	1,500	400		400	100	200	2,600
1970	2,000	250	950	800	250	550	4,800
1990	850	200	500	500	200	300	2,550

A similar story of division and weakness presents itself if we look at the political parties associated with the labour movement. At the beginning of the twentieth century, the left embraced many different and often competing tendencies: the *Possibilists* led by Paul Brousse, who were active in municipal socialism; the *Allemanists*, led by Jean Allemane, who preferred more direct forms of workers' action to parliamentary politics; the *Blanquists*, followers of the nineteenth-century revolutionary Auguste Blanqui, and the *Vaillantists*, grouped around Edouard Vaillant, who was to become a central figure in the international socialist movement; the Marxist *Guesdists*, with strong support in the industrial north (especially the textile industry); the independent socialists like Jean Jaurès and Alexandre Millerand, who mixed republicanism with strong social concerns; and various other groups including anarchists. Deep ideological differences concerning the political position of socialism in the Third Republic were not altogether surmounted when in 1905, under pressure from their counterparts in the Second International, the French socialists decided to form a single party: the *Parti Socialiste Français – Section Française de l'Internationale Ouvrière* (SFIO).

As in the case of many other European socialist movements, the internal divisions, already severely tested by the call for national unity during the First World War, proved too great to withstand the shock of the Russian Revolution and the Communist Party emerged in 1920. The question of participation in the government of the bourgeois republic continued to divide French socialism, until under Leon Blum, a left united against fascism was able to govern independently. In the period after the Second World War, socialists participated in government with centre parties and even came to support De Gaulle at the beginning of the Fifth Republic, but remained overshadowed in membership and electoral terms by a strong Communist Party (we will examine some of the reasons for the PCF's strength later).

In the early days of labour organisation, the divided socialist movement (and, in the case of the *Guesdists*, the threat of subordination of labour to party) held few attractions for the CGT. Later, whereas the Communist Party maintained strong ties with the working class through its link with the CGT and its 'mass and class' policies (and largely because the Communist Party occupied this political space after 1920), the Socialist Party failed to achieve real mass working-class support; indeed, its electoral success after 1970 owed much to a strategy of winning over middle-class voters. It is thus little wonder that the socialist leader Michel Rocard, convening a gathering for the 'renewal of the party' after the electoral defeat of March 1993, should confess humbly to the foreign delegates present: 'France may be a great power, but the French PS is, of all the parties of the International, the one which carries the least weight on its home ground, and this has been so since 1920.'[5]

In studying the French labour movement in the twentieth century, the historian is presented not with a linear progression but a series of overlapping phases with some underlying features, notably the heterogeneity of the working class, a problematic relationship between the labour movement and parties of the left, and a relatively (in relation to Britain and Germany) slow rate of industrialisation and patchy industrial concentration. The two world wars of the twentieth century undoubtedly affected the place of the working class in French society, accentuating labour shortages and leading employers to diversify recruitment and re-think strategies for the deployment of labour.

The key to working-class development must however be sought in the development of capitalism itself.[6] In this respect the period before the First World War was crucial. As is pointed out by Goetschy and Rozenblatt, the legacy of the nineteenth century has been difficult to determine.[7] In France as in most other European countries, the formation of the working class took place in the four decades preceding the First World War; indeed, some social historians place the start of the twentieth century in 1880.[8] Already before 1914 employers had begun to experiment with 'rationalised' forms of work as a response to labour shortages; after 1920, these 'Taylorised' forms of work organisation began to take root in certain sectors of the French economy, particularly in car production, whilst in many other sectors production was still based on small units and craft methods of production. This dualism has remained characteristic of the French labour market.

Labour Markets

The number of workers rose from the beginning of the twentieth century to the 1970s, but unevenly over time. Between 1906 and 1931, the number of workers increased by two million to reach a total of seven million. By the time of the 1954 census, 6.5 million workers (34.5 per cent of the labour force) were recorded. The number of workers in France peaked in 1975 at 8.5 million. Since then, numbers have decreased: the 1981 census recorded 8 million workers (with 700,000 of them unemployed), and by 1989, the number had gone down to 7.3 million (of whom 1.2 million were women) out of a labour force of 22.4 million.[9] Of these, it is estimated that around 5 million work in industry.[10]

Massive changes have taken place in the sectoral distribution of the workforce over the course of the twentieth century but the pace of change in the first half of the century was slow. In 1911, around 39 per cent of the labour force worked in agriculture, 33 per cent in industry and 28 per cent in the tertiary sector. In 1945, 36 per cent worked in the primary sector, 30 per cent in the secondary and 34 per cent in the tertiary. In 1990, the figures were 7 per cent, 29 per cent, and 64 per cent respectively. The peak for the proportion of the labour force in industry occurred in 1974, at 42 per cent of the workforce.

Until recently, the orthodox view was that of the French working class as a late developer: an immature working class, because of late industrialisation, failed to develop a strong, centralised labour movement.[11] However, some interesting work has been done on the idea of 'proto-workers', which suggests that, rather than a unilinear process of proletarianisation, overlapping processes of rural and industrial change took place over a long period.[12] One of the main features of the French workforce, certainly up until the end of the nineteenth century and carrying on into the first half of the twentieth century, was a highly mobile working class with strong rural roots. Thus France saw the emergence of proto-industrial districts, with many workers working from home or intermittently also working in the fields at harvest time. Thus Verret talks of the doubly incomplete process in France of 'proletarianisation of peasants' and of 'workerisation of proletarians'.[13]

It was not until the 1950s that the major break with the countryside took place. Until then, around one-third of French working people still worked in agriculture. This means that possibly the greatest social upheaval in France's history has taken place in a short space of time (in the latter half of the twentieth century). However, set against this, the number of industrial workers has remained globally stable in the post-war period, increasing slowly but steadily until the late 1960s and then falling with the onset of economic crisis. It is in the tertiary sector that the biggest growth has taken place.

Also of note is the survival in France, for longer than in Britain or to a lesser extent Germany, of independent workers. Rather than merely continuing the nineteenth-century forms of artisanal production, this phenomenon appears to have been a specific response to the development of capitalism at the beginning of the twentieth century. Thus between 1896 and 1936 a new group of *travailleurs isolés* appears in surveys. In 1901 these accounted for 22 per cent of the working population: they include 2.2 million *petits patrons*, 0.6 million home workers and 1.4 million irregular workers. In 1906, they represented 24 per cent of the working population.[14]

Labour biographies show that the practice of switching from paid manual labour to artisanal or retail activities (for instance, in periods of unemployment, or when militant workers faced 'blacklists'), common in the nineteenth century, still occurred in the early twentieth century. Crossick and Haupt observe that the high rate of social mobility of the group of artisanal workers and small shopkeepers 'must also have served to hinder the development of anything comparable with common class relationships' in the period before 1914.[15] The existence of these 'independent' workers, lacking firm alliances with either the working class or the lower middle classes, helped to blur class boundaries. However, as Steven Zdatny shows in his study of artisans, by 1925 consciousness of a separate artisan status had emerged, bringing independent workers out of the working class and into the lower middle class. The political expression of artisanal class consciousness was always problematic, however, and Zdatny charts its division into left- and right-wing populist movements.[16]

On the whole, industrial concentration remained weak, but in some industrial sectors the large factory appeared on the scene between 1880 and 1914. In 1906 each employer employed on average 4.3 persons, and the situation did not change much until the end of the war. The average factory employed 240 workers and there were 189 establishments employing more than 1,000 workers, accounting for a total of 436,000 workers.[17] This was the period described by Patrick Fridenson as a 'Taylorian turning point', with France borrowing heavily but in piecemeal fashion from scientific work organisation theories and adapting them to French practices of paternalism and bureaucracy.[18] Concentration remained weak in older industries, but became particularly visible in mining and especially in metals in the early twentieth century.

The new car industry – the mainstay of Tayloristic practices – was in 1913 concentrated in fewer than fifty firms with a total of 33,000 workers, mainly in the west of the Paris region and around Lyon: Renault's Billancourt plant employed 4,400 workers in 1914, and between 32,000 and 34,000 in 1945.[19] By 1931, over half the workforce worked in firms employing over a hundred people, and a quarter of the workforce was in factories with more than 500 employees.[20] Almost 20 per cent were in very small units with fewer than ten employees, and around 30 per cent in factories employing between ten and one hundred people. In 1962, 37 per cent of the industrial workforce worked in establishments with more than 500 employees, and although the figure rose to 45 per cent in 1974, it had fallen again to 38 per cent in 1983.[21]

Historians today rightly lay emphasis on the diversity of working-class experience. Noiriel pays particular attention to the stratification of the working class in different periods, linking it with the supply of skilled male industrial labour. In the early twentieth century, and particularly after the devastation of the Great War, employers had two solutions to the problem of labour scarcity: rationalisation and recourse to labour reserves (peasants, women and immigrants).[22] The former, linked with mechanisation and Taylorisation, brought about the creation of a new stratum of the workforce, the specialised worker or OS (semi-skilled machine operators).

Often these OS were the new peasant or immigrant recruits. In 1891, 12 per cent of wage earners were immigrants; they were particularly concentrated in certain sectors and certain regions such as mining and metal extraction in the Lorraine, where as many as three-quarters of labourers were immigrants in the 1910s. Gary Cross shows clearly that, because of France's peculiar demographic structure, immigration functioned as a 'safety valve' in the French labour market. As a result, France opened its doors to immigration much earlier than other European countries, and indeed as early as the 1920s the French state sought to regulate immigration in ways which other advanced capitalist countries adopted only in the second half of the twentieth century.[23] By 1931, 2.7 million immigrants (or 7.1 per cent of the total population) worked in France.

In the 1930s, however, economic crisis hit the labour reserves first, and up to one-third of the immigrant population was sent home.[24] Later, in the 1950s, France once again looked to immigration to boost the production effort, but by the 1970s the need for OS had dried up as those sectors which had earlier promoted Tayloristic rationalisation sought new forms of restructuring, and again immigrants felt the brunt of mass redundancies. However, in the 1980s and 1990s, France has found it less easy than in the 1930s to dismiss the immigrant labour reserve, and considerable social problems arising from difficulties of integration remain.

Women, on the other hand, have become central to new forms of work organisation in the latter half of the twentieth century, involving intellectualisation and tertiarisation of work. Arguably women have always had a high activity rate in France, albeit as a casual and peripheral workforce, and in this sense the 1930–1950 period constitutes an exception due first to economic crisis and then to the post-war fears of unemployment for demobilised soldiers. This view of women's place in the working class seems to suggest a link between earlier traditions of women's work in 'proto-industrialisation', with women working in the fields and in cottage industries, and later rates of female activity.

Perhaps because of this tradition, France has a higher proportion of married women in the workforce than Britain or Germany. Women accounted for 30 per cent of labour force in 1866 and 37.7 per cent in 1906. The growth of women's employment was at that time linked with the rise of industry. The increase in the number of women employed in industry during this period was quite marked in absolute terms although not in relative terms: women formed 35 per cent of the industrial labour force in 1876, but only 33.9 per cent in 1906.[25] During the inter-war and post-war periods the proportion of women in the industrial workforce continued to fall, and conversely women became less active in industry and more active in the tertiary sector. In 1962 women represented 34.6 per cent of the French working population, compared with 40.7 per cent in 1982.

The period 1930–1950, however, saw the creation of a relatively homogeneous and structured workforce. This was the era of the skilled factory worker (*le métallo de chez Renault*), but it also depended on a sub-stratum of semi-skilled OS. The stabilisation of collective bargaining in the new regime of capital accumulation – the move from an economy based on heavy industry to a consumer society – favoured the former category of worker and even made him the central figure in the working class, but worsening conditions for the OS led to a series of wildcat strikes in the 1970s and signalled the limits of Taylorist production methods.

Noiriel links the importance of the post-war generation of skilled workers (those born between the wars) with other social trends marking the transition to the consumer society, the beginnings of industrial sociology as a discipline, and the organisation of occupational classifications by the *Institut National de Statistique et d'Etudes Economiques* (INSEE) based on three groups, labourers, OS and professional workers (skilled workers).[26] The stabilisation of the working class, which started in the 1930s and continued into the 1960s, was also linked with political affiliation: in 1958, 36 per cent of the working class voted communist, and in 1973, 33 per cent voted similarly. The relative stability of the communist vote during this period contrasts with the 1980s: in 1981, 24 per cent of workers voted communist, while in 1986 the figure was 20 per cent and in 1989 only 12 per cent.

These figures support the idea of a stable and class-conscious working class during the post-war period and the break-up of class solidarities in the 1970s. The 1950–1970 period is particularly interesting because this idea of a homogeneous, class-conscious working class must bear some relation to the astonishing growth of the French economy (all the more astonishing because during this period the working population as a whole was stagnating). Studies have shown the main factor in France's economic growth was a more efficient, more productive workforce, linked with rationalisation, large-scale production and work intensification and also with a relatively high level of workers' skills.[27] This was a fairly rigid workforce; in the 1960s, the replacement of labour with capital meant a stagnation of the demand for labour and inflation of qualifications leading to polarisation. Not surprisingly, this was a time when sociologists began talking about a labour aristocracy, and when conflicts started to highlight the marginal nature of the bottom segment of the working class.

In the 1960s, the progressive disintegration of this homogeneity was reflected in sociological studies on the effects of technology, suggesting that a cycle of technological and industrial development had come to an end. Theories about the 'new working class' became popular: Mallet, for instance, argued that newer high technology industries were moving away from assembly line mass production and thereby creating a new stratum of skilled, technical workers who could form the vanguard of a new movement for greater job control and participation in decision-making.[28] The May 1968 movement, whose rhetoric focused on qualitative issues, seemed to reinforce these theories.

However, while many of the strike movements after 1968 adopted new forms of protest (for example, the famous occupation of the Lip watch factory in 1973 and the establishment of a workers' cooperative) and often drew attention to working conditions rather than pay, the main actors were the OS of traditional factories rather than the 'new working class'. The question of whether the French economy has moved towards a new form of wage regulation remains open. The working class remains stratified, and the dualism of the workforce presents itself today, albeit in a different form, along the lines of the secondary/tertiary sector divide, the public/private sector divide and the core/periphery divide.

Arguably, the multiple divisions among French workers may be seen as one of the reasons for the weakness of the labour organisations in that they posed challenges which these organisations found themselves poorly equipped to take up. From the start, French trade unions had difficulty in organising a significant number of women; until 1920, women needed the permission of their husbands to become trade union members. Barely one-tenth of the CGT's members in 1911 were women, and some unions such as the print-workers' union refused to allow women to join, although as Barbara Mitchell notes 'concrete changes in organisational attitudes and policies did occur' during this period,[29] and by 1919 almost one-third of trade union members were women. Conscious moves to organise women and address questions of equality of pay and treatment were sparked off particularly by the (relatively early) 1946 law stipulating equal pay for equal work. In 1952, the CGT set up a journal specifically for women members, which was re-named *Antoinette* in 1955 (and discontinued in 1992).

From 1948, the CGT set up various women's committees within the confederation. The position of the CFTC/CFDT was more problematic because of the view inspired by the Catholic Church that women should look after the family; it was not until the 1970s that the CFDT took up issues connected with women at work. The slightly higher proportion of women members in the CGT than other confederations (18 per cent in 1970, compared with only 14 per cent for the CFDT)[30] has declined as the structure of work has changed away from manual industrial work towards office employment. However, women have always been seriously under-represented in French trade unions despite their sizeable presence in the workforce.

Immigrants have also been under-represented, but to a lesser extent. France is unique in having been a host to immigration since the nineteenth century, and a large proportion of the immigrants have been workers: 50.8 per cent of them in 1901, 66.9 per cent in 1931 and 64 per cent in 1975.[31] The presence of large numbers of immigrant workers, and particularly their concentration in certain urban areas and certain sectors, have provoked various reactions from French workers ranging from xenophobia to solidarity; as Lequin notes, 'the recurrent hostility of the world of labour towards foreigners is as old as their presence'.[32]

In the face of often violent conflicts between foreign (mainly Italian, Belgian or Polish) and French workers, especially in the construction industry, the CGT sought to affirm solidarity between immigrants and nationals. However, a trade union strategy emerged only slowly; it was not until 1924 that the CGT set up a national office for organising immigrants.[33] Cross notes that the French trade unions had two choices, to unionise immigrant workers or to seek political regulation of migratory flows. The CGT, in line with its 'policy of presence' after 1921, chose the regulatory path and had some success in instituting nationality quotas in areas (mainly Paris) where the tripartite employment placement offices retained a measure of control over local labour market conditions, although at national level attempts to set up corporatist regulation of immigration faltered in the 1920s. The CGTU, on the other hand, attempted to organise immigrants around class-based demands but with limited success: only around 8 per cent of Polish workers (1925) and 6 per cent of Italian workers joined CGTU unions.[34]

The weakness of the unions in industry, where immigrants were concentrated, accounted largely for their failure to overcome obstacles to the organisation of immigrant workers, including the different expectations and prospects of migrant labour, the often temporary nature of their migration and a concerted effort on the part of employers and the state to prevent 'contamination' of immigrants by communist ideas. The law recognised trade union rights for Tunisians and Algerians in 1932, and in 1936 for European workers only in Morocco.[35] After the CGTU and CGT joined ranks in 1935, the regulatory approach predominated and Cross makes it clear that the majority wing of organised labour in France colluded in setting up a 'new foreign labour system' in which immigrant workers had no citizenship rights.[36]

In the post-war period, as the CGT looked increasingly to the large factories, the labour movement had more success in organising a relatively stable immigrant population. Indeed, the political and social organisations of the French working class formed important channels of socialisation for immigrants in the post-war period, largely because the dominant political model of integration made it difficult for immigrants to organise separately. Immigrant workers were particularly active in the strike movements of the 1970s, which involved many unskilled or low-skilled factory workers. At the same time the main union confederations moved towards a more conscious policy of support for specific demands of immigrant workers. Statistics on participation by immigrants in trade union activities are notoriously hard to obtain because of the prevailing political view that they should not be treated as a separate demographic category, but studies of the composition of congress delegations suggest that the number of immigrants taking part in such activities rose significantly in the 1970s, at least for the CGT (from 1.7 per cent of delegates in 1972 to 5.2 per cent in 1975). Adam suggests that in the late 1970s the relative number of immigrant workers in the CGT (6.3 per cent) was approaching the proportion of immigrants in the workforce (7.5 per cent).[37] Levels of unionisation were lower for the other confederations, reflecting the working class bias of the CGT.

The example cited at the beginning of the chapter serves to highlight the ambiguous nature of the relationship between the French labour movement and immigrant workers: Renault-Billancourt, for decades the bastion of the CGT and the symbol of the French working class, employed a substantial number of immigrant workers, particularly to fill the least interesting and dirtiest jobs. In 1967 for instance, foreign workers accounted for 72 per cent of all unskilled workers taken on and 32 per cent of the total workforce.[38] The turnover rate was very high. These figures help to throw light on the success of the Communist Party in the post-war period, which was not only as Noiriel argues based on a growing homogenisation of the workforce (which as we have seen was only relative), but also reflected the party's capacity to incorporate the marginalised sections of society behind a common goal.

Occupation and Class

In the nineteenth century, the French worker was defined by a craft knowledge or a trade, or else was designated a *journalier* (day worker) or *manoeuvre* (labourer). The term worker (*ouvrier*) came to mean a manual worker in general. The vocabulary changed because of the emergence of Taylorised forms of work organisation in the 1920s, and then in the 1940s because of the spread of classification structures which formalised distinctions between skill levels. Much of France's inter-war labour legislation was linked with the problem of classifications; the metal industry was (as was usually the case in bargaining) the first to introduce a classifications structure for pay and bargaining, which in 1946 was extended across the country (the Parodi-Croizat decrees).

A new codification of socio-professional categories, based on the 1946 structure, was established after the Second World War and included four main categories of worker: foremen/supervisors, skilled workers (having a trade, involving formal or on-the-job training), OS or specialised workers (having a designated task to perform, whether training was involved or not), and labourers (performing simple tasks with no training). As a result of these classifications which over-emphasised the skilled nature of many machine jobs, the 1954 census overestimated the position of skilled workers, recording 130,000 supervisory staff, 2,139,000 skilled workers and 192,000 apprentices, with only 1,314,000 OS (basically assembly/machine workers) and 766,000 labourers.[39]

After 1968 the classifications changed. In 1975 the categories of labourer and OS disappeared, leaving a distinction between skilled and unskilled workers, while supervisory staff were moved to an intermediate category. Thus three levels of employee remained, workers, intermediate category (supervisory and technical) and cadres (various management levels). In the 1982 survey, new classifications appeared. Skilled workers accounted for 4.1 million (52.6 per cent of workers), of whom 1.5 million worked in artisanal crafts, 1.6 million in industry, 0.4 million in transport, stocks and maintenance, 0.6 million were drivers. The census recorded 3.4 million unskilled workers (43.6 per cent of workers), of whom 1 million worked in artisanal trades and 2.4 million in industry. Agricultural workers accounted for 0.3 million (3.8 per cent of the workforce).[40]

The first forms of legal trade unionism in France were based on crafts (*métiers*). French trade unionism at the turn of the century represented a rejection of new working methods which diluted craft skills and therefore reduced workers' autonomy. Scott's study of the Carmaux glass workers around the turn of the century shows the central importance of mechanisation and de-skilling in leading highly skilled workers to unionise and strike. Across France as a whole, Scott notes, a high correlation existed between mechanisation and strike activity from 1864 to 1913.[41] The CGT recruited mainly in older professions, and unionisation rates were lower in newer sectors (textiles, steel and metals, chemicals).

Revolutionary syndicalism is often seen as a transitionary period for the French labour movement, and certainly as new forms of industrial organisation emerged the CGT too underwent a crisis as its leadership sought to encourage structural change. However, as Scott insists, the process of change was far from linear and in the case of the glass workers the initial period of protest did not necessarily result in the development of a strong class consciousness because other, less skilled workers came to replace the craftsmen. At the same time, France saw the development of a reformist unionism linked to a strong corporate identity, which has left deep corporatist traces in the French workers' movement.[42]

Transformations in the structure of industry were slow to emerge in the twentieth century, and trade unions for their part had difficulty in adapting to changes in workforce composition and organisation. The CGT became a mass union only in 1936 when, at Renault for example, around half the workforce was unionised. It was also at this time that unions started to attempt to organise cadres (supervisory and technical staff) and immigrants. Unions changed in nature from being defensive organisations to aspirant representative organisations, developing demands for workplace representation and collective bargaining. In the 1970s the dominant image changed again as the focus moved to the unskilled worker, particularly with the rise of new themes in trade unionism associated with the new direction of the *Confédération Française Démocratique du Travail* (formerly the *Chrétiens Confédération Française des Travailleurs Français*). The emphasis now lay not so much on representation as on conflict and moves towards *autogestion* (workers' self-management) as expressed in the celebrated occupation of the Lip factory and the strike at *Joint Français*.

Undoubtedly this change in union direction coincided with a new consciousness of social stratification and its consequences. In the 1980s and 1990s, the notion of class became separated from skills and occupation, and trade unions are today in search of an occupational model as the class basis of an occupational militancy (of a trade union type if not actually organised by trade unions) increasingly based on public service workers becomes more and more ambiguous. In the 1980s, qualified workers were less likely than other workers to join a trade union (14 per cent as opposed to 25 per cent for workers as a whole, according to a 1988 study),[43] but in general it is true to say that trade union activity does not define working-class experience in the latter part of the twentieth century.

Culture, Class and Consumption

If the link between skill, class and political activity has gradually broken down over the course of the twentieth century, social and cultural determinants of class values present a more mixed picture. According to Dewerpe, the French worker's situation at the beginning of the 1950s had not altered radically since the 1920s, but the introduction of indirect wages, access to leisure activities and the institutionalisation of trade unions all slowly modified the lifestyle of workers in the post-war period.[44] New social habits linked with a rationalised factory system, although this still employed only a minority of workers, imposed themselves on a wider mass of workers still characterised by the workshop and homeworking as the idea of a homogeneous working class became grafted onto a heterogeneous mass of workers.

Nevertheless, social mobility has in general terms been restricted. At the start of the twentieth century, a very limited proportion of workers (well under 10 per cent) could hope to work their way out of their class. Supervisory hierarchies were not very well developed; as in the nineteenth century, the exit route was through setting up a small business, but the capital outlay required for such a self-starter was prohibitive.

Studies in the 1970s seemed to suggest that the traditional idea of the 'hereditary proletariat' was breaking down,[45] but this reflected a newer pattern of diversity within the working class itself (due to the extension of schooling, women workers, the improvement of living and working conditions, the development of informal work and technological change) rather than a breakdown of the barrier separating it from other classes. However, social heredity has since then become more rigid: if in 1970 the rate was 43 per cent, in the 1980s it was around 50 per cent. INSEE figures confirm the rigidity of French society: in 1984, 66 per cent of workers' children remained workers, while 10 per cent occupied clerical posts and 14 per cent had made it into management.[46] Eight per cent of workers' children were classed as independent (self-employed) workers (a slightly higher proportion than for other social backgrounds), which tends to confirm Albertini's hypothesis that towards the end of the twentieth century the artisanat has re-emerged to provide a form of social mobility for workers, although on a very small scale.[47] The age of the hereditary proletariat seems to have been limited to the post-war productivity boom, which was one of relative stability for the French working class. In the latter half of the twentieth century it has given way to an age of hereditary exclusion.

The affirmation of an independent working-class culture played an important role in projects for workers' political autonomy in the early twentieth century, notably in the *Bourses du Travail*. It has however been observed that the First World War removed much of the impetus from such projects.[48] In the 1930s the relationship between political activism and culture changed dramatically, however, as class conflicts intensified; many radical theatre groups and writing and reading circles emerged. These movements usually involved only a minority of activists, who found it difficult to maintain their independence from the Communist Party; later, in the period following the Second World War, this radical, working-class cultural identity became closely associated with the PCF, and since the 1970s its decline has been associated with the disappearance of the party's hegemony.[49]

Even in the 1930s, however, the relationship between class

consciousness and culture remained ambiguous. For example, the achievement of paid holidays under the Popular Front opened up new leisure possibilities which at least allowed aspirations for greater social mobility. There is no doubt that in the second half of the twentieth century workers enjoyed a rise in their standard of living, as the following table shows:

Table 8.2. Evolution of Household Disposable Income[50]

Socio-professional category of head of household	1962–1970 (index 100 in 1962)	1970–1979 (index 100 in 1970)	1979–1983 (index 100 in 1979)
Upper management	112	109	90
Middle management	125	114	95
Clerical staff	141	118	98
Workers}	143}	128	100
Agricultural workers}	153]		
Farmer	151	118	96
Indep. professional	143	122	97
Unwaged	160	153	112
Total	139	125	100

As a result of higher disposable income and the growth of common lifestyles promoted by the mass media, differences in social behaviour between workers and other classes have decreased. Verret is in no doubt that the post-war consumer society has led to a real improvement in workers' living standards: in 1975, a working-class family with two children enjoyed the same level of household equipment and consumer goods as a qualified engineer's family in 1954.[51] It is not therefore surprising that attitude surveys have shown a decline in feelings of class identity; between 1976 and 1983 the proportion of the French population identifying itself as 'working class' fell from 27 per cent to 22 per cent.[52]

Workers continued nevertheless to behave in different ways from other classes. In 1988 they were less likely than other classes to own their own home, own a dishwasher, invite friends round to eat or go out to dinner. Despite specific government projects in favour of a 'democratisation' of cultural life, studies of cultural life and leisure activities in France show that class differences in leisure consumption (for example, workers participate in fewer activities outside the home and take fewer holidays) remain strong. However, the notion of class no longer seems relevant as a mobilising force (in terms of party politics), as the fate of the Communist Party has shown.

Economic and Political Identity and the Role of the French State

Employers' attitudes have often been seen as a major determinant of the structure of industrial relations in France, and in particular the development of a combative, class-conscious trade unionism in response to employers' refusal to negotiate.[53] Employers' refusal to develop bargaining has also been cited as a reason for the strong role of the state in industrial relations, a major feature of France's 'exceptionalism' as an advanced industrial society. In the French case it is certainly hard to distinguish historically between repressive and paternalistic attitudes, in that the corollary of paternalism certainly was the repression of organised labour at least until the latter half of the twentieth century. It took the shock of 1936 for employers to allow the idea of collective bargaining in the firm (despite the earlier law of 1919 on workplace agreements), the shock of 1968 for the state to force employers to accept trade unions in the firm, and the traumatic victory of the left in 1981 for French employers to give their employees the right to 'express themselves' (*droit d'expression*).

In many ways paternalism can also be linked with the primary/secondary sector distinction, with large companies developing social sub-structures in order to ensure social reproduction of labour at the start of the twentieth century, in a context of a shortage of skilled labour and a high degree of labour turnover as well as low factory discipline. Again, if we generalise very crudely, the same can be said of the situation today, where there is a relatively high degree of worker protection in larger firms and little or no protection in small firms. In very small firms (under ten workers) there is no legal obligation to set up any mechanisms for worker representation or allow trade union sections, although workers may ask for joint bodies to be set up for a group of small firms, for example on a building site. In slightly larger firms there is either widespread flouting of the law or deliberate attempts to get round the law (for instance, by employing forty-nine rather than fifty employees in order to avoid having to set up a *comité d'entreprise*).

Another feature of French 'exceptionalism' throughout the twentieth century has been the regulation of industrial conflict. France has paid little attention to the regulation of strikes and according to Adam, of all Western countries it is the nation where strikes are the least defined and regulated. In France, the link between strikes and negotiation is seen as particularly weak, and this is another reason why unions traditionally view themselves as combat organisations rather than negotiating partners.[54] The right to strike was granted in 1864 for the private sector only, and reaffirmed in the preamble to the 1946 Constitution. Strikes are recognised by law as a 'concerted stoppage of work with a view to win acceptance of professional demands'; in other words they must concern solely workplace demands, and therefore political strikes or general strikes are strictly illegal. Participation in a strike is not seen as a breach of the individual work contract, which is suspended under a law passed in 1950. A serious offence committed during a strike can however be legitimate cause for dismissal. The right to work has primacy over the right to strike: therefore, pickets are not allowed to prevent workers from entering premises. On these grounds, occupation of factories or any other actions preventing machinery from being used, for instance, constitute a serious offence and therefore a sackable offence. Apart from these conditions, the law does not regulate strikes in the private sector.

In the public sector, the situation is different. Where the state has legislated on strikes it has been as an employer, with the aim of ensuring that the state functions smoothly. With the 1946 Constitution, public sector workers achieved the right to strike except in certain cases vital to the state's security. This right was refined in 1963 by a law requiring five days' notice for strikes, through recognised unions. Police, prison warders, judges, prefects, air traffic controllers, Interior Ministry officials and members of the armed forces are forbidden to strike – although this does not seem to prevent them from doing so. A minimum service is stipulated in radio and TV and in education. French law also distinguishes between different types of work stoppage, in the sense of the restrictions mentioned above and also to prevent (mainly public sector) workers from carrying out tactical strikes.

Adam sees the lack of regulation of private sector strikes, and particularly trade unions' relative indemnity from judicial pursuit, as a hangover from France's past, as a result of which the labour movement 'has always considered illegality as a necessity of action.'[55] In fact, strikes have not traditionally been a trade union weapon as such and the lack of a real link between strikes and negotiation has meant that industrial conflicts have only constituted a weak factor of integration. Industrial relations in twentieth-century France have seen a large number of wildcat strikes, with unions more often following than leading.

The Olsonian paradox of collective action (with its central question: 'why join a trade union'?) seems particularly appropriate in France, where unions have adopted a confrontational stance instead of developing a network of services for members as in Germany. Thus the low level of finances available for strike actions has discouraged long, focused strike actions and encouraged instead short, symbolic stoppages. Employers' refusal to recognise trade unions in the workplace until they were forced to do so in 1969, coupled with a tradition of 'blacklisting' of union members, undoubtedly made it harder for unions to organise workers and plan industrial action.

Some authors have recently suggested, however, that the reason for the weakness of French trade unions lies not so much with the employers' strategies as with the organisational inefficiency of the unions themselves.[56] The trends throughout the twentieth century in France are so persistent that it seems difficult to attribute them solely, or even mainly, to organisational weaknesses. Rather, a combination of employer hostility, a takeover by the state of many of the functions which in other countries are regulated by collective bargaining and a general political climate of distrust of intermediate institutions between the state and the citizen have forced the labour movement into a series of choices regarding its organisation and activities.

The legal and constitutional framework has undoubtedly had a major impact on the French labour movement. Universal manhood suffrage was achieved by the alliance of revolutionary forces in 1848, so French labour did not have to struggle for suffrage as many European labour movements did. Unlike Britain, however, where earlier industrialisation and rationalisation of industry had given the labour movement more economic muscle, the French working class was shaped by the struggle for economic and social status. Paul Thibaud sums up the difference thus: if England invented trade unionism, France invented socialism.[57] This also meant that, like Germany, the French labour movement was to a large extent centred on the state. It also harboured a deep distrust of bourgeois politics, fed by scandals and more importantly by state repression. It was faced with a double refusal; that of the employers to recognise collective action, and that of the state to recognise the working class as a collective actor.

The idea of institutionalisation of trade unions arrived much later in France than in Germany, beginning in 1936 but developing in earnest only in the post-war period after 1945. The legalisation of trade unions in 1884, as has been stressed elsewhere, arose from a desire to control the nascent labour movement rather than from a genuinely liberal development of radical politics; thus, as Roger Magraw insists, the idea of a 'social reform bloc' within French politics at the turn of the century does not sustain analysis, despite Millerand's attempts to formulate plans for a new relationship between the state, employers and trade unions.[58] For the political parties of the left, the unwillingness of the Third Republic's political elite to concede social reform posed major tactical problems and thus aggravated the divisions within the socialist movement about the best means of achieving social change. Millerand's entry into a republican government in 1899 brought these divisions out into the open.

Julliard's basic idea is that 'the situation of the [French] working class with regard to the nation as a whole has always been contradictory: it is both politically integrated and socially marginalised.'[59] Because the labour movement did not have the opportunity to influence working conditions through collective bargaining, it sought to make virtue out of necessity by developing a strategy of confrontation in relation to both employers and the state, which seemed to be on the employers' side. This is the essence of the notion of 'autonomy' to which the French labour movement has clung and which Julliard sees as central to its development. It means complete independence from the state and political parties on one hand, and the rejection of any hint of 'partnership' with the employers on the other. In the inter-war period the labour movement's ambivalence towards the state found expression in an outright split between the communist CGTU (*Confédération Générale du Travail Unitaire*) and a mainstream reformist CGT. Whilst the former maintained a hostile stance towards the state, the CGT pursued a policy of representation in state institutions (*la politique de la présence*). As this ideological and tactical division suggests, the First World War provided the labour movement with the first opportunities to think in terms of a closer relationship between workers and the state.

Because of the failure of early attempts to integrate social demands and political rights, the French left had to wait until it was able to gain a majority in parliament in order to decisively influence the social policy of the state. It achieved this in 1936 when the union of socialist and communist forces allowed the left to form a government. However, the transition to a left-wing government so traumatised sections of the employers and the right that it left lasting traces in French political life and created expectations of revolutionary change when a (supposedly united) left next came to power in 1981. To some extent the Fourth Republic furthered the social reform which had been so lacking in the Third Republic, by affirming rights of association and rights to strike, and by strengthening worker representation in the workplace through the *comités d'entreprise* (workplace committees). Yet the exclusion of the PCF from political office from 1947 served to underline the separation between the labour movement and the state.

Traditionally, the French labour movement sees the social legislation of the twentieth century as 'working class achievements', gained by painful struggle from a hostile state wedded to employers' interests. It is true that labour legislation in France has often resulted directly from either widespread industrial unrest (as in the case of 'contractual policy' of the early 1970s) or from the election of 'popular' left governments, as in the historic Matignon agreement of 1936 which introduced paid holidays, established workers' delegates in firms with over ten employees and laid down an obligation to bargain. However, it is also true that the two wars provided an opportunity for the establishment of a 'social pact' which left its mark on labour legislation in the immediate post-war periods; thus the year 1919 saw the introduction of the eight-hour law, the first pension state scheme and collective bargaining. The period after the Second World War saw a further shift in social regulation, with a greater emphasis on collective bargaining and the establishment of bipartite or tripartite administration of social affairs. According to Dewerpe, 1936 marks a turning point in the direction of social reform. Before 1936, employers conserved or even increased their powers within the firm through restrictive regulations; after 1936, and particularly in the post-war period, reforms began to modify social relationships and attenuate the arbitrary powers of employers.[60]

With the left divided between socialist and communist wings after 1920, French workers could hardly expect the left parties to attain political power and thereby grant them the social reforms they wanted. However, the threat of fascism in the 1920s and 1930s brought the labour movement – both the trade unions and the political parties of the left – back together, resulting in the election of the Popular Front left-wing coalition in 1936. For the French workers, accustomed to being shut out of power, the expectations simply proved too much; popular euphoria erupted into strikes and occupations. Leon Blum's Popular Front government undoubtedly gave French workers reforms with more than symbolic value (the forty-hour week and paid holidays) and drew them to the negotiating table, showing employers by their exclusion from talks that the state and the workers together could threaten the employers' power. But this experiment in workers' empowerment proved to be short-lived, and early in 1937 Blum announced a 'pause' in the reforms.

The legacy of the Popular Front coloured the French labour movement's experiences during the Second World War. For Roger Magraw, 'the period of World War Two should be viewed, essentially, as a logical continuation of the social conflicts of the previous years – for Vichy symbolised the revenge of the far right for the humiliations of the Popular Front and the Resistance became involved in an ideological civil war.'[61] For French people the wartime period brought such painful choices that it still remains a taboo subject, and historians have only with difficulty been able to piece together an account of workers' experience of life under German occupation in the north and a collaborationist government in the south. Despite these problems, historians rightly see the Vichy period as fundamental to the debate which underlies studies of the French working class in the twentieth century, the question of integration into French society and politics.

On one hand, Vichy provided the conditions for the development of corporatist industrial relations, some elements of which would later be taken up in Gaullist plans for modernisation. On the other, the Resistance offered the chance to integrate social and national concerns (but obviously at the price of huge personal sacrifice). Under Vichy, workers' rights were suspended, including the right to strike or indeed to formulate any autonomous demands at all, and the national labour confederations were outlawed. Yet the chance to practice some kind of *politique de la présence* tempted some labour leaders: probably the most famous of these is René Belin, a close associate of Jouhaux in the CGT who became Minister of Labour in the Vichy government. Belin's Charter of Labour (4 October 1941) set up 'social committees' in companies with more than 100 employees, to allow management and labour to work together, and by 1944 such committees were operating in two-thirds of the firms concerned.[62] But we know that such attempts to 'pacify' workers did not always have the desired effect and opposition to increased intensification of work was expressed in numerous short protest strikes. We know also that workers were proportionally under-represented in active collaboration and over-represented in the Resistance movement: they accounted for nearly 50 per cent of *Resistants* in the Loire area, with metalworkers alone making up 23 per cent. A large proportion of the deportees were also workers.[63] In the south, too, similar figures are given for workers in the Resistance.[64]

Work itself became the focus of Resistance because increasingly to work at all meant to work for Germany. This was made explicit in the September 1942 law giving the Vichy government the power to force workers to carry out any job deemed necessary, and in the law of February 1943 which established the *Service de Travail Obligatoire* (forced labour) for young workers. The introduction of the STO provided a huge boost to the Resistance as many young workers escaped into the underground movement to avoid deportation to Germany.

The leading role played by the Communist Party in organising and maintaining the Resistance goes a long way towards explaining the party's popularity in the post-war period. The PCF was the single biggest party throughout the Fourth Republic, whilst the Socialists remained for a long time tainted by the ease with which many of their leaders had given in to Petain. The experience of the Second World War allowed the Communist Party to assimilate nationalism into its discourse.

The post-war legacy of the Resistance movement may also be seen in numerous measures taken immediately after the war. The political rights and freedoms of the labour movement now became enshrined in the constitution. Perhaps more importantly, the post-war institutionalisation of labour movement took place largely through the creation of social insurance schemes which owed much to the Resistance. As the American historian Richard Kuisel has controversially pointed out, some of the corporatist features of the Vichy regime were also to play a role in the new order based on *dirigisme* (economic planning involving representatives of labour and capital).[65] Kuisel sees Vichy and the Resistance as parallel forces in the modernisation process. In the economic sphere, too, wartime did not disrupt the long-term trends in economic development; rather, it widened the gap between older and newer industries and, as in the 1914–1918 period, encouraged the intensification of work through Taylorised practices, thus contributing to economic modernisation. In other words, 'modernity' may be seen as a more or less continuous process beginning just before the First World War and gradually intensifying around the time of the Second World War, regardless of party political discontinuities and external upheavals. Reinforcing these long-term political and economic developments, the notion of a gradual *embourgeoisement* of workers through the development of consumer culture in the 1950s and 1960s would seem to support the modernity argument.

The establishment of the social security system in 1946 meant a new form of institutionalisation of the labour movement within the State, just as the preamble to the Constitution of the Fourth Republic (1946) guaranteed for the first time the basic civil rights of workers including the right to strike. According to Touraine, the creation of the social security system 'at the double initiative of the CGT and General De Gaulle' signified 'the clearest expression of the will to integrate' labour in 'a society subject to circumstantial and structural changes which threaten its internal cohesion and therefore its capacity to be an actor'.[66] Touraine's point about the link between De Gaulle and the PCF, both seeking to integrate workers into the nation (since, for the PCF, the workers constitute the authentic nation), is backed up by Herrick Chapman's 1991 study of workers in the aircraft industry in the post-war period, where he argues that Gaullist-style *dirigisme* fostered the growth of the CGT but along reformist lines, despite the CGT's undoubted ties with the PCF.[67]

There is some merit in the modernisation analysis, but it still begs the question of the real extent of labour integration. As Magraw points out, the events of May–June 1968 proved the 'assimilation' theorists spectacularly wrong and revealed the underlying social immobilism of the post-war years.[68] More recently, writers such as Adam have made great play of the dangers posed by increasing institutionalisation of the trade unions since the 1970s, which he sees notably in effective state and employer subsidies of trade unions through the organisation of 'social' elections (works councils, joint industrial tribunals and Social Security administration funds) and the payment of workplace trade union officials.[69] Such reliance on the state has arguably cushioned the unions from the financial effects of the drastic fall in membership and prevented them from looking beyond state-centred solutions. Some authors have even argued that the weakness of French trade unions can largely be attributed to the role of the state, because state recognition of certain trade unions has prevented the development of a wider culture of organisation and mobilisation.[70]

On another level, the choice made by the labour confederations at various points in the twentieth century to follow developments on the political left – in the 1930s, and later in the 1970s when the CGT and CFDT's 'joint action' pact echoed the political 'union of the left' – and to work in support of the election of a left-wing government reveals a fundamental weakness of the French labour movement in its attitude towards the state. On one hand, a constant theme of the discourse of both the unions and the left-wing parties in France (particularly the PCF) is that no serious reform can come from the state but must be won by workers' own struggle; on the other hand, grass-roots mobilisation seems so often to be sacrificed in favour of political power. This contradiction helps to explain the disarray of the trade unions in the face of left-wing governments after 1981. Socialist governments either could not find the means or lacked the political will to bolster organised labour; the trade unions for their part could not take advantage of the few opportunities offered to them, such as the Auroux laws on workers' rights.

The 1982–1983 Auroux laws constitute the major labour reform of the 1980s period of socialist government. Of particular note are the provisions giving workers 'right of expression' (the right to regular meetings to voice concerns about working conditions or other matters) and making regular negotiations between employers and workers' representatives obligatory, especially on issues such as working time and new technologies. Some unions, particularly the CGT and FO, disliked the emphasis on individual rather than collective (i.e. trade union) rights of workers, and found it difficult to adjust to a new strategy of closer cooperation with employers which the Auroux laws sought to promote.

More generally, the social reform record of the Socialist party in government was patchy. The major reforms of the period were generally held to be the lowering of the retirement age to sixty for men and fifty-five for women, and the introduction of a safety-net (but not universal) minimum income (*Revenu Minimum d'Insertion* or RMI) in 1988. However, by 1990 the differences between right and left on social reforms, as on economic policy, appeared very slight (and in fact the RMI was initially launched as a pilot project in right-wing-run *départements*). The Socialist Party, which by now of course was no longer the party of the workers but represented a much wider electorate, had lost its specificity as the party (or at least, a constituent member of the bloc) of social reform; the Communist Party, which maintained a class-specific stance, saw its electoral support shrink to 4.6 per cent in the first round of the 1993 legislative elections.

The Role of Other Classes and Social Groups

France's history is remarkable for the role played in the eighteenth and particularly in the nineteenth centuries by a revolutionary bourgeoisie, thus leading to a strong tradition of class cooperation. Julliard sees the role of intellectuals and the emphasis on national values and patriotism as especially important in the formation of the organised labour movement.[71] At the same time this revolutionary alliance in the nineteenth century fuelled mutual distrust which was later to provide favourable conditions for the development of revolutionary syndicalism, the ultimate expression of class antagonism.

Around the turn of the century, the relationship between the labour movement and the socialist middle classes was distinctly uneasy. Jaurès and Millerand undoubtedly enjoyed the absolute support of the local mining constituency, but the miners constituted a special group of workers with their own lifestyle and political behaviour. Within the wider labour movement Millerand's attempts to modernise labour relations were treated with the utmost suspicion. The metal workers' leader Merrheim's work with the economist Delaisi also earned him suspicion among his colleagues, within a labour movement solidly rooted in *ouvriérisme*.

Overall, *ouvriérisme* has won out in the twentieth-century French labour movement: the great moments of the movement's history are not shared with other classes, with the exception of the Resistance movement (but even in this case, the PCF later appropriated many of the symbols and values of the Resistance for the working class). The events of May–June 1968, far from sealing the gulf between workers and intellectuals, simply revealed it.

Given the fairly high degree of impermeability of class barriers, and given a well-documented sense of social space in France, both of which have been enduring features of twentieth-century France, two questions spring to mind. First, what has happened in recent years to break down the generational reproduction of social values in the working class and work-based cultures?[72] Second, throughout the twentieth century, what has been the role of outside institutions in integrating the working class into wider French society? The role of other social groups and institutions has not been studied systematically for France; here we shall look briefly at the Church, the army, the family and the educational system.

The Church had an obvious influence on the French labour movement through Christian trade unionism, which promoted the idea of cooperation in the firm. This idea has skirted the fringes of 'yellow' unionism or house unionism on one hand, and on the other has embraced industrial democracy notably through Marc Sangnier's Sillon movement, which at the beginning of the twentieth century advocated the granting of citizenship rights in the firm, a theme taken up in the 1982–1983 Auroux laws. Later, the goal of workers' self-management (*autogestion*), with the development in the 1960s of an alternative, non-communist left associated with the CFDT also emerged. Christian ethics have been prominent in the paternalist strand of the French employers, and form an important base within the French employers' federation, the *Conseil National du Patronat Français* (CNPF). Thus Yves Poirmeur sees the creation of the CFTC in November 1919 as the fruit of a meeting between on the one hand workers and employers, upset by the anti-clericalism of the CGT, and on the other hand 'social' priests sensitive to the social doctrine of the Church.[73]

Whilst Christian teaching has undoubtedly had a direct influence on the development of trade unionism in the CFTC and later the CFDT, it has also been a factor of division and has indirectly influenced the development of other forms of trade unionism in France. *Force Ouvrière*'s firm rejection of all forms of 'collaboration' within the firm and within the state (hence its active campaign against De Gaulle's 1969 proposal to create an upper house of parliament based on interest groups and regional representation) reflects its fiercely *laïque* stance. The idea of cooperation or participation has constituted a dividing line in the French labour movement throughout the twentieth century, and mirrors the Christian/neutral divide. Throughout the twentieth century, the map of Catholicism in France has closely resembled the geography of the right-wing vote.[74] On the other hand, anti-clericalism has played an important part in the radicalism which made rural areas like the Midi, the Centre and the Limousin constant bastions of the left. For these reasons the relationship between Christian social teaching and the labour movement in France – as yet largely unexplored – offers scope for further research.

The role of the army is difficult to analyse. At the beginning of the twentieth century the relationship between the working classes and the army posed problems because the popular (conscript) army, with two-year conscription (raised to three years in 1913), was used regularly to repress strikes and not infrequently opened fire on workers. To trade unionists, the events of Montceau-les-Mines in 1901,[75] or Draveil-Villeneuve-Saint Georges in 1908 (when soldiers killed six strikers) revealed not that the army itself was fundamentally hostile to workers (despite the aftermath of the Dreyfus affair) but that the true face of the state was repression. Before 1914, the CGT devoted much energy to trying to maintain links with workers called up for military service, mainly through the *Sou du soldat* solidarity fund, and conducted campaigns denouncing poor conditions for soldiers in barracks, but with little effect. Governments in France have continued to use the conscript army against strikers, mainly as reserve workers in public sector strikes and this appears to have been largely accepted; however, the conscription of striking miners in 1964 in order to force them back to work backfired on De Gaulle as the miners gained widespread public sympathy. Given such a troubled history, it is far from clear that the army could have worked as an integrative factor; rather, in placing the state on the side of employers against strikers, it has tended to reinforce antagonisms between the working class and the rest of French society.

The family has always exerted a primary pull in French society, and numerous surveys show that the family provides the major focus of sociability and socialisation for all French people, but especially for the working class. Verret, writing in 1979, pointed out that the working class is characterised by an attachment to the family. No other class spent as much time outside work in the home: 52 per cent of workers ate all meals at home (but only 42.6 per cent of white-collar workers did so). In 1962, workers married earlier than other socio-professional groups and had more children per household.[76] Noiriel notes that, particularly during the periods of relative homogeneity of the working class when occupational heredity was at its strongest, integration into the working class took place first through the family and then through apprenticeship and work, at the same time as wider socialisation in French society was happening; for the post-war generation of workers, war and Resistance occurred in these crucial phases of adolescence and early childhood.[77] Agnès Pitrou's 1976 doctoral research on families and the transmission of norms and cultural heritage concludes that the family helps to maintain social stratification and sees clear differences in behaviour according to class.[78]

As we have seen, the family was backed up in its socialisation role by school and apprenticeship. While some scholars have drawn links between schooling and social integration,[79] others have cast doubt on the ability of the education system to deliver a sufficiently coherent and powerful model to overcome the pull of local and particularly Church ties. What emerges very strongly from the history of the early labour movement in France is the role of self-taught workers, and the importance placed by activists on workers' culture. Bernard Charlot and Madeleine Figeat, who have traced the relationship between education and workers' identity in the twentieth century, identify the central tension between State provision of education and employer provision of training on one hand, and the labour movement's desire for worker autonomy on the other. They distinguish between three main phases.[80] In the first phase, between 1851 and 1919, the debate hinged on whether to train workers in the workplace or set up professional schools. The professional schools catered overwhelmingly for lower middle class children; the majority of working class children (80–90 per cent) received no professional education. Apprenticeship was badly organised and received little support from either employers or trade unions. Labour activists' ideas remained close to those of Proudhon, who saw education as inseparable from workplace learning. Training was considered to belong to the workers themselves and therefore became a condition for association and for working-class emancipation. Such ideas corresponded to a labour movement largely defined by skill; Moss and others have highlighted the disparity between this militancy of skilled, urban, male workers and the mass of unskilled, often female, proto-workers.[81] By 1908, a crisis was beginning to develop. The machine-worker was no longer a skilled worker on a universal machine but an unskilled worker servicing a specialised machine. Although many syndicalist leaders thought that the crisis would be temporary, Taylorism in fact deepened.

The second period, from 1919 to 1959, saw the state take charge of the education and training system, with the emphasis on training semi-skilled machine operators and technicians to boost productivity. During this period the workers could no longer aspire to control youth training directly; they had to seek control indirectly through state institutions, reinforcing the institutionalisation of the labour movement. The final period, between 1959 and the 1980s, saw several major reforms. It was during this phase that the relationship between the working class and its younger generations broke down, and in which the apprenticeship system finally collapsed. Far from being integrated into the workforce, youth was used as a reserve labour force in competition with existing workers; whereas in the early twentieth century young entrants to the labour market had lower skill levels than the existing work force, in the late twentieth century they have higher skill levels. The scarcity of jobs and the changing nature of work, caused notably by technological change but also by changes in markets and production constraints, have caused a breakdown in the system of social reproduction which goes a long way towards answering the questions posed at the beginning of this section.

Space and Place

Studies of local industrial development and class formation are still relatively rare in France (although there is a growing body of literature by US scholars on the period 1815–1914),[82] but they have yielded a rich seam of information. Trempé's study of the miners of Carmaux is a classic in its sheer scope and detail, but concentrates on a highly exceptional group of workers.[83] Noiriel has similarly looked at the steelworkers of

Lorraine over a century of change and restructuring.[84] Yves Lequin, a pioneer in this field with his study of the Lyon area, has continued to stimulate thought on the relationship between urbanisation and working-class development.[85] Following Lequin, Michel Pigenet offers valuable insights into the way the Cher department in the nineteenth century acquired a clear industrial and class identity; within the department, towns and villages took on a specific character, and within towns particular areas housed particular workers. Thus the centre of Vierzon housed skilled workers, porcelain workers lived in Vierzon-Ville and metalworkers lived in outlying Vierzon-Villages.[86] Also, the stability of local populations varied according to various factors such as industry, geographical proximity to other departments and communications. By the time of the *Belle Epoque*, the period when the local working class developed into a 'class for itself', the working class had become sedentarised: from multiple activities, the working population had settled into an identifiable group, albeit with skilled/unskilled, occupational and geographical divisions within it.

French geographers such as Joel Pailhé have emphasised the importance of locality over other factors such as company culture, citing the 1990 Peugeot dispute which was centred at the Mulhouse plant rather than Sochaux.[87] However, the precise nature of local loyalties – town, province or region – remains rather unclear. Michel Verret notes that the working class is essentially an urban class because of the organisation of capitalism; towns are the driving force of capitalist society. In France, this central fact needs to be seen in perspective: in 1968, Verret notes, 20.8 per cent of working-class households were still in rural communes with fewer than 2,000 inhabitants and 16.7 per cent in towns with less than 20,000 inhabitants, making a total of 37.5 per cent in villages or small towns (as opposed to 22.1 per cent of white-collar workers).[88] The key to this is to be found in France's industrial geography: Verret notes that rural regions form a 'network of industrialisation', that is, the coexistence of agriculture and industry through the development of commuter villages. Such areas account for 86.7 per cent of French households if the Paris area (19.8 per cent) is taken into account. Only 13.3 per cent of workers were living in the 'deep countryside' in 1968.[89]

Given the profound and often overlapping divisions which cut across French society and which in the 1980s and 1990s manifested themselves in the debate about European integration, the link between geographical and class identity would appear to offer a very fruitful field for future research.

Conclusion

We have seen that, in the case of France, although it is possible to map out the objective boundaries of class identity at different moments in the twentieth century, these boundaries fluctuate considerably over time and within them the relationships between different groups of workers shift. Moreover, the subjective class identity of French workers has undergone substantial changes. The French working class has always been heterogeneous, with multiple allegiances and layers of consciousness. To a large extent, employers' determination to preserve control and the strong central role of the state have facilitated united class action, particularly in the early part of the twentieth century.

However, the labour movement – the trade unions and the political parties of the left – have only very rarely been able to mobilise a large section of French workers. In 1936, workers rallied behind the first united left-wing government in French history. In the post-war period, the liberation and the reconstruction of the French economy gave workers a moral justification for their demands, while mass factory production (representing a small but economically key sector of the economy) provided the symbolic framework for working-class action. However, at that time the political parties of the left remained divided, with the Socialist Party centrally involved in the Fourth Republic and the stronger Communist Party in permanent opposition. Thus the old debate pitting reform against revolution has maintained its force in France, even if it has lost most of its meaning, and opposition to other parties or unions remains an important factor in determining organisational identity within the French labour movement.

Rather than specific political circumstances, we have seen that long-term changes in the labour process, or the 'structure of work',[90] have to a large extent determined the organisational response of French workers. The two world wars appear to have formed part of this process of change, rather than halting it temporarily or forcing it to change direction. Periods of economic crisis and mass unemployment have had the effect, first of reinforcing the homogenisation of the 'core' of French workers and then (as in the period since 1970) of breaking down class solidarities as in the 1930s. Political events have also played a part; for example, the political mood of post-war France and its long-term effects on the PCF accompanied and strengthened the formation of a 'hereditary proletariat'. This example serves to underline the fact that, while economic forces may tend towards convergence, political circumstances often reflect deep-seated social realities in different nations.

Notes

1. See 'Adieu à la classe ouvrière', *La Marche du Siècle* (television programme), June 1992.
2. Lebaube, 'L'avenir ouvrier', *Le Monde*, 24 June 1992.
3. See for example Noiriel (1986), pp. 209–10.
4. Robert (1992), pp. 120–1.
5. Reported in *Le Nouvel Observateur*, 8 July 1993.
6. Noiriel (1986), p. 265.
7. Goetschy and Rozenblatt (1992), p. 405.
8. See for example Bouvier and Braudel (1982).
9. INSEE (1990).
10. Verret, speaking on *La Marche du Siècle*, June 1992.
11. This is the thrust of Marxist analysis, but the idea is also evident in work by authors like Stearns (1971).
12. See the extremely valuable work done by Dewerpe (1989).
13. Verret (1982), p. 16.
14. Dewerpe (1989), p. 98.
15. Crossick and Haupt (1984), p. 7.
16. Zdatny (1990).
17. Dewerpe (1989), p. 104.
18. Fridenson (1987), pp. 1031–60.
19. Dewerpe (1989), p. 104.
20. Noiriel (1986), p. 123.
21. Borne (1988). Note that these figures exclude very small establishments with fewer than ten employees, so the level of concentration is exaggerated.
22. Noiriel (1986), p. 128.
23. Cross (1983).
24. Noiriel (1986), p.172.
25. Dewerpe (1989), p. 140.
26. Noiriel (1986), p. 195.
27. See Sylvester (1978).
28. See Mallet (1975).
29. Mitchell (1987), pp. 124–73.
30. Adam (1985), p. 53.
31. Figures based on tables in appendix, Noiriel (1988).
32. Lequin (1988), p. 389.
33. Cross (1983), p. 144.
34. Cross (1983), p. 145.
35. See Mouriaux and Wihtol de Wenden (1987), pp. 795–6.
36. Cross (1983), pp. 144–8.
37. Adam (1985), p. 55.

38. Tripier (1990), p. 166.
39. INSEE (1990).
40. Ibid.
41. Scott (1974), p. 4.
42. Segrestin (1985).
43. Herpin et al (1988), p. 59. Note that this INSEE figure for overall rate of unionisation is generally held to be overestimated.
44. Dewerpe (1989), p. 148.
45. Bertaux (1977).
46. INSEE (1988), p. 61.
47. Albertini (1988), p. 203–4.
48. Rebérioux (1975), p. 9.
49. Lequin (1982), p. 72–3.
50. Herpin et al (1988), p. 54 (INSEE statistics).
51. Verret, speaking on *La Marche du Siècle*, June 1992.
52. Magraw (1992), p. 313.
53. See Rojot (1986), pp. 1–16.
54. Adam (1985), p. 145.
55. Adam (1981), p. 106.
56. See Bevort and Labbé (1992).
57. Thibaud (1984), pp. 79–86.
58. Magraw (1992), pp. 21–3.
59. Julliard (1988), p. 23.
60. Dewerpe (1989), pp. 166–167.
61. Magraw (1992), p. 307.
62. Fridenson and Robert (1992), pp. 140–2.
63. Ibid., p. 145.
64. Magraw (1992), p. 308.
65. Kuisel (1984). For a discussion of these issues within a case study of the workings of Social Committees in northern mines, see Kourchid (1990).
66. Touraine (1990), p. 372.
67. Chapman (1991).
68. Magraw (1992), p. 311.
69. Adam (1985).
70. See Sellier and Sylvestre (1986).
71. Julliard (1988), pp. 25–9.
72. See Linhart and Malan (1988).
73. Poirmeur (1987), p. 47.
74. See Todd (1991), pp. 89–105.
75. Quoted in Jennings (1990), p. 37.
76. Verret (1979), p. 120.
77. Noiriel (1986), p. 204.

78. Pitrou (1976). It is interesting to note that the role of the family in the transmission of social norms and the reproduction of class structures, a popular research topic of the 1970s, has fallen out of favour in recent years.
79. See for example J. and M. Ozouf (1964).
80. Charlot and Figeat (1985).
81. Moss (1976).
82. See, for example, Acampo (1989); Berlanstein (1984); Hanagan (1989).
83. Trempé (1971).
84. Noiriel (1984).
85. Lequin (1977).
86. Pigenet (1990).
87. Pailhé (1990).
88. Verret (1979), pp. 55–6.
89. Ibid., p. 90.
90. Lequin (1977).

Bibliography

Acampo, E., *Industrialisation, Family Life and Class Relations: Saint-Chamond 1815–1914*, Berkeley, 1989

Adam, G., *Histoire des grèves*, Paris, 1981

——, *Le pouvoir syndical*, Paris, 1985

Albertini, J.-M., *Bilan de l'économie française*, Paris, 1988

Berlanstein, L. R., *The Working People of Paris 1971–1914*, Baltimore, 1984

Bertaux, D., *Destins personnels et structures de classe*, Paris, 1977

Bevort, A. and Labbé, D., *La CFDT: Organisation et audience depuis 1945*, Paris, 1992

Borne, D., *Histoire de la société française depuis 1945*, Paris, 1988

Bouvier, J. and Braudel, F., *Histoire économique et sociale de la France*, Paris, 1982

Charlot, B. and Figeat, M., *Histoire de la formation des ouvriers, 1789–1984*, Paris, 1985

Chapman, H., *State Capitalism and Working-class Radicalism in the French Aircraft Industry*, Berkeley, 1991

Cross, G. H., *Immigrant Workers in Industrial France: The Making of a New Laboring Class*, Philadelphia, 1983

Crossick, G. and Haupt, H.-G., *Shopkeepers and Master Artisans in Nineteenth-century Europe*, London, 1984
Dewerpe, A., *Le monde du travail en France, 1800–1950*, Paris, 1989
Fridenson, P., 'Un tournant taylorien de la société française (1904–18)', *Annales ESC*, no. 5, September–October 1987, pp. 1031–60
—— and Robert, J.-L., 'Les ouvriers dans la France de la Seconde Guerre Mondiale: un bilan', *Le Mouvement Social*, no. 158, January–March 1992, pp. 117–46
Goetschy, J. and Rozenblatt, R., 'France: the Industrial Relations System at a Turning Point?' in A. Ferner and R. Hyman, *Industrial Relations in the New Europe*, Oxford, 1992, pp. 404–44
Hanagan, M. P., *Nascent Proletarians: Class Formation in Post-revolutionary France*, Cambridge, MA, 1989
Herpin, N. et al., 'Les conditions de vie des ouvriers', *Economie et statistique*, no. 208, March 1988, pp. 53–9
INSEE, *Tableaux de l'économie française*, Paris, 1988
INSEE, *Annuaire rétrospectif de la France 1948–88*, Paris, 1990
Jennings, J., *Syndicalism in France: A Study of Ideas*, Basingstoke, 1990
Julliard, J., *Autonomie ouvrière*, Paris, 1988
Kourchid, O., 'Un leadership industriel en zone interdite: la Société des Mines de Lens et la Charte du Travail', *Le Mouvement Social*, no. 151, April–June, 1990, pp. 55–78
Kuisel, R., *Le capitalisme et l'Etat en France. Modernisation et dirigisme au XXe siècle*, Paris, 1984
Lequin, Y., *Les ouvriers de la région lyonnaise 1848–1914*, Lyons, 1977
——, 'Jalons pour une histoire de la culture ouvrière en France', *Milieux*, nos. 7–8, October–January, 1981, pp. 70–9
——, *La Mosaïque France*, Paris, 1988
Linhart, D. and Malan, A., 'Individualisme professionnel des jeunes et action collective', *Travail et emploi*, nos. 36–7, June–September, 1988, pp. 9–18
Magraw, R., *A History of the French Working Class*, Vol.II. *Workers and the Bourgeois Republic 1871–1939*, Oxford, 1992
Mallet, S., *The New Working Class*, tr. by A. and B. Shepherd, Nottingham, 1975
Mitchell, B., *The Practical Revolutionaries*, New York, 1987
Moss, B., *The Origins of the French Labor Movement: The Socialism of Skilled Workers 1830-1914*, Berkeley, 1976
Mouriaux, R. and Wihtol de Wenden, C., 'Syndicalisme et islam', *Revue Française de Science Politique*, vol. 37, no. 6, December, 1987, pp. 794–819
Noiriel, G., *Longwy: immigres et proletaires, 1880–1980*, Paris, 1984
——, *Les ouvriers dans la société française: XIXe–XXe siècles*, Paris,

1986

——, *Le Creuset français: Histoire de l'immigration IXe–XXe siècles*, Paris, 1988

Ozouf, J. and M., Le thème du patriotisme dans les manuels primaires, *Le Mouvement Social*, no. 49, 1964, pp. 5–31

Pailhé, J., Pour une géographie des pratiques syndicales, *Modern and Contemporary France*, no. 41, April, 1990, pp. 7–12

Pigenet, M., *Les ouvriers du Cher (fin XVIIIe siècle–1914)*, Paris, 1990

Pitrou, A., Relations entre générations et insertion sociale, Thèse de doctorat de 3e cycle, LEST, Aix-en-Provence, 1976

Poirmeur, Y., 'Activité politique et organisations syndicales', in N. Decoopman et al., *L'actualité de la Charte d'Amiens*, Amiens, 1987, pp. 37–64

Rebérioux, M., 'Culture et militantisme', *Le Mouvement Social*, no. 91, April–June, 1975, pp. 3–12

Robert, J.-L., 'Le syndicalisme des salariés', *Cahiers français*, no. 255, 1992, pp. 118–23

Rojot, J., 'L'évolution de la politique des employeurs français vis-à-vis des organisations syndicales', *Travail et societe*, vol. 11, no. 1, January, 1986, pp. 1–16

Scott, J. W., *The Glass Workers of Carmaux*, Cambridge, MA, 1974

Segrestin, D., *Le phénomène corporatiste*, Paris, 1985

Sellier, F. and Sylvestre, J.-J., 'Unions' Policies in the Economic Crisis in France', in R. Edwards et al, *Unions in Crisis and Beyond*, London, 1986, pp. 173–227

Stearns, P., *Revolutionary Syndicalism and French Labor: A Cause without Rebels*, New Brunswick, 1971

Sylvestre, J.-J., *Les inégalités de salaire: marché du travail et croissance économique*, Paris, 1978

Thibaud, P., 'L'éléphant sauvage', *CFDT Aujourd'hui*, no. 66, March–April, 1984, pp. 79–86

Todd, E., *The Making of Modern France*, Oxford, 1991

Touraine, A., 'La crise du système de relations professionnelles', in J.D. Reynaud et al, *Les systèmes de relations professionnelles*, Paris, 1990, pp. 371–77

Trempé, R., *Les mineurs de Carmaux*, 2 vols., Paris, 1971

Tripier, M., *Les immigrés dans la classe ouvrière française*, Paris, 1990

Verret, M., *L'espace ouvrier*, Paris, 1979

——, *Le travail ouvrier*, Paris, 1982

Zdatny, S. M., *The Politics of Survival: Artisans in Twentieth Century France*, Oxford, 1990

–9–

European Labour Movements and the European Working Class in Comparative Perspective

Stefan Berger

Historians of Labour have long been pre-occupied by questions of exceptionalism. Almost every national labour movement has its exceptional history, or rather historiography. The exceptional success of the Swedish labour movement in governing its country throughout much of the period from the 1930s to the 1980s has been explained in terms of the weakness of the political right in Sweden and the peculiar class alliances that the SDAP was able to strike in the 1930s and the 1950s. British exceptionalism is usually connected to the early integration of the labour movement into the state, and the high dependency on powerful trade unions. The French labour movement's precocious winning of universal male suffrage in February 1848 combined with continuing social and political exclusion (the June days, the Bonapartist coup of 1851, the massacre of the Communards) to set French working class and labour movement history apart. It is precisely in the lack of political and social integration that German labour is held to have had a peculiar history. The exceptional strength of anarchism in Spanish labour history and the long reign of fascist dictatorship in Spain made for theories of a Spanish special path. The pillarisation of Dutch society is held to have been responsible for the peculiar development of working-class identities in The Netherlands, while the 'subversivism' of the Italian working class sets the Italian case apart from other West European countries.

Theories of special paths and exceptionalisms in Labour history underline the importance of national circumstances for the development of the Western European working class and its labour movements. However, if every labour movement and every working class was in some sense peculiar or exceptional, it would be impossible to talk about special paths of some countries as judged against an alleged norm that other countries represent. Furthermore, the country studies in this volume demonstrate that any long-term look at working class and labour movement history in Western Europe in the twentieth century brings out a plethora of similarities. The working class and its labour movement in twentieth century Western Europe increasingly faced similar problems and circumstances which called for similar responses. This point is often missed in synchronic comparisons, as national movements and classes faced analogous problems at different times in the twentieth century. Hence, only a long-term view allowing for diachronic comparisons can fully comprehend the Western European dimension of many features of national labour movements and working classes.

For most chapters it is notable that the twentieth century does not begin in 1900, but rather at some point in the last third of the nineteenth century. It is the three decades from the 1860s to the 1880s which can be seen as important decades for the political awakening of the working class and the emergence of labour movements in Western Europe. Male suffrage was granted or extended in France, Britain, Spain and Germany, and political parties as well as trade unions began to emerge in Sweden, The Netherlands, Britain, Germany and Italy.

Within the twentieth century the two world wars mark important turning points for labour-movement and working-class history. The First World War had revealed that the solidarity of class, the internationalism of the labour movement, was paralleled and overlaid by national solidarity which, in August 1914, won the day in almost every national working class in Europe. The process of nationalisation of the working class was well advanced in many Western European countries. In Germany, Britain and France the educational system was particularly important in creating feelings of national identity amongst workers. The unification of Germany by Bismarck, the republican legacy of the French revolution, and the civilising mission of the British Empire all served as important methods of integration for the national working class.

This process of nationalisation was much less marked in Italy or Spain, where the educational system on the whole had failed to overcome the regional identities of most Italians and Spaniards by the beginning of the twentieth century. Italian imperialism in Africa and the Spanish colonial wars could not really accommodate large sections of the working class within the framework of an illiberal state. The hated imposition of Piedmontese state structures on the whole of Italy after the unification of the country also did not help to 'make Italians'. Significantly, therefore, the Italian labour movement was (next to the Russian and the Irish ones) one of the few to condemn the outbreak of war in August 1914 and opt for non-participation.

War not only revealed the strength of national identity amongst the workers of different countries, it also contributed twice in the twentieth century to an accelerated change in the composition of the working class, changing the position of workers in the market place and in society significantly. Whether social change was the result of war or of long-term social processes will remain a matter for contentious debate for a long time to come. However, many of the chapters in this volume underline the significance of war for changes in working-class customs and behaviour, social and political values and material conditions.

Furthermore the social geography, structure and cohesion of whole nations was considerably affected by the two world wars. They were times of crisis for the nations involved. To bring the working class firmly behind the war effort, governments had to make concessions to workers and their economic and political interest organisations. As organised Labour emerged strengthened from both wars, they managed to push through important political and social reforms (particularly in the areas of social welfare and social policy), thereby integrating the working class more firmly into their respective nation-states. At the same time, however, the link between war and integration of labour is by no means straightforward; after all, the First World War led to the emergence of communist parties in almost every European country, and in Italy and Germany it led to near-revolution followed by a fascist backlash.

Nevertheless it remains true to say that those countries which did either not participate in the two World Wars, like Spain or Sweden, or which were only passive victims of the war, like The Netherlands, experienced a development of labour relations different from the countries which were major combatants in both world wars. The absence of warfare in Sweden, for example, partly explains the state's lack of interest in mobilising and controlling its population to the same degree as other Western European nations. In turn, the state proved less willing to use repressive means against the emerging labour movement. However, marginality in the two major military conflicts in Europe this century alone cannot be a sufficient criteria for the Swedish labour movement's relatively smooth integration into the Swedish state, as the example of Spain amply demonstrates. Without participating in both world wars, class conflict and class militancy in this country were among the highest in Western Europe, and culminated in a bloody civil war in the 1930s. Apart from a short period in the 1930s the repressive nature of the Spanish state throughout much of the twentieth century hindered the self-expression of the working class and the emergence of an effective labour movement until the late 1970s.

War between nations and civil war did contribute to a politicisation and radicalisation of many workers in Western European societies. Social hardship endured at home and in the trenches could easily turn into social protest which sometimes took the form of political revolt, especially in defeated nations. Germany in 1918 experienced a full-blown revolution which swept the pre-war political system aside and ushered in a parliamentary republic. In The Netherlands the socialist party leader Troelstra announced a revolution in 1918 under the influence of developments in Germany. Without the backing of much of his own party, let alone a majority of Dutch workers, this call to arms soon collapsed.

Amongst the victorious nations of the First World War, there was also often much talk of revolution. This was most pronounced in Italy, where the factory occupations and the political turmoil of the *biennio rosso* brought the country to the brink of revolution. In Britain the widespread industrial conflicts in and after the First World War, coupled with political initiatives like the 'Hands off Russia' campaign in 1920, brought a flair of revolutionary rhetoric to some industrial regions and cities. Even a non-participant in the war, like Spain, under the impression of events in Russia, saw an abortive general strike and attempt at revolution in August 1917 followed by three years of political insurrection and turmoil in the South, the so-called Bolshevik triennium.

Much of this revolutionary or potentially revolutionary sentiment owed something to specific regional or local time, place and circumstance which brought the revolutionary traditions within national labour movements to the fore. The existence of different ideological identities amongst workers represented by different political organisations is clearly visible in the history of twentieth-century Western European Labour. Broadly speaking one can distinguish between revolutionary and evolutionary identities, but rarely were these identities clear-cut. Workers and their organisations could often switch from one identity to the other, depending on the contingent circumstances of the particular situation they found themselves in.

The major break between revolutionary and evolutionary socialism occurred during and immediately after the First World War, when many socialist parties split into left and right wings. After 1918 these developed into communist and social democratic parties in all Western European countries. The immediate reason for this split, which was to divide Labour until the end of the Cold War in 1989, was the successful Bolshevik revolution in Russia and Lenin's insistence on the formation of communist parties across Europe. However, the divisions between evolutionary and revolutionary socialism, with revolutionary anarchism playing a major role in some regions of Spain, Italy and The Netherlands, were already highly visible in all Western European labour movements long before 1914. In Britain, Sweden and The Netherlands evolutionary socialism dominated working-class politics throughout the twentieth century, while Italy, Spain and France had a more revolutionary tradition, based on higher levels of militancy of workers. Germany had both one of the largest Social Democratic Parties and the strongest Communist Party in Western

Europe after the First World War. When the country was divided in 1949 the deep split between revolutionary and evolutionary traditions in the German labour movement was translated into separate states by the advent of the Cold War. While the GDR in its forty-year existence saw itself as the inheritor of the communist struggle for working-class emancipation, West Germany experienced a 'social democratisation' of its society.

On the whole it is fair to say that in twentieth-century Western Europe it was the reformist rather than the revolutionary tradition which came to dominate. This trend was visible already well before 1914, when even the allegedly orthodox Marxist German socialists showed little inclination to smash the state and instead proved keen to participate in and cooperate with the institutions of the state where they had the opportunity to do so. The relative ease with which national labour movements could be integrated into the states of Western Europe had little to do with some kind of treachery by political or social labour aristocracies. Instead, it was mostly based on a recognition by labour movements that they could gain political and social reforms by cooperating with the state rather than confronting it head on.

However, there is no linear forward march of reformism within the labour movements of Western Europe, and the dominant reformist trends in Western European labour movements remained shot through with revolutionary traditions. Especially in the first half of the century, there were strong anarchist and syndicalist traditions in parts of Spain, Italy and The Netherlands. Almost all national labour movements were characterised by interesting ambiguities as far as their ideological orientation was concerned. Broadly reformist parties, like the Swedish socialists, the Independent French socialists led by Jean Jaurès and the British ILP adopted the general strike as a political weapon before the First World War. In the 1930s the broadly reformist Spanish PSOE became radicalised by its successful recruitment of southern landless labourers with broadly anarchic orientations. On the other hand there existed currents both in the mainly syndicalist French CGT after 1908 and the Spanish CNT between 1917 and 1923 which became increasingly reformist as the unions concentrated to a greater extent on elections and union leaders became enmeshed within the state machinery.

If evolutionary socialism in the long run remained the dominant form of political identity of Western European workers, this can be related to a number of developments. First, the emergence of the Western European welfare state became a major vehicle of integration for the working class. Where the state neglected social provision for workers, like in Spain until the advent of the Second Republic in 1931, reformism found it more difficult to win the hearts and minds of workers in the face of compeling revolutionary ideologies. The strong revolutionary rethoric of the Spanish

Socialist Party in the 1930s is highly illuminating in this respect. On the other hand, the social reforms introduced in Italy in 1912 had an immediate impact on the willingness of the Italian Socialist Party to consider cooperation with the government. The early development of welfare states in countries like Britain, Germany and Sweden made for a smoother integration of the working class, the more so as interest organisations were allowed participation in the administering of the welfare state. Especially in Sweden, and in The Netherlands in the 1930s, where much of the welfare was administered by the unions, the welfare state greatly increased class solidarity, and at the same time insured the unions against decline in difficult economic times, as the receipt of welfare remained dependent on trade union membership.

France and Spain provide examples of the opposite. Here, unions play no role in welfare administration and they offer few benefits to members. Hence French and Spanish workers have few incentives to join unions, and trade union density has remained low throughout the twentieth century. At times of industrial militancy, however, the mobilisation rate of French and Spanish workers has often been very high, indicating that the unions could rely on non-organised members in the event of a strike.

Second, the ideological identities of Western European workers have had much to do with the attitude of the state and other social classes towards workers and their independent interest organisations. Electoral deals or even government coalitions were struck between bourgeois parties and working-class parties in Sweden, Britain, The Netherlands, Italy and Germany in the first half of the twentieth century. Reformist tendencies were usually strengthened by such cooperation.

The degree and success of this cooperation depended heavily on the different traditions of liberalism in Western Europe; the reactions of liberals towards working-class parties were crucial for the ideological identity of labour movements. Where authoritarian, state-oriented Liberals were dominant, as in Germany and Spain, they tended to agree to anti-socialist legislation, permanently alienating workers and their organisations. Both Wilhelmine Germany and the Cánovas restoration in Spain saw widespread persecution of socialists and the social and political isolation of labour movement activists. Where the liberals held on to genuinely liberal demands of democratisation and liberty, as in Sweden and Britain, the labour movement found it far easier to strike a deal with liberals and follow reformist strategies. In those countries trade unions and working-class parties were recognised early on, which in turn strengthened reformism further. Both countries knew high levels of anti-socialism and anti-union legislation was intermittently passed by parliament, and yet the level of opposition to labour movements was qualitatively different to more authoritarian states such as Spain and Italy.

In Germany, Italy and Spain the victory of fascism in the inter-war period marked the highpoint of state persecution of the labour movement. Instead of integrating organised Labour, the state opted to crack down on independent worker representation (more thoroughly in Germany than in Italy or Spain), denying workers a genuinely independent voice. All three fascist states were characterised by increased exploitation of workers by their employers, largely through longer working hours, lower wages and an intensification of work rhythms. Autonomous trade unions were outlawed and strikes were declared illegal. State-run organisations, in which membership was often compulsory, were set up instead.

However, the legacy of fascism for workers in several Western European societies has been ambiguous. Workers were not necessarily united by the common experience of repression, and rarely did they develop a more revolutionary identity under fascism; on the contrary, the working-class identity experienced a process of fragmentation in the workplace as well as in the neighbourhoods. Fascist regimes were capable of winning at least partial working-class support by granting high job security and introducing a competitive wage structure with benefits and possibilities for upward social mobility especially for young and fit workers. The experience of war, with its massive destruction of cities and great upheaval of millions of people, increased this sense of fragmentation.

It was also under fascism and – reformulated on a more liberal basis – increasingly after the Second World War (although in Spain not until the 1960s and 1970s) that growing state intervention in the economy under a generally accepted Keynsian model of economics led to forms of corporatism developing in many Western European states. Corporatism, with its implicit recognition of labour as bargaining partner, contributed significantly to the integration of the working class into Western European nation-states after 1918.

Third, in those countries occupied by Germany in the Second World War the experience of resistance often lowered levels of class conflict and drew different political groups closer together. The *Résistance* in France certainly contributed not only to the emergence of a mass communist party after 1945 but also to the integration of the PCF into the republican framework of post-war France. In The Netherlands there was a widespread feeling of renewal after 1945 which would do away with the pillarisation of Dutch society (i.e. the peculiar construction of social identities around Catholic, Protestant and non-religious 'pillars'). It was in this climate that the PvdA was founded as a people's party, not a class party, after the Second World War.

Where the resistance was not only directed against foreign occupation but also against national government, as in Italy, it lacked this inter-class cooperation and therefore the effect could be quite different. Mainly due to the industrial and political militancy of the years 1943 and 1944, Italian workers close to the PCI continued to believe in an insurrectionary path to socialism long after 1945. Italian communists never shared a particular national myth with other classes to the same degree as the French communists did.

Fourth, reformism was also strengthened by an electoral dilemma of working-class parties in Western Europe. A more popular form of politics based heavily on inter-class cooperation was replaced by class politics in the first half of the twentieth century. Liberal labour movements were destroyed by the impact of class politics in Germany in the 1860s, in Sweden in the 1880s, and in Spain during the First World War. Even in Britain the Labour Party in the inter-war years managed to overcome and partly inherit the popular radical Liberal tradition which had strong roots in the working class.

However, nowhere in Western Europe at any time in the twentieth century could working-class support alone ensure a majority in elections. The success of electoral socialism therefore had to rely either on multi-class support or on cooperation with other parties. Sometimes the broadening of the parties' working-class base could rely on strong popular, inter-class republican traditions based on an alliance of skilled workers, small employers, small farmers and petty bourgeois elements, as in parts of Northern Italy, France and Spain. Both the German and the Dutch parties in the inter-war period took their first tentative steps from being class parties to catch-all parties. Increasingly in the twentieth century working-class parties attracted non-working class support and the party membership became more heterogeneous, with workers often being only the largest of the minority groups forming the party at large. However, at the same time it has to be emphasised that most working-class parties had serious difficulties in overcoming the widespread mistrust and outright hostility of large sections of the middle classes long after their transformation to catch-all parties. This was particularly notable in the cases of the British Labour Party and the Dutch PvdA. The prominent role of middle-class intellectuals, for example in the French, Dutch and Italian labour movements, did not have straightforward implications for the outlook of these movements. Intellectuals tended to be well represented amongst both the reformist and the revolutionary wings of European labour movements.

Fifth, full and lasting integration of workers into the Western European nation-states was only achieved under the conditions of the Western European 'economic miracle' in the 1950s and 1960s. The integrating effect of this long economic boom period on workers and the reformist orientation of Western European labour movements cannot be overestimated. If the economic crisis after the First World War led either to the failure of corporatist experiments, like in Britain, or to their authoritarian restructuring by fascist dictatorships – often on the employers' terms – the economic prosperity after the Second World War ensured the smooth functioning of corporatism for almost three decades and more.

When the long post-war economic boom came to an end in the late 1960s and 1970s, working-class radicalism flared up in several Western European countries. The first half of the 1970s saw a long unofficial strike movement taking hold of several key industries in Sweden. The industrial militancy of May–June 1968 in France backed up the student protests and threatened for a short period to bring down the government. The 'Hot Autumn' in Turin in 1969 showed the continued potential of the Italian workers for industrial militancy. Spain in the final years of the fascist dictatorship saw a major wave of strikes in its industrial centres between 1973 and 1976.

However, this passing phase of militant workerism could not turn the clock back on the effective social democratisation of the Western European labour movement. The Dutch socialists transformed their party from a class to a people's party between 1933 and 1935; the re-orientation of the German Social Democratic Party away from a mere class party which can be traced back to the inter-war period, found its final conclusion in the adoption of the Bad Godesberg programme in 1959. The rapid industrialisation and modernisation of Western European societies in the two decades after the Second World War led to the emergence of a 'new working class' with different and above all heterogeneous political and economic identities. As long as the identities of workers had been shaped by the world of production, the world of the factory, labour movements successfully appealed to man as worker. But increasingly throughout the twentieth century workers came to identify themselves as consumers. Political loyalties and social stratification became blurred as a result. In many Western European countries, most successfully in Britain, the political Right was able to address itself to workers as consumers. As the attitudes and outlooks of workers changed, labour movements adapted to that change by loosening their ties to their erstwhile most important clientele.

As the working class began to decline in numbers and importance and as its identity became less linked to the fortunes of the labour movement, class solidarity, from being a *leitmotif* of the Western European labour movement, came increasingly to be seen as an anachronism. The Italian Socialist Party never had a strong base of working-class support, but under the leadership of Bettino Craxi after 1976 it lost what little support it still had amongst workers. Equally, the French socialist party's success after the 1970s would have been unthinkable without strong middle-class support. In the 1980s the Spanish Socialist party experienced its own Bad Godesberg; under González the social democratisation of the once firmly-Marxist PSOE found its ultimate conclusion in a deep alienation from the trade union movement. Its electoral success became at least partly based on a broad alliance between the middle classes of Northern Spain and the agricultural labourers of the South, while at the same time, it also proved able to retain strong working-class support in northern Spain.

In the countries of Southern Europe generally the communist parties, partly through their closer links with unions and partly because of their emphasis on class policies, have been far more successful in retaining the loyalty of workers. And yet on the one hand, the emergence of Euro-Communism in the 1970s demonstrated an increasing willingness of communists to abandon the revolutionary tradition and work within the boundaries of the existing state; in fact, the Italian Communist Party in the 1980s looked much more like a Social Democratic Party than did the Italian Socialists. On the other hand the decline of the communist parties, most markedly in Spain and France in the 1980s, only underlined the weakening of class as a political factor in twentieth-century Western Europe. The most successful working-class parties of the 1980s and 1990s have at the same time remained at a distance from organisations of organised labour, notably trade unions, while continuing to appeal successfully to the 'salaried classes' (i.e. blue- and white-collar workers including a large segment of the new middle classes below the level of management).

Sixth, the ideological identity of workers has often been linked to economic conditions in the industrialisation process. If such a connection can be maintained at all, there seems to be a negative relationship between the degree of social deprivation and political class consciousness. Landless agricultural labourers in southern Spain, for example, lived in dire poverty, and yet there were only sporadic revolutionary outbursts until 1931 which made any sustained organisation of workers impossible. The depression in the 1930s and in the 1970s reduced rather than increased the militancy of Western European workers and weakened the labour movements right across the board. By contrast, some of the most important gains for the Western European working class were achieved in times of rising living standards and economic boom. Significantly, the backbone of the organised labour movement were artisans, skilled workers and the generally better-off workers.

Seventh, employers' strategies played an important part in the development of working-class identities. Initially, everywhere in Western Europe, employers reacted negatively towards the emergence of independent workers' organisations. There were efforts to stamp out trade unionism via the foundation of company unions, tied housing, employers' control of welfare and, generally, the creation of multiple divisions within the working class through a complex system of rewards in money, benefits and social status for some workers only. Paternalism was often linked to combatting independent trade unionism, like in the iron-work communities (*järnbruk*) in Sweden, the Krupp or Stumm empires in Germany, the steel and shipping companies in the Basque country or the shipyards in Göteborg. At times the employers took refuge in ferocious counter-attacks against the advances of worker representation. This was the case, for example, in Spain and Britain in the 1890s, and in Germany in the 1920s. The setting up of powerful employers' federations in Western Europe in the first decades of the twentieth century was also clearly in reaction to the successes of a growing labour movement.

Where employers were supported by a strong and authoritarian state, as in Germany, Spain and Italy at various times in the twentieth century, employers were successful in keeping unions out of the workshops for a considerable time. However, in the course of the twentieth century, employers in every country discussed here found it more convenient to come to some sort of understanding with the unions. Increasingly, strong unions were seen as partners regulating workers' protest, a process which was seen as beneficial for the whole industry. Hence collective bargaining procedures were established in every Western European country: in Britain in the second half of the nineteenth century, in Sweden after the 1905 engineering industry agreement, in Germany just before and during the First World War.

The refusal to accept trade unions was probably fiercest in Spain, Italy and France. In Spain the unions could make limited headway in the First World War, in Italy the Giolittian period still saw widespread reluctance on the part of major employers to cooperate with unions, and in France it was only the shock of the Popular Front government in 1936 which made them accept collective bargaining.

The increasing integration of trade unionism into collective bargaining procedures and the subsequent concentration of trade unions on 'bread and butter' questions had important repercussions on the relationship between trade unions and working-class parties in all Western European countries. Where unions were affiliated to working-class parties, as in Britain and Sweden, their statutory rights over the party were often considerable. Their integration and reformism inherently strengthened reformist tendencies in the working-class parties. Yet even where this was not the case, as in Germany, mass unions retained very close links to working-class parties, held a *de facto* veto power over any party decision, and contributed significantly to shaping the increasingly reformist outlook of working-class parties.

Only recently, over the course of the 1980s, did a process of decoupling trade unions from working-class parties set in. This was strongest in Spain, where the neo-liberalism of the governing PSOE went unchecked by an impotent UGT. The latter turned its back on the socialists, but as the PSOE became less and less dependent on working-class support for electoral success, this move did not have much consequence.

As the working class in every Western European country becomes only one group amongst others which support left-wing parties, the strong ties between unions and parties of the left are under threat. Increasingly, as the discussions in Britain in the late 1980s and early 1990s clearly demonstrate, the links are perceived as a burden. Ultimately, this is a consequence of the declining importance of the class cleavage for explaining political allegiance after the Second World War; with the emergence of social democratic people's parties in all Western European countries, there was a functional delineation of tasks between political parties and trade unions. For example, the close links between the Dutch trade union federation NVV and the socialist party were never rebuilt after 1945, and the German DGB almost immediately declared its party political neutrality, although it retained close links with the SPD.

The regionalisation and localisation of labour history is another important aspect emerging from these essays. In many respects it is not so much national developments which have conditioned the outlook and organizational capacity of Western European workers and their labour movements, but regional and local environments which contributed to highly specific local and regional milieus and identities. As one can speak of industrialising regions in Western Europe rather than industrialising nations, so one should also consider the working class and labour movement in their regional setting more than in their national one. Such emphasis on regional and local developments also draws attention to the crucial impact the timing of industrialisation had on the relation between the working class and the labour movement. As the Swedish case reminds us, if the socialists actually arrived at the same time as the industrialisation process got under way, they tended to grow strongly. If however, they arrived late on the scene, as was most obviously the case in Britain, then they were confronted by other political groups with alternative identities offered to and accepted by workers. In the latter case it would only be after a long political battle that the socialists would be able to win the majority of working-class support.

Furthermore, only the regional and local approach promises to provide answers to the question which is of central concern to all chapters in this book: how successful have labour movements been in the twentieth century in uniting the bulk of the working class behind their organisations and programmes? The picture which emerges from these pages is one of great difficulties in all countries in uniting workers behind the labour movement. If there was a time in which the Western European working class was coming together, it was probably most visibly the turn of the century, between the last two decades of the nineteenth century and the first two decades of the twentieth century. In that period a view of a proletariat which would grow in numbers and become ever-more homogeneous was most justified. Employers' repression, the exclusion from civil society, political discrimination and an often self-confident and assertive labour-movement and working-class culture combined to produce what could justifiably be called the 'heroic age' of working class struggle. However, division was at least equally important as unity, as far as the political orientation of the Western European working class was concerned.

Amongst the various dividing lines, regional divisions played a major role. This is especially obvious in Italy, where regional divisions hindered significant advances of the labour movement at crucial times, as in the *biennio rosso*, where the failure to synchronise risings across Italy led to the ultimate failure of revolution. The Labour Party in Britain throughout the twentieth century remained very much a party of the northern regions of England and the Celtic fringe, while the Catholic regions of The Netherlands and Germany remained largely untouched by support for socialists.

Skill divisions also remained central to the internal stratification of the working class in all Western European societies. The emergence of the labour movement in Western Europe was firmly linked to the organising capacity of skilled workers and artisans in the early manufacturing centres. Political identities were often formed along skill lines, although ultimately attempts generally to link groups of workers to particular ideologies have to be regarded with a pinch of salt. Certainly after 1918 the socialist leadership in Western Europe aimed at organising what it perceived to be the more respectable working class while the anarchists and communists concentrated on the less-skilled, the 'true' proletarians. In urban Spain by the 1930s the anarchists organised the poorer, marginalised sections of society, while the socialists looked to the more respectable working class for support. Similarly in Germany, the more respectable working class tended to support the Social Democrats in the 1920s, whilst the communists were more successful amongst the unskilled and the unemployed. The formal institutionalisation of skill differences was at the same time a conscious effort by employers in several Western European countries to prevent the effective unionisation of the workforce.

The importance of housing for the emergence of a political working-class identity should not be underestimated. On the one hand it was in the 'red quarters' of major cities like Barcelona, Paris, Berlin and London that a genuine labour movement culture took hold in the 1920s. Vociferous neighbourhood associations in several major cities in Western Europe certainly helped the labour movement to get a foothold amongst local workers, as the Dutch and British cases clearly show. With the improvement of housing in the course of the twentieth century, working-class culture became increasingly centred on the family. This had important repercussions for the publicness of working-class life. Retreat into the family (familialism) meant that working-class life was less grounded in neighbourhoods, and consequently neighbourhoods could not be the basis for a particular labour movement milieu anymore.

The divisions between agricultural labourers and industrial workers took very different forms in Western Europe. Of great importance was the question of land ownership. Where the land was in the hands of large estate owners, the landless labourers often had different interests and developed quite different political identities from areas in which the land was divided between small but independent farmers. Class distinctions tended to be much sharper where large-scale agricultural enterprises dominated. However, whereas the repressive brutality of agricultural social relations in Friesland, Groningen, Andalucia, Apulia and Calabria radicalised many agricultural labourers who became supporters of revolutionary labour movements, the more benevolent agricultural paternalism in Germany's eastern provinces made it difficult for working-class parties and trade unions to make much headway in rural areas. Small farmers in Germany, in northern and central Spain and in the Veneto and northeastern Lombardy also remained largely immune to the advances of the labour movement, whilst in some parts of Northern Italy, such as the Po valley, share-croppers and farm labourers gave strong support to the labour movement. As the Italian chapter points out, certainly before 1914 Italian socialism had a semi-rural character, the centre of its strength being in Emilia-Romagna. Equally, in the Midi and the Centre of France, sections of the French small-holding peasantry developed stable and strong 'red' traditions.

Ethnic tensions between workers marked a further dividing line which made it difficult for the labour movement to unite workers behind its banners. Some British cities, such as Liverpool or Glasgow became notorious for the rivalry between the Irish and the English/Scottish. Midlands car workers and East End dockers earned themselves a reputation for their racist outlook. Imperialism and jingoism did not leave the British working class and its labour movement unaffected. In Germany, the Ruhr area saw significant tension between Polish and German workers before 1914 and the treatment of foreign slave workers in Nazi Germany also revealed high levels of racism amongst the German working class. In the economic crisis of the 1980s and 1990s, tensions between foreigners and Germans reached fever-pitch in some rundown working class quarters of major German cities, such as Bremen and Hamburg. Here, the extreme right-wing *Republikaner* won some of their most impressive election victories. Similar problems with large immigrant communities occurred in France in the 1930s, 1980s and 1990s with at times violent clashes between foreign and French workers. However, the Western European labour movement for the most part tried hard to affirm solidarity amongst workers of different ethnic origin; the French CGT's efforts to unionise immigrant workers, the Swedish SDAP's extremely progressive legislation on more equality for immigrants in Sweden, and the German SPD's efforts to reach out for Polish support before 1914 are but a few examples.

Religious divisions remained very marked throughout much of the twentieth century in Western European societies. In Germany, the SPD failed to significantly break into the Catholic working class in all but two elections in the late 1960s and early 1970s. In Britain, despite the non-conformist roots of the ILP and High Church Christian socialist traditions, the Anglican Church, the Catholic Church and a good deal of non-conformism always remained firmly in the anti-socialist camp, the Anglican Church being widely known as the 'Tory party at prayer'. The Catholic Church in Spain and Italy was widely used to guarantee social control by the elites, without necessarily gaining much support from the urban working class. Catholicism in Brabant made it almost impossible for the Dutch labour movement to find a foothold in that province. An important Catholic associational culture, most marked in Germany and The Netherlands, underpinned the religious separation of Catholic workers. Strong Catholic trade unions in France, Italy, The Netherlands and Germany rivalled the dominance of socialist and anarchist trade unions in these countries.

Cultural divisions often prevented the labour movement from making inroads into the working class. The relationship between labour-movement culture and working-class culture often remained distant. Whereas the former was a culture of self-improvement, sobriety, respectability and prudence and, at least in part, adopted its models from bourgeois culture, the latter was increasingly part of a growing leisure industry in the twentieth century whose commercial aspects were usually deplored by organised workers. People's halls and people's parks, week-long fiestas, vibrant youth and women's movements, theatre groups, study circles and the labour press all largely appealed to organised workers. They preached to the converted, and rarely managed to bridge the gulf to either popular or working-class culture. With the decline of the working class in the second half of the twentieth century, and with the competing claims of mass media and mass culture, the labour movement sub-culture is threatened by extinction almost everywhere. Higher geographic mobility of workers, new forms of housing and work experience have also contributed to the erosion of a once-vibrant labour-movement culture in Western Europe.

A central division of the Western European working class throughout its twentieth century history was the division of gender. Workers took over the view of women as housewives and mothers from bourgeois models. Bourgeois gender stereotypes were reinforced by the fascist regimes of Spain, Italy and Germany which massively discriminated against women. It was a sign of working-class respectability right across Western Europe if a working-class wife did not have to go out for work. Socialist unions often upheld such strict gender divisions; demands for a family wage were often linked to the argument that women should not enter the labour market. Unions neglected organisation amongst women, and tended to see women in employment as a threat to higher male wages. Only a small elite amongst the organised workers were willing to consider women as equal partners at work and in the family.

Women showed at times very high levels of politicisation and potential for social protest, for example in Spain in the period of galloping inflation between 1916 and 1919 and in Germany in the final years of the First World War. Things began to change more thoroughly in favour of women from the 1960s and 1970s when the women's movement made great strides in Western Europe, leaving its impact on the working class and labour movement alike. Increasingly, working-class parties have introduced gender-based quota-systems, and policies of positive discrimination have even found their way into trade unions to encourage women trade union officials.

The number of women in employment has increased substantially in the second half of the twentieth century which makes it impossible for unions to ignore them. Trade unionisation of women was most successful in Sweden, where trade union density amongst women workers currently exceeds that among men. As far as their political identity was concerned, women in Sweden tended to vote more for left-wing than for right-wing parties throughout the 1980s. The Swedish example contrasts sharply with France, where the percentage of women in the work force compares well with other Western European states, but their trade unionisation has made little headway (as has that of men, one should probably add). Women made up nearly 40 per cent of the French labour force in the early 1900s, but they were nevertheless ignored by the labour leadership.

In the light of all these divisions, labour historians across Western Europe have begun to question the usefulness of class as an instrument of analysis. Whereas much labour history in the 1960s and 1970s was underpinned by that 'grand narrative' of class, labour history from the

1980s onwards has tended to stress the diversity and heterogeneity of working-class experiences in the twentieth century. Clearly this trend is connected to current social and political developments. Notions of class have lost their image as a mobilising force in all Western European countries at the end of the twentieth century; social class has become only one cleavage amongst others. As all chapters in this book show, class situations were invariable uneven and diverse and class interests and identities were constructed on often fragile and contingent grounds throughout much of the twentieth century.

Apart from the weakening of class as a social reality and an analytical concept, the breakdown of communism in Eastern Europe and the rise of environmental concerns and movements in the West have contributed to a much-commented on crisis of socialism in Western Europe at the end of the twentieth century. A growing recognition of the destructive potential of the belief in progress and rising living standards, underpinning the utopia of the labour movement, brought not only communist but also social democratic visions into ill repute. Added to these ideological problems are practical organisational changes. In the 1980s, for example, the increasing sectoral division led to growing difficulties of trade unions to stick to centralised bargaining procedures in the face of employers' demands for more flexible localised bargaining. The increasing decentralisation of industrial relations is threatening the coherence of union movements all over Western Europe. And yet, despite all of these weaknesses, the crisis should not be overemphasised. If one compares the state of Western European societies at the end of the twentieth century with the ambitions and aims of the labour movement at the beginning of the twentieth century, one can only conclude that the history of the labour movement in twentieth century Western Europe has been a success story. There are major working-class parties in every Western European country. Especially after 1945 they had considerable political success in shaping the outlook of their societies as parties of government. Emancipation of workers, democratisation of society, the principles of a welfare state and broad educational opportunities for all, closer cooperation between nation states, the major aims of the labour movement have all been achieved in the course of the twentieth century. Whether this already means that Social Democracy has outlived its useful purpose, as Ralf Dahrendorf has frequently argued, remains doubtful. In advanced capitalist societies, solidaristic values and social as well as political rights need constant defence against the ever-encroaching forces of individualist egotism.

Appendix

Statistical Data

Trade Union Membership (thousands)

Year	France[1]	Germany [1]	Great Britain	Italy	Netherlands[1,2]	Spain[1,2]	Sweden[1]
1900	800[2]	680	2022	n.a	n.a.	172[3]	44
1914	700[3]	1500	4145	962[1]	266	n.a.	101
1920	1000[4]	8033	8348	4650[2]	684	932[4]	280
1930	900[5]	4717	4842	n.a	625	1494[5]	583
1950	n.a.	5279 4700*	9289	5830	1160	n.a.	1587
1960	1993[6]	6379 6200*	9835	3908	1354	n.a.	1938
1970	2000[7]	7713 7090*	11187	5530	1524	n.a.	2438
1980	1200[8]	7883 8807*	12947	9006	1790	2800	3334
1990	2500[9]	7938 9600*[2]	9900	10145	1653	1900[6]	3836

Notes:

France

n.a. = Figure not available.

Sources: C. Tilly and E. Shorter, *Strikes in France 1830–1968*, Cambridge, 1978; H. Bouzonnie, 'L'évolution des effectifs syndicaux depris 1912: essai d'interprétation', *Revue Francaise des Affairs Sociales*, no. 4, 1987, pp. 52–82; P. Rosanvallon, *La question syndicale*, Paris, 1988

1 CGT, CFTC/CFDT and FO only: white-collar union excluded.
2 800 of which only about 200 CGT. Figures relate to 1906.
1910: 977.
1911: 1029.

3 700 of which half CGT.
4 CGT (but J.-L. Robert, 'Le syndicalisme des salariés', *Cahiers français*, no. 255, p. 119, 1992: between 1500 and 2000 – surely exaggerated; Tilly and Shorter between 1053 and 1153). No figures for Christian trade unions.
1921: CGT: 373, CGTU:500.
5 Tilly and Shorter.
1932: CGT: 258, CGTU 533.
1935: CGT: 600, CGTU 200.
1936: 5000 (temporarily!), CGT and CGTU reunited. CFTC has 400 members.
6 CGT: 1993; FO:400; CFTC between 700 and 455 (say 600 as CFTC figures recognised as more reliable than most): total approaching 4 million (Bouzonnie, 1987, p. 60).
7 CGT 2000, CFTC 250, FO 800, CFDT 950 (i.e. so, 3.9 million: Robert, p. 121; again, these figures may be slightly inflated).
8 Rosanvallon.
9 Robert. Figures vary between Rosanvallon's low figure of 1.2 million and Robert's more optimistic 2.5 for 1990 or thereabouts; reality is probably nearer Rosanvallon's figure.

Germany

1 Social democratic unions: Freie Gewerkschaft, ADGB, DGB.
Sources: G. Hohorst, J. Kocka, G. A. Ritter, *Sozialgeschichtliches Arbeitsbuch II. Materialien zur Statistik des Kaiserreiches 1870–1914*, 2nd edition, Munich, 1979; D. Petzina, W. Abelshauser, A. Faust, *Sozialgeschichtliches Arbeitsbuch III. Materialien zur Geschichte des Deutschen Reiches 1914–1945*, Munich, 1978; R. Rytlewski, M. Opp de Hipt, *Die Bundesrepublik Deutschland in Zahlen 1945/49–1980*, Munich, 1987; Statistisches Bundesamt (ed.), *Datenreport 1992. Zahlen und Fakten über die Bundesrepublik Deutschland*, Bonn, 1992; R. Rytlewski and M. Opp de Hipt, *Die Deutsche Demokratische Republik in Zahlen 1945/49–1980*, Munich, 1987; Graham Timmins, 'Trade Unions and German Re-Unification: the Social Dimension' in Jonathan Osmond (ed.), *German Reunification: A Reference Guide and Commentary*, London, 1992, p. 175.
2 Figure relates to 1989.
* FDGB membership in the GDR.

Italy

1 C. Seton-Watson, *Italy from Liberalism to Fascism, 1870–1925*, London, 1967, p. 298.

2 N. Pernicone, 'The Italian Labour Movement', in E. Tannenbaum and E. Noether, *Modern Italy: A Topical History Since 1801*, New York, 1974, pp. 208–9.

Netherlands

1 Membership of all trade unions combined. Source: Centraal Bureau voor de Statistiek.
2 Figures include pensioners.

Spain

n.a. = Figure not available.

1 Affiliation to PCE\CC.OO and PSOE\UGT 1976–1990 (in thousands)

Year	PCE	CC.00	PSOE	UGT
1970	202[a]	30[a]	9[a]	7[a]
1980	70–80[b]	778[b]	97[b]	1.472
1990	n.a.	999	213[c]	666[c]

[a] For 1976.
[b] For 1981.
[c] For 1988.

2 Sources: Richard Gillespie, *The Spanish Socialist Party: A History of Factionalism*, Oxford, 1989, pp. 320–337; José Félix Tezanos, 'Continuidad y cambio en le socialismo español', in Tezanos et al, *La Transición Democrática Española*, Madrid, 1989, pp. 438–39; Alvaro Soto Carmona, 'Comisiones obreras en la transición y consolidación democrática. De la asamblea de Barcelona a la huelga general del 14–D (1976–1988)', in David Ruiz (ed.), *Historia de Comisiones Obreras (1958–1988)*, Madrid, 1993, p. 507.
3 Figure relates to 1904.
4 Figure relates to 1919–1920.
5 Figure relates to 1931.
6 Figure relates to 1989.

Sweden

1 Year	LO	TCO[a]	SACO[b]	SR[c]
1900	44	–	–	–
1914	101	–	–	–
1920	280	–	–	–
1930	553	20[d]	–	10[e]
1950	1278	272	16	21
1960	1486	394	42	16
1970	1680	658	81	19
1980	2127	1033	174	–[f]
1990	2230	1276	330	–

[a] Central organisation for white-collar workers.
[b] Central organisation for professional associations.
[c] Organisation for senior civil servants and army officers.
[d] TCO did not exist then. This figure is for predecessor organisations.
[e] SR did not exist then. This figure is for predecessor organisations.
[f] By this date SR has merged with SACO, which has become SACO/SR.

Labour Party Membership (thousands)

Year	France[1]	Germany[1]	Great Britain (total)[1]	Italy	Netherlands[1] SDAP/ PvdA	SDP/ CPN	Spain[1,2,3]	Sweden[1]
1900	35[2]	384[2]	375	19[1]	3	–	172[4]	44
1914	76[3]	1086	1612	47[1]	26	1	n.a.	84
1920	110[4]	1012[3]	4359	216[1]	48	2	932[5]	143
1930	137[5]	1037	2346	n.a[2]	61	1	1496[6]	227
1940	610[6]	875[4]	n.a.	n.a[2]	n.a.	n.a.	n.a.	n.a.
1950	355[7]	629[5]	5920	2812[3]	106	27	n.a.	722
1960	120[8]	650	6328	2282[3]	143	11[2]	n.a.	801
1970	85[9]	820	6222	2013[3]	99	11[3]	n.a.	890
1980	160[10]	987	6811	2253[3]	113	16	2796	1205
1990	n.a.	928[6]	5287	1933[3]	–	–	1881[7]	838[2]

Notes:

France

n.a. = Figure not available.

1 Section Française de l'Internationale Française/Parti Socialiste (PS) and Parti Communiste (PC) Français only (PC from 1920).
Sources: D. S. Bell and E. Shaw, *The Left in France*, Nottingham, 1983; Neill Nugent and David Lowe, *The Left in France*, London, Basingstoke, 1982; J. Touchard, *La Gauche en France depuis 1900*, Paris, 1977.
2 Figure relates to 1906.
3 PS 1910: 56.
4 PS 110 (Nugent, p. 137), 120 (Touchard, p. 138); PC 50. Figures relate to 1921.
5 PC 32. Figures relate to 1932.
1933: PS 130; PC 28 ('rock-bottom': Touchard, p. 138).
1937: PC 330 (Touchard).
6 1937: PS 280; PC 330.
7 PS 338 (postwar peak). PC 800. Figures relate to 1946.
8 PC 320 (Touchard, p. 324), (Nugent, 86: 430). Figures relate to 1956.
9 PC 850. Figures relates to 1965.
10 PC 700. Figures relate to 1977. ('putative' membership according to Bell and Shaw, p. 141; tallies with most other general estimates).

Germany

1 Sozialdemokratische Partei Deutschlands (SPD) only. Sources: Dieter Fricke, *Handbuch zur Geschichte der deutschen Arbeiterbewegung*, 2 vols., Berlin, 1987; Heinrich August Winkler, *Von der Revolution zur Stabilisierung. Arbeiter und Arbeiterbewegung in der Weimarer Republik 1918–1924*, Berlin, 1984, p. 243; Heinrich August Winkler, *Der Weg in die Katastrophe. Arbeiter- und Arbeiterbewegung in der Weimarer Republik 1930–1933*, 2nd ed., Berlin, 1990, p. 589; R. Rytlewski and M. Opp de Hipt, *Die Bundesrepublik Deutschland in Zahlen 1945/49–1980*, Munich, 1987, p. 166; Alf Mintzel and Heinrich Oberreuter (eds), *Parteien in der Bundesrepublik Deutschland*, 2nd ed., Bonn 1992, p. 568; Statistisches Bundesamt (ed.), *Datenreport 1992*, Bonn, 1992, p. 182.

Figures for the German communist parties in the twentieth centuries are as follows:

Kommunistische Partei Deutschlands (KPD):
1919 (year of its foundation): 106.656
1921 (after merger with USPD left): 359.000
1929: 135.160
1933: (just before its dissolution): 252.000
1950: 183.550
1954: (just before its dissolution): 79.027
1960: (estimate of illegal organisation): 7.000

Deutsche Kommunistische Partei (DKP):
1968: (year of its foundation): 9.085
1970: 33.410
1980: 40.000
1988: 47.513

Sozialistische Einheitspartei Deutschlands (SED):
1946 (after the merger of KPD and SPD in the Soviet zone): 1.298.415
1950: 1.750.000
1961: 1.610.769
1971: 1.909.859
1981: 2.172.110
1989: 2.300.000

Partei des Demokratischen Sozialismus (PDS), (successor party to the SED):
1995: 123.751

Sources: Hermann Weber, *Die Wandlung des deutschen Kommunismus. Die Stalinisierung der KPD in der Weimarer Republik*, 2 vols, Frankfurt am Main, 1969; vol. 1, pp. 361–95; Patrick Major, *The Death of the German Communist Party (KPD). Communism and Anticommunism in West-Germany, 1945–1956*, Oxford, 1996 (forthcoming); Manfred Wilke, Hans-Peter Müller, Marion Brabant, *Die Deutsche Kommunistische Partei (DKP). Geschichte/Organisation/Politik*, Cologne, 1990, p. 152; R. Rytlewski and M. Opp de Hipt, *Die Deutsche Demokratische Republik in Zahlen 1945/49–1980*, Munich, 1987, p. 130.

2 For 1905, first year when reliable data are available.
3 For 1919.
4 For 1947.
5 For 1952.
6 For mid-1991.

Great Britain

n.a. = not available

n.c. = not compiled

	Year	Individual Members	Trade Union Members	Co-Op. Societies Members	Socialist Societies Members
1					
	1900	n.a.	353	n.a.	23
	1914	n.a.	1572	1526	33
	1920	n.c.	4318	n.a.	42
	1930	277	2011	32	26
	1950	908	4971	31	9
	1960	790	5513	20	5
	1970	680	5519	16	8
	1980	348[a]	6407	53[b]	n.a.
	1990	311	4922	54[b]	n.a.

[a] New basis for calculation introduced.
[b] This figure is a joint one for Co-Operative Societies and Socialist Societies together.

Italy

1 PSI only
2 Clandestine party at this time; membership estimated to be very small.

3 Total figure for PCI and PSI together. Separately:
1950: PCI, 2,112,593; PSI, 700,000
1960: PCI, 1,792,974; PSI, 489,337
1970: PCI, 1,507,047; PSI, 506,533
1980: PCI, 1,751,323; PSI, 502,211
1990: PCI, 1,264,790; PSI, 669,003

Netherlands

1 Source: SDAP/PvdA 1900–1930 Kendal (1975); 1950–1980 *Compendium voor politiek en samenleving in Nederland* (1988); 1990 PvdA. SDB/CPN Boet e.a. (1986).
2 For 1959. (CPN)
3 No figure for 1970 available – reasonable assumption is of about 11,000 members between 1967–1973.

Spain

n.a. = not available.

1 Major Sources: Manuel Tuñon de Lara, *El Movimento Obrero en la Historia de España*, Barcelona, 1977, Vol. II, pp. 40, 121, 129, 258, 275–276, Vol. III, pp. 135, 178–187; Manuel Contreras, *El PSOE en la Segunda República: Organización e Ideología*, Madrid, 1981, pp. 55, 85; José Félix Tezanos, 'continuidad y Cambio en el Socialismo Español', in Tezanos et al, *La Transición Democrática Española*, Madrid, 1989, pp. 438–439.

2

Year	Socialists		Anarchists	Communists (PCE)[a]	Total
	PSOE	UGT			
1900	n.a.	26	34[b]	n.a.	171[c,d]
1915	14	112	27[f]	n.a.	n.a.
1920	54	211	550[f]	6[g]	932
1930	18	277	536[h]	1[h]	1496[h]
1936	60	n.a.	559	60	n.a.

[a] Figures for Communist party membership during the Second Republic are not as rigorous as those of the PSOE and are no doubt inflated. The PCE set up its own independent labour federation, the *Confederación General del Trabajo Unitario* (General Confederation of Unitary Labour) in April 1934, but in November 1935 it joined the UGT.

[b] *Federación Regional Española de Sociedades de Resistencia* (Spanish Regional Federation of Trade Unions). Operated between 1900 and 1906. Figures for membership taken from *El Socalista*, 26 October 1900.

[c] The vast disparity between figures for the Socialist and anarchist union federations and the total number of affiliates given for 1904 is due to the fact that before 1918–1919 large numbers of independent unions operated. For example in 1899 a large independent textile federation, the *Federación de la Industria Textil Española* (Federation of the Spanish Textile Industry) was set up in Catalonia. It only operated for two years but at its high point it claimed between 50,000 and 70,000 workers. See *Revista Fabril*, 7 June 1900.

[d] For 1905.

[e] For 1910.

[f] Confederatión Nacional del Trabajo (CNT) (National Labour Confederation). Anarcho-syndicalist labour confederation founded in 1910. The 1919 figures give those actually affiliated at the time of the Confederation's 1919 congress. Representatives of 714,028 workers actually attended.

[g] For 1921.

[h] For 1931.

3 In the absence of government data for union membership the data is based on information from union sources. This has been particularly difficult to collect for the years prior to 1920 when a large number of small, local unions still existed.
4 Figure relates to 1904.
5 Figure relates to 1919–20.
6 Figure relates to 1931.
7 Figure relates to 1989.

Sweden

1 Source: Social Democratic Party Annual Report 1992.
2 Note that the collective affiliation of union members came to an end in this year.

Union Density Rate

Year	France[1]	Germany[1]	Great Britain[1]	Italy	Netherlands[1,2]	Spain[1]	Sweden[1]	
							a	b
1900	4[2]	5	12.7	n.a	n.a.	4.1[2]	12	–
1914	5.7[3]	18[2]	23.0	c.10[1]	17	n.a.	15	–
1920	n.a.	53	45.2	n.a	36	20.6[3]	31	–
1930	n.a.	34	25.4	n.a	30	27.3[4]	45	24
1940	n.a.	n.a.	n.a.	n.a	n.a.	n.a.	n.a.	n.a.
1950	n.a.	33	44.1	50.8[2]	39	n.a.	76	47
1960	18.5	37	44.2	28.5	38	n.a.	78	50
1970	20	36	48.5	38.5	36	n.a.	80	63
1980	20[4]	38	52.6	49	39	33.8[5]	83	84
1990	10[5]	34[3]	37.7	39.3	24	16.4[6]	81	80

Notes:

France

1 Sources: Jean-Louis Robert, 'Le syndicalisme des salariés', *Cahiers français*, no. 255, 1992, pp. 118–23;
Huguette Bouzonnie, 'L'évolution des effectifs syndicaux depuis 1912: essai d'interprétation', *Revue Française des Affaires Sociales*, no. 4, 1987, pp. 52–82; Guy Caire, *Les syndicats ouvriers*, Paris, 1971. G. Groux and R. Mourians, *La CGT: Crise et Alternative*, Paris, 1992.
There are no density figures for the inter-war and post-war periods. This is because the trade union figures were always seen as unreliable and therefore any attempt to quantify the 'real' proportion of union members would have been too difficult, that is until a more recent generation of researchers found ways to estimate it. The gap in figures may also reflect a change in the way the trade union question has been tackled in the past, i.e. mainly by historians looking at the development of events and much less interested in quantitative data.

2 CGT: 'barely' 4 per cent (of 'wage-earners': Mouriaus and Groux 1992, p. 77). Overall union density slightly less than 10 per cent. Figures relate to 1906.

3 (Using above figure of union membership i.e. 700 out of total workforce of 12.15million), 5.7 per cent for all unions not just CGT (CGT less than half of this).

4 1982: 18.2 per cent (OECD figure); 13 per cent (INSEE).

5 c.10 per cent (Rosanvallon: 9 per cent), (OECD: 12 per cent 1988).

Germany

n.a. = Figure not available.

1 Sources: Hartmut Kaelble, *A Social History of Western Europe 1880–1980*, London, 1989, p. 85; Jelle Visser, 'The Strength of Union Movements in Advanced Capitalist Democracies: Social and Organizational Variations', in Marino Regini (ed.), *The Future of Labour Movements*, London, 1992, p. 19.
2 Figure relates to 1910.
3 Figure relates to 1989.

Great Britain

n.a. = Figure not available.

1 Density refers to percentage of civilian workforce in employment.

Italy

1 Seton-Watson, London, 1967, p. 298.
2 A. Ferner and R. Hyman, 'Italy: Between Political Exchange and Micro-Corporatism', in A. Ferner and R. Hyman (eds), *Industrial Relations in the New Europe*, Oxford, 1992, p. 545. Figures for 1950–1990.

Netherlands

n.a. = Figure not available.

1 Source: 1914–1930, Visser, J. 'In search of inclusive unionism. A comparative analysis' unpublished PhD thesis, University of Amsterdam, 1987; 1950–1990, CBS size of working class is dependent labour force. Source: 1920–1980, Visser (1987); 1990 CBS.
2 Figures exclude pensioners.

Spain

n.a. = Figure not available.

1 The figures for 1900–1931 have been calculated by Angel Smith, but they can only be regarded as a very rough guide. There are two reasons for this. First, there is an almost complete absence of government data on trade union membership. The only official figures available were drawn up by the *Instituto de Reformas Sociales* in 1904, and given the large number of small, local, unions which existed in Spain before 1917–18 unaffiliated to any labour federation, this is the only year for

which it has been possible to make an approximation. The figures for 1919–20 and 1931 are based on trade union sources, and given the rapid growth of the CNT and UGT, who in these years affiliated the great majority of unionised workers they can be regarded as reasonably accurate. However, there is a further problem with respect to the census data for 1900, 1920 and 1930 used to calculate the total number of workers. Apart from being of dubious reliability it makes no distinction (with the exception of 1920) between employers and non-employers. In the case of agriculture even the figures for 1920 do not help a great deal because there is no breakdown of peasants who owned or rented land and landless labourers. In these circumstances it has been necessary to make a series of estimates as to the percentage of the active population in agriculture, industry and commerce which may be defined as workers. The most significant decision has been to consider that 40 per cent of the agrarian population was waged. Overall, workers have been defined as the waged population in its broadest sense. In the service sector, public administration, domestic service and the liberal professions have been included, though the police, army and clergy have been excluded.

2 Figure relates to 1904.
3 Figure relates to 1919–20.
4 Figure relates to 1931.
5 The estimate of trade union density for 1980 is taken from Víctor Péréz Díaz, *El Retorno de la Sociedad Civil,* Madrid, 1987, p. 234.
6 Figure relates to 1989. The figure for 1989 is to be found in Richard Gillespie, 'The break up of the "Socialist family": Party-union relations in Spain, 1982–1989', *West European Politics*, vol. 13, no. 1, 1990, p. 54.

Sweden

1 a Manual workers
  b White collar workers

Note: Union density of manual workers, including agricultural workers.

Size of Working Class (millions)

Year	France[1]	Germany[1]	Great Britain[1]	Italy	Netherlands[1]	Spain[1]	Sweden
1900	3.1[2]	15.427[2]	n.a.	n.a.	n.a.	4.2[2]	0.1
1914	4.7[3]	n.a.	17.1[2]	9.3[1]	1.62	n.a.	0.1
1920	n.a.	16.024[3]	18.0[3]	9.3[2]	1.89	4.5[3]	0.4
1930	7.0[4]	16.158[4]	19.6[4]	7.7[3]	2.30	5.5[4]	0.6
1940	n.a.	17.577[5]	n.a.	n.a	n.a.	n.a.	n.a.
1950	6.5[5]	9.9	21.4[5]	9.7[4]	2.83	n.a.	1.3
1960	n.a.	12.63	22.5[6]	10.9[5]	3.35	n.a.	1.5
1970	8.5[6]	12.5	25.0[7]	9.9[6]	3.97	n.a.	1.7
1980	8.0[7]	10.92	25.4[8]	10.0[7]	4.88	n.a.	2.1
1990	6.7[8]	10.68[6]	n.a.	n.a	6.41	n.a.	2.1

Notes:

France

1 Statistics before 1950 are generally held to be not too reliable; also census classifications changed between 1975 and 1981 and some caution needs to be exercised in comparing between years; figures are approximate. Figures available only for census years (as shown).
2 Figure relates to 1901.
3 Figure relates to 1911.
4 Some authors have 7.5. Figures relate to 1931.
5 6.5 = 34.5 per cent of labour force. Figures relate to 1954.
6 Figure relates to 1975.
7 Figure relates to 1981.
1982: 7.0 (census figures).
8 Census figures.

Germany

1 Sources: D. Petzina, W. Abelshauser, A. Faust, *Sozialgeschichtliches Arbeitsbuch III. Materialien zur Statistik des Deutschen Reiches 1914–1945*, Munich, 1979; R. Rytlewski and M. Opp de Hipt, *Die Bundesrepublik Deutschland in Zahlen 1945/49–1980*, Munich, 1987; Statistisches Bundesamt (ed.), *Datenreport 1992*, Bonn, 1992.
2 Figure relates to 1907.
3 Figure relates to 1925.
4 Figure relates to 1933.

5 Figure relates to 1939.
6 Figure relates to 1989.

Great Britain

1 Given the limitations of the official statistics, and the necessarily problematic definition of 'the working class', these figures are the best available. The occupational classification system used in the 1901 census cannot be made consistent with the systems used thereafter. The best that can be attempted is an estimate of the number of manual workers in 1901 as being 12,395,000. Furthermore, from 1971 onwards the category of non-manual workers includes employers and proprietors. Whereas some or all of the previously defined non-manual workers might be considered to be (at least nominally) 'working class', no such assumption can be made from 1971. It might be simplest, therefore, to identify the 'working class' simply with the category of manual workers. Again, estimates of the number of non-manual workers for 1971 and 1981 based upon the earlier definition can be made, and stand at 10,177,000 and 12,205,000 respectively, the corresponding percentages being 40.7 per cent and 48.0 per cent. However, such estimates should be used with extreme caution.

Year	Non-manual workers		Manual workers	
	thousands	%	thousands	%
1911	3433	18.7	13685	74.6
1921	4094	21.2	13920	72.0
1931	4841	23.0	14776	70.3
1951	6948	30.9	14450	64.2
1961	8478	35.9	14022	59.3
1971	11072	44.3	13949	55.7
1981	13278	52.3	12128	47.7

Note: The percentage is a percentage of the total occupied population, the remainder (1911–1961) being comprised of employers and proprietors.

2 Figure relates to 1911.
3 Figure relates to 1921.
4 Figure relates to 1931.
5 Figure relates to 1951.
6 Figure relates to 1961.
7 Figure relates to 1971.
8 Figure relates to 1981.

Italy

1 Figure relates to 1911.
2 Figure relates to 1921.
3 Figure relates to 1931.
4 Figure relates to 1951.
5 Figure relates to 1961.
6 Figure relates to 1971.
7 Figure relates to 1981.

Netherlands

n.a. = Figure not available.

1 Figures exclude pensioners.
Size of working class is dependent labour force.
Source: 1920–1980, J. Visser 'In search of inclusive unionism. A comparative analysis' unpublished PhD thesis, University of Amsterdam, 1987; 1990 CBS

Composition Dutch labour force, 1899–1991, absolute figures (in thousands)

Year	Agriculture and fishing	Manufacturing	Utilities, transport, Communication, Mining, Construction	Trade, Services (incl. others and unknown	Total
1899	592	452	261	616	1921
1909	641	547	351	721	2259
1920	641	706	481	891	2719
1930	655	822	576	1126	3179
1947	747	1043	639	1437	3866
1960	447	1279	780	1663	4169
1971	291	1257	841	2346	4735
1981	271	1042	851	2943	5108

Source: Centraal Bureau voor de Statistiek.

Spain

1 The census figures used to calculate the total number of workers, apart from being of dubious reliability, make no distinction (with the exception of 1920) between employers and non employers. In the case

of agriculture even the figures for 1920 do not help a great deal because there is no breakdown of peasants who owned or rented land and landless labourers. In these circumstances it has been necessary to make a series of estimates as to the percentage of the active population in agriculture, industry and commerce which may be defined as workers. The most significant decision has been to consider that 40 per cent of the agrarian population was waged. Overall, workers have been defined as the waged population in its broadest sense. In the service sector public administration, domestic service and the liberal professions have been included, though the police, army and clergy have been excluded.

2 Figure relates to 1904.

3 Figure relates to 1919–20.

4 Figure relates to 1931.

Index

Index